CERTIFICATE

FINANCIAL ASPECTS
OF MARKETING

First edition 1991
Third edition September 1993

ISBN 0 7517 4006 3 (previous edition 0 86277 476 4)

British Library Cataloguing-in-Publication Data

A catalogue record for this book
is available from the British Library

Published by

BPP Publishing Limited
Aldine House, Aldine Place
London W12 8AW

We would like to acknowledge the substantial contribution made to the first edition of this text by Mr David S M Hatton CA, BCom.

We are grateful to the Chartered Institute of Marketing, the Institute of Chartered Secretaries and Administrators, the Chartered Association of Certified Accountants and the Chartered Institute of Management Accountants for permission to publish past examination questions. The suggested solutions have been prepared by BPP Publishing Limited.

CONTENTS

PREFACE

The examinations of the Chartered Institute of Marketing are a demanding test of students' ability to master the wide range of knowledge and skills required of the modern professional marketer. The Institute's rapid response to the pace of change is shown both in the content of the syllabuses and in the style of examination questions set.

BPP's experience in producing study material for professional examinations is unparalleled. Over the years, BPP's Study Texts and Practice & Revision Kits have helped students to attain the examination success that is a prerequisite of career development.

This Study Text is designed to prepare students for the Certificate in Marketing examination in Financial Aspects of Marketing. It provides comprehensive and targeted coverage of the syllabus (reproduced on pages (vii) and (viii)) in the light of recent developments and examination questions (analysed on pages (ix) and (x)).

BPP's Study Texts are noted for their clarity of explanation. They are reviewed and updated each year. BPP's study material, at once comprehensive and up to date, is thus the ideal investment that students of the Certificate in Marketing can make for examination success.

The September 1993 edition of this Study Text

Changes made in this edition include the following.

(a)   The text has been updated for all relevant recent developments.

(b)   An example is given of the radical effect of the new accounting standard FRS 3 on the profit and loss account.

BPP Publishing
September 1993

If you wish to send in your comments on this Study Text, please turn to page 345.

INTRODUCTION

Syllabus

Aims and objectives

- To develop the student's capacity to see the financial implications of marketing activities.

- To develop the student's ability to apply basic financial techniques in the context of marketing activities.

- To develop the student's understanding of the essential characteristics of 'financial position'.

- To develop the student's competence in interpreting financial reports.

<table>
<tr><td>Content</td><td></td><td>Chapter(s) in
this Text</td></tr>
<tr><td>(a)</td><td>Introduction</td><td>1</td></tr>
</table>

    (i)   The role of financial analysis and control in marketing.

    (ii)   Differences in accounting for order-getting, order filling and manufacturing activities.

    (iii) Cost/benefit of financial information.

    (iv) Organisational considerations: locating the accounting department relative to marketing.

<table>
<tr><td>(b)</td><td>Analysis of current position</td><td>2 - 4</td></tr>
</table>

    (i)   In broad terms, the key aspects of financial position of any enterprise.

- Liquidity
- Profitability
- Financial structure/capability

    (ii)   Construction and interpretation of:

- balance sheet;
- profit and loss account;
- funds/cash flow statement;
- value added statement.

    (iii) In detailed terms, financial analysis to show the current allocation of marketing effort (and its productivity) within a given enterprise using:

- segmental analysis;
- matrix analysis;
- productivity analysis;
- mission analysis.

INTRODUCTION

(c) *Planning for the future*

Consideration needs to be given to financial concepts that focus on decision-making. The impact of time, scale, learning, risk and inflation need to be introduced, as well as criteria of a non-financial nature. All these topics are to be developed via specific reference to marketing activities.

(i) Short-run decision making:

- cost-volume-profit analysis;
- relevant costing;
- setting budgets and standards.

(ii) Long-run decision making:

- differential costing;
- project appraisal (using discounting and non-discounting approaches).

(iii) Sources of finance: alternative sources relevant to short, medium and long-run horizons.

(d) *Controlling the outcome of marketing activities*

(i) A distinction must be made between controllable and uncontrollable financial flows. This can be done by means of:

- accountability planning;
- responsibility accounting.

(ii) Control systems design: the principles of control in a systems framework, with specific reference to marketing activities.

(iii) Variance analysis: the identification and investigation of variances; when to investigate; causal factors; adaptive responses.

(iv) The operation of budgetary control system and links with motivational issues.

Hints and tips from the examiner

'The importance of ensuring future generations of marketing managers are "financially literate" cannot be over emphasised. The focus must be on the students' ability to demonstrate their understanding of financial data and its business implications. Numbers are only surrogates: what really matters are the underlying activities.'

The format of the examination paper

The examination paper consists of eight questions in three sections, A, B and C. All questions carry 25 marks. The candidates must choose one question from sections A and C and two questions from section B. Discount tables are provided in the examination.

INTRODUCTION

Analysis of past papers

This brief analysis of the last five papers should help you to see the scope of recent examination questions.

June 1993

Section A
1 Limitations of conventional P & L account for marketing management
2 Profit v cash flows; relevance to marketing

Section B
3 Pros and cons of different methods of project appraisal
4 Budget for transport department of haulage company
5 Patterns of financial flows of product life cycle
6 Viability of a promotion

Section C
7 Selecting projects with highest ROI; calculating ROI
8 Controllable v uncontrollable costs

December 1992

Section A
1 Valuation of tangible and intangible fixed assets
2 Measurement and assessment of liquidity; impact of marketing on liquidity

Section B
3 Absorption costing
4 Size of orders; marketing cost per order
5 Sunk costs and decision-making
6 Role of cost analysis in pricing decisions

Section C
7 Responsibility accounting system
8 Usefulness of ratio analysis

June 1992

Section A
1 Distinguish between liquidity and profitability
2 Calculate financial ratios for potential new customer and assess creditworthiness

Section B
3 The importance of a qualifying adjective for 'cost'.
4 Financial appraisal of a new product; pricing strategy
5 Methods of financing a fleet of distribution vehicles
6 Sales budget by month by line

Section C
7 Performance measures for divisional appraisal
8 Assess performance by territory, line, customer group; further information required for a thorough evaluation

INTRODUCTION

December 1991

Section A
1 How an enterprise's financial position might affect marketing activity
2 Effect of inflation on usefulness of information contained in financial reports

Section B
3 Calculations based on revenue and cost characteristics of a product
4 Decision making: whether to accept an order at a given price
5 The use of cost data based on absorption principles; decision making with apportioned versus fixed costs
6 Investment appraisal using different methods

Section C
7 Prepare budget for a sales office and compare yearly actual figures
8 Evaluating performance of sales persons

June 1991

Section A
1 Methods of financing sales made on credit terms
2 Analyse the financial statements of a prospective credit customer

Section B
3 Categories of cost in terms of planning, decision-making and control
4 Segmental analysis of sales and related costs
5 Financial appraisal of a new product; pricing strategy
6 Analysis of sales results given by product, territory and customer

Section C
7 Discuss the calculation of the rate of return of an investment; ROI as a performance measure of marketing operations
8 Sales variances; explain standard setting for marketing activities

How to use this BPP Study Text

The study text itself is structured as far as possible to correspond with the order in which the syllabus itself is laid out and you should work through each part in order.

Each part of the text is divided into chapters which deal with individual subjects in the syllabus. At the end of each chapter you will find a number of short questions which test your knowledge of the material which you have just read.

If you can provide complete answers to each of these short questions then you should try the relevant illustrative question for the chapter. These are located towards the back of the text and the relevant question number is indicated at the end of each chapter.

When you have checked your solution against ours and have understood the reasons for any differences then you are ready to proceed to the next chapter or part of the text.

This systematic approach will ensure that you have a thorough understanding of each aspect of the syllabus before you move on to a fresh one.

INTRODUCTION

Study checklist

This checklist is designed to help you chart your progress through this Study Text and thus through the Institute's syllabus. You can record the dates on which you complete your study of each chapter, and attempt the corresponding illustrative questions. You will thus ensure that you are on track to complete your study in good time to allow for revision before the exam.

	Text chapters	*Illustrative questions*
	Ch Nos/Date Comp	Ques Nos/Date Comp

Analysing the current financial position

	Text chapters	Illustrative questions
The role of accounting in marketing	1	1
Financial accounts	2	2
Interpretation of accounts	3	3
Limitations of historical cost accounts	4	4

Planning for the future

	Text chapters	Illustrative questions
Budgeting	5	5
Costs for decision making	6	6
Costing systems: standard costing	7	7
Costing systems: absorption and marginal costing	8	8
Cost-volume-profit analysis (breakeven analysis)	9	9
Pricing decisions	10	10
Decision-making techniques	11	11
Sources of finance	12	12

Control

	Text chapters	Illustrative questions
Variance analysis	13	13
Measuring performance	14	14

PART A

ANALYSING THE CURRENT
FINANCIAL POSITION

Chapter 1

THE ROLE OF ACCOUNTING IN MARKETING

This chapter covers the following topics.

1.   The role of accounting in marketing
2.   Profit or cash
3.   The costs and benefits of financial information

---

1.   THE ROLE OF ACCOUNTING IN MARKETING

1.1   Everyone has their own idea of what accounting is. Most people know that it is something to do with business, and most assume that it is something to do with the money that the business owns. For those who aspire to a career in marketing management, as in any sector of business, finance cannot remain a vague and shadowy discipline, the sole responsibility of professional accountants. Throughout your CIM studies you will be expected to demonstrate your understanding of the financial implications of the marketing strategies which you propose.

1.2   The concepts, techniques and disciplines of accounting provide a framework for the essential and fundamental process of business planning and control. Resources in their many forms (plant, people, materials and stock) are the organisation's lifeblood and accounting is the discipline dedicated to monitoring, maintaining and improving the 'health' of the business. The responsibility for that state of health cannot be abdicated to the accountants. Every manager's action can and does have an impact on the overall well-being of the operation and it is essential that those developing marketing strategy:

(a)   understand the impact of their decisions on the finances of the business;

(b)   are able to work effectively with the finance professionals in the business;

(c)   are competent in the use of financial techniques necessary in the day to day management and planning for their own departments.

1.3   Business exists to achieve agreed objectives, the organisation's corporate objectives. In the private sector these are likely to be profit based and in the non-profit making public and charity sectors they require provision of a level of service or output within the constraints of the available funding. Whatever the nature of the objectives, every organisation is faced with the same constraints: limited resources.

1.4 The task of management involves making a series of decisions about how best to use these scarce resources in pursuit of the organisation's objectives. Decisions between the alternatives available are made easier by making comparisons in the common denominator of the financial context.

1.5 This process of decision-making is not without its risks. Decisions are about influencing future events, which cannot be predicted accurately. The process of planning, based on careful analysis of the past and current position, aims to minimise the risks of future failure by careful allocation of the operation's scarce resources. Systems of control are developed to monitor performance as plans are implemented and to alert managers to deviations and changes which require their action and attention if the desired goals are to be attained.

1.6 There are three dimensions to the financial comparisons which can aid decision making:

(a) looking back at the organisation's financial history and records to identify similar situations and to draw conclusions and trends from the information;

(b) to examine published information of other organisations for any indicators which may aid decision making;

(c) forecasts of the future based on assumptions.

1.7 Using financial analysis as a framework for planning for the future is a sound basis because one of the major objectives of most private sector businesses is to provide a satisfactory financial return for the owners of the business: *the profit concept.*

1.8 Financial involvement in marketing planning can therefore be determined by three main phases:

(a) analysis of the past to establish the basis for planning;

(b) planning in order to set objectives and to understand how they will be achieved;

(c) control over the activities in order to use feedback to decide how well the objectives are being achieved and instigating corrective action where necessary.

This can be represented diagrammatically as follows.

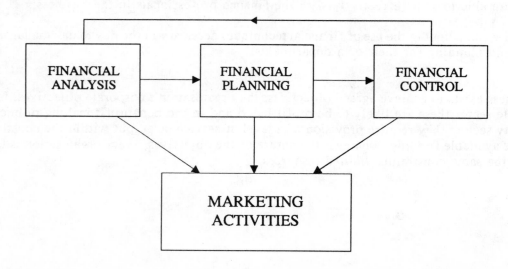

The accounting department relative to marketing

1.9 The relative importance of good communications between the marketing and accounting functions cannot be over-emphasised. The reasons for communication will be varied, reflecting the different roles which might be undertaken by the accounting function. There are three important accounting roles, and they produce three different forms of output, all of which are relevant to the marketing department.

(a) *Financial accounting*. For public limited companies (plcs) the financial accounts are published in a glossy document called the annual report and accounts, and which may include both statutory information and some general statements on the health and prospects of the business. It will include a *balance sheet*, a *profit and loss account* and a *cash flow statement*. It may also include an optional *value added statement*. These components will be discussed later in this text. Private limited companies also produce financial accounts. The annual report also includes a *directors' report* and a *chairman's report* which talk about the past and future of the company in general terms.

Financial accounting is important to marketing activities because the financial effects of marketing activities must be recorded properly and accurately. The financial accounting function does not aid the decision-making process, merely acting as a recorder of historic events.

(b) *Management accounting*. As part of a continuous process within a company management accounts will be produced, usually on a monthly or quarterly basis, which are not available to outside users. These accounts are much more operationally drawn and are intended to help the decision making process within the company. They may well include a comparison of performance to date against a predetermined target as budget and assess that performance against the budget for the full year. Remember that one of the objectives of the business will be to satisfy the return required by the owners, and hence there is a need to constantly focus attention on that anticipated return.

The management accounting function should therefore interact very closely with the marketing function as an aid to analysis, planning *and* control.

(c) *Corporate finance*. This department may be categorised as 'finance' rather than 'accounting'. It may be called 'treasury management'. It is concerned with financial management, in the sense that it is concerned with ensuring that sufficient funds are available to the business in order for it to pursue its objectives. The funds must be in an appropriate form for both their specific purpose and for the business as a whole. Marketing activities are not usually separately funded, but are included in the financial plans produced in the management accounting function. We will look at funding and sources of finance in more detail in a later chapter.

The users of published accounts

1.10 We will look at financial accounts in more detail in the next chapter. We need to consider here *why* financial accounts are prepared. Financial accounts are required to be published by statute but are also designed to meet the needs of various different users. These users might want information about a business for one or more of the following reasons.

(a) The *owners* will want to know how well the company is doing, so they can decide how much profit to withdraw from the business for their own use.

(b) *Managers* need information about the company's financial situation as it is currently and as it is expected to be in the future. This is to enable them to manage the business efficiently and to take effective control and planning decisions.

(c) *Suppliers* will want to know about the company's ability to pay its debts.

(d) *Customers* need to know that the company is a secure source of supply and is in no danger of having to close down.

(e) *Providers of finance to the company* will want to ensure that the company is able to keep up with interest payments, and eventually to repay the amounts advanced.

(f) The *Inland Revenue* will want to know about business profits in order to assess the tax payable by the company.

(g) *Employees of the company* have a right to information about the company's financial situation, because their future careers and the size of their wages and salaries are dependent on it.

(h) *Financial analysts and advisers* need information for their clients or audience. For example, stockbrokers will need information to advise investors in stocks and shares; credit agencies will want information to advise potential suppliers of goods to the company; and journalists need information for their reading public.

Exercise

Obtain copies of as many company reports which contain published accounts as possible. These can be obtained from a variety of sources, including via the *Financial Times* annual report service. Examine the content of the accounts.

Do not be concerned with some of the more technical aspects of financial information but look at the layout of the accounts. It would be useful if you could obtain copies of similar documents from a couple of your major competitors or customers and compare the basic layout and information available. You may also note how useful this report has become as a means of communicating a public relations message to the shareholders and potential shareholders, to banks and to other users.

1.11 In short, there are a great many people who have any number of reasons for wanting information about a business. That in itself is a good reason for a business to take the trouble to record and analyse all its transactions, but in addition there are two other reasons.

(a) There are some legal requirements to prepare financial information.

(b) There are Statements of Standard Accounting Practice (SSAPs), which are legally binding and which accountants are obliged to implement. These are gradually being replaced by Financial Reporting Standards (FRSs).

1.12 Included in these groups are those audiences which marketing professionals refer to as the 'financial public' and to whom corporate public relations and publicity activity are frequently targeted. Their perceptions and confidence in the financial health and prospects for the business are essential to the long term survival and growth of the operation. Communicating with them is increasingly recognised as an important aspect of marketing activity. Understanding the basis of the financial needs of these market segments will mean you are better equipped to devise strategies and communicate messages to influence them.

2. PROFIT OR CASH

2.1 As marketing professionals you are well aware of the need for corporate objectives to be quantified. You will also be well versed in the concept of the need to satisfy the consumer. Owners of a business are in a sense the ultimate consumer in that they will need an acceptable return for their financial commitment to the business. The return is usually expressed as profit. If the owner or shareholder is not satisfied with his or her return then he or she may decide to sell their investment in the business and reinvest somewhere else. For this reason the determination of profitability is extremely important and the impact on profitability of the various alternative projects before a decision is made is of great significance.

2.2 We can define profit in very simple terms as follows.

$$P = S - E$$

Where   P = Profit
        S = Sales value (or revenue)
        E = Expenses (or costs)

2.3 As a very simple example, suppose that you buy a cheap jacket for £8. You then sell it to a friend for £10. Obviously, you are now £2 better off, and this £2 represents your *profit*.

2.4 The relationship between profit and cash in the above example is simple and direct. The £2 profit was represented by £2 in cash. But what if your friend had given you an IOU for the £10, to be paid in one month's time? You have still made a profit of £2 on the sale of your jacket, but you are £8 worse off in terms of cash than you were before you touched the jacket. This very basic example shows the difference between profit and cash. In the case of limited companies, the distinction between profit and cash is usually described in terms of profitability and liquidity.

Profitability v liquidity

2.5 The following definitions are important.

(a) *Liquidity* can be defined as a state of having access to liquid assets, where liquid assets are cash or assets which can be converted quickly and easily into cash.

(b) *Profitability* may be defined as the profit achieved per £ of investment.

2.6   It is important to note the significance of both these states to a company and we can demonstrate the significance using a diagram.

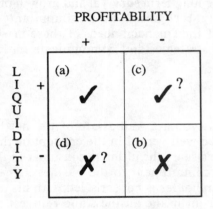

2.7   The four states demonstrated by this diagram can be described in terms of ability to survive.

(a)   The company which is both profitable and liquid will survive as it can pay bills as they become due and it can attract investment because it is profitable.

(b)   A company which is neither liquid or profitable will not survive. It cannot pay bills as they become due and it cannot attract investment because it is not profitable and it therefore will not give a good return to the investor.

(c)   This situation is harder to determine. The company has money to pay bills in the short term but it is unprofitable and therefore would not be expected to survive in the long term.

(d)   The company in this situation would have difficulty surviving in the short term as it cannot pay its bills. However, its profitability should attract long term investment.

Note. Limited companies are not allowed to continue trading if they cannot pay bills as they fall due. Liquidity is therefore very important to them.

2.8   The implications for marketing liquidity and profitability are highlighted by the difference between the accounting for 'order getting' versus 'order filling'.

Order getting versus order filling

2.9   The most evident divergence between marketing and its financial treatment is that the specific marketing effort is primarily directed at getting an order placed by a customer. There may well be a time lag between the time of the majority of the marketing effort (its expense) and the time when the benefits to the business will be seen. A typical example would be advertising, which may be heavy in the introductory and growth years of a product's life but relatively light in maturity and decline. It could therefore be reasonably argued that the benefits of the initial advertising expenditure are not felt until much later and that, under the rules of matching revenue and expense, the cost of advertising should be spread over the life cycle of the product. Here, however, the concept of *prudence* is generally observed by accountants. The view that prevails is that the revenues from sales in future periods are not certain and it is therefore more prudent to write off the costs of advertising as they arise.

2.10 We have also highlighted another area of divergence between the marketing effort and the accounting treatment of that effort. Marketing is often charged with filling the order book. For a business to earn a satisfactory financial return it must sell goods or services at a price which exceeds its costs *and* the sale must take place. This is not the same as making an order or producing the goods for possible sale at some future point in time. Unless there is a contract that specifically states anything to the contrary, a sale is not recognised until the goods have been delivered to, and accepted by the customer.

2.11 You will note that the payment for goods or services is not mentioned in the above definition. A sale is recognised by the accountant when delivery takes place and the goods are accepted. In practice you will find that the production of an invoice is the signal for recognition of a sale. The invoice is only produced when an order and goods delivered are matched, or when some record of services rendered is signed as completed by an operational manager. However, the customer may not have paid for those goods and services and indeed may not do so for a month or so. Nevertheless a sale will be recognised at this time and a profit statement can be prepared. The profit on the transaction will be defined by:

$$\text{PROFIT} = \text{SALES VALUE} - \text{EXPENSES}$$

2.12 The important aspect in determining what revenues and costs to include is related to the activity involved. It is rather like your electricity bill at home which usually arrives at the end of every quarter of the year. Simply because you have not got a bill at the end of the second month of the quarter does not suggest that you have not used some electricity. You therefore still have a liability to pay a bill relating to that period in time even though its value has not been itemised for you. Accountants would recognise this expense because you have used the resource, even though you do not know exactly what the cost is and despite the fact that you have not paid for it yet. They will usually guess at the possible cost based on past experience.

2.13 It is similarly important for marketing professionals to recognise that a business which is increasing its revenue, perhaps as a result of increased sales effort, is not necessarily increasingly profitable. If new sales are won on the basis of substantially increased marketing costs, or by offering significant discounts, it is possible to increase revenue without increasing profits.

For example, a business sells its products for £10 each and in period 1 sales = 10 units and total expenses £80.

Period 1

$$
\begin{array}{lll}
\text{Profit} & = \text{revenue} & - \text{expenses} \\
\text{£20} & \text{£100} & \text{£80}
\end{array}
$$

Period 2

After an increased expenditure on marketing support, costs increase by £20 and sales increase to 12 units.

$$£20 = £120 - £100$$

Although revenue has increased by 20% the profit has stayed the same.

2.14 Alternatively if the additional sales are earned by offering significant discounts so that the sales price per unit becomes £8 each, it can be seen that both revenue and profit can actually fall, despite sales volume rising, to 12 units each.

$$£16 = £96 - £80$$

Again, you must note that we only mention the profit, revenue and expense. We do not talk about cash. The customer may not pay us for some time and we may not pay our marketing consultant for some time. However, the activity of the transaction has been clearly defined and the accountant will recognise this activity in his or her profit and loss account.

2.15 It is important not to mix up the concepts of profit and cash. Making a profit does not mean that your business is generating cash, as you can see above. An accountant would suggest that a transaction can have made a profit or a loss based on the activities that have taken place despite the fact that a customer has not paid for his or her goods and services, and that the business has not yet paid its sales staff, its advertising agency or its electricity bill. The activities involved indicate a sale has been made and that expenses have been incurred (but not paid) in making that sale. This fundamental principle will crop up again and again and you must be sure that you fully understand it.

3. THE COSTS AND BENEFITS OF FINANCIAL INFORMATION

3.1 All information has a cost. It is true that a company *must* produce certain information, for externally published accounts. In the decision-making process, however, the level of financial information required will usually depend on the relative cost of the information compared to the benefit that is expected from having the information for the decision. In many cases the benefit will represent a reduction of risk when making the decision.

3.2 Obviously, the more critical the decision, in terms of both the cost and the reversability of the decision, then the more financial information is required and the more one is prepared to pay to obtain it. Consider the differences in the following situations.

(a) A large conglomerate is considering introducing a new product line. Projected costs are £15m over the next five years. The company is having some difficulty in estimating annual unit sales and total income.

(b) One of the sales staff needs a new car. The cost of the car is approximately £12,500. The company's policy is to find the cheapest possible insurance.

3.3 It is clear that the cost of the information on sales required in the first situation will be much higher than that in the second situation. In (a) the company will probably spend hundreds of thousands of pounds collecting market research information because the decision to produce, once made, will be very difficult to reverse and the costs of production are very high. On the other hand, in situation (b), the cost of the information will probably consist of a few telephone calls to insurance brokers and the cost of staff time lost in making the calls. The relative saving compared with this cost is quite low.

4. CONCLUSION

4.1 This chapter has introduced you to the fundamental principles underlying the accounts which are produced for publication. Although these accounts are relevant to your CIM studies, they are aimed at so many user groups and determined to such a large extent by statute that they are unlikely to be of great use in your practical experience within your business. Within that environment there should be much greater detail available upon which to structure your decisions provided the data relates entirely to your own business. The published accounts of companies are, however, relevant in understanding the basic financial health of a company and may provide some insight into fundamental trends and strategies being adopted.

TEST YOUR KNOWLEDGE
The numbers in brackets refer to paragraphs of this chapter

1   Why is accounting useful to the marketing manager? (1.2)

2   What are the three main roles of the accounting function in relation to marketing activities? (1.9)

3   What kinds of people use published accounts and why? (1.10)

4   What is a simple definition of profit? (2.5)

5   How is liquidity defined? (2.5(a))

6   How is profitability defined? (2.5(b))

7   What factors need to be taken into account when considering the need for financial information? (3.2)

Now try question 1 at the end of the text

Chapter 2

FINANCIAL ACCOUNTS

This chapter covers the following topics.

1. The regulatory framework
2. The balance sheet
3. Fixed assets
4. Current assets
5. Liabilities
6. Capital and reserves
7. The profit and loss account
8. Cash flow statements
9. The statement of source and application of funds
10. The value added statement

---

1. THE REGULATORY FRAMEWORK

1.1 Unincorporated businesses in the UK can prepare their financial statements in any form they choose. However, companies are required to comply with the provisions of the Companies Act 1985 in preparing their financial statements and are also subject to the provisions of Statements of Standard Accounting Practice (SSAPs) and their successors Financial Reporting Standards (FRSs). Public limited companies which are listed on the Stock Exchange must comply with Stock Exchange requirements.

1.2 These regulations provide the 'framework' which gives authority to company accounts. We will look at the bodies which produce these rules briefly, to give you an idea of how and why such regulations exist. You need not concern yourself with the details of any of the legislation or accounting standards.

Company law

1.3 In 1985, all existing companies legislation was brought together in a number of consolidating Acts, of which by far the most important is the Companies Act 1985 (CA 1985). This was substantially amended on the enactment of the Companies Act 1989 (CA 1989).

1.4 Since the United Kingdom became a member of the European Community (EC) it has been obliged to comply with legal requirements decided on by the EC. It does this by enacting UK laws to implement EC directives.

Accounting Standards (FRSs and SSAPs)

1.5 Until recently a body called the Accounting Standards Committee was responsible for producing SSAPs. The ASC had been set up by some of the big UK accountancy bodies. The main purposes of the SSAPs were to narrow areas of difference and variety in accounting practice and encourage disclosure of accounting policies and departures from the accounting treatments prescribed by the standards.

1.6 In 1991 the ASC was disbanded and new regulatory arrangements were put into effect, the following bodies being formed.

Financial Reporting Council (FRC)

1.7 The FRC covers a wide constituency of interests at a high level. It guides the standard setting body (see below) on policy and ensures that its work is properly financed. It also funds and oversees the Review Panel (see below). Members are drawn from users, preparers and auditors of accounts.

Accounting Standards Board (ASB)

1.8 The ASB is responsible for producing Financial Reporting Standards.

Urgent Issues Task Force (UITF)

1.9 The UITF is an offshoot of the ASB. Its function is to tackle urgent matters not covered by existing standards, and for which, given the urgency, the normal standard setting process would not be practicable.

The Review Panel

1.10 The Review Board is chaired by a barrister and it is concerned with the examination and questioning of departures from accounting standards by large companies. The Panel can force companies to revise their accounts if it is felt necessary.

1.11 You do not need to know any details of the regulatory framework, but this general outline helps to put financial accounts into perspective.

2. THE BALANCE SHEET

2.1 We are going to look at all the statements from a set of accounts in turn in this chapter. We will examine each statement and each function of the statement, starting with the balance sheet.

ARC LIMITED
BALANCE SHEETS AT 31 DECEMBER

	19X0		19X1	
Fixed assets	£'000	£'000	£'000	£'000
Plant, machinery and equipment, at cost		17,600		23,900
Less accumulated depreciation		9,500		10,750
		8,100		13,150
Current assets				
Stocks	5,000		15,000	
Trade debtors	8,600		26,700	
Prepayments	300		400	
Cash at bank and in hand	600		-	
	14,500		42,100	
Current liabilities				
Bank overdraft	-		16,200	
Trade creditors	6,000		10,000	
Accruals	800		1,000	
Taxation	3,200		5,200	
Dividends	3,200		6,000	
	13,000		38,400	
Net current assets		1,500		3,700
Loans				
15% debenture stock		600		750
Net assets		9,000		16,100
Capital and reserves				
Ordinary shares of £1 each		5,000		5,000
10% preference shares of £1 each		1,000		1,000
Profit and loss account		3,000		10,100
		9,000		16,100

2.2 Before we look at the balance sheet in any detail, or even define it, we need to look at the *accounting equation*. This is the rule by which accounts are constructed and it explains why the 'net assets' and the total of 'share capital and reserves' are both equal to £16,100,000 in 19X1 in the balance sheet shown above. Don't worry if you don't understand this section: come back to it at the end of the chapter.

The accounting equation

2.3 The assets of a business are always equal to its liabilities (assets and liabilities are described later). This is knows as the accounting equation, and we can write it as:

$$\text{Liabilities} = \text{Assets}$$

2.4 Capital is the amount invested by the owners in the business and the business owes it to the owners (in a similar way to owing money to creditors). So we can add this into the equation and get:

$$\text{Capital} + \text{Liabilities} = \text{Assets}$$

2.5 We can introduce the idea of net assets where *net assets* just means the difference between total assets and total liabilities.

The accounting equation is:

$$\text{Capital} + \text{Liabilities} = \text{Assets}$$

but this could equally well be written:

$$\text{Capital} = \text{Assets} - \text{Liabilities}$$

Since the second part of this equation is what we call net assets, we can write, even more simply:

$$\text{Capital} = \text{Net assets}$$

2.6 Another way of understanding the accounting equation is to look at the accounts which are produced by a company. They will always produce:

(a) a balance sheet at a given date;

(b) a profit and loss account detailing the results of the operation of the business over a period in time (usually one year).

The importance aspect to notice here is the time periods referred to. A balance sheet is a picture of the affairs of the company at a point in time, for example on 31 December. By 3 January the next year some cash may have been received, some paid, some sales made and so on and therefore the balance sheet on that day will be different.

2.7 The profit and loss account on the other hand refers to trading activity over a period of time.

2.8 Now if we compare two basic balance sheets with each other, one being produced exactly one year after the other, what do you expect to have changed within the basic accounting equation?

One hopes that the business in that time will have made a profit. Profit is the return generated by the business for the owners and everything that is owed to the owners is referred to as 'capital'. If we assume that there has been no other change to the capital figure then:

$$\text{Profit} = \text{Change in net assets}$$

because the accounting equation must always balance. We would surely have expected the net assets to change over the year that the business has traded (it will have sold goods; paid its suppliers; maybe bought some other assets and be due money from its customers) but the accounting equation will remain in balance. The change in the net assets must equal the profit over the period.

The balance sheet

2.9 Particular aspects to note about the balance sheets shown above are as follows.

(a) The balance sheet is headed up 'as at 31 December 19X1'. This is telling the user that it is a picture of the affairs of the company at a point in time. Over time this picture will change.

(b) Comparative figures (figures for the previous period) are always given to indicate movement. They should be prepared on a consistent basis and usually refer to the balance sheet one year ago.

(c) The accounting equation balances. In the example the capital investment (or shareholders' funds) equals the net assets.

(d) The capital investment in the business has risen by (£16,100,000 - £9,000,000) = £7,100,000 between the two years. This usually means that the business made a profit after tax of £7,100,000 (although there can be other explanations). The movement in the shareholders' funds (capital and reserves) is exactly matched by a movement in the net assets (or capital employed).

2.10 We stated above that the balance sheet is a picture of the affairs of the company at a point in time. To expand on this description, the balance sheet is a statement of the assets, liabilities and capital of a business at a given moment in time. It captures in a 'snapshot', frozen at a single moment in time, a picture of something which is dynamic and continually changing.

2.11 The most important factor to consider when dealing with all the items in the balance is *valuation*. How would you expect a lease on a warehouse to be valued? At cost? at current value? These questions concerning valuation of both assets and liabilities are very important and we will consider them as we describe each item in the balance sheet in turn.

3. FIXED ASSETS

3.1 An *asset* is a possession which has a value to the business, Examples of assets are factories, office buildings, warehouses, delivery vans, lorries, plant and machinery, computer equipment, office furniture, cash and also goods held in store awaiting sale to customers, and raw materials and components held in store by a manufacturing business for use in production.

3.2 Some assets are held and used in operations for a long time. An office building might be occupied by administrative staff for years; similarly, a machine might have a productive life of many years before it wears out. Other assets are held for only a short time. The owner of a newsagent shop, for example, will have to sell his newspapers on the same day that he gets them, and weekly newspapers and monthly magazines also have a short shelf life. The more quickly a business can sell the goods it has in store, the more profit it is likely to make. That is the meaning of the phrase 'business is brisk'.

3.3 Assets in the balance sheet are divided into:

(a) fixed assets; and
(b) current assets.

Fixed assets

3.4 A fixed asset is any asset, tangible or intangible, acquired for retention by a business for the purpose of providing a service to the business, and not held for resale in the normal course of trading. Examples of fixed assets include the following:

(a) a salesman's car which is used by the business for three years;

(b) a 20 year lease on a warehouse;

(c) a new computerised order processing system which will not be obsolete for at least five years.

3.5 To be classed as a fixed asset in the balance sheet of a business, an item must satisfy two further conditions.

(a) Clearly, it must be used by the business. For example, a shareholder's own house would not normally appear on the business balance sheet.

(b) The asset must have a 'life' in use of more than one year (strictly, more than one 'accounting period' which might be more or less than one year).

3.6 A *tangible* fixed asset is a physical asset, that is, one that can be touched. It has a real 'solid' existence. The salesman's car mentioned above is tangible.

An *intangible* fixed asset is an asset which does not have a physical existence. It cannot be 'touched'. The expense of acquiring patent rights or developing a new product would be classified as an intangible fixed asset. The value of a brand name also comes under this category.

Valuation of fixed assets

3.7 The valuation of fixed assets can cause some problems. In the past, fixed assets, whether tangible or intangible, were valued at their *historic cost*. This figure is easy to determine as it is usually the price paid in money for the asset when it was bought. If the asset was exchanged for another asset, then a valuation of the asset given in consideration at the time of sale should give a historic cost value.

3.8 The problems with this method of valuation are:

(a) the historic cost of the asset may be very different from the current value of an asset, particularly in the case of buildings and land which may have increased in value over the years; and

(b) the historic cost of the asset does not represent the true value of the asset to the business in terms of the future economic benefit expected to arise from the asset.

3.9 The first of these problems has been solved in published accounts by allowing an alternative method of valuation. Fixed assets may be revalued to their current value in the balance sheet. Any excess of the revalued amount over the historic cost is not a 'profit' because the asset has not actually been sold to *realise* that profit. This means that the excess cannot just be added to profit.

3.10 For example, suppose a warehouse was bought for £30,000 in 19X2. In 19X5 the warehouse was revalued to a current value of £50,000. The difference of £20,000 is not a profit that the business has actually received yet and so it cannot be added to profit and given out to the shareholders in the form of dividends.

3.11 The question of the economic value of an asset to a business is not usually tackled by financial accounts as historic cost or revaluation figures are straightforward, objective and make accounting easy. In the decision-making process, however, the economic value of an asset might be very important. The value to the business is usually considered in terms of *deprival value*.

3.12 *Deprival value* is an important concept, which you may find rather difficult to understand at first, and you should read the following explanation carefully.

   (a) The deprival value of an asset is the loss which a business entity would suffer if it were deprived of the use of the asset.

   (b) 'Value to the business' reflects the extra funds which would be required to maintain the operating capability of the business entity if it suddenly lost the use of an asset.

3.13 Value to the business, or deprival value, can be any of the following values.

   (a) *Replacement cost*. In the case of fixed assets, it is assumed that the replacement cost of an asset would be its *net replacement cost* (NRC), its gross replacement cost minus an appropriate provision for depreciation to reflect the amount of its life already 'used up'.

   (b) *Net realisable value* (NRV), which is what the asset could be sold for, net of any disposal costs.

   (c) *Economic value* (EV), or utility, which is what the existing asset will be worth to the company over the rest of its useful life.

3.14 The choice of deprival value from one of the three values listed will depend on circumstances. The decision tree on the next page illustrates the principles involved in the choice.

3.15 If the asset is worth replacing, its deprival value will always be net replacement cost. If the asset is not worth replacing, it might be disposed of straight away, or else it might be kept in operation until the end of its useful life.

3.16 You may therefore come across a statement that deprival value is the lower of:

   (a) net replacement cost; and
   (b) the higher of net realisable value and economic value.

3.17 We have already seen that if an asset is not worth replacing at the end of its life, the deprival value will be NRV or EV. However, there are many assets which will not be replaced either:

(a) because the asset is technologically obsolete, and has been (or will be) superseded by more modern equipment; or

(b) because the business is changing the nature of its operation and will not want to continue in the same line of business once the asset has been used up.

3.18 Such assets, even though there are reasons not to replace them, would still be valued (usually) at net replacement cost, because this 'deprival value' still provides an estimate of the operating capability of the company.

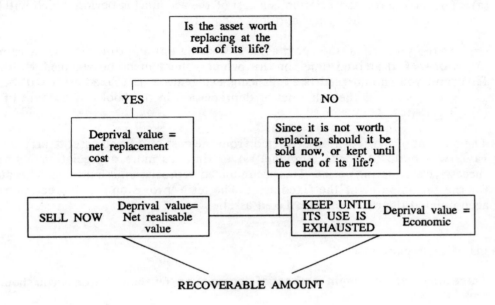

Fixed assets and depreciation

3.19 Fixed assets might be held and used by a business for a number of years, but they wear out or lose their usefulness in the course of time. Every tangible fixed asset has a limited life. The only exception is freehold land.

3.20 The accounts of a business try to recognise that the cost of a fixed asset is gradually consumed as the asset wears out. This is done by gradually writing off the asset's cost in the profit and loss account over several accounting periods. For example, in the case of a machine costing £1,000 and expected to wear out after ten years, it might be appropriate to reduce the balance sheet value by £100 each year. This process is known as depreciation. Please note that this does not represent a movement in cash. It simply reflects a permanent devaluation of the value of the asset to the business.

3.21 Let us imagine, for example, that a balance sheet was drawn up four years after the asset was purchased. The amount of depreciation which would have accumulated would be 4 × £100 = £400. The machine would then appear in the balance sheet as follows.

	£
Machine at original cost	1,000
Less accumulated depreciation	400
Net book value*	600

* Net book value = the value of the asset in the books of account, net of depreciation. After ten years the asset would be fully depreciated and would appear in the balance sheet with a net book value of zero.

Depreciation in the accounts of a business

3.22 When a fixed asset is depreciated, two things must be accounted for.

(a) The charge for depreciation is a cost of the accounting period which will be charged as an expense in the profit and loss account.

(b) At the same time, the fixed asset is wearing out and diminishing in value, and so the value of the fixed asset in the balance sheet must be reduced by the amount of depreciation charged. The balance sheet value of the fixed asset will be its 'net book value' which is the value net of depreciation in the books of account of the business.

3.23 The amount of depreciation deducted from the cost of a fixed asset to arrive at its net book value will build up (or 'accumulate') over time, as more depreciation is charged in each successive accounting period. This accumulated depreciation is a provision because it provides for the fall in value of the fixed asset. The term 'provision for depreciation' refers to the accumulated depreciation of a fixed asset.

Methods of depreciation

3.24 There are several different methods of depreciation. Of these, the ones you should know about are:

(a) the straight-line method;
(b) the reducing balance method; and
(c) the machine hour method (sometimes called the units of output method).

The straight line method

3.25 This is the most commonly used method of all. The total depreciable amount is charged in equal instalments to each accounting period over the expected useful life of the asset. (In this way, the net book value of the fixed asset declines at a steady rate, or in a 'straight line' over time.)

3.26 The annual depreciation charge is calculated as:

$$\frac{\text{Cost of asset minus residual value}}{\text{Expected useful life of the asset}}$$

Example: straight line depreciation

3.27 (a) A fixed asset costing £20,000 with an estimated life of 10 years and no residual value would be depreciated at the rate of:

$$\frac{£20,000}{10 \text{ years}} = £2,000 \text{ per annum}$$

(b) A fixed asset costing £60,000 has an estimated life of 5 years and a residual value of £7,000. The annual depreciation charge using the straight line method would be:

$$\frac{£(60,000 - 7,000)}{5 \text{ years}} = £10,600 \text{ per annum}$$

The net book value of the fixed asset would be:

	After 1 year £	After 2 years £	After 3 years £	After 4 years £	After 5 years £
Cost of the asset	60,000	60,000	60,000	60,000	60,000
Accumulated depreciation	10,600	21,200	31,800	42,400	53,000
Net book value	49,400	38,800	28,200	17,600	7,000*

* its estimated residual value.

3.28 Since the depreciation charge per annum is the same amount every year with the straight line method, it is often convenient to state that depreciation is charged at the rate of x per cent per annum on the cost of the asset. In the example in Paragraph 3.27(a) above, the depreciation charge per annum is 10% of cost (10% of £20,000 = £2,000).

3.29 The straight line method of depreciation is a fair allocation of the total depreciable amount between the different accounting periods, provided that it is reasonable to assume that the business enjoys equal benefits from the use of the asset in every period throughout its life.

The reducing balance method

3.30 The reducing balance method of depreciation calculates the annual depreciation charge as a fixed percentage of the net book value of the asset, as at the end of the previous accounting period.

3.31 For example, suppose that a business purchases a fixed asset at a cost of £10,000. Its expected useful life is 3 years and its estimated residual value is £2,160. The business wishes to use the reducing balance method to depreciate the asset, and calculates that the rate of depreciation should be 40% of the reducing (net book) value of the asset. (The method of deciding that 40% is a suitable annual percentage is a problem of mathematics, not financial accounting, and is not described here.)

The total depreciable amount is £(10,000 - 2,160) = £7,840.

The depreciation charge per annum and the net book value of the asset as at the end of each year will be as follows:

	£	Accumulated depreciation £
Asset at cost	10,000	
Depreciation in year 1 (40%)	4,000	4,000
Net book value at end of year 1	6,000	
Depreciation in year 2 (40% of reducing balance)	2,400	6,400 (4,000 + 2,400)
Net book value at end of year 2	3,600	
Depreciation in year 3 (40%)	1,440	7,840 (6,400 + 1,440)
Net book value at end of year 3	2,160	

3.32 You should note that with the reducing balance method, the annual charge for depreciation is higher in the earlier years of the asset's life, and lower in the later years. In the example above, the annual charges for years 1, 2 and 3 are £4,000, £2,400 and £1,440 respectively.

3.33 The reducing balance method might therefore be used when it is considered fair to allocate a greater proportion of the total depreciable amount to the earlier years and a lower proportion to later years, on the assumption that the benefits obtained by the business from using the asset decline over time.

The machine hour method of depreciation

3.34 As the name of this method implies, it is a method of depreciation which might be considered suitable for plant and machinery, where it is assumed that the fixed asset wears out through use rather than over time. Instead of calculating a depreciation charge relating to a period of time, depreciation is calculated according to the number of hours of use made of the machine by the business during the course of the period.

3.35 The life of the asset is estimated in hours (or miles or other conventional units) and each unit is given a money value for depreciation purposes. The rate of depreciation is calculated as:

$$\frac{\text{Cost of the asset minus estimated residual value}}{\text{Estimated useful life of the asset in hours of used time}}$$

Example: the machine hour method

3.36 A business purchases a machine at a cost of £45,000. Its estimated useful life is 8,000 hours of running time, and its estimated residual value is £5,000.

The rate of depreciation by the machine hour method will be:

$$\frac{£(45,000 - 5,000)}{8,000 \text{ hours}} = £5 \text{ per machine hour}$$

3.37 Suppose that the actual use of the machine each year is:

	Hours
Year 1	3,000
Year 2	1,500
Year 3	2,500
Year 4	1,000
	8,000 hours

We can calculate the annual depreciation charge and net book value of the machine as at the end of each year as follows:

Year	Depreciation charge in the P & L account of the year £	Accumulated depreciation as at end of the year £	Fixed asset at cost £	Net book value as at end of the year £
Start of life			45,000	45,000
Year 1 (3,000 × £5)	15,000	15,000	45,000	30,000
Year 2 (1,500 × £5)	7,500	22,500	45,000	22,500
Year 3 (2,500 × £5)	12,500	35,000	45,000	10,000
Year 4 (1,000 × £5)	5,000	40,000	45,000	5,000
	40,000			

3.38 This method is sometimes modified so as to base each year's depreciation on the number of units produced by the machine in that year, rather than on the number of hours in which the machine is active. In this case the depreciation method is referred to as the units of output method.

Applying a depreciation method consistently

3.39 It is up to the business concerned to decide which method of depreciation to apply to its fixed assets. Once that decision has been made, however, it should not be changed and the chosen method of depreciation should be applied consistently from year to year.

3.40 Similarly, it is up to the business to decide what a sensible life span for a fixed asset should be. Again, once that life span has been chosen, it should not be changed unless something unexpected happens to the fixed asset.

3.41 It is permissible for a business to depreciate different categories of fixed assets in different ways. For example, if a business owns three cars, then each car would normally be depreciated in the same way (for example by the straight line method) but another category of fixed asset, say, photocopiers, might be depreciated using a different method (for example by the machine hour method).

Exercise

A lorry bought for a business cost £17,000. It is expected to last for five years and then be sold for scrap for £2,000. Usage over the five years is expected to be:

Year 1	200 days
Year 2	100 days
Year 3	100 days
Year 4	150 days
Year 5	40 days

Required

Work out the depreciation to be charged each year under:

(a) the straight line method;
(b) the reducing balance method (using a rate of 35%); and
(c) the machine hour method.

Solution

(a) Under the straight line method, depreciation for each of the five years is:

$$\text{Annual depreciation} = \frac{£17,000 - 2,000}{5} = £3,000$$

(b) Under the reducing balance method, depreciation for each of the five years is:

Year	*Depreciation*		
1	35% × £17,000	=	£5,950
2	35% × (£17,000 - £5,950)		
	= 35% × £11,050	=	£3,868
3	35% × (£11,050 - £3,868)		
	= 35% × £7,182	=	£2,514
4	35% × (£7,182 - £2,514)		
	= 35% × £4,668	=	£1,634
5	Balance to bring book value down to £2,000		
	= £4,668 - £1,634 - £2,000	=	£1,034

(c) Under the machine hour method, depreciation for each of the five years is calculated as follows:

Total usage (days)	=	200 + 100 + 100 + 150 + 40	
	=	590 days	
Depreciation per day	=	$\frac{£(17,000 - 2,000)}{590}$ =	£25.42

Year	*Usage* *(days)*	*Depreciation (£)* *(days x £25.42)*
1	200	5,084.00
2	100	2,542.00
3	100	2,542.00
4	150	3,813.00
5	40	1,016.80
		14,997.80

(The answer does not come to exactly £15,000 because of the rounding carried out at the 'depreciation per day' stage of the calculation.)

3.42 The treatment of brands for accounting purposes has been the subject of some considerable debate over the past few years. Companies whose existence is determined by the strength of its brands wished to reflect the value of the brands on their balance sheets, since they would then most truly reflect the worth of the company. Initially this was particularly true of companies which felt vulnerable to a takeover threat when the balance sheet looked a little weak.

The inclusion of a value for the brand has however led to two problems.

(a) Who should value the brands and exactly what valuation methodology should be adopted?

(b) If the brand names are to be included as a fixed asset, should they be depreciated?

3.43 The valuation debate still rolls on but usually it is the directors of the business who ascribe a value to the brand name. The depreciation issue is a little more sensitive. Most public companies (plc's) would wish to minimise the charges against profit. As a result companies will argue that the brand value should not be depreciated unless there is a permanent diminution in the value of the brand. In multi-brand companies this is likely to be reasonable since as one brand declines another will be on its development stage. In a single brand company however it may be dangerous because competitor activity may result in a sudden decline in sales and hence a massive reduction in the value of the brand will occur. (Consider what happened to Perrier when problems occurred in the production process.)

Investments

3.44 An *investment* might also be a fixed asset. Investments are commonly found in the published accounts of large limited companies. A large company A might invest in another company B by purchasing some of the shares or debentures of B. These investments would earn income for A in the form of interest or dividends paid out by B. If the investments are purchased by A with a view to holding on to them for more than one year, they would be classified as fixed assets of A.

4. CURRENT ASSETS

4.1 Current assets are either:

(a) items owned by the business with the intention of turning them into cash within one year; or

(b) cash, including money in the bank, owned by the business.

These assets are 'current' in the sense that they are continually flowing through the business.

Current assets and the cash cycle

4.2 The definition in (a) above needs explaining further. Let us suppose that a trader, Chris Rhodes, runs a business selling motor cars, and purchases a showroom which he stocks with cars for sale. We will also suppose that he obtains the cars from a manufacturer, and pays for them in cash on delivery.

(a) If he sells a car in a cash sale, the goods are immediately converted into cash. The cash might then be used to buy more cars for re-sale.

(b) If he sells a car in a credit sale, the car will be given to the customer, who then becomes a debtor of the business. Eventually, the debtor will pay what he owes, and Chris Rhodes will receive cash. Once again, the cash might then be used to buy more cars for sale.

4.3 In this example:

(a) the cars (goods) held in stock for re-sale are current assets, because Chris Rhodes intends to sell them within one year, in the normal course of trade;

(b) any debtors are current assets, if they are expected to pay what they owe within one year;

(c) cash is a current asset.

4.4 The transactions described above could be shown as a cash cycle.

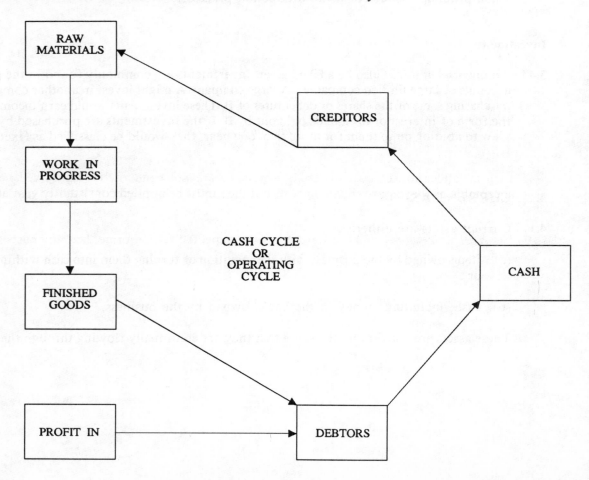

Cash is used to pay creditors for goods bought which are then sold. Sales on credit create debtors, but eventually cash is earned from the sale. Some, perhaps most, of the cash will then be used to replenish stocks.

4.5 The main items of current assets are therefore:

(a) stocks;
(b) debtors;
(c) cash.

Stocks

4.6 It is important to realise that cars are current assets of Chris Rhodes in the above example because he is in the business of buying and selling them, that is, he is a car trader. If he also has a car which he keeps and uses for business purchases, this car would be a fixed asset. The distinction between a fixed asset and a current asset is not what the asset is physically, but for what purpose it is obtained and used by the business.

4.7 Stock is defined as a quantity of goods which are for resale. They can exist either in their original form (for example as the component parts which when assembled make up a car, provided the company is in the business of manufacturing and selling cars), or as work in progress (as a part-assembled car) or as finished goods awaiting resale.

Stock valuation

4.8 Once again, the important question of valuation arises when considering the assets of the business. The basic rule of stock valuation is that stock should be valued at the lower of cost or net realisable value.

4.9 *Cost* is the amount paid for the stock in cash terms. This is easy to determine when there are very few items of individually recognisable stock. When there are large quantities of the same items in stock, it is necessary to assign the cost to each item. This is not always easy as the cost per item may have varied during the year. There are various methods which are used for such an allocation of cost to stock, which we are not concerned with here. They are all acceptable as they approximate to cost, but they must be applied consistently year after year.

4.10 *Net realisable value (NRV)* is defined as the expected selling price, less any costs still to be incurred getting the stock ready for sale and then selling it.

4.11 The basic concept here is that stocks (along with all current assets) should be valued at the *minimum* that could be obtained in cash if they were sold. We will see shortly that this applies to debtors in much the same way as it does to stock.

Example: stock valuation

4.12 Suppose that the marketing department holds quite a large quantity of stock items as samples. Unused sample items are returned to stock and therefore, at the year end, stock held by the marketing department must be valued. The four stock items held by the marketing department carry the following costs and NRVs.

Stock item	Cost	NRV
	£	£
A	27	32
B	14	8
C	43	55
D	29	40
	113	135

What is the total value that should be placed on the stock?

Solution

4.13 The value of stock is £107.

Stock item	Cost	NRV	Lower of cost/NRV
	£	£	£
A	27	32	27
B	14	8	8
C	43	55	43
D	29	40	29
	113	135	107

4.14 There are some other categories of current assets.

(a) *Short term investments*. These are stocks and shares of other businesses, currently owned but with the intention of selling them in the near future. For example, if a business has a lot of spare cash for a short time, its managers might decide to 'have a flutter' on the Stock Exchange, and buy shares in, say, Marks and Spencer, ICI or GEC. The shares will later be sold when the business needs the cash again. If share prices rise in the meantime, the business will make a profit from its short-term investment.

(b) *Prepayments*. These are amounts of money already paid by the business for benefits which have not yet been enjoyed but will be enjoyed within the next accounting period. Suppose, for example, that a business pays an annual insurance premium of £240 to insure its premises against fire and theft, and that the premium is payable annually in advance on 1 December. Now, if the business has an accounting year end of 31 December it will pay £240 on 1 December, but only enjoy one month's insurance cover by the end of the year. The remaining 11 months' cover (£220 cost, at £20 per month) will be enjoyed in the next year. The prepayment of £220 would therefore be shown in the balance sheet of the business, at 31 December, as a current asset.

A prepayment might be thought of as a form of debtor. In the example above, at 31 December the insurance company still owes the business 11 months' worth of insurance cover.

Debtors

4.15 A *debtor* is a person, business or company who owes money to the business. Just as a business might buy goods on credit, so too might it sell goods to customers on credit. A customer who buys goods without paying cash for them straight away is a debtor. For example, suppose that C sells goods on credit to D for £6,000 on terms that the debt must be settled within 2 months of the invoice date, 1 October. If D does not pay the £6,000 until 30 November, D will be a debtor of C for £6,000 from 1 October until 30 November.

4.16 A debtor is an asset of a business. When the debt is finally paid, the debtor 'disappears' as an asset, to be replaced by 'cash at bank and in hand'.

4.17 Although it is convenient to think of debtors as customers who buy goods on credit, it is more accurate to say that a debtor is anyone who owes the business money. Continuing the example of an insurance policy, if a business makes an insurance claim for fire damage, the insurance company would be a debtor for the money payable on the claim.

4.18 A distinction can be made between:

   (a) trade debtors, which are customers who still owe money for goods or services bought on credit in the course of the trading activities of the business; and

   (b) other debtors (anyone else owing money to the business).

The value of current assets in the balance sheet

4.19 Current assets must never be valued at more than their *net realisable value*, which is the amount of cash they will eventually earn the business when they are sold, minus the further costs required to get them into a condition for sale and to sell them. For example:

   (a) debtors are valued at the cash value of the debt, that is at their net realisable value;

   (b) stocks of goods are usually valued at their historical cost. However, if the net realisable value (NRV) of stocks is less than their cost, the stocks will be value at NRV instead of cost. In other words, stocks of goods are valued at the lower of their cost and net realisable value. In normal circumstances, the lower of the two amounts is cost.

Bad debts

4.20 One of the areas that is important to any business is its sales. Marketing effort is usually focused on obtaining orders. Accountants do not, however, recognise the sale until the goods or services are delivered to the customer and an invoice is raised. Some sales, however, do not get paid for despite the good intentions of the selling company.

4.21 Customers who buy goods on credit might fail to pay for them, perhaps out of dishonesty or perhaps because they have gone bankrupt and cannot pay. Customers in another country might be prevented from paying by the unexpected introduction of foreign exchange control restrictions by their country's government during the credit period.

4.22 For one reason or another, a business might decide to give up expecting payment and to write the debt off as a 'lost cause'. If it seems unlikely that cash will be received to extinguish that debt, then the amount of the debt will be 'written off' as an expense to the profit and loss account.

4.23 For example, if Alfred's Mini-Cab Service sends an invoice for £300 to a customer who subsequently does a 'moonlight flit' from his office premises, never to be seen or heard of again, the debt of £300 must be written off. It might seem sensible to record the business transaction as:

Sales £(300 - 300) = £0.

However, bad debts written off are accounted for as follows.

(a) Sales are shown at their invoice value in the trading account. The sale has been made, and gross profit should be earned. The subsequent failure to collect the debt is a separate matter, which is reported in the P & L account.

(b) Bad debts written off are shown as an expense in the profit and loss account.

4.24 In our example of Alfred's Mini-Cab Service:

	£
Sale (in the trading account)	300
Bad debt written off (expense in the P & L account)	300
Net profit on this transaction	0

4.25 Obviously, when a debt is written off, the value of the debtor as a current asset falls to zero. If the debt is expected to be uncollectable, its 'net realisable value' is nil, and so it has a zero balance sheet value.

4.26 A bad debt which has been written off might occasionally be paid unexpectedly. The only accounting problem to consider is when a debt written off as bad in one accounting period is subsequently paid in a later accounting period. The amount paid should be recorded as additional income in the profit and loss account of the period in which the payment is received.

A provision for doubtful debts

4.27 When bad debts are written off, specific debts owed to the business are identified as unlikely ever to be collected.

However, because of the risks involved in selling goods on credit, it might be accepted that a certain percentage of outstanding debts at any time are unlikely to be collected. Although it might be estimated that, say, 5% of debts will turn out bad, the business will not know until later which specific debts are bad.

4.28 Suppose that a business commences operations on 1 July 19X4, and in the twelve months to 30 June 19X5 makes sales of £300,000 (all on credit) and writes off bad debts amounting to £6,000. Cash received from customers during the year is £244,000, so that at 30 June 19X5, the business has outstanding debtors of £50,000.

	£
Credit sales during the year	300,000
Add debtors at 1 July 19X4	0
Total debts owed to the business	300,000
Less cash received from credit customers	244,000
	56,000
Less bad debts written off	6,000
Debtors outstanding at 30 June 19X5	50,000

Now, some of these outstanding debts might turn out to be bad. The business does not know on 30 June 19X5 which specific debts in the total £50,000 owed will be bad, but it might guess (from experience perhaps) that 5% of debts will eventually be found to be bad.

4.29 When a business expects bad debts amongst its current debtors, but does not yet know which specific debts will be bad, it can make a *provision for doubtful debts*.

4.30 A 'provision' is a 'providing for' and so a provision for doubtful debts provides for future bad debts, as a prudent precaution by the business. The business will be more likely to avoid claiming profits which subsequently fail to materialise because some debts turn out to be bad.

(a) When a provision is first made, the amount of this initial provision is charged as an expense in the profit and loss account of the business, for the period in which the provision is created.

(b) When a provision already exists, but is subsequently increased in size, the amount of the *increase* in provision is charged as an expense in the profit and loss account, for the period in which the increased provision is made.

(c) When a provision already exists, but is subsequently reduced in size, the amount of the *decrease* in provision is recorded as an item of 'income' in the profit and loss account, for the period in which the reduction in provision is made.

4.31 The balance sheet, as well as the profit and loss account of a business, must be adjusted to show a provision for doubtful debts. *The value of debtors in the balance sheet must be shown after deducting the provision for doubtful debts.* This is because the net realisable value of all the debtors of the business is estimated to be less than their 'sales value'. After all, this is the reason for making the provision in the first place. The net realisable value of debtors is the total value of debtors minus the provision for doubtful debts.

4.32 In the example above, the newly created provision for doubtful debts at 30 June 19X5 will be 5% of £50,000 = £2,500. This means that although total debtors are £50,000, eventual payment of only £47,500 is expected.

(a) In the P & L account, the newly created provision of £2,500 will be shown as an expense.

(b) In the balance sheet, debtors will be shown as follows.

	£
Total debtors at 30 June 19X5	50,000
Less provision for doubtful debts	2,500
	47,500

Debtors are thus shown at net realisable value.

Other provisions

4.33 A provision for doubtful debts is not the only type of provision you will come across in accounting. Companies legislation defines a provision as 'any amount written off or retained by way of providing for depreciation, renewals or diminution in value of assets or retained by way of providing for any known liability of which the amount cannot be determined with substantial accuracy.'

4.34 A good example for the marketing manager relates to sales of goods which carry a warranty, for example car sales. Under the terms of the sale we recognise that for a period of time the company will bear the cost of replacing parts if it becomes necessary. Since we have recognised the sales revenue in one period (provided we are in the business of selling cars), then the concept of prudence would suggest to the accountant that there may well be a cost in future periods that relates to that sale. Rather like the example of a 5% provision for bad debts, we do not know which parts will need replacement on a car by car basis, but history will indicate what types of equipment need replacing and what the cost will be. As a result it is usual to set up a warranty provision at the time of the sale.

5. LIABILITIES

5.1 A *liability* is something which is owed to somebody else. 'Liabilities' is the accounting term for the debts of a business.

(a) A bank loan or bank overdraft is a liability.

(b) Amounts may be owed to suppliers for goods purchased but not yet paid for: for example, a boatbuilder might buy some timber on credit from a timber merchant, which means that the boatbuilder does not have to pay for the timber until some time after it has been delivered. Until the boatbuilder pays what he owes, the timber merchant will be his *creditor* for the amount owed.

(c) Taxation may be owed to the government. A business pays tax on its profits but there is a gap in time between when a company declares its profits and becomes liable to pay tax and the time when the tax bill must eventually be paid.

5.2 A distinction is made between:

(a) current liabilities; and
(b) long-term liabilities.

5.3 *Current liabilities* are debts of the business that must be paid within a fairly short period of time (by convention, within one year). In the accounts of limited companies, the Companies Act 1985 requires use of the term 'Creditors: amounts falling due within one year' rather than 'current liabilities' although they mean the same thing.

5.4 Examples of current liabilities are:

(a) loans repayable within one year;

(b) a bank overdraft;

(c) trade creditors;

(d) bills of exchange which are payable by the business;

(e) taxation payable;

(f) 'accrued charges'. These are expenses already incurred by the business, for which no bill has yet been received.

5.5 It is often argued that a bank overdraft is not a current liability, because a business is usually able to negotiate an overdraft facility for a long period of time. If an overdraft thus becomes a more permanent source of borrowing, it is really a long-term liability. However, you should normally expect to see an overdraft as a current liability, since banks reserve the right to demand repayment at short notice.

5.6 *Long-term liabilities* (or *deferred liabilities*) are debts which are not payable within the 'short-term' and so any liability which is not current must be long-term. Just as 'short-term' by convention means one year or less, 'long-term' means more than one year. In the accounts of limited companies, the Companies Act 1985 requires use of the term: 'Creditors: amounts falling due after more than one year'.

Examples of long-term liabilities

5.7 (a) Loans which are repayable after one year, such as a bank loan or a loan from an individual to a business, are long term liabilities.

(b) A mortgage loan, which is a loan specifically secured against a freehold property, is also long term. (If the business fails to repay the loan, the lender then has 'first claim' on the property, and is entitled to repayment from the proceeds from the enforced sale of the property.)

(c) Debenture or debenture loans. These are usually found in larger limited companies' accounts. Debentures are securities issued by a company at a fixed rate of interest. They are repayable on agreed terms by a specified date in the future. Holders of debentures are therefore lenders of money to a company. Their interests, including security for the loan, are protected by the terms of a trust deed.

Creditors

5.8   A *creditor* is a person to whom a business owes money. A business does not always pay immediately for goods or services it buys. It is a common business practice to make purchases on credit, with a promise to pay within 30 days, or two months or three months of the date of the bill or 'invoice' for the goods. For example, if A buys goods costing £2,000 on credit from B, B might send A an invoice for £2,000, dated say 1 March, with credit terms that payment must be made within 30 days. If A then delays payment until 31 March, B will be a creditor of A between 1 and 31 March for £2,000.

5.9   *Note.* A *trade creditor* is a person to whom a business owes money for debts incurred in the course of trading operations, and in an examination question, this term might refer to debts still outstanding which arise from the purchase from suppliers of materials, components or goods for resale.

6.   CAPITAL AND RESERVES

6.1   The capital and reserves figures in the balance sheet represent the *shareholders' funds*. These funds consist of the original capital contributed by the shareholders (the cost of the shares) plus the profits the business has made over the years, which are accumulated in the profit and loss account balance.

Share capital

6.2   The money put into the business by its owners is called *capital*. In accounting, capital is an investment of money (funds) with the intention of earning a return. A business proprietor invests capital with the intention of earning profit. As long as that money is invested, accountants will treat the capital as money owed to the proprietor by the business. Shareholders have invested money in a business and this investment is included within the 'shareholders funds' or 'capital and reserves' section of the balance sheet.

6.3   The capital in a limited company consists of share capital. When a company is set up for the first time, it issues shares, which are paid for by investors, who then become shareholders of the company. Shares are denominated in units of 25p, 50p, £1 or whatever seems appropriate. The 'face value' of the shares is called their *nominal value*.

Reserves

6.4   We have already explained the relevance of the profit and loss account as a reserve. Other reserves may be created by a company for a variety of reasons. One example is a *revaluation reserve*. This is where the excess of revalued fixed assets over cost is taken.

Preference shares

6.5   Preference shareholders do not 'own' the business as the shareholders do. Preference shares are just a means of paying a fixed amount to shareholders every year, in the same way as debenture loans, usually expressed as a percentage of the nominal value of the shares.

7.   THE PROFIT AND LOSS ACCOUNT

7.1   We now turn to the profit and loss account. Once again, as an example, let us look at the accounts of ARC Ltd.

ARC LIMITED
PROFIT AND LOSS ACCOUNTS FOR THE
YEARS ENDED 31 DECEMBER

	19X0	19X1
	£'000	£'000
Sales	53,470	98,455
Cost of sales	40,653	70,728
Gross profit	12,817	27,727
Distribution and selling expenses	2,317	4,911
Administration expenses	1,100	2,176
Operating profit	9,400	20,640
Interest paid	–	(280)
Interest received	100	40
Profit before taxation	9,500	20,400
Taxation	3,200	5,200
Profit after taxation	6,300	15,200
Dividends		
Preference (paid)	100	100
Ordinary: interim (paid)	1,000	2,000
final (proposed)	3,000	6,000
Retained profit for the year	2,200	7,100

7.2   The profit and loss account has already been mentioned as a statement in which revenues and expenditure are compared to arrive at a figure of profit or loss. Many businesses try to distinguish between a gross profit earned on trading, and a net profit. They prepare a statement called a trading, profit and loss account: in the first part of the statement (the trading account) revenue from selling goods is compared with direct costs of acquiring or producing the goods sold to arrive at a gross profit figure; from this, deductions are made in the second half of the statement (the profit and loss account) in respect of indirect costs (overheads).

7.3   The trading, profit and loss account is a statement showing in detail how the profit (or loss) of a period has been made. The owners and managers of a business obviously want to know how much profit or loss has been made, but there is only a limited information value in the profit figure alone. In order to exercise financial control effectively, managers need to know how much income has been earned, what various items of costs have been, and whether the performance of sales or the control of costs appears to be satisfactory. The management accounting function will produce trading accounts which are much more detailed than the profit and loss account shown here.

7.4   Particular items to note are as follows.

(a)   The profit and loss account in the example is stated for a period of a year. Comparative figures for the previous payroll are always given.

(b) The section which arrives at trading (or operating) profit is not given in detail in published accounts. Statute only requires that turnover, operating profit, profit before tax, taxation, profit after tax and dividends are detailed on the profit and loss account. However there is a lot of information regarding certain items of cost which are deducted before arriving at operating profits. This detail will be included in the notes to the accounts, which are also published.

(c) An adjustment for opening and closing stock is made in cost of sales to reflect the fact that the costs associated with opening stock, although incurred by the business last year, are in fact associated with sales for this year. Similarly, closing stock costs will be related to sales next year. This is just an exercise to match costs to benefits.

(d) The profit retained in the business (£7,100,000 in 19X1) is exactly equal to the movement in the shareholders' funds in the example balance sheet (see Section 2). Although there may be reasons for this not to be so, it is usual that this profit is the major part of any movement in these funds as indicated on the balance sheet.

7.5 Most of the marketing expenses will appear in this section. The main types of expenses in this category are as follows.

(a) *Selling and distribution expenses*. These are expenses associated with the process of selling and delivering goods to customers and in published accounts they will include marketing expenses. They include the following items.

(i) Salaries of marketing and sales directors and management.

(ii) Salaries and commissions of sales staff.

(iii) Travelling and entertainment expenses of sales people.

(iv) Marketing costs (including advertising, market research costs and sales promotion expenses).

(v) Costs of running and maintaining delivery vans.

(vi) Discounts allowed to customers for early payment of their debts. For example, a business might sell goods to a customer for £100 and offer a discount of 5% for payment in cash. If the customer takes the discount, the accounts of the business would not record the sales value at £95; they would instead record sales at the full £100, with a cost for discounts allowed of £5.

(vii) Bad debts written off. Sometimes debtors fail to pay what they owe, and a business might have to decide at some stage of chasing after payment that there is now no prospect of ever being paid. The debt has to be written off as 'bad'. The amount of the debt written off is charged as an expense in the profit and loss account. Bad debts will be described more fully in a later section.

(b) *Administration expenses*. These are the expenses of providing management and administration for the business. They include the following items.

(i) Salaries of directors, management and office staff
(ii) Rent and rates
(iii) Insurance
(iv) Telephone and postage
(v) Printing and stationery
(vi) Heating and lighting

FRS 3 Reporting financial performance

7.6 A new accounting standard, FRS 3 *Reporting financial performance* has changed the format of the profit and loss account for some (mainly large) companies. The illustrative example shown below indicates the changes made. You should not worry about the effect or importance of the changes, but you should familiarise yourself with the new format because you will need to understand it when you see it in published accounts.

7.7 The main function of the new format is to show how discontinued (sold or closed-down) activities affected the profit and los account for the year. This allows comparisons with future years when such discontinued activities no longer have an impact on the company's results.

Illustrative example

7.8 PROFIT AND LOSS EXAMPLE 1

	1993 £m	1993 £m	1992 as restated £m
Turnover			
Continuing operations	550		500
Acquisitions	50		
		600	
Discontinued operations	175		190
		775	690
Cost of sales		(620)	(555)
Gross profit		155	135
Net operating expenses		(104)	(83)
Operating profit			
Continuing operations	50		40
Acquisitions	6		
		56	
Discontinued operations	(15)		12
Less 1992 provision	10		
		51	52
Profit on sale of properties in continuing operations		9	6
Provision for loss on operations to be discontinued			(30)
Loss on disposal of discontinued operations	(17)		
Less 1992 provision	20		
		3	
Profit on ordinary activities before interest		63	28
Interest payable		(18)	(15)
Profit on ordinary activities before taxation		45	13
Tax on profit on ordinary activities		(14)	(4)
Profit on ordinary activities after taxation		31	9
Minority interests		(2)	(2)
(Profit before extraordinary items)		29	7
(Extraordinary items - included only to show positioning)		-	-
Profit for the financial year		29	7
Dividends		(8)	(1)
Retained profit for the financial year		21	6

	1993	1992 as restated
Earnings per share	39p	10p
Adjustments (to be itemised and an adequate description to be given)	Xp	Xp
Adjusted earnings per share	Yp	Yp

(Reason for calculating the adjusted earnings per share to be given.)

PROFIT AND LOSS ACCOUNT EXAMPLE 2 (to operating profit line)

	Continuing operations		Discontinued operations	Total	Total
		Acquisitions			1992 as
	1993	1993	1993	1993	restated
	£m	£m	£m	£m	£m
Turnover	550	50	175	775	690
Cost of sales	(415)	(40)	(165)	(620)	(555)
Gross profit	135	10	10	155	135
Net operating expenses	(85)	(4)	(25)	(114)	(83)
Less 1992 provision			10	10	
Operating profit	50	6	(5)	51	52
Profit on sale of properties	9			9	6
Provision for loss on operations to be discontinued					(30)
Loss on disposal of the discontinued operations			(17)	(17)	
Less 1992 provision	—	—	20	20	—
Profit on ordinary activities before interest	59	6	(2)	63	28

Thereafter example 2 is the same as example 1.

7.9 The standard also requires various explanatory notes in the accounts which need not concern us here.

What goes into the balance sheet and profit and loss account?

7.10 We have already seen the basis of accounting and the importance of the accounting equation. All accounting is completed by the use of a double entry system, which is another way of expressing the accounting equation. It is defined by the terms 'debit' and 'credit' and for every debit that must be an equal and opposite credit.

7.11 All accounts are included within the balance sheet and profit and loss account. In general terms the impact of the debits and credits is summarised as follows.

Debit	Credit
Asset or expense	Liability or revenue

7.12 This may confuse you a little because you will look at your bank statement and see that your balance is positive (and hence an asset to you) but money you pay in always appears as a credit on the statement. Remember, however, that your account from the bank's point of view is the other way round. If your account is in funds then they owe you the money and so it is a liability from their perspective and hence it is said to be *in credit*. Similarly if you have an overdraft it is shown as a debit balance because you owe the bank money, so it is an asset from the bank's perspective.

7.13 The table above does indicate another problem. When do we treat a particular item as an asset and when is it an expense? When does a transaction give rise to a liability and when is that transaction referred to as revenue? Buying a new car for the marketing director, for example, will result in the company buying a fixed asset and paying out cash. Hence the transaction has been accounted entirely within the 'asset' section of the balance sheet in that we have increased our fixed assets and reduced our cash balance. Yet if we are in the business of selling soap powder and we sell £10,000 of goods on credit (the customer paying sometime in the future), then we will recognise sales revenue within the profit and loss account, but be owed money by the customer and hence increase our assets (debtors).

7.14 In addition, we will pay the salesperson's salary at the end of the month. Here we will have an expense of the business which has been incurred in the effort of generating sales, so we recognise a cost or expense in the profit and loss account and reduce our cash asset.

The importance of the above examples is to emphasise that items can simply affect the balance sheet and not affect the profit and loss account. So now we must understand the rules that determine how to treat transactions.

Capital and revenue items

7.15 The distinction between capital and revenue items can be described in very general terms.

(a) *Capital* items are related to financing decisions, such as the purchase of a fixed asset and how the purchase is to be financed.

(b) *Revenue* items are related to trading decisions, that is the sale, purchase and expense, transactions associated with normal trading.

7.16 The distinction between capital and revenue items can be important for a variety of reasons.

(a) Obviously the type of decision-making involved will be very different for revenue and capital items.

(b) The accounting treatment for capital items is different to that of revenue items, as we have seen.

Exercise

State whether each of the following items should be classified as 'capital' or 'revenue' expenditure or income for the purpose of preparing the trading, profit and loss account and the balance sheet of the business.

(a) Purchase of leasehold premises.

(b) Annual depreciation of leasehold premises.

(c) Solicitors' fees in connection with the purchase of leasehold premises.

(d) Costs of adding extra storage capacity to a mainframe computer used by the business.

(e) Computer repairs and maintenance costs.

(f) Profit on the sale of an office building.

(g) Revenue from sales by credit card (for example Access or Visa).

(h) Cost of new machinery.

(i) Customs duty charged on the machinery when imported into the country.

(j) 'Carriage' costs of transporting the new machinery from the supplier's factory to the premises of the business purchasing the machinery.

(k) Cost of installing the new machinery in the premises of the business.

(l) Wages of the machine operators.

Solution

(a) Capital expenditure.

(b) Depreciation of a fixed asset is revenue expenditure.

(c) The legal fees associated with the purchase of a property may be added to the purchase price and classified as capital expenditure. The cost of the leasehold premises in the balance sheet of the business will then include the legal fees.

(d) Capital expenditure (enhancing an existing fixed asset).

(e) Revenue expenditure.

(f) Capital income (net of the costs of sale).

(g) Revenue income.

(h) Capital expenditure.

(i) If customs duties are borne by the purchaser of the fixed asset, they may be added to the cost of the machinery and classified as capital expenditure.

(j) Similarly, if carriage costs are paid for by the purchaser of the fixed asset, they may be included in the cost of the fixed asset and classified as capital expenditure.

(k) Installation costs of a fixed asset are also added to the fixed asset's cost and classified as capital expenditure.

(l) Revenue expenditure.

2: FINANCIAL ACCOUNTS

Items appearing in both the balance sheet and the trading, profit and loss account

7.17 A few items appear in both the trading, profit and loss account and also the balance sheet.

(a) *Net profit.* The net profit in the profit and loss account is the profit for the financial year or other period which is then added to the proprietor's capital in the balance sheet.

(b) *Expenses incurred but not yet paid for.* The cost of goods purchased by a business and then re-sold before the business has paid for them will be included in the trading account (cost of goods sold) and in the balance sheet (as a creditor).

(c) The *value of goods sold on credit*, for which payment is still owed. Credit sales are included in the trading account, and unpaid debts are debtors in the balance sheet.

(d) The *cost of goods purchased but not yet sold by the business* will appear in the balance sheet as stocks held at the end of one accounting period (current assets) and will become a cost of goods sold in the trading account in a subsequent accounting period when the goods are eventually sold.

Another important item which is relevant both to the profit and loss account and the balance sheet is depreciation.

8. CASH FLOW STATEMENTS

8.1 We will use ARC Ltd's cash flow statement as an example in this section.

ARC LIMITED
CASH FLOW STATEMENT FOR THE YEAR ENDED 31 DECEMBER 19X1

	£'000	£'000
Net cash inflow from operating activities		2,390
Returns on investments and servicing of finance		
Interest received	40	
Interest paid	(280)	
Dividends paid	(5,100)	
Net cash outflow from returns on investments and servicing of finance		(5,340)
Taxation		
Corporation tax paid (including advance corporation tax)	(3,200)	
Tax paid		(3,200)
Investing activities		
Payments to acquire tangible fixed assets	(11,800)	
Receipts from sales of tangible fixed assets	1,000	
Net cash outflow from investing activities		(10,800)
Net cash outflow before financing		(16,950)
Financing		
Repurchase of debenture loan	150	
Net cash inflow from financing		150
Decrease in cash and cash equivalents		(16,800)

Notes to the cash flow statement

1   *Reconciliation of operating profit to net cash inflow from operating activities*

	£'000
Operating profit	20,640
Depreciation charges	5,050
Loss on sale of tangible fixed assets	700
(Increase)/decrease in stocks	(10,000)
(Increase)/decrease in debtors	(18,200)
Increase/(decrease) in creditors	4,200
Net cash inflow from operating activities	2,390

2   *Analysis of changes in cash and cash equivalents during the year*

	£'000
Balance at 1 January 19X1	600
Net cash inflow/(outflow)	(16,800)
Balance at 31 December 19X1	(16,200)

3   *Analysis of the balances of cash and cash equivalents as shown in the balance sheet*

	19X0	19X1	Change in year
	£'000	£'000	£'000
Cash at bank and in hand	600	-	(600)
Bank overdrafts	-	(16,200)	(16,200)
	600	(16,200)	(16,800)

4   *Analysis of changes in finance during the year*

	Debenture loan £'000
Balance at 1 January 19X1	600
Cash inflow/(outflow) from financing	150
Balance at 31 December 19X1	750

8.2 It can be argued that 'profit' does not always give a useful or meaningful picture of a company's operations. Readers of a company's financial statements might even be misled by a reported profit figure.

(a) Shareholders might believe that if a company makes a profit after tax, of say, £100,000 then this is the amount which it could afford to pay as a dividend. Unless the company has sufficient cash available to stay in business and also to pay a dividend, the shareholders' expectations would be wrong.

(b) Employees might believe that if a company makes profits, it can afford to pay higher wages next year. This opinion may not be correct: the ability to pay wages depends on the availability of cash.

(c) Creditors might consider that a profitable company is a *going concern* (it can pay all debts). However:

(i)   if a company builds up large amounts of unsold stocks of goods, their cost would not be chargeable against profits, but cash would have been used up in making them, thus weakening the company's liquid resources;

(ii)   a company might capitalise large development costs, having spent considerable amounts of money on R & D, but only charge small amounts against current profits. As a result, the company might show reasonable profits, but get into severe difficulties with its liquidity position. (This is roughly the problem that led to the collapse of the old Rolls Royce company in 1971.)

(d)   Management might suppose that if their company makes a historical cost profit, and reinvests some of those profits, then the company must be expanding. This is not the case: in a period of inflation, a company might have a historical cost profit but a current cost accounting loss, which means that the operating capability of the firm will be declining.

(e)   Survival of a business entity depends not so much on profits as on its ability to pay its debts when they fall due. Such payments might include 'profit and loss' items such as material purchases, wages, interest and taxation etc, but also capital payments for new fixed assets and the repayment of loan capital when this falls due (say on the redemption of debentures).

8.3   From these examples, it may be apparent that a company's performance and prospects depend not so much on the 'profits' earned in a period, but more realistically on liquidity: cash flows.

8.4   In the 1970s a view was put forward that the traditional profit and loss statement should be replaced (or at least supplemented) by a cash flow statement. A financial reporting standard, FRS 1 *Cash flow statements* was published which requires larger companies to produce a cash flow statement as shown above.

8.5   The aim of a cash flow statement should be to assist users:

(a)   to assess the enterprise's ability to generate positive net cash flows in the future;
(b)   to assess its ability to meet its obligations to service loans, pay dividends etc;
(c)   to assess the reasons for differences between reported profit and related cash flows;
(d)   to assess the effect on its finances of major transactions in the year.

The statement therefore shows changes in cash and cash equivalents rather than working capital. The opening and closing figures given for cash etc will be those shown in the balance sheet. Cash equivalents are highly liquid short-term investments.

8.6   The statement should classify cash receipts and payments as resulting from investing, financing or operating activities. Examples of each are:

(a)   investing - making loans, acquiring/disposing of fixed assets;

(b)   financing - borrowing/repaying money, making an issue of shares, paying dividends;

(c)   operating activities - receipts from customers, payments to employees and suppliers, any other cash flows from transactions not classified as investing or financing.

The advantages of cash flow accounting

8.7 The advantages of cash flow accounting are as follows.

(a) Survival in business depends on the ability to generate cash. Cash flow accounting directs attention towards this critical issue.

(b) Cash flow is more comprehensive than 'profit' which is dependent on accounting conventions and concepts.

(c) Creditors (long and short-term) are more interested in an entity's ability to repay them than in its profitability. Whereas 'profits' might indicate that cash is likely to be available, cash flow accounting is more direct with its message.

(d) Cash flow reporting provides a better means of comparing the results of different companies than traditional profit reporting.

(e) Cash flow reporting satisfies the needs of all users better:

   (i) for management, it provides the sort of information on which decisions should be taken (in management accounting, 'relevant costs' to a decision are future cash flows); traditional profit accounting does not help with decision-making;

   (ii) for shareholders and auditors, cash flow accounting can provide a satisfactory basis for stewardship accounting;

   (iii) as described previously, the information needs of creditors and employees will be better served by cash flow accounting.

(f) Cash flow forecasts are easier to prepare, as well as more useful, than profit forecasts.

(g) Cash flows can in some respects be audited more easily than accounts based on the accruals concept.

(h) Cash flows are more easily understood than income and costs which are matched with each other.

(i) Cash flow accounting should be both retrospective and forward-looking, including a forecast for the future. This is of great information value to all users of accounting information.

(j) Forecasts can subsequently be monitored by the publication of variance statements which compare actual cash flows against the forecast.

9. THE STATEMENT OF SOURCE AND APPLICATION OF FUNDS

9.1 An example of a statement of source and application of funds is shown below. Companies had to produce these as part of their published accounts until they were replaced by cash flow statements.

ARC LIMITED
STATEMENT OF SOURCE AND APPLICATION OF FUNDS
FOR THE YEAR TO 31 DECEMBER 19X9

	£'000	£'000
Source of funds		
Profit before taxation		20,400
Adjustments for items not involving the movement of funds		
Depreciation	5,050	
Loss on sale of fixed assets	700	
		5,750
Total funds generated from operations		26,150
Funds from other sources		
Issue of debenture stock	150	
Sale of fixed assets	1,000	
		1,150
Total sources of funds		27,300
Application of funds		
Dividends paid	5,100	
Taxation paid	3,200	
Purchase of fixed assets	11,800	
		20,100
		7,200
Increase/(decrease) in working capital		
Increase in stocks	10,000	
Increase in debtors	18,100	
Increase in prepayments	100	
Increase in trade creditors	(4,000)	
Increase in accruals	(200)	
		24,000
Movement in net liquid funds		(16,800)
		7,200

9.2 Although these statements are no longer obligatory, they can be useful in certain circumstances.

Definition of funds

9.3 In the very broadest sense, funds can be described as *purchasing power*. On a very basic level, purchasing power is cash. *Working capital* is the net investment made in current assets and current liabilities. More simply, it is the difference between current assets and current liabilities.

9.4 The statement is for the same period as the profit and loss account, calculated at the same point in time as the balance sheet. It shows the movement of funds in and out of the business and reconciles the net movement to the change in working capital.

The need for a funds flow statement

9.5 Because neither the profit and loss account nor the balance sheet gives a satisfactory explanation of how a business obtains and uses its funds, the statement of source and application of funds (often called a funds flow statement) has been introduced to fill the 'information gap'.

9.6 A funds flow statement is a method of showing where a business gets its funds from and how those funds are then applied. In particular it shows the extent to which profits have contributed towards the supply of funds, and it indicates whether a business is generating enough funds to meet all its needs, or whether it might be in a position where its liquidity is deteriorating (and likely to deteriorate further in the future).

9.7 Another way of looking at a funds flow statement is to say that it reconciles the amount of profit earned in a period of time with the increase or decrease in liquid funds during the same period. 'Liquid funds' are cash and bank balances (either in credit or in overdraft) and also short-term investments which could be disposed of quickly for cash.

9.8 The profit and loss account gives information about sales minus the matching cost of sales in an accounting period. It does not explain whether the size of the profit earned is big enough to provide sufficient funds (enough cash) to keep the business *solvent*. This is partly because profit does not look at cash received or paid, but at income *earned* and expenses *owed*.

9.9 Profit is an important source of funds and these funds may be used for various purposes.

(a) *To buy new fixed assets*. The purchase cost of a fixed asset (the cash required for the purchase) will exceed the amount set aside as a depreciation charge in the profit and loss account because the depreciation charge is spread across several years.

(b) *To invest in stocks or debtors*. Money may be spent on building up stock levels and if the extra stocks are unsold at the end of an accounting period, they will not yet have earned any profit. In other words, funds may be applied to build up stocks without any immediate return of profit. An increase in the amount of debtors means that a business is making more sales (and claiming the profit from these sales in the profit and loss account) without actually receiving the funds (cash) which it eventually expects from its sales, and it is therefore sometimes said that a business which sells more goods on credit is 'investing in its debtors'.

9.10 At the same time, profits are not the only source of funds to a business. A company can raise more funds by issuing new shares or by raising a loan. For example, consider these scenarios.

(a) If a company issues 100,000 shares with a nominal value of £1 each at a price of £2.50 per share there would be an increase in funds (cash) of £250,000. This source of funds would be shown in the company's balance sheet by increasing its shareholders funds by the same amount.

(b) If a company buys the assets of another business for £300,000 and pays for these assets by issuing 80,000 £1 shares valued at £3.75 each to the owners of the business taken over:

(i)   shareholders funds would increase by £300,000; and

(ii) these funds would be simultaneously 'applied' to purchase the business's assets for £300,000.

9.11 Just as a profit and loss account does not describe the flow of funds into or out of a business, neither does a balance sheet. A balance sheet is a 'static' statement of a business entity's position at one point in time. By comparing a balance sheet at the start of one year with a balance sheet at the end of the year, it is possible to note the differences as an indication of sources or applications of funds. For example:

(a)   an increase in issued share capital and share premium in the balance sheet at the end of the year would indicate that shares have been issued during the year to obtain funds;

(b)   an increase in stocks and debtors at the end of the year (compared with the start of the year) would show that the business has 'applied' or invested funds in these items;

(c)   a decrease in loan stock or borrowings at the end of the year would indicate that funds have been applied to repay a loan during the year.

However, although a comparison of two balance sheets gives some indication of sources and applications of funds, it does not provide a complete picture. In particular, it would not show how much profit has been earned and how those profits have been used.

So in preparing a funds flow statement we start with profit before tax as a source of funds and try to minimise the amount of 'netting off' of funds flow to show how funds have been generated and applied.

10.   THE VALUE ADDED STATEMENT

10.1 One final statement needs to be understood although it is not used extensively by companies and as a result has not reached a standard uniformity of layout. This is the *value added statement*. It attempts to show how wealth is created by a business by relating to stages of the business process.

10.2 Suppose for example that a company buys raw materials and components which cost £2,000. By committing resources (labour time, machine time, capital funds) to production and sales, the raw materials and components are transformed into finished goods which are sold for £11,000. The business entity, as a unit or 'team' will have created extra wealth of £11,000 - £2,000 = £9,000. In other words, £9,000 will have been added to the value of bought-in materials and components.

10.3 Another way of expressing the same idea is that the £2,000 of bought-in materials and components represent the value of the output of other business entities: supplier firms. The company itself creates output which has a value of £11,000. As a result of its own efforts, it has added £9,000 to value.

10.4 The business entity is a 'team' consisting of:

(a) employees;
(b) fixed assets and machinery;
(c) providers of capital (shareholders and long-term creditors).

10.5 Value added is the wealth created by the 'team' and it should be used to reward the members of the 'team'. However, some of the value added may have to be paid out in taxation, and the company might also wish to reinvest some money. Value added can therefore be thought of as a 'cake', with slices being cut for:

(a) employees;
(b) depreciation (which is a form of reinvestment);
(c) dividends;
(d) interest payments;
(e) taxation;
(f) retained profits.

10.6 A value added statement is particularly informative for employees, because it presents accounting data in a relatively simple manner which is more easily understood than a profit and loss account. Some companies have actually negotiated wages bonus schemes for productivity on the basis of improvements in added value.

10.7 A typical example of a value added statement for a manufacturing company would be as follows.

		Current year			Previous year	
	£'000	£'000	%	£'000	£'000	%
Turnover		1,120			1,006	
Bought-in materials and services		784			710	
Value added		336			296	
Applied the following way:						
(a) To pay employees (wages, pensions and fringe benefits)		232	69		202	68
(b) To pay providers of capital:						
(i) Interest on loans	23		7	17		6
(ii) Dividends to shareholders	23		7	22		7
		46			39	
(c) To pay government:						
Corporation tax payable		8	2		12	4
(d) To provide for maintenance and expansion of assets:						
(i) Depreciation	24		7	20		7
(ii) Retained profits	26		8	23		8
		50			43	
Value added		336	100		296	100

There is some scope for differences in the definition of each item in the statement. Given that there is no regulated format for value added statements, a wide variety of methods of presentation have developed in practice.

As a result it is difficult to use the value added statement to compare different companies or even the same company over a period in time. There are no specific rules or regulations government how the statement should be computed and hence the intention of producing these statements may be lost because of differing approaches to specific items of disclosure and hence differing treatments.

10.8 If you are presented with a value added statement during your CIM studies you should read the headings and explanations carefully. The answer to most questions will be contained within the words used to describe the various elements of the value added statement. You should then rely on your understanding of the various elements which comprise the basic aspects of accounting and state any assumptions you may need to make as clearly as possible.

11. CONCLUSION

11.1 This chapter has led you from the accounting equation into its expanded version as defined by the published balance sheet and profit and loss account. The formats described are those that appear under statutory provision in the annual report and accounts of a public listed company. Remember, however, that companies will also produce historic accounts for internal purposes which will be prepared under similar conventions. These are usually produced either monthly or quarterly and are used to monitor progress and health against predetermined budgets. We will deal with this aspect of accounting in a later chapter.

11.2 The following points are of particular importance.

(a) A balance sheet is a snapshot of the financial position of a business at a point in time.

(b) A profit and loss account measures the operational performance of the company over a period of time.

(c) Capital items are concerned with financing decisions. Revenue items are concerned with trading decisions.

(d) Certain items may appear in the profit and loss account which are simply accounting entries which do not involve the movement of cash. They reflect a prudent approach to the reduction in the value of assets. These will include depreciation, provision for bad debts and other provisions against known future liabilities.

(e) The funds flow statement is an analysis where a business gets its fund and how those funds are utilised.

11.3 Financial terms have been defined in this chapter and you should be able to reproduce these definitions, not just for the purposes of the examination, but to enable you to communicate effectively with financial staff. The main definitions are given briefly here.

(a) Assets are things of value that a business owns or has use of.

(b) Fixed assets are assets which are acquired for use within a business with a view to facilitating the generation of revenue (and consequently profits).

(c) Current assets are assets which are owned by the business which are intended to be turned into cash within one year.

(d) Liabilities are financial obligations to someone else.

(e) Creditors are people to whom the business has a financial obligation.

(f) Debtors are people who have a financial obligation to us.

(g) Capital is the money put into a business by the owners and it is therefore owed by the business to the owners.

(h) Gross profit is the profit shown after the purchase or production cost of the goods sold is deducted from the value of sales.

(i) Net profit is the gross profit, plus any other income from sources other than the sale of goods, minus other expenses of the business which are not included in the cost of goods sold.

11.4 This chapter is very long and it has covered a great deal of material. It would be wise to go back and study the whole chapter again, even if you think you have understood everything. The contents of this chapter are fundamental to an understanding of financial and accounting matters. Although some items may be expanded upon later in the text, you are advised to attempt to grasp the logic of accounting now as laid out in this chapter. It is important that you should put these matters in context by obtaining some published accounts (perhaps for your own company) and studying what they are trying to do.

TEST YOUR KNOWLEDGE

The numbers in brackets refer to paragraphs of this chapter

1   Outline the function and purpose of:

   (a)   the Financial Reporting Council; (1.7)
   (b)   the Accounting Standard Board. (1.8)

2   What is the accounting equation in its simplest form? (2.3)

3   What effect does profit have on the accounting equation? (2.8)

4   Give a definition of a fixed asset. (3.4)

5   Give three methods of valuing a fixed asset. (3.8 - 3.12)

6   What are the different methods of depreciation? (3.24)

7   Define current assets. (4.1)

8   Briefly explain the cash cycle. (4.4)

9   What is 'net realisable value'? (4.10)

10 What is the accounting treatment for a bad debt in the profit and loss account? (4.22)

11 What is a liability? (5.1)

12 Write down a list of the items which appear in the profit and loss account. (7.1 - 7.5)

13 Explain the difference between capital expenditure and revenue items. (7.15)

14 Give examples of two items which will appear in both the balance sheet and the profit and loss account. (7.17)

15 What are the main advantages of cash flow accounting? (8.7)

16 What is the purpose of a funds flow statement? (9.6)

17 What information is shown in a value added statement? (10.5)

Now try question 2 at the end of the text

Chapter 3

INTERPRETATION OF FINANCIAL STATEMENTS

This chapter covers the following topics.

1. Analysing financial statements
2. Profit margin, asset turnover and return on capital employed
3. Earnings per share
4. Gearing
5. Operational ratios
6. Liquidity ratios

---

1. ANALYSING FINANCIAL STATEMENTS

1.1 The profit and loss account and the balance sheet are both sources of useful information about the condition of a business. The analysis and interpretation of these statements can be carried out by calculating certain ratios, between one item and another, and then using the ratios for comparison, either:

(a) between one year and the next for a particular business, in order to identify any trends, or significantly better or worse results than before; or

(b) between one business and another, to establish which business has performed better, and in what ways. You should be very careful, when comparing two different businesses, to ensure that the accounts have been prepared in a similar way. Different accounting treatments of a similar situation may vastly distort these comparisons. If during your studies you are presented with financial data from two different companies without any additional information, it is always sensible to state your assumption that they have both been prepared on a similar and consistent basis.

1.2 We will use the set of accounts from Chapter 2 as a basis for our analysis. The balance sheet and profit and loss account are shown again together here as a reminder.

ARC LIMITED
BALANCE SHEETS AT 31 DECEMBER

	19X0		19X1	
Fixed assets	£'000	£'000	£'000	£'000
Plant, machinery and equipment, at cost		17,600		23,900
Less accumulated depreciation		9,500		10,750
		8,100		13,150
Current assets				
Stocks	5,000		15,000	
Trade debtors	8,600		26,700	
Prepayments	300		400	
Cash at bank and in hand	600		-	
	14,500		42,100	
Current liabilities				
Bank overdraft	-		16,200	
Trade creditors	6,000		10,000	
Accruals	800		1,000	
Taxation	3,200		5,200	
Dividends	3,200		6,000	
	13,000		38,400	
Net current assets		1,500		3,700
Loans				
15% debenture stock		600		750
Net assets		9,000		16,100
Capital and reserves				
Ordinary shares of £1 each		5,000		5,000
10% preference shares of £1 each		1,000		1,000
Profit and loss account		3,000		10,100
		9,000		16,100

ARC LIMITED
PROFIT AND LOSS ACCOUNTS FOR THE
YEARS ENDED 31 DECEMBER

	19X0	19X1
	£'000	£'000
Sales	53,470	98,455
Cost of sales	40,653	70,728
Gross profit	12,817	27,727
Distribution and selling expenses	2,317	4,911
Administration expenses	1,100	2,176
Operating profit	9,400	20,640
Interest paid	-	(280)
Interest received	100	40
Profit before taxation	9,500	20,400
Taxation	3,200	5,200
Profit after taxation	6,300	15,200
Dividends		
Preference (paid)	100	100
Ordinary: interim (paid)	1,000	2,000
final (proposed)	3,000	6,000
Retained profit for the year	2,200	7,100

2. PROFIT MARGIN, ASSET TURNOVER AND RETURN ON CAPITAL EMPLOYED

2.1 There are three principal ratios which can be used to measure how efficiently the operations of a business have been managed. These are:

(a) profit margin;
(b) asset turnover;
(c) return on capital employed (ROCE).

Profit margin

2.2 *Profit margin* is the ratio of profit to sales, and may also be called 'profit percentage'. For example, if a company makes a profit of £20,000 on sales of £100,000 its profit percentage or profit margin is 20%. This also means that its costs are 80% of sales. A high profit margin indicates either of the following.

(a) *Costs are being kept well under control*. If the ratio of costs to sales goes down, the profit margin will automatically go up. For example, if the cost: sales ratio changes from 80% to 75%, the profit margin will go up from 20% to 25%.

(b) *Sales prices are high*. For example, if a company sells goods for £100,000 and makes a profit of £16,000, costs would be £84,000 and the profit margin 16%. Now if the company can raise selling prices by 20% to £120,000 without affecting the volume of goods sold or their costs, profits would rise by the amount of revenue increase (£20,000) to £36,000 and the profit margin would also rise (from 16% to 30%).

2.3 The profit referred to above is usually the Profit Before Interest and Tax (PBIT), also known as the operating profit. In the accounts of ARC Ltd, the PBIT for 19X1 is £20,640,000 and for 19X0, £9,400,000.

The profit margins for the two years are:

19X1	*19X0*
$\dfrac{20,640}{98,455} = 21\%$	$\dfrac{9,400}{53,470} = 18\%$

2.4 During your studies you may be presented with information which compares different businesses within a group of companies and you may be given much more detail than the basic information which is contained in the published profit and loss account. In these cases you can make up your own ratios to help understand the business provided you apply then constantly. For example, it is not unusual to fund some costs expressed as a percentage of turnover such as marketing costs which may be quoted as 6% turnover. Similarly it may be useful to know that over time the revenue (turnover) generated per person in the sales force has risen by 20% from one year to another (but be careful not to draw too many conclusions here since the price of the product may have doubled in the same period, so perhaps your sales force is now less efficient).

Asset turnover

2.5   *Asset turnover* is the ratio of sales turnover in a year to the amount of capital employed. For example, if a company has sales in 19X4 of £720,000 and has assets of £360,000, the asset turnover will be:

$$\frac{£720,000}{£360,000} = 2 \text{ times}$$

This means that for every £1 of assets employed, the company can generate sales turnover of £2 per annum. To utilise assets more efficiently, managers should try to create a higher volume of sales and a higher asset turnover ratio. For example, suppose that our firm with assets of £360,000 can increase its sales turnover from £720,000 to £900,000 per annum. The asset turnover would improve to:

$$\frac{£900,000}{£360,000} = 2.5 \text{ times}$$

2.6   In the accounts of ARC Ltd, the asset turnover for 19X1 and 19X0 is:

19X1	*19X0*
$\frac{98,455}{16,100} = 6.1$ times	$\frac{53,470}{9,000} = 5.9$ times

2.7   The significance of this improvement is that if a business can create more sales turnover from the same amount of assets it may make larger profits (because of the increase in sales) without having to increase the size of its investment. This is not always the case and we used an example in Chapter 1 to show that increasing revenue does not necessarily lead to increased profits. However, as a generalisation it is reasonable.

Return on Capital Employed (ROCE)

2.8   *Return on Capital Employed* (ROCE) is the amount of profit as a percentage of capital employed. If a company makes a profit of £30,000, we do not know how good or bad the result is until we look at the amount of capital which has been invested to achieve the profit. £30,000 might be a good sized profit for a small firm, but this would not be good enough for a 'giant' firm such as Marks and Spencer. For this reason, it is helpful to measure performance by relating profits to capital employed, and because this seems to be the only satisfactory ratio or percentage which judges profits in relation to the size of business, it is sometimes called the *primary ratio* in financial analysis.

2.9   You may already have realised that there is a mathematical connection between return on capital employed, profit margin and asset turnover:

$$\frac{\text{Profit}}{\text{Capital employed}} = \frac{\text{Profit}}{\text{Sales}} \times \frac{\text{Sales}}{\text{Capital employed}}$$

ie   ROCE   =   Profit margin   ×   Asset turnover

This is important. If we accept that ROCE is the single most important measure of business performance, comparing profit with the amount of capital invested, we can go on to say that business performance is dependent on two separate 'subsidiary' factors, each of which contributes to ROCE:

(a) profit margin;
(b) asset turnover.

For this reason, just as ROCE is sometimes called the primary ratio, the profit margin and asset turnover ratios are sometimes called the *secondary ratios*.

2.10 The implications of this relationship must be understood. Suppose that a return on capital employed of 20% is thought to be a good level of business performance in the retail trade for electrical goods.

(a) Company A might decide to sell its products at a fairly high price and make a profit margin on sales of 10%. It would then need only an asset turnover of 2.0 times to achieve a ROCE of 20%.

(b) Company B might decide to cut its prices so that its profit margin is only $2\frac{1}{2}$%. Provided that it can achieve an asset turnover of 8 times a year, attracting more customers with its lower prices, it will still make a ROCE of $2\frac{1}{2}$% × 8 = 20%.

2.11 Company A might be a department store and company B a discount warehouse. Each will have a different selling price policy, but each, in its own way, can be effective in achieving a target ROCE. In this example, if we supposed that both companies had capital employed of £100,000 and a target return of 20% or £20,000:

(a) company A would need annual sales of £200,000 to give a profit margin of 10% and an asset turnover of 2 times;

(b) company B would need annual sales of £800,000 to give a profit margin of only $2\frac{1}{2}$% but an asset turnover of 8 times.

The inter-relationship between profit margin and asset turnover

2.12 A higher return on capital employed can be obtained by increasing the profit margin or the asset turnover ratio. The profit margin can be increased by reducing costs or by raising selling prices.

However, if selling prices are raised, it is likely that sales demand will fall, with the possible consequences that the asset turnover will also decline. If higher prices mean lower sales turnover, the increase in profit margin might be offset by the fall in asset turnover, so that total return on capital employed might not improve.

3: INTERPRETATION OF FINANCIAL STATEMENTS

Example: profit margin and asset turnover

2.13 Suppose that Swings and Roundabouts Ltd achieved the following results in 19X6:

Sales	£100,000
Profit	£5,000
Capital employed	£20,000

The company's management wish to decide whether to raise its selling prices. They think that if they do so, they can raise the profit margin to 10% and by introducing extra capital of £55,000, sales turnover could be increased to £150,000.

You are required to evaluate the decision in terms of effect on ROCE, profit margin and asset turnover.

Solution

2.14 At present, ratios are:

Profit margin	5%
Asset turnover	5 times
ROCE (5/20)	25%

With the proposed changes, the profit would be 10% × £150,000 = £15,000, and the asset turnover would be:

$$\frac{£150,000}{£75,000} = 2 \text{ times, so that the ratios might be:}$$

Profit margin	×	Asset turnover	=	ROCE	
10%	×	2 times	=	20%	$\left\{\dfrac{£15,000}{£75,000}\right\}$

In spite of increasing the profit margin and raising the total volume of sales, the extra assets required (£55,000) only raise total profits by £(15,000 - 5,000) = £10,000.

The return on capital employed falls from 25% to 20% because of the sharp fall in asset turnover from 5 times to 2 times.

This does not mean that the management of the company would not raise its prices. However, the financial analysis has provided them with another piece of the decision-making jigsaw. It may be that this is a weakness in the SWOT analysis because the owners of the business, although very happy with the increase profitability may not be happy with the reduced ROCE. The management must judge which aspect is most acceptable.

Note. SWOT analysis is a management tool used to establish a clear picture of the organisation's current position or the viability of a project or strategy. SWOT stands for *strengths* and *weaknesses*, *opportunities* and *threats*. You will come across SWOT analysis frequently during your CIM studies and you will be competent in its use by the time you take your Diploma examinations.

2.15 The ROCE of ARC Ltd for 19X1 and 19X0 is:

$$
\begin{array}{cc}
19X1 & 19X0 \\
\dfrac{20,640}{16,100} = 128\% & \dfrac{9,400}{9,000} = 104\%
\end{array}
$$

Whose return and whose capital employed?

2.16 Most of the providers of finance to a business expect some return on their investment.

(a) Trade creditors and other current liabilities merely expect to be paid what they are owed.

(b) A bank charges interest on overdrafts.

(c) Interest must be paid to the holders of loan stock.

(d) Ordinary shareholders also expect a dividend. However, any retained profits kept in the business also represent funds 'owned' or 'provided' by them.

2.17 The return that we discussed above could apply equally to any one of the groups of interested parties listed in Paragraph 2.15. Equally the capital employed definition will change depending on exactly who we are considering. The most widely used ratio, however, refers to the company as a whole. Businesses own assets, both fixed assets and net current assets, which are used to generate profits (where net current assets are defined as current assets less current liabilities). These assets can only be funded in two ways. We can either borrow money or we can ask the shareholders to provide the funds. So to arrive at the capital employed in the business we should add the total of shareholders funds to the total long term borrowings of the company. The return used is the profit before interest and tax because we are trying to measure how effective our operations are at generating profits, so we omit the cost of borrowing the money from the calculation.

2.18 We can now see that our equation has become:

$$
\text{ROCE} = \frac{\text{PBIT}}{\text{Sales}} \times \frac{\text{Sales}}{\text{Capital employed}} = \frac{\text{PBIT}}{\text{Capital employed}}
$$

2.19 You will often need to be aware of this ratio during your analysis of companies particularly in case studies. Be careful in your analysis because the definition is often difficult to analyse. The difficulty is in how to define long term borrowings.

(a) Should we include any overdrafts which are included in current liabilities?

(b) Current liabilities may also include an element of long term borrowing that is due to be paid within one year.

2.20 In most cases you will not be troubled with these decisions because the case study will not identify the elements of cash in current assets, overdrafts in current liabilities or borrowings in current liabilities. If they do, however, the clear thinker will simply choose a path to take, state the assumption made and apply it consistently. Given the choice you should effectively determine whether the overdrafts and borrowings due in under one year are part of the long term funding strategy of the company; if they are then include them in capital employed, if not include them as simply part of net current assets.

2.21 The one vital point to remember is that a single ratio is nearly meaningless. What is important is the movement in that ratio over time and the comparison of that ratio with other companies in a similar business. Only then can any conclusions be drawn.

2.22 We mentioned before the most common ratio used to determine ROCE for the business as a whole. There are others, such as the return generated purely for the shareholders. They are entitled to the entire profit after tax. So their return is exactly that, the profit after tax. Their capital is simply the money they have invested in the business being, the share capital and reserves. Hence:

$$\text{Return on shareholder's capital} = \frac{\text{Profit after tax}}{\text{Share capital plus reserves}}$$

For ARC Ltd, the calculations will be:

19X1	*19X0*
$\frac{15,200}{16,100} = 94\%$	$\frac{6,300}{9,000} = 70\%$

You are unlikely to need to calculate this or any other variation on the basic ratio. However, be aware that variations can exist.

3. EARNINGS PER SHARE

3.1 Another method of calculating the return due to the ordinary shareholders is contained in the earnings per share calculation. This simply divides the earnings which are due to the shareholders (which is profit after tax) divided by the average number of ordinary shares in issue whilst the profit was generated. You will not need to calculate this figure but it is widely used by investors, potential investors and stock market analysts as one of the basic measures of success. As a result trends in EPS are very important and a decline in the EPS is often frowned upon.

4. GEARING

4.1 We have now seen a company is financed by different types of capital and that each type expects a return in the form of interest or dividend.

4.2 Gearing is a method of comparing how much of the long-term capital of a business is provided by equity (ordinary shares and reserves) and how much is provided by investors who are entitled to interest or dividend before ordinary shareholders can have a dividend themselves. These sources of capital are loans and preference shares, and are sometimes known collectively as 'prior charge capital'.

4.3 Gearing is usually calculated using one or other of two basic calculations.

4.4 The first method, commonly known as the debt:equity ratio, is defined as:

$$\frac{\text{Long term loans}}{\text{Equity (ordinary shares + reserves)}} \times 100\%$$

Long term loans will normally exclude overdrafts, whilst equity will exclude any preference shares. In your studies, equity will usually equate to the total of shareholders funds (but you should be aware that if items such as preference shares are included in the figure for shareholders funds they are, in effect, a source of long-term debt since they do not usually carry any voting rights, and should be included as part of the debt section of the equation). Again, however, the key is consistency since it is generally the level of the ration and its movement which is important. As a guideline the figure should not exceed 100%.

4.5 The second method measures the level of long term debt as a percentage of all funding raised by the company. Hence the calculation is:

$$\frac{\text{Long term debt}}{\text{Ordinary share capital + reserves + long term debt}} \times 100\%$$

A figure in excess of 50% is again usually felt to be getting a little high.

4.6 In the case of ARC Ltd, the gearing figures are:

19X1

$$\frac{750}{5,000 + 10,100 + 750} = 4.7\%$$

19X0

$$\frac{600}{5,000 + 3,000 + 600} = 7.0\%$$

Why is gearing important?

4.7 Gearing can be important when a company wants to raise extra capital, because if its gearing is already too high, we might find that it is difficult to raise a loan. Would-be lenders might take the view that ordinary shareholders should provide a fair proportion of the total capital for the business and that at the moment they are not doing so. Unless ordinary shareholders are prepared to put in more money themselves (either by issuing new shares or by retaining more profits), the company might be viewed as a bad business risk.

4.8 If excessive gearing indicates that more loans should not be made to a company, we must now ask the question 'what is excessive gearing?'

Unfortunately, there is no hard and fast answer to this question. The 'acceptable' level of gearing varies according to the country (average gearing is higher among companies in Japan than in Britain), the industry, and the size and status of the individual company within the industry. The more stable the company is, the more 'safe' higher gearing should be.

4.9   The advantages of gearing (of using debt capital rather than equity capital) are as follows.

   (a)   Debt capital is cheaper, because:

      (i)   the reward (interest or preference dividend) is fixed permanently, and therefore diminishes in real terms if there is inflation. Ordinary shareholders, on the other hand, usually expect dividend growth;

      (ii)   the reward required by debt-holders is usually lower than that required by equity holders, because debt capital is often secured on company assets, whereas ordinary share capital is a more risky investment;

      (iii)   payments of interest attract tax relief, whereas ordinary (or preference dividends do not.

   (b)   Debt capital does not normally carry voting rights, but ordinary shares usually do. The issue of debt capital therefore leaves pre-existing voting rights unchanged.

   (c)   If profits are rising, ordinary shareholders will benefit from gearing because earnings per share grow at a faster rate in a highly geared company.

4.10   The main disadvantage of gearing is that if profits fall even slightly, the profit available to shareholders will fall at a greater rate.

Gearing and earnings

4.11   One of the reasons why high gearing might be considered risky for lending is that the more loan capital a business has, the bigger becomes the size of profit before interest and tax (PBIT) which is necessary to meet demands for interest payments.

5.   OPERATIONAL RATIOS

5.1   Having dealt with the ratios which are used to analyse the overall strength and performance of a business it can now turn to rather shorter term operating ratios which reflect the businesses cash management.

5.2   Working capital has already been defined as the difference between current assets (mainly stocks, debtors and cash) and current liabilities (such as trade creditors and a bank overdraft).

   (a)   *Current assets* are items which are either cash already, or which will soon lead to the receipt of cash. Stocks will be sold to customers and create debtors; and debtors will soon pay in cash for their purchases.

   (b)   *Current liabilities* are items which will soon have to be paid for with cash. Trade creditors will have to be paid and a bank overdraft is usually regarded as a short-term borrowing which may need to be repaid fairly quickly.

   In published balance sheets, the word 'current' is applied to stocks, debtors, short-term investments and cash (current assets) and amounts due for payment within one year's time (current liabilities).

5.3   The ability to operate a business successfully involves the understanding of how cash will be exchanged for stocks of raw materials, which will be turned into a finished product, which may then be stockpiled awaiting sale, which will then be sold on credit terms creating a debtors, and which finally will be exchange for cash from the customer.

5.4   You will note that we may have to pay our supplier a long time before we receive cash for the sale of our goods. In the meantime we may have to pay stock storage charges, will incur expenses in producing our finished goods, may incur marketing costs and so on. The ability to minimise the period from payment for goods at one end of the operating cycle to receiving cash for our sales at the other end of the cycle can be critical to our performance.

5.5   As a result the finance function will monitor the *turnover periods*. A 'turnover' period is an (average) length of time.

   (a)   In the case of stock turnover, it is the length of time an item of stock is held in stores before it is used.

      (i)   A raw materials stock turnover period is the length of time raw materials are held before being issued to the production department.

      (ii)   A work in progress turnover period is the length of time it takes to turn raw materials into finished goods in the factory.

      (iii) A finished goods stock turnover period is the length of time that finished goods are held in a warehouse before they are sold.

      (iv) When a firm buys goods and re-sells them at a profit, the stock turnover period is the time between their purchase and their sale.

   (b)   The debtors turnover period, or debt collection period, is the length of the credit period taken by customers or the time between the sale of an item and the receipt of cash for the sale from the customer.

   (c)   Similarly, the creditors turnover period, or period of credit taken from supplies, is the length of time between the purchase of materials and the payment to suppliers.

5.6   These ratios, usually expressed in days, measure how long or how many times the business is exchanging cash during any aspect of the cash cycle over a period of time.

5.7   For example, the debtor turnover period links the sale turnover (or revenue) to the level of debtors in the business. Hence:

$$\frac{\text{Debtors}}{\text{Sales turnover}}$$

describes the level of debtors compared with the sales turnover. So the ratio for ARC Ltd is:

19X1	*19X0*
$\dfrac{26{,}700}{98{,}455}$	$\dfrac{8{,}600}{53{,}470}$

This can be expressed in days. You will note that the turnover is generated over one year or 365 days, or 12 months. By multiplying our ratio by 365 we recognise that the debtors are on average:

19X1	*19X0*
$\dfrac{26,700}{98,455} \times 365 = 99$ days	$\dfrac{8,600}{53,470} \times 365 = 59$ days

or

19X1	*19X0*
$\dfrac{26,700}{98,455} \times 12 = 3.25$ months	$\dfrac{8,600}{53,470} \times 12 = 1.93$ months

Another way of expressing this is to say that, in 19X1, the business has 99 days sales outstanding.

5.8 There are difficulties again with this measurement.

(a) The debtor figure quoted in the balance sheet may not include only trade debtors but also include debtors, say, for sale of capital goods (for example, we sold one of our retail shops but have not been paid yet). Hence there may be a distortion. In your studies assume the debtors are all trade debtors unless told otherwise and state your assumption.

(b) We know that the balance sheet shows only a point in time but turnover is generated over a period of time. We also know that ratio analysis is only useful when a trend is to be established. In a cyclical business such as selling fireworks we probably will not get a very meaningful analysis if we compare the balance sheet ratios gained from the accounts at the end of March against those on 5 November.

(c) What we really want is to compare average debtors against the sales turnover, but we will not usually be given that information.

5.9 We can, of course, do similar turnover calculations for stock turnover period:

$$\frac{\text{Average finished goods stocks (use closing stock)}}{\text{Total cost of goods sold in the period}} \times 365 \text{ days}$$

and for credit taken from suppliers:

$$\frac{\text{Average trade creditors (use closing creditors)}}{* \quad \text{Total purchase in the period}} \times 365 \text{ days}$$

* Cost of sales can be substituted on an approximation

5.10 The calculations of these ratios for ARC Ltd are as follows.

	19X1	*19X0*
Stock turnover period	$\dfrac{15,000}{70,728} \times 365 = 77$ days	$\dfrac{5,000}{40,653} \times 365 = 45$ days

	19X1	*19X0*
Creditor's payment period	$\dfrac{1,000}{70,728} \times 365 = 5$ days	$\dfrac{800}{40,653} \times 365 = 7$ days

Again these can be expressed in days or months depending on the period of time referred to in the denominator of each equation. The problem again with these ratios is that you will not usually be given the necessary information in your exam.

5.11 The importance of understanding these ratios is their impact on cash requirements. An increase in the stock turnover ratio or in the debtor turnover ratio means that more money is being tied up in funding working capital and this may not be desirable. Finance departments should keep a constant check and control on these ratios since they may highlight a problem which might not otherwise by recognised in time.

6. LIQUIDITY RATIOS

6.1 The word 'liquid', when applied to an asset, means 'readily converted into cash' and a firm's liquidity is defined by its ability to convert its assets into cash to meet all the demands for payments when they fall due.

6.2 The most liquid asset, of course, is cash itself (or a bank balance). The next most liquid assets are short-term investments (stocks and shares) because these can be sold quickly for cash should this be necessary. Debtors are fairly liquid assets because they should be expected to pay their bills in the near future. Stocks are the least liquid current asset because they must first be sold (perhaps on credit) and the customers given a credit period in which to pay before they can be converted into cash.

6.3 Current liabilities are items which must be paid for in the near future. When payment becomes due, enough cash must be available to make the payment. The managers of a business must therefore make sure that a regular supply of cash comes in (from current assets) at all times to meet the regular flow of payments.

6.4 There are two common liquidity ratios:

(a) the current ratio or working capital ratio;
(b) the quick ratio or liquidity ratio or *acid test ratio*.

The *current ratio* or *working capital ratio* is the more commonly used and is the ratio of current assets to current liabilities.

6.5 The current ratio is calculated as:

$$\frac{\text{current assets}}{\text{current liabilities}}$$

The quick ratio is calculated as:

current assets less stock
current liabilities

The exclusion of stock reflects the greater length of time it would take to realise the stock.

6.6 A 'prudent' current ratio is sometimes said to be 2:1. In other words, current assets should be twice the size of current liabilities. This is a rather simplistic view of the matter, because particular attention needs to be paid to certain matters.

    (a) *Bank overdrafts*. These are technically repayable on demand, and therefore must be classified as current liabilities. However, many companies have semi-permanent overdrafts in which case the likelihood of their having to be repaid in the near future is remote. It would also often be relevant to know a company's overdraft limit and this may give a truer indication of liquidity than a current or quick ratio.

    (b) Are the year-end figures are *typical* of the year as a whole? This is particularly relevant in the case of seasonal businesses. For example, many large retail companies choose an accounting year end following soon after the January sales and their balance sheets show a higher level of cash than would be usual at any other time in the year.

6.7 In practice, many businesses operate with a much lower current ratio and in these cases, the best way to judge their liquidity would be to look at the current ratio at different dates over a period of time. If the trend is towards a lower current ratio, we would judge that the liquidity position is getting steadily worse.

6.8 For example, the liquidity ratios of two firms A and B are as follows.

	1 Jan	1 Apr	1 July	1 Oct
Firm A	1.2 : 1	1.2 : 1	1.2 : 1	1.2 : 1
Firm B	1.3 : 1	1.2 : 1	1.1 : 1	1.0 : 1

We would say that firm A is maintaining a stable liquidity position, whereas firm B's liquidity is deteriorating. We would then begin to question firm B's continuing ability to pay its bills. A bank, for instance, would need to think carefully before granting any request from Firm B for an extended overdraft facility.

6.9 The *quick ratio* is used when we take the view that stocks take a long time to get ready for sale, and then there may be some delay in getting them sold, so that stocks are not particularly liquid assets. If this is the case, a firm's liquidity depends more heavily on the amount of debtors, short-term investments and cash that it has to match its current liabilities.

6.10 A 'prudent' quick ratio is 1:1. In practice, many businesses have a lower quick ratio (such as 0.5:1), and, as with the current ratio, the best way of judging a firm's liquidity would be to look at the trend in the quick ratio over a period of time. The quick ratio is also known as the *liquidity ratio* and as the *acid test ratio*.

6.11 The liquidity ratios for ARC Ltd would be calculated as follows.

	19X1	*19X0*
Current ratio	$\dfrac{42,100}{38,400} = 1.1:1$	$\dfrac{14,500}{13,000} = 1.1:1$
Quick ratio	$\dfrac{42,100 - 15,000}{38,400} = 0.7:1$	$\dfrac{14,500 - 5,000}{13,000} = 0.7:1$

This shows a good stability in the liquidity position.

Exercise

Calculate liquidity and working capital ratios from the accounts of the RMC Group, a manufacturer of products for the construction industry. (*Note.* In an examination you would be expected to comment on the results you obtain.)

	1988 £m	*1987* £m
Turnover	2,065.0	1,788.7
Cost of sales	1,478.6	1,304.0
Gross profit	586.4	484.7
Current assets		
Stocks	119.0	109.0
Debtors (note 1)	400.9	347.4
Short-term investments	4.2	18.8
Cash at bank and in hand	572.3	523.2
Creditors: amounts falling due within one year		
Loans and overdrafts	49.1	35.3
Corporation taxes	62.0	46.7
Dividend	19.2	14.3
Creditors (note 2)	370.7	324.0
	501.0	420.3
Net current assets	71.3	102.9
Notes		
1 Trade debtors	329.8	285.4
2 Trade creditors	236.2	210.8

Solution

	1988		*1987*	
Current ratio	$\dfrac{572.3}{501.0}$	$= 1.14$	$\dfrac{523.2}{420.3}$	$= 1.24$
Quick ratio	$\dfrac{453.3}{501.0}$	$= 0.90$	$\dfrac{414.2}{420.3}$	$= 0.99$
Debtors' payment period	$\dfrac{329.8}{2,065.0} \times 365$	$= 58$ days	$\dfrac{285.4}{1,788.7} \times 365$	$= 58$ days
Stock turnover period	$\dfrac{119.0}{1,478.6} \times 365$	$= 29$ days	$\dfrac{109.0}{1,304.0} \times 365$	$= 31$ days
Creditors' turnover period	$\dfrac{236.2}{1,478.6} \times 365$	$= 58$ days	$\dfrac{210.8}{1,304.0} \times 365$	$= 59$ days

---

7. CONCLUSION

7.1 The interpretation of financial data is the key to the understanding of any business, either in a practical application or during your studies. Companies as large as GEC have been effectively managed for many years simply by ensuring that the ratios relevant to their businesses were kept within acceptable limits.

7.2 These are the important to be lessons learned from this chapter.

(a) Ratios are a useful measure when in comparison with something else: either the company's history, or a competitor or an industry norm.

(b) Consistency in calculation and in the base data is important otherwise we could end up comparing apples and oranges.

(c) Return on capital employed is the product of two other ratios:

ROCE = profit margin × asset turnover

(d) Gearing is a measure of how funds have been generated to buy assets. Remember if those funds have been entirely generated from operations then the money has been effectively raised by the shareholders.

(e) There are two main measures for gearing. Neither is more correct than the other but both are widely used. Be consistent in your approach.

(f) Proper control of cash is vital to the continued financial strength of any company. Marketing managers should be aware of the debtor collection periods (also known as the debtor turnover or day sales outstanding) which is measured as:

$\dfrac{\text{Average debtors}}{\text{Annual turnover}} \times 365$ days

(g)   Two important tests of a business liquidity are:

(i)   the current ratio $\qquad = \dfrac{\text{current assets}}{\text{current liabilities}}$

(ii)   the quick or acid test ratio $\qquad = \dfrac{\text{current assets (excluding stocks)}}{\text{current liabilities}}$

TEST YOUR KNOWLEDGE
The numbers in brackets refer to paragraphs of this chapter

1   Write down the formula which shows the ROCE broken down into the secondary ratios. (2.9)

2   Explain two ways a business may change its overall ROCE? (2.10, 2.11)

3   What is EPS? (3.1)

4   Why is gearing important? (4.6, 4.7)

5   What is the link between debtors and sales turnover and why should these be monitored together? (5.7, 5.8)

6   What ratios would you use to determine whether a business could pay its liabilities as they fall due? (6.3, 6.4)

Now try question 3 at the end of the text

Chapter 4

LIMITATIONS OF HISTORICAL COST ACCOUNTS

This chapter covers the following topics.

1. Criticisms of historical cost accounting
2. Alternatives to historical cost accounting

---

1. CRITICISMS OF HISTORICAL COST ACCOUNTING

1.1 Traditionally, there have been two main reasons for the preparation of accounts. The first is to fulfil the needs of the owners of a business. The directors of a company, who manage its day-to-day affairs, are required by law to provide the shareholders with stewardship accounts. These are intended to help the shareholders assess the effectiveness with which their investment is being managed. They should give a *true and fair view* of the profit or loss for the accounting period and the state of affairs of the company at the balance sheet date. Published accounts are, of course, used by several other groups of people, for example potential investors, employees and creditors. These published accounts are usually produced once a year.

1.2 Secondly, accounts are prepared for management. These are intended to assist the managers of a business in controlling that business and in making decisions about its future. Management accounts are produced more frequently than published accounts, usually monthly (although sometimes quarterly).

1.3 Although the information needs of internal and external users differ considerably, it has become increasingly clear that accounts prepared on a traditional historical cost basis can present financial information in a misleading manner. The greatest criticisms of traditional accounting concepts have stemmed from their inability to reflect the effects of changing price levels.

1.4 Inflation of nearly 8% after the second world war gave rise to some interest in inflation accounting for a few years, but this dwindled as the rate of inflation fell in the early 1950s. In the late sixties, the interest in alternative accounting bases was revived, not only because inflation rates had again become significant, but also because the fundamental purpose of accounts was being questioned. The accounting profession now recognises that treatment of inflation is only one aspect of the problem of finding a superior accounting system. Not surprisingly, progress in this area has been slow.

1.5 Before mentioning the various alternatives, we should first consider the criticisms of historical cost accounting in more detail.

(a) *Fixed asset values are unrealistic.*
The most striking example is property. Although it is a statutory requirement that the market value of an interest in land should be disclosed in the directors' report if it is significantly different from the balance sheet figure, and although some companies have periodically updated the balance sheet values, in general there has been a lack of consistency in the approach adopted and a lack of clarity in the way in which the effects of these changes in value have been expressed. If fixed assets are retained in the books at their historical cost, *unrealised holding gains* are not recognised. This means that the total holding gain, if any, will be brought into account during the year in which the asset is realised, rather than spread over the period during which it was owned.

There are, in essence, two points to be considered.

(i) Although it has long been accepted that a balance sheet prepared under the historical cost concept is an historical record and not a statement of current worth, many people now argue that the balance sheet should at least give an indication of the current value of the company's tangible net assets.

(ii) The prudence concept requires that profits should only be recognised when realised in the form either of cash or of other assets the ultimate cash realisation of which can be assessed with reasonable certainty. It may be argued that recognising unrealised holding gains on fixed assets is contrary to this concept.

On balance, the weight of opinion is now in favour of restating asset values. It is felt that the criticism based on prudence can be met by ensuring that valuations are made as objectively as possible (as in the case of property, by having independent expert valuations) and by not taking unrealised gains through the profit and loss account.

(b) *Depreciation is inadequate to finance the replacement of fixed assets.*
This criticism is generally well understood and you will appreciate that what is important is not the replacement of one asset by an identical new one (something that rarely happens) but the replacement of the operating capability represented by the old asset.

Another criticism of historical cost depreciation is that it does not fully reflect the value of the asset consumed during the accounting year. Whilst this point is obviously closely related to the first, it can be overcome whilst still retaining insufficient profits to finance replacement.

(c) *Holding gains on stocks are included in profit.*
During a period of high inflation the monetary value of stocks held may increase significantly while they are being processed. The conventions of historical cost accounting lead to the realised part of this holding gain (known as stock appreciation) being included in profit for the year. It is estimated that in the late 1970s nearly half the declared profits of companies were due to stock appreciation.

This problem can be illustrated using a simple example. At the beginning of the year a company has 100 units of stock and no other assets. Its trading account for the year is shown below.

TRADING ACCOUNT

	Units	£		Units	£
Opening stock	100	200	Sales (made 31 December)	100	500
Purchases (made 31 December)	100	400			
	200	600			
Closing stock (FIFO basis)	100	400			
	100	200			
Gross profit	-	300			
	100	500		100	500

Apparently the company has made a gross profit of £300. But, at the beginning of the year the company owned 100 units of stock and at the end of the year it owned 100 units of stock and £100 in cash (sales £500 less purchases £400). From this it would seem that a profit of £100 is more reasonable. The remaining £200 is stock appreciation arising as the purchase price increased from £2 to £4.

The criticism can be overcome by using a capital maintenance concept based on physical units rather than money values.

(d) *Profit (or losses) on holdings of net monetary items are not shown.*
In periods of inflation the purchasing power, and thus the value, of money falls. It follows that an investment in money will have a lower real value at the end of a period of time than it did at the beginning. A loss has been made. Similarly, the real value of a monetary liability will reduce over a period of time and a gain will be made.

(e) *The true effect of inflation on capital maintenance is not shown.*
To a large extent this follows from the points already mentioned. It is a widely held principle that distributable profits should only be recognised after full allowance has been made for any erosion in the capital value of a business. In historical cost accounts, although capital is maintained in nominal money terms, it may not be in real terms. In other words, profits may be distributed to the detriment of the long-term viability of the business because more is distributed than the company can afford.

(f) *Comparisons over time are unrealistic.*
This will tend to an exaggeration of growth. For example, if a company's profit in 1964 was £100,000 and in 1984 £500,000, a shareholder's initial reaction might be that the company had done rather well. If, however, it was then revealed that with £100,000 in 1964 he could buy exactly the same goods as with £500,000 in 1984, the apparent growth would seem less impressive.

Exercise

Outline the basis on which tangible assets are valued in financial reports, giving specific examples.

Solution

Asset valuation in general is a controversial area. An asset has a future value to the business but it is difficult to quantify that value in terms of financial accounting. Assets can be fixed or current assets; they can also be categorised as intangible or tangible assets.

Tangible assets have traditionally been valued at historical cost (or original cost). A factory, say, purchased for £500,000 will be shown in the balance sheet at a value of £500,000. This value will be reduced over a period of time (the useful life of the factory) by deducting depreciation to reflect the consumption of value as the factory wears out, thus leaving the *net book value* in the balance sheet.

Historical cost does not tend to reflect the true economic value of tangible assets. As a result, alternative approaches to valuation may be used, or have been attempted in the past. It is now possible to revalue *fixed assets* and show the current value of the asset in the balance sheet. This does not allow the business to make a 'profit' on the revaluation (the difference between the revaluation figure and the historical cost figure) as this 'profit' is not put through the trading profit and loss account, but through reserves instead.

When inflation was very high in the UK it was felt that assets in the balance sheet should be valued in a way which recognised the effects of inflation. This would remove the distorting effects of changes in the purchasing power of money and make financial accounts more comparable on a yearly basis. There are alternative methods to show the effects of inflation, the most well known being current cost accounting (CCA) and accounting for current purchasing power (CPP). Neither of these methods was popular and consequently they are not mandatory now in the preparation of financial accounts, although some companies produce some kind of CCA or CPP accounts voluntarily.

Current assets are valued in the balance sheet at historical cost. This is subject to the concept of prudence in that, if the net realisable value (NRV) of an asset is lower than its cost, then it should be valued at NRV. This valuation concept is usually applied to stock, but the same applies to debtors as the total value of debtors is adjusted to reflect bad and potentially bad debts.

---

2. ALTERNATIVES TO HISTORICAL COST ACCOUNTING

2.1 The points mentioned above have demonstrated some of the accounting problems which arise in times of severe and prolonged inflation. Of the various possible systems of accounting for price changes most can be divided into two categories:

(a) general price change bases and in particular current purchasing power (CPP);

(b) current value bases: the basic principles of all these are:

    (i) to show balance sheet items at some form of current value rather than historical cost;

    (ii) to compute profits by matching the current value of costs at the date of consumption against revenue.

The current value of an item will normally be based on replacement cost, net realisable value or economic value.

2.2 In the UK an attempt was made to implement a system of CPP accounting with the publication in 1974 of Provisional Statement of Standard Accounting Practice 7 (PSSAP 7). The principal feature of the system was that profit for the year was calculated after an adjustment designed to reflect the effect of general price inflation on the purchasing power of equity shareholders' funds.

2.3 CPP accounting did not catch on and in 1980 a decisive step was taken in the direction of a current value basis of accounting. SSAP 16 *Current cost accounting* was published for a trial period of three years beginning in March 1980. The system of current cost accounting (CCA) advocated by SSAP 16 did not attempt to cater for general price inflation; instead, profit for the year was to be calculated after allowing for the effects of price increases specifically on the operating capability of the particular business.

2.4 The principal features of CCA are as follows.

(a) In the balance sheet, assets are stated at their 'value to the business'. This may be a replacement cost, net realisable value or economic value depending on the circumstances.

(b) In the profit and loss account holding gains are excluded from profit. A holding gain is the difference between value to the business of an asset and its original cost. If X buys an item for £100 and sells it for £150 there will be an HC profit of £150 - £100 = £50. If the replacement cost of the item at the date of sale is £130, in CC terms there will be an operating gain of £150 - £130 = £20 and a holding gain of £130 - £100 = £30. Current cost accounting recognises operating gains only as profit; historical cost accounting does not differentiate between holding and operating gains, and recognises both as profit.

2.5 SSAP 16 encountered a good deal of criticism on both practical and theoretical grounds. In 1988 the standard was withdrawn. It is unclear whether any future standard will be based on CCA or an alternative system.

3. CONCLUSION

Historical cost accounts have a number of deficiencies in times of rising prices. In the UK attempts to deal with the problem have centered mainly on a system of current cost accounting introduced by SSAP 16 in 1980. Compliance with SSAP 16 was never widespread even amongst the companies (mainly public companies) within its scope. Now that the standard has been withdrawn the position is likely to deteriorate further. Unless the Accounting Standards Board produces a new inflation standard, historical cost accounts are likely to be the only accounts routinely produced in the UK.

TEST YOUR KNOWLEDGE
The numbers in brackets refer to paragraphs of this chapter

1 Name two important reasons for preparing accounts. (1.1, 1.2)

2 Why do some businesses revalue fixed assets periodically for accounts purposes? (1.5)

3 What are holding gains on stock? (1.5)

4 What does CPP accounting aim to show? (2.2)

5 How does current cost accounting treat holding gains? (2.4)

Now try question 4 at the end of the text

74

PART B
PLANNING FOR THE FUTURE

Chapter 5

BUDGETING

This chapter covers the following topics.

1. Budgeting
2. Analysing costs
3. Flexible budgets
4. Budgetary control and cost control
5. Cash budgets
6. Behavioural aspects of budgeting

---

1. BUDGETING

1.1 Businesses must concentrate on both short term and long term objectives if they are to be successful. Having established a long term corporate plan management should develop a coordinated short term plan which is designed to steer the business towards those long term goals. This means that the business should use a process which concentrates management action on those areas that can be changed in the short term, which will eventually lead to the success of the longer term corporate plan. This is usually done by way of a budget. The budget draws together the necessary actions and coordinates the activities of management. In this chapter we will look at budgeting in fairly general terms before looking at specific aspects of costs, pricing, and so on, in the next few chapters.

The purpose of budgeting

1.2 Budgets have several different purposes. 'Budgets are designed to carry out a variety of functions: planning, evaluating performance, co-ordinating activities, implementing plans, communicating, motivating and authorising actions' (Horngren, *Cost accounting: a managerial emphasis*).

The purpose of a budget might be as follows.

(a) To *compel planning*. This is probably the most important feature of budgeting because planning forces management to look ahead, set targets, anticipate problems and give the organisation purpose and direction.

(b) To *communicate ideas and plans* to everyone affected by them. A formal system is necessary to ensure that each person is aware of what he or she is supposed to be doing.

(c) To *co-ordinate the activities of different departments or sub-units of the organisation*. This concept of co-ordination implies, for example, that the purchasing department should base its budget on production requirements and that the production budget should in turn be based on sales expectations. Although straightforward in concept, co-ordination is remarkably difficult to achieve, and there is often 'sub-optimality' and conflict between departmental plans in the budget so that the efforts of each department are not fully integrated into a combined plan to achieve the company's best targets.

(d) To *provide a framework for responsibility accounting*, whereby managers of budget centres are made responsible for the achievement of budget targets for the operations under their personal control.

(e) To *establish a system of control*. Budgetary control usually involves the feedback of actual results for comparison against the budget plan.

1.3 In order to achieve these various objectives the budgets should be broken down into relevant business segments. These should naturally fit both the products and the markets in which the company operates or is intending to operate. This will be set in the context of the overall marketing plan and hence must be consistent with that plan. The setting of budgets in a financial framework gives management the ability to plan and control performance against a pre determined yardstick. Because we are dealing with the future we will have to make assumptions on the outcome of various events. One thing is certain: the budget will be wrong! Circumstances change, outcomes change, timing of events changes. As a result, a budget is not to be seen as a static document. By measuring performance against this yardstick management will continually re-evaluate the overall anticipated result of the series of decisions and actions, and will produce forecasts and flexed budgets which better match the results to date and anticipated results for the rest of the year.

1.4 This does not necessarily means that the budget does not remain in place. After some roundabout and repeated processes, a final budget will be agreed with the company's management committee (usually the board of directors). This will remain in place throughout the year as an agreed quantified plan of actions and policies which are defined to achieve the corporate objectives. The flexed budget is slightly different.

1.5 A *flexible budget* recognises the existence of fixed, variable and mixed (semi-fixed, semi-variable) costs, and it is designed to change so as to relate to the actual volumes of production and sales in a period. We will look at the definition of fixed and variable costs in section 2 of this chapter. Flexible budgets may be used in one of two ways.

(a) *At the planning stage*. For example, suppose that a company expects to sell 10,000 units of output during the next year. A master budget (the fixed budget) would be prepared on the basis of these expected volumes. However, if the company thinks that output and sales might be as low as 8,000 units or as high as 12,000 units, it may prepare contingency flexible budgets, at volumes of, say 8,000, 9,000, 11,000 and 12,000 units. The advantages of planning with flexible budgets include:

(i)   finding out well in advance the costs of lay-off pay, idle time and so on if output falls short of budget;

(ii) deciding whether it would be possible to find alternative uses for spare capacity if output falls short of budget (for example, could employees be asked to overhaul their own machines instead of paying for an outside contractor?);

       (iii)   estimating the costs of overtime, sub-contracting work or extra machine hire if sales volume exceeds the fixed budget estimate, and finding out if there is a limiting factor which would prevent high volumes of output and sales being achieved.

  (b) Flexible budgets are used *retrospectively* at the end of each month (control period) or year, to compare actual results achieved with what results should have been under the circumstances. Flexible budgets are an essential factor in budgetary control.

       (i)   Management needs to be informed about how good or bad·actual performance has been. To provide a measure of performance, there must be a yardstick (budget or standard) against which actual performance can be measured.

       (ii)   Every business is dynamic, and actual volumes of output cannot be expected to conform exactly to the fixed budget. Comparing actual costs directly with the fixed budget costs is meaningless.

       (iii)   For useful control information, it is necessary to compare actual results at the actual level of activity achieved against the results that should have been expected at this level of activity (the flexible budget).

1.6   Finally there is the *forecast*. This is a revision or latest prediction of the results of the business for the period under consideration (usually a year). It will be produced at different stages in the year and hence will be a mixture of results already achieved and the latest views on how management action and market conditions will affect the remaining period. It is not therefore a formally agreed plan and hence may not be aiming to achieve the same set of corporate objectives as set in the budget because of changing circumstances.

2.   ANALYSING COSTS

2.1   Cost classification is extremely important in the context of the budgeting process. We will consider the different methods of analysing costs here.

Fixed and variable costs

2.2   One way of analysing and classifying costs is into:

  (a) fixed costs; and
  (b) variable costs.

Some items of expenditure are part-fixed and part-variable or 'mixed' costs, but in cost accounting, mixed costs are divided into their fixed and their variable elements.

2.3   The distinction between fixed and variable costs lies in whether the amount of costs incurred will go up as the volume of activity goes up, or whether the costs will remain the same, regardless of the volume of activity. For example:

  (a) direct material costs will rise as more units of a product are manufactured, and so they are variable costs, varying with the volume of production;

  (b) sales commission is often a fixed percentage of sales turnover, and so is a variable cost that varies with the level of sales (but not with the level of production);

    (c)   telephone call charges are likely to increase if the volume of business expands, and so they are a variable overhead cost, varying with the volume of production and sales;

    (d)   the rental cost of business premises is a constant amount, at least within a stated time period, and so it is a fixed cost that does not vary with the level of activity conducted on the premises.

Direct and indirect costs

2.4   We have already mentioned the need to budget for both the product and the market place in which we operate or intend to operate. This type of matrix based approach is also adopted in budgeting within the financial framework. As well as being either fixed or variable, costs can also be described as direct or indirect.

2.5   Materials, labour costs and other expenses can be classified as direct costs or indirect costs.

    (a)   A *direct* cost is a cost that can be traced in full to the product or service (or department) that is being costed.

        (i)   Direct materials costs are the costs of materials that are known to have been used in making and selling a product (or even providing a service).

        (ii)   Direct labour costs are the specific costs of the workforce used to make a product or provide a service. Direct labour costs are established by measuring the time taken for a job, or the time taken in 'direct production work'. Traditionally, direct labour costs have been restricted to wage-earning factory workers, but in recent years, with the development of systems for costing services, the costs of some salaried staff might also be treated as a direct labour cost.

        (iii)   Other direct expenses are those expenses that have been incurred in full as a direct consequence of making a product, or providing a service, or running a department (depending on whether a product, a service or a department is being costed).

    (b)   An *indirect* cost is a cost that is incurred in the course of making a product, providing a service or running a department, but cannot be traced directly and in full to the product, service or department.

        (i)   Indirect materials costs are therefore those which are not charged directly to a product, such as coolants or cleaning materials.

        (ii)   Indirect labour costs are labour costs which are not charged directly to a product for example a supervisor's salary.

        (iii)   Indirect expenses are expenses which are not charged directly to a product, such as building insurance or water rates.

2.6   Here is another definition of direct and indirect costs, that you might find useful later.

    (a)   A direct cost is a cost which can be identified with and *allocated* to a cost centre (perhaps a department) or cost unit (a product).

(b) An indirect cost is a cost which cannot be directly allocated, but which can be *apportioned* to, or *absorbed* by, cost centres or cost units. Indirect costs are commonly referred to as overheads.

Hence the cost of the marketing director is indirect since his role should cover all areas of activity, but a specific brand support can be considered to be a direct cost.

2.7 Of course, life is not always quite as simple as these definitions would suggest. There will be occasions when costs may seem to be of both a fixed and variable nature. For example, factory rent is fixed only if you produce at the current levels of activity. Increasing sales activity may result in the need for most factory space.

2.8 Similarly it is difficult sometimes to differentiate direct costs from indirect costs. By-products are a classic example where costs can be incurred to produce two different products but the allocation is different.

2.9 In your studies you should be aware of these pitfalls and in the examination you should make logical assumptions which are clearly stated.

3. FLEXIBLE BUDGETS

Accuracy of budgets

3.1 It is important that budgets should be as accurate as possible in estimating both the fixed costs in any period, and the variable costs of output. Failure to achieve a sufficiently accurate budget would mean that:

(a) plans will be made on false assumptions of costs and profits;

(b) in budgetary control, comparisons of actual results with the budget would give meaningless control information.

3.2 There are many practical difficulties in attempting to plan accurately, some of which cannot be overcome. Unnecessary inaccuracies, however, should be avoided.

(a) If a business is seasonal, so that at some times of the year output is low, whereas at other times there is a requirement for overtime and casual labour, the budget during high and low activity months should allow for expected changes in costs (for example overtime pay, holiday pay, lay-off pay and so on).

(b) Many managers prepare estimates of next year's spending by adding an allowance for inflation on the current year's spending. This approach to budgeting is slapdash; individual cost items should be budgeted carefully, and the timing of inflationary increases, if known, (as with the date of wage settlements) should be allowed for.

The necessity of flexible budgets

3.3 We have seen that flexible budgets may be prepared in order to plan for variations in the level of activity above or below the level set in the fixed budget. It has been suggested however, that since many cost items in modern industry are fixed costs, the value of flexible budgets in planning is dwindling.

(a) In many manufacturing industries, plant costs (depreciation, rent and so on) are a very large proportion of total costs, and these tend to be fixed costs.

(b) Wage costs also tend to be fixed, because employees are generally guaranteed a basic wage for a working week of an agreed number of hours.

(c) With the growth of service industries, labour (wages or fixed salaries) and overheads will account for most of the costs of a business, and direct materials will be a relatively small proportion of total costs.

3.4 Flexible budgets are nevertheless necessary, and even if they are not used at the planning stage, they must be used for budgetary control variance analysis because:

(a) material costs are variable costs;

(b) labour costs, although often fixed, are treated as variable costs in order to measure efficiency of working (productivity) for control purposes.

3.5 Within the area of overheads, promotional support may be considered to be variable in that it is a discretionary spend and may be revised if predictions of sales volume change.

Where to start

3.6 In overall business terms the budget tries to put into a financial framework the predicted result of all the activities that will go together towards achieving the overall corporate objectives.

3.7 The budgeting process should enable a business to produce the following as an overall master budget.

(a) *A budgeted profit and loss account*. This shows how much profit or loss the business is planning to make over the budget period. The business should expect to make a profit, but the budget will show whether an overall loss or a loss in a particular department might be incurred.

The total profit and loss account budget will often be sub-divided into *departmental budgets*; (a budgeted profit and loss account for each department, division or other profit centre in the organisation.

(b) A *cash budget*. A business needs to make sure that it will have enough cash to continue operating, or that an overdraft facility is available with a bank to cover the expected need.

Profit and cash flows are not the same thing. A business can be profitable but run out of cash, and so be forced into liquidation. The purpose of a cash budget is to forecast what cash flows should be, and whether the cash resources of the organisation should be sufficient.

(c) *An end-of-period budgeted balance sheet.* From the budgeted profit and loss account, the cash budget and the balance sheet as at the start of the period, it should be possible to prepare an estimated balance sheet as at the end of the budget period.

3.8 The process necessary to bring these documents together will involve a wide variety of people and in most cases a budgetary committee will be set up with representations from each of the key functional departments being represented. The initial task is to identify the critical factor which will drive all other costs and revenues. In most cases this will be sales. The interface between sales and production is fundamental here since the function of the sales and marketing department is to provide for the needs of the customer whilst maximising the benefit to the business. This usually results as a process in the maximisation of sales volumes, but it is no good believing that the business can sell 10,000 units in the year if our production capacity is 9,000 units and there are no available capacity alternatives that can be considered within the time frame.

3.9 There are occasions when budgeting does not begin with the sales budget, because there is a shortage of a key resource which prevents the business from selling as much as it could. For example there could be a shortage of skilled labour, of raw materials or of machine capacity. In these situations there is a *limiting budget factor*, and this becomes the key budget factor or principal budget factor on which the budget should be based. Budgeting would start by looking at the problem of how to maximise profits within the resource constraints.

In the absence of resource shortages, sales is the principal budget factor and is therefore the first budget to be prepared.

Preparing the sales budget

3.10 Since the sales budget is usually the budget from which cost budgets and the budgeted P & L account are developed, it is obviously very important that the estimated sales in the budget should be reasonable and realistic.

3.11 It is not easy to forecast sales with any degree of accuracy, because the future in business is always uncertain. All that a business can do is try to put as much care as possible into preparing the sales budget, and there are several methods that can be used to forecast likely sales.

(a) Future sales values can be estimated on the basis of what sales have been in the past. Allowances can be made for sales price increases, and whether there is an upward or downward trend in sales volume over time.

(b) For new products, there is no historical data on which to base a sales forecast. An organisation might therefore ask its salespeople to prepare their own sales forecasts or they might commission a market research survey as a means of forecasting sales.

(c) An organisation might already have signed sales contracts with commercial customers, in which case estimates of sales can be based on contract agreements.

3.12 An organisation might produce a large number of products or services, and sell them in a wide geographical area. In such cases, sales budgets should be prepared for each product or product group and for each region or area.

3.13 For many organisations, sales have seasonal peaks and troughs, with heavy selling periods at some times of the year, and not much selling at other times. Seasonal variations in sales should be recognised in the budgets for each control period (in the monthly or quarterly budgets).

Other functional budgets

3.14 Once the sales budget has been prepared, a manufacturing organisation can go on to prepare a production budget. Goods may be produced for stock or sold out of stock, therefore planned production and sales volumes are not necessarily the same amount. The production budget in units will be equal to the sales budget in units plus the budgeted increase in finished goods stock or minus the budgeted decrease in finished goods stocks.

3.15 Once the production budget has been prepared it is possible to prepare the budgets for the resources needed to produce the required output.

The resource budgets will include the following.

(a) The materials usage budget will be prepared, stated in quantities and perhaps cost, for each type of material used.

(b) The machine utilisation budget will show the operating hours required on each machine or group of machines.

(c) The labour budget will be prepared for all grades of labour, both direct and indirect, showing the number of hours needed and the wages cost.

3.16 A materials *usage* budget is a plan for the cost of materials that will be used or consumed during the budget period. The materials *purchases* budget, in contrast, is the plan for the cost of materials that will be purchased in the period. The cost of materials consumed and the cost of materials purchased will differ by the amount of increase or decrease in stocks of materials between the beginning and the end of the budget period.

3.17 Budgets for marketing and administration costs must also be prepared. Many cost items will be fixed, although there may be some variable costs, which vary with the volume of sales (for example sales commission). Some of the marketing budget will have to be prepared in conjunction with the sales budget since, for existing products, the level of sales anticipated will rely on the marketing support. The balance of the budget may well be determined by the activity anticipated from new products which may be launched during the year or which may be bunched in a further period.

Exercise

The actual expenditure of the Eastern Regional office of Cain Ltd during the 12 months to 30 November 19X1 was as follows.

	£	£
Salaries		
Branch manager	24,000	
Salesmen (5 @ £15,000)	75,000	
Office secretary	7,500	
		106,500
Commissions (based on sales of £4m)		
Branch manager (0.1%)	4,000	
Salesmen (0.9%)	36,000	
		40,000
Travel and entertainment		
Averaging £35 per salesman per day for an annual average of 225 days per salesman		39,375
Office expenses		
Rent, utilities, suppliers and so on		25,000
Total branch expenditure		210,875

In preparing the budget for the next 12 months the following facts are anticipated.

(a)   The branch manager's salary will rise by £2,000.

(b)   Each salesman's base salary will remain unchanged, but the commission rate will increase to 1.0%.

(c)   The office secretary's salary will be increased by £60 per month.

(d)   Two additional salesmen are to be employed, on the same terms as the existing sales force.

(e)   The sales quota for the branch will be £5m.

(f)   Travel and entertainment expenses are likely to increase by 4% per salesman-day.

(g)   A special promotional campaign will be undertaken at the cost of £25,000.

(h)   The office expenses will rise by 10%.

Required

Prepare the 1991/92 budget for the Eastern sales office.

Solution

	£	£
Salaries		
Branch manager £(24,000 + 2,000)	26,000	
Salesmen (7 @ £15,000)	105,000	
Office secretary £7,500 + (£60 × 12)	8,220	
		139,220
Commissions		
Branch manager (£5,000,000 × 0.1%)	5,000	
Salesmen (£5,000,000 × 1.0%)	50,000	
		55,000
Travel and entertainment		
(225 × £35 × 1.04 × 7)		57,330
Office expenses		
Rent, utilities etc (£25,000 × 1.10)		27,500
Promotional campaign		25,000
		304,050

---

4. BUDGETARY CONTROL AND COST CONTROL

4.1 Budgetary control is the practice of establishing budgets which identify areas of responsibility for individual managers (production managers, brand managers and so on) and of regularly comparing actual results against expected results. The most important method of budgetary control is *variance analysis*, which involves the comparison of actual results achieved during a control period (a month, or four weeks) with a flexible budget. The differences between actual results and expected results are called variances and these are used to provide a guideline for control action by individual managers (or a guideline for altering the master budget in the light of actual events). Variance analysis calculations will be covered in detail in a later chapter.

4.2 Budgetary control is defined as 'the establishment of budgets relating the responsibilities of executives to the requirements of a policy, and the continuous comparison of actual with budgeted results, either to secure by individual action the objective of that policy or to provide a basis for its revision'.

4.3 You should notice from this definition that individual managers are held responsible for investigating differences between budgeted and actual results, and are then expected to take corrective action or amend the plan in the light of actual events.

4.4 The administration of budgetary control may be the responsibility of the budget committee, with most of the detailed work of communicating variance information and co-ordinating control efforts organised on behalf of the committee by the accounting department. The accountant will normally prepare the period statements of variances, and ensure that the managers responsible are aware of the need to consider control action about particular variances which have arisen. Hence the marketing manager will receive a regular statement on sales value, specific costs and so forth.

The wrong approach to budgetary control

4.5   The wrong approach to budgetary control is simply to compare actual results against a fixed budget. Consider the following example.

Sidewinder Ltd manufactures a single product, the varmint. Budgeted results and actual results for June 19X2 are shown below.

	Budget	Actual results	Variance
Production and sales of the varmint (units)	2,000	3,000	
	£	£	£
Sales revenue (a)	20,000	30,000	10,000 (F)
Direct materials	6,000	8,500	2,500 (A)
Direct labour	4,000	4,500	500 (A)
Maintenance	1,000	1,400	400 (A)
Depreciation	2,000	2,200	200 (A)
Rent and rates	1,500	1,600	100 (A)
Other costs	3,600	5,000	1,400 (A)
Total costs (b)	18,100	23,200	5,100
Profit (a) − (b)	1,900	6,800	4,900 (F)

Note. (F) denotes a favourable variance and (A) an adverse or unfavourable variance. Adverse variances are sometimes denoted as (U) for unfavourable.

4.6   (a)   In this example, the variances are meaningless for purposes of control. Costs were higher than budget because the volume of output was also higher; variable costs would be expected to increase above the budgeted costs in the fixed budget. There is no information to show whether control action is needed for any aspect of costs or revenues.

(b)   For control purposes, it is necessary to know whether:

(i)   actual costs were higher than they should have been to produce and sell 3,000 units of varmint;

(ii)   actual revenue was satisfactory from the sale of 3,000 units of varmint;

(iii)   whether the volume of units made and sold has varied from the budget favourably or adversely.

All these aspects are relevant to the decision making process in which the marketing manager will be a key individual.

The correct approach to budgetary control

4.7   The correct approach to budgetary control is:

(a)   to identify fixed and variable costs; and

(b)   to produce a flexible budget. It is preferable to use 'marginal or incremental costing' techniques, and keep fixed costs at the same amount in the flexed budget as in the original master budget. We will discuss marginal costing a little later in the text.

4.8 In the previous example of Sidewinder Ltd, let us suppose that we have the following estimates of cost behaviour:

(a) direct materials and maintenance costs are variable;

(b) although basic wages are a fixed cost, direct labour is regarded as variable in order to measure efficiency/productivity;

(c) rent and rates and depreciation are fixed costs;

(d) other costs consist of fixed costs of £1,600 plus a variable cost of £1 per unit made and sold.

We will ignore the absorption of fixed costs into product costs, and any under- or over-absorption of overhead; we shall use marginal costing principles.

4.9 Now that the cost behaviour patterns are known, a budget cost allowance can be calculated for each item of expenditure. This allowance is shown in a flexible budget as the expected expenditure on each item for the relevant level of activity. The budget cost allowances are calculated as follows.

(a) Variable cost allowances, for example material cost allowance
= original budget × (3,000 units/2,000 units)

= £6,000 × 3/2 = £9,000

(b) Fixed cost allowance
= as original budget

(c) Semi-fixed cost allowances
= original budgeted fixed costs plus (3,000 units × variable cost per unit)

For example, other costs allowances
= £1,600 + (3,000 × £1) = £4,600

4.10 The budgetary control (variance) analysis should be as follows.

	Fixed budget (a)	Flexible budget (b)	Actual results (c)	Total variance (b) − (c)
Production and sales (units)	2,000	3,000	3,000	
	£	£	£	£
Sales revenue	20,000	30,000	30,000	0
Variable costs				
Direct materials (i)	6,000	9,000	8,500	500 (F)
Direct labour (ii)	4,000	6,000	4,500	1,500 (F)
Maintenance (iii)	1,000	1,500	1,400	100 (F)
Semi-variable costs				
Other costs (iv)	3,600	4,600	5,000	400 (A)
Fixed costs				
Depreciation (v)	2,000	2,000	2,200	200 (A)
Rent and rates (v)	1,500	1,500	1,600	100 (A)
Total costs	18,100	24,600	23,200	1,400 (F)
Profit	1,900	5,400	6,800	1,400 (F)

Analysis

(a) In selling 3,000 units, the expected profit should have been, not the fixed budget profit of £1,900 but the flexible budget profit of £5,400. Instead, actual profit was £6,800, £1,400 more than we should have expected. One of the reasons for the improvement is that, given output and sales of 3,000 units, costs are lower than expected (and sales revenue exactly as expected):

			£	
(i)	Direct materials cost variance		500	(F)
(ii)	Direct labour cost variance		1,500	(F)
(iii)	Maintenance cost variance		100	(F)
(iv)	'Other costs' cost variance		400	(A)
(v)	Fixed cost expenditure variances			
	1	Rent and rates	100	(A)
	2	Depreciation	200	(A)
			1,400	(F)

(b) Another reason for the improvement in profit above the fixed budget profit is the sales volumes. Sidewinder Ltd sold 3,000 units of varmint instead of 2,000 units, with the result that:

		£	£
(i)	Sales revenue increased by		10,000
(ii)	Variable costs increased by		
	Direct materials	3,000	
	Direct labour	2,000	
	Maintenance	500	
	Variable element of other cost	1,000	
(iii)	Fixed costs are unchanged		6,500
(iv)	Profit increased by		3,500

(c) For purposes of budgetary control it is useful to note in our example that:

	£	£
Sales price per unit of varmint		10.00
Variable cost per unit		
Direct material	3.00	
Direct labour	2.00	
Maintenance	0.50	
Other costs	1.00	
Total variable costs		6.50
Contribution per unit		3.50

The sales volume variance was 1,000 units favourable (3,000 - 2,000). The difference between the profit in the fixed budget and the flexible budget = 1,000 units (F) × £3.50 per unit = £3,500 (F). Now check the calculation in (b) above, which gives the same result (using a method of calculation which usually takes longer to carry out). Do not worry about fully understanding this variance analysis calculation at this stage. Detailed explanations of how the variance calculations work are dealt with in a later chapter.

(d) A full variance analysis statement would be:

	£	£
Fixed budget profit		1,900
Variances:		
Sales volume (margin)	3,500 (F)	
Direct materials cost	500 (F)	
Direct labour cost	1,500 (F)	
Maintenance cost	100 (F)	
Other costs	400 (A)	
Rent and rates expenditure	100 (A)	
Depreciation expenditure	200 (A)	
		4,900 (F)
Actual profit		6,800

4.11 Investigation of the variances, with a view to deciding whether control action is required, will be carried out for those variances which seem significantly large, by the manager responsible for the area of operations concerned. Large favourable variances should be checked, as well as adverse variances, in order to find out what has happened and why. In our example, the sales manager may be asked to check why sales were 50% higher than budgeted and the production manager may be asked to explain the large favourable variance in labour costs. The adverse variances are probably insufficiently large, in this example, to warrant an investigation.

Cost control and cost reduction

4.12 Budgetary control is the basis of a cost control system which requires managers to be held responsible for aspects of a budget or plan. They are also responsible for differences between the actual results and the budget or plan. The reporting system provides management with information to enable them to identify which costs and revenues are in need of management action to keep them under control.

4.13 Cost reduction, in contrast, is concerned with bringing down expenditure levels and spending less than before without reducing the quality of the products or service. Cost reduction implies 'cuts' whereas cost control implies keeping costs within planned and acceptable limits. Do not make the common error of confusing these two terms.

Controllable costs

4.14 Budgetary control reporting systems must report costs to the managers who are accountable for them and the concept of the *controllable or managed cost* is an important one. This is 'a cost, chargeable to a budget or cost centre, which can be influenced by the actions of the person in whom control of the centre is vested. It is not always possible to pre-determine responsibility, because the reason for deviation from expected performance may only become evident later. For example, sales promotional budgets and actual performance may be at variance because of a high level of redemptions of coupons or similar devices.

4.15 In contrast, a non-controllable cost is a cost over which the manager of a cost or budget centre has no control. It would be incorrect to attempt to hold the manager responsible for any variance occurring on such a cost.

5.   CASH BUDGETS

5.1   When a budgeted profit and loss account has been prepared, a cash budget can be drawn up. The cash budget shows the expected receipts of cash and payments of cash during the forthcoming budget period.

5.2   Receipts of cash may be from cash sales, payments by debtors, the sale of fixed assets, the issue of new shares or loan stock, the receipt of interest and dividend from investments outside the business and so on.

Not all of these are profit and loss account items. For example the issue of new shares or loan stock does not appear in the profit and loss account. The new shares or loan stock will appear as additions to the balance sheet.

5.3   Payments of cash may be for the purchase of stocks, payment of wages or other expenses, the purchase of capital items, the payment of interest, dividends or taxation.

5.4   It is important for you to remember that profit and cash flow during a period need not be the same amount and indeed will not usually be the same. The reasons for the difference between profit and cash flow might be familiar to you already. They are as follows.

(a)   There are some items in the profit and loss account which are not cash flow items. For example depreciation is a charge against profit but is not a cash flow.

(b)   There are some sources of cash income which are not fully reported, or not reported at all, in the P & L account. These include the cash earned from the sale of fixed assets.

(c)   There are some payments which are not reported fully, or at all, in the P & L account, such as the payment for new capital equipment (fixed assets) the payment of dividend and taxation, and the repayment of loans.

(d)   Increases in the volume of working capital tie up funds and reduce the cash inflow. For example an increase in debtors represents sales on credit (and so profit) without cash income yet having been received. This is normally an important element in any sales campaign which is often overlooked by marketing managers but can have a higher adverse impact on profitability since borrowing funds costs money (interest).

5.5   The purpose of the cash budget is to forewarn managers as to what the cash position of the business will be; for example whether it will run up an overdraft and if so, how large the overdraft will be. Managers will also wish to be forewarned of a cash surplus so that they can make plans to take full advantage of the excess cash resources.

5: BUDGETING

Example: receipts from sales

5.6   CB Ltd has the following sales budget for the forthcoming year.

Sales

	£
1st quarter	120,000
2nd quarter	150,000
3rd quarter	210,000
4th quarter	240,000
	720,000

Assume even quantities of sales per month during each quarter. 10% of sales are for cash. 30% of customers pay after one month. 60% of customers pay after two months.

There are no opening debtors at the start of the year.

Required

Calculate the expected cash receipts from sales during each quarter, and for the year as a whole.

Solution

5.7   The cash received from debtors in any quarter will be equal to the sales for the quarter plus the opening debtors brought forward from the previous quarter, less the closing debtors carried forward to the next quarter.

Closing debtors at the end of one quarter are the opening debtors at the beginning of the next quarter.

The first step is to calculate the closing debtors at the end of each quarter. Check the following workings carefully.

	1st quarter £	2nd quarter £	3rd quarter £	4th quarter £
Sales per month	40,000	50,000	70,000	80,000
Closing debtors				
From sales in month 1	0	0	0	0
From sales in month 2 (60%)	24,000	30,000	42,000	48,000
From sales in month 3 (90%)	36,000	45,000	63,000	72,000
Closing debtors	60,000	75,000	105,000	120,000

	1st quarter £	2nd quarter £	3rd quarter £	4th quarter £	Total £
Opening debtors	0	60,000	75,000	105,000	0
Sales	120,000	150,000	210,000	240,000	720,000
	120,000	210,000	285,000	345,000	720,000
Closing debtors	60,000	75,000	105,000	120,000	120,000
Cash received	60,000	135,000	180,000	225,000	600,000

Total cash received is £600,000, and closing debtors are £120,000. The cash received plus the increase in debtors in the year (£120,000) add up to the total sales figure of £720,000.

Cash payments for materials

5.8　Having calculated the materials purchased during each period, the cash paid for the materials will depend on how much credit is taken from suppliers.

　　　The cash paid to suppliers will be equal to the purchases for the period plus the opening creditors brought forward from the previous period, less the closing creditors carried forward to the next period.

Example: payments for purchases

5.9　CP Ltd expects to purchase the following quantities of materials from suppliers.

	£
1st quarter	90,000
2nd quarter	120,000
3rd quarter	60,000
4th quarter	150,000
	420,000

Credit is taken from suppliers, and 40% of purchases are paid for after one month and 60% are paid for after two months. There were no creditors at the start of the year.

Required

Calculate the cash payments in each quarter and for the year as a whole.

Solution

5.10　The calculations are similar to those for calculating receipts from customers.

	1st quarter £	2nd quarter £	3rd quarter £	4th quarter £	
Monthly purchases	30,000	40,000	20,000	50,000	
Amount owing					
From purchases month 1 (0%)	0	0	0	0	
From purchases month 2 (60%)	18,000	24,000	12,000	30,000	
From purchases month 3 (100%)	30,000	40,000	20,000	50,000	
Closing creditors	48,000	64,000	32,000	80,000	
	£	£	£	£	£
Opening creditors	0	48,000	64,000	32,000	0
Purchases	90,000	120,000	60,000	150,000	420,000
	90,000	168,000	124,000	182,000	420,000
Closing creditors	48,000	64,000	32,000	80,000	80,000
Cash paid to suppliers	42,000	104,000	92,000	102,000	340,000

Here it is evident that some of our customers do not pay immediately (buying on credit). But then we do not pay our suppliers immediately and so we can fund our cash requirements by a similar delay in our payments.

Cash payments for other items

5.11 To budget the cash payments for other items, you need to follow just a few simple rules.

 (a) When cost items are spread across each month or quarter of the year in the profit and loss account, make sure that the cash budget records the amount of cash *actually paid* during each month or quarter.

 (b) Notional costs, which are non-cash items, should not appear in a cash budget. Depreciation is one example of an item that must not appear in a cash budget because they are not cash flows.

 (c) Capital expenditures on fixed assets should be included in full, if they are paid for during the period.

 (d) Include any other cash flows, such as capital raised from loans or government grants.

Operating cash flow and total cash flow

5.12 Cash flow refers to the flow of money into and out of a business. It might help to distinguish between operating cash flow and total cash flow.

5.13 Operating cash flow is the cash flowing into and out of the business as a consequence of the operations of the business. It includes cash received from sales and cash paid for materials, labour and other expenses to pay for the day-to-day running of the business.

5.14 Operating cash flows exclude financing cash flows which are items of cash receipts or cash payments which are not directly connected to business operations. They include the following.

 (a) Cash raised from owners putting capital into the business.

 (b) Cash raised from new loans.

 (c) Cash paid as dividends.

 (d) Cash paid for the purchase of new fixed assets. The fixed assets will be used for operational work, but the full cost of fixed assets is not attributable to a single budget period.

 (e) Interest charges on a loan or overdraft.

5.15 The reason for sometimes distinguishing between operating cash flows and total cash flows is that a business might be paying out more in cash than it is receiving, because of its non-operational cash flows (repayments of loan capital, fixed asset purchases and so on). However, the business may be earning a net cash surplus from operations which is masked by the total cash outflow. Managers may wish to see the positive cash flow from operations highlighted because a business that is earning a net cash surplus from operations *should be* financially sound, in the longer term at least. A business that is failing to earn a net cash surplus from its operations, on the other hand, could be in serious trouble!

6. BEHAVIOURAL ASPECTS OF BUDGETING

6.1 An important feature of control in business is that control is exercised by managers, ie by people. Their attitude towards control information will colour their views on what they should do with it. Some 'behavioural' problems that can arise are as follows.

(a) The managers who set the budget or standards are often not the managers who are then made responsible for achieving budget targets.

(b) The goals of the organisation as a whole, as expressed in a budget, may not coincide with the personal aspirations of individual managers.

(c) Control is applied at different stages by different people. A supervisor might get weekly control reports, and act on them; his superior might get monthly control reports, and decide to take different control action, which may or may not coincide with the efforts of his subordinate. Different managers can get in each others' way, and resent the interference from others.

6.2 As a result it is important that managers 'own' their budget and are sufficiently motivated to ensure that actions are followed up and problems highlighted.

6.3 A poor attitude to budgeting is not uncommon. It is often seen as additional work, outside the scope of managerial responsibility; or it is seen as too time consuming or too restricting or it is too difficult to predict the future. It may be seen as a device to threaten the underperformers within an organisational structure. It is often seen as a power base, with the result that slackness is built into the budgets resulting in further underperformance since the corporate objectives get lost in the political manoeuvrings. These behavioural attitudes can largely be overcome by use of communication. The executive of the company must ensure that the management team are aware of the company goals and are motivated to achieve them. This is then backed up by the regular communication of progress against those budgets and further down the management structure into the areas of responsibility where different objectives have been agreed.

Motivation

6.4 If management decisions are to be taken in the organisation's best interests, it is necessary not only to provide good information for decision making, but also to ensure that management and employees are motivated to work towards the goals of the organisation.

6.5 Motivation is what makes people behave in the way that they do.

(a) It comes from individual attitudes, or group attitudes. Individuals will be motivated by personal desires and interests. These may be in line with the objectives of the organisation, and some people 'live for their jobs'. Other individuals see their job as a chore, and their motivations will be unrelated to the objectives of the organisation they work for.

(b) Motivation can be 'positive', individuals might be trying to act in ways which help to achieve the objectives of the organisation; it can be 'negative', hostile to the objectives of the organisation; and it can be 'indifferent'.

(c) Motivating influences can be weak or strong. Strong influences are more likely to prod people into action than weaker influences.

6.6 Charles T Horngren defined motivation as 'the need to achieve some selected goal and the resulting drive that influences action toward that goal', and he suggested that motivation has two aspects.

(a) Direction, or *goal congruence*. Goal congruence exists when managers working in their own best interests also act in harmony with the goals of top management (the organisation as a whole). 'Obtaining goal congruence is essentially a behavioural problem', nevertheless a system can be designed so as to evoke the required behaviour.

'Should standards and budgets be relatively tight or loose? Should performance be judged on the basis of sales, gross profit, contribution, . . . return on investment, or on some other basis? Should central corporate costs be fully allocated to divisions and departments? There are no clear-cut answers to these questions. A method that works well in one organisation may flop in the next. Nevertheless, the answers must be framed in terms of the predicted motivational impact of the various alternatives'.

(b) Strength of purpose, or *incentive*. 'Incentive is concerned with getting subordinates to run rather than walk toward the desired goals'. Systems which evaluate the performance of managers (of parts of the organisation under their control) are considered to be means of providing incentive, just as wage bonus systems are sometimes considered to provide an incentive to employees to be more productive.

6.7 Several writers have suggested that a behavioural approach, which links motivation to productivity, should be taken when setting a standard level of efficiency.

(a) There is likely to be a de-motivating effect where an ideal standard of performance is set, because adverse efficiency variances will always be reported.

(b) A low standard of efficiency is also de-motivating, because there is no sense of achievement in attaining the required standards.

(c) It ought to be possible to set standards which motivate employees to achieve a certain level of productivity above current standards of performance.

6.8 Individuals will not be motivated to achieve their targets for performance if they are kept in ignorance of how well or badly they are performing. There should be regular and timely feedback of information of actual results, and a comparison of actual results with targets.

Ideally, the information that is fed back (for example variance reports) should draw managers' attention to those results where some control action might be necessary.

6.9 Many researchers agree that pay can be an important motivator when there is a formal link between higher pay (or other rewards, such as promotion) and achieving budget targets. Individuals are likely to work harder to achieve budget if they know that they will be rewarded for their successful efforts.

6.10 There are problems with using pay as an incentive, however. Briefly, these are as follows.

(a) Higher pay or bonuses will be tied to the achievement of short term budget targets. There is a danger that the long term interests of the organisation will be subordinated to short term interests.

(b) The budget targets must be challenging, but fair, otherwise individuals will become dissatisfied. Pay can be a de-motivator as well as a motivator!

6.11 There is some evidence that rewards based on a formal performance evaluation system do give individuals an incentive to achieve a good performance level. On the other hand, there are circumstances in which individual incentive schemes do not work.

(a) When an individual's work performance is dependent on work done by other people (and much work involves co-operation and interdependence with others), an individual bonus scheme is not always effective, since individual performance can be impaired by what other people have done.

(b) Incentive schemes are most effective when there is a short time-scale between effort and reward. Incentive schemes are less effective for long-term achievements, since effort and reward are too distant in time from each other.

(c) There is evidence that the effectiveness of incentive schemes wears off over time, as acceptable 'norms' of working are re-established.

6.12 A serious problem that can arise is that formal reward and performance evaluation systems can encourage dysfunctional behaviour. 'Many investigations have noted the tendency of managers to pad their budgets either in anticipation of cuts by superiors or to make the subsequent variances more favourable. Perhaps of even more concern are the numerous examples of managers making decisions in response to performance indices, even though the decisions are contrary to the wider purposes of the organisation.' An example of this behaviour is the reluctance of investment centre managers to replace old equipment, because this might reduce the ROCE of their investment centre. (Investment centres are discussed in a later chapter.)

Behavioural problems with budgeting

6.13 Budgeting is a multi-purpose activity. In technical terms, it is a plan based on a prediction of future events, and it is used to plan the acquisition of supplies, funds and facilities. In addition, budgeting is used for the following purposes.

(a) As a framework for the delegation of authority within the organisation, by setting targets for managers to achieve.

(b) As a means of co-ordinating inter-related activities.

(c) For top managers to exercise personal power, for example by criticising or vetoing budgets of their subordinates.

(d) To motivate individual managers and employees, by giving them a sense of purpose.

6.14 A poor attitude or hostile behaviour towards the budgetary control cycle can begin at the planning stage. If managers are involved in preparing a budget the following may happen.

(a) Managers may complain that they are too busy to spend much time on budgeting.

(b) They may build in 'slack' to their expenditure estimates and lobby for a high budget expenditure allowance.

(c) They may argue that formalising a budget plan on paper is too restricting and that managers should be allowed flexibility and room for manoeuvre in the operational decisions they take.

(d) They may set budgets for their budget centre without trying to co-ordinate their own plans with those of other budget centres.

(e) They may base future plans on past results, instead of using the opportunity for formalised planning to look at alternative options and new ideas.

6.15 A further problem is that managers may *not* be involved in the budgeting process. Instead, they might have their budget decided for them by senior management or administrative decision. It is hard for people to be motivated to achieve targets set by someone else.

6.16 Poor attitudes also arise when a budget is *implemented*.

(a) Managers might put in only just enough effort to achieve budget targets, without trying to beat targets.

(b) A formal budget might encourage rigidity and discourage flexibility in operational decision-making.

(c) Short-term planning in a budget can draw attention away from the longer term consequences of decisions.

(d) Managers might tolerate slapdash and inaccurate methods of recording (classifying and codifying) actual costs, resulting in costs being allocated to the wrong cost centre or area of responsibility.

(e) Co-operation and communication between managers might be minimal.

(f) Managers will often try to make sure that they spend up to their full budget allowance, and do not overspend, so that they will not be accused of having asked for too much spending allowance in the first place.

Motivation and the use of control information

6.17 The attitude of managers towards the accounting control information they receive might reduce the information's effectiveness. The sorts of attitude that might be found are as follows.

(a) Management accounting control reports could well be seen as having a relatively low priority in the list of management tasks to be seen to. Managers might take the view that they have more pressing jobs on hand than looking at routine control reports.

(b)   Managers might resent control information coming from the accountant, which they see as part of a system of trying to find fault with their work. This resentment is likely to be particularly strong when budgets or standards are imposed on managers without allowing them to participate in the budget-setting process. When managers resent control reports, they are likely to adopt a hostile and defensive attitude.

(c)   If budgets are seen as pressure devices to push managers into doing better, control reports will be resented.

(d)   Managers may not understand the information in the control reports, because they are unfamiliar with accounting terminology or principles.

(e)   Managers might have a false sense of what their objectives should be. A production manager, for example, might consider it more important to maintain quality standards regardless of cost, and a service department manager might similarly think that his department must maintain a certain level of service, regardless of expense. They would then dismiss adverse expenditure variances as inevitable and unavoidable.

(f)   If there are flaws in the system of recording actual costs, managers will dismiss control information as unreliable.

(g)   Control information might be received weeks after the end of the period to which it relates, in which case managers might regard it as out-of-date and no longer useful.

6.18 Two management theorists, Argyris and Hopwood, have analysed in detail the human problem of budgeting. In summary they identified the following.

(a)   Budgets are viewed as pressure devices to force the lazy employees to work harder. The reaction to attempts to improve efficiency is to infuse resistance in the workforce and hence widen any gulf between the management and its employees.

(b)   The controllers of budgets are seen to be the accountants. The sceptical view is that the accountant is only looking for the negative or adverse variance which identifies lack or performance. This leads to lack of interest on the part of the business sector who should own their budget and hence can lead to underperformance.

(c)   Over stringent use of budgets as the sole measure of performance will result in arguments in attributing blame and interdepartmental disputes can arise. Management time is then wasted in settling such disputes.

(d)   Budgets are used to express the style of the manager. Employees who dislike their supervisors style will blame the budget as a surrogate.

(e)   Budgets are manipulated by cunning and political managers to their own ends.

(f)   Budgets often fail to reflect corporate objectives clearly.

(g)   Budgets fail to recognise the different groups which will be measured in this way. The target for managers may conflict with the employee's aspiration for performance levels.

6.19 Although budgeting might seem to be a technical process, it depends heavily on the expectations, guesses, opinions and aspirations of managers because the future is always uncertain. The more uncertain the future, the more valuable a budget will be for an organisation, but there will also be more scope for political bargaining over resource allocations. Behind the essential technical facade of the budgetary procedures lies a previous less formal bargaining process in which the managers compete for organisational resources.

6.20 It is a widely-adopted practice for historical cost information to be used to estimate budget requirements. In a crude form, next year's budget is often based on last year's figures; nevertheless, managers use skill and cunning to finalise their estimates. Reasons are found for increasing estimates, and 'padding' is incorporated to allow for anticipated cuts when top management reduces budget expenditure levels by arbitrarily cutting x per cent from every manager's claim.

6.21 The political aspects of budgets are perhaps inevitable and unavoidable, but they reduce the value of the budget and the control systems that go with it.

6.22 A budget should be formulated so as to achieve the overall objectives of the organisation, at least within the short term. However, organisational objectives are very rarely clearly defined (and one organisation is likely to have a number of different objectives anyway). Different managers will perceive their objectives differently, and so the budget demands of managers will frequently be incompatible. The conflicting demands of different departments are accentuated by the following.

(a) The lack of social interaction between people in different departments. Arguments with acquaintances and colleagues will usually be less fierce and uncompromising than those with strangers.

(b) The different and often conflicting sources of information for each department.

(c) Different, or even competing, reward structures.

6.23 Although the budgeting process remains as the primary means of setting short term goals within any organisation, its usefulness is limited because it emphasises profits without any other goals being identified. And yet the revenues and costs which go to making this profit are subject to a great deal of manipulation by budget centre managers.

Budgets for planning and separate budgets for control?

6.24 Once decided, however, budgets become targets. As targets, they can motivate managers to achieve a high level of performance. But how difficult should targets be? And how might people react to targets of differing degrees of difficulty in achievement? Hopwood cited research by Atkinson, who made a distinction between the following.

(a) A manager's tendency to achieve success, and the factors contributing towards this tendency.

(b) A manager's tendency to avoid failure, and the factors contributing towards this.

6.25 Atkinson found the following.

(a) If a manager's tendency to achieve success is stronger than the tendency to avoid failure, budgets with targets of intermediate levels of difficulty were the most motivating, and stimulated a manager to better performance levels. Budgets which were either too easy to achieve or too difficult were de-motivating, and managers given such targets achieved relatively low levels of performance.

(b) A manager's tendency to avoid failure might be stronger than the tendency to achieve success. (This is likely in an organisation in which the budget is used as a pressure device on subordinates by senior managers, as researched by Argyris). In such a situation, Atkinson found that managers were discouraged from trying to achieve budgets of intermediate difficulty and tended to avoid taking on such tasks, with the consequence that their level of performance was poor, worse than if budget targets were either easy or very difficult to achieve.

6.26 As a result of the above, two rather distinct budgetary needs are established; the need for planning and decision making based on reasonable expectations and the need for motivationally based budgets where the targets may need to be more difficult. This approach is often informally adopted by managers. For example, sales managers will agree formally to a budget level of sales or finance but will task individuals within the sales team with targets which cumulatively exceed the formally agreed budget.

Participation in the budgeting process

6.27 Another view is that participation in the budgeting process will improve motivation and so will improve the quality of budget decisions and the efforts of individuals to achieve their budget targets.

6.28 Participation in the budgetary process is a topic which readily elicits a stock opinion from students that participating in decision making improves standards of performance. Hopwood draws attention to the widely varying degrees of participation: 'In ranging from an open process of group decision-making to a process of consultation under the strict supervision of the more powerful, from a radical plan of action, through the soft and sentimental to a scheming manipulative intent, it appears that participation can mean almost anything to anyone.'

6.29 Conventional 'wisdom' about participation and the implementation of decisions is that when individuals participate in decision making, they will be more satisfied with their job and colleagues and they will be more productive: there will be fewer communications problems, and when circumstances change, the individuals can adapt more quickly and readily to adjust their plans accordingly.

6.30 Hopwood questioned the wisdom of generalising research findings. The degree of participation required to achieve a better implementation of decisions will depend on circumstances. Participation certainly appears to raise morale, but it is by no means clear that it also improves productivity and performance.

6.31 Hopwood argued that the *acceptance* of decisions can be improved with participation, but what about the *quality* of decisions? Does group decision-making (participation) improve the quality of decisions? Some research has found that, perhaps contrary to expectations, groups tend to opt for decisions with higher payoffs but greater risks than individual decision-takers. However, greater risk-taking does not necessarily mean better decisions.

6.32 His conclusions about the quality of decisions were as follows.

(a) The degree of participation which is most likely to produce the best quality of decisions will vary according to circumstances, depending, for example, on what the decisions are about and who would be affected by them, the functional department in which the decisions are taken (for example personnel decisions lend themselves more readily to participation than finance or production decisions), the number of subordinates involved and their capabilities, and the experience of the senior manager. Participation is unlikely to be beneficial where the decision involves matters adversely affecting the subordinates (for example a shutdown of a factory or department).

(b) 'It is simply naive to think that participative approaches are always more effective than more authoritarian styles of management or vice versa. The critics as well as the advocates of participative management would therefore be wise to direct their energies towards identifying the situations in which a variety of decision making styles are effective, rather than towards universalistic claims for the applicability or otherwise of any single approach.'

7. CONCLUSION

7.1 (a) A budget is a quantified plan of action for a forthcoming period.

(b) The principal budget factor should be identified at the beginning of the budgetary process, and the budget for this is prepared before all the others.

(c) Cash budgets are important in the planning process because they give advanced warning of any cash surpluses or deficits.

(d) Budgets are important to the achievement of the overall corporate objective. However, unless these goals are properly communicated into relevant divisions of the business in specific terms which are controllable by that division, the process will not achieve its own objectives.

(e) Managers and staff have motivations which may be outside the corporate flow and which need to be recognised and harnessed.

TEST YOUR KNOWLEDGE

The numbers in brackets refer to paragraphs of this chapter

1 What is a budget and what is its purpose? (1.1, 1.3)

2 Define fixed costs and variable costs and give an example of each. (2.3)

3 Define direct and indirect costs and give an example of each. (2.5)

4 Why is it important for budgets to be accurate? (3.1)

5 What are the contents of a master budget? (3.7)

6 What is the correct approach to budgetary control? (4.7)

7 Which items will be included in receipts and payments on a cash budget? (5.2-5.3)

8 When might it be important to distinguish between operating cash flow and total cash flow? (5.12 - 5.13)

9 Why do managers often have a poor attitude to budgeting? (6.2)

10 Why is motivation important to the control process? (6.7)

11 How does employee participation in budgeting help the company achieve its goals? (6.27-6.32)

Now try question 5 at the end of the text

Chapter 6

COSTS FOR DECISION MAKING

This chapter covers the following topics.

1. Types of decision
2. Relevant costs and non-relevant costs
3. Fixed costs and variable costs: attributable costs
4. Other rules for relevant cost identification
5. Limiting factor analysis
6. Make or buy problems
7. Accepting or rejecting orders
8. Shutdown problems
9. Assumptions and qualitative factors

---

1. TYPES OF DECISION

1.1 Managers must make decisions about what should be done. Decisions arise from the existence of a choice about what to do and a decision is the selection of the choice that seems best from those available. It helps to be able to identify what the various types of decision are.

There are different ways of categorising decisions. One useful analysis of decisions is into five categories.

(a) *Routine planning decisions:* typically, budgeting. Budgeting decisions commonly analyse fixed and variable costs, together with revenues, over a one year period. They are also often concerned with how to make the best use of scarce resources.

(b) *Short-run problem decisions:* typically, unforeseen 'one-off' special decisions of a non-recurring nature, where the costs and benefits are all obtained within a relatively short period. For example, should a contract be accepted or rejected? What price should be quoted in the tender for a contract?

(c) *Investment or disinvestment decisions:* for example, should an item of equipment be purchased? Should a department be shut down? Decisions of this nature often have long-term consequences, so that the 'time value of money' must be allowed for, and discounted cash flow techniques applied. DCF decisions are dealt with separately in another chapter.

(d) *Longer-range decisions:* decisions made once and reviewed infrequently, but which are intended to provide a continuing solution to a continuing or recurring problem. Shillinglaw (1963) called these 'quantitative policy decisions', and they include decisions about selling and distribution policies (for example should goods be sold through middlemen or direct to customers? What type of customer should the sales force attempt to attract? What should the company's discount policies be? Should a new product or service be launched?)

(e) *Control decisions:* should disappointing performance be investigated, given that the benefits expected must exceed the costs from investigation and control?

1.2 *Pricing decisions* are sometimes put into a category of their own, but pricing decisions span most of the range of decision categories above: routine pricing decisions are made at periodic price reviews. 'One-off' short run pricing decisions might be made for specific jobs or contracts or to dispose of surplus stocks; long range decisions about price must be made for services, products or product ranges and some control decisions might have to be made about prices. For example, are excessive discounts being allowed?

1.3 The reason it is helpful to identify different categories of decision is that the nature of the costs and benefits that are relevant to the decision are likely to differ in some respects between each type of decision.

(a) Routine planning decisions are often based on estimates of fixed and variable costs, and the application of cost-volume-profit analysis, ie marginal costing techniques.

(b) Short run 'one-off' decisions call for the identification of incremental or differential costs, and the distinction between sunk costs and opportunity costs. Opportunity costs are relevant to ranking decisions.

(c) Investment decisions are of a longer-term nature, and so *the time value of money* becomes an additional element in the decision.

(d) For long range decisions, it has to be recognised that in the long run all costs are variable, and so costs that are fixed in the short run can be made to change over time. Similarly, surplus operating capacity can be eliminated over time, just as a restricted supply of scarce resources or a limited operating capacity might be overcome in the longer term.

(e) Control decisions tend to make more use of restrospective information, such as the comparison of actual costs or profits against budget. Variance analysis might then indicate what control decisions, if any, should be taken.

Contribution

1.4 Before we go any further we must define a term which will be used frequently from now on.

Contribution is defined as the excess of sales value over variable cost *or* the contribution made towards covering fixed costs and making a profit.

Contribution is important because it is a measurement which ignores fixed costs. In decision-making, the fixed costs should be ignored. Contribution is therefore a better measure than profit. It can be given in terms of total production or contribution per unit.

2. RELEVANT COSTS AND NON-RELEVANT COSTS

2.1 The costs which should be used for decision making are often referred to as *relevant costs*. We can define relevant costs as those costs appropriate to aiding the making of specific management decisions.

2.2 A relevant cost is a future cash flow arising as a direct consequence of the decision under review. Only relevant costs should be considered in decision making, because it is assumed that in the long run future profits will be maximised if the 'cash profits' of the company, ie the cash earned from sales minus the cash expenditures on making and selling the goods, are also maximised.

Costs which are *not* relevant include the following:

(a) past costs, or money already spent, such as R & D work already done;

(b) future spending already committed by separate previous decisions (we will spend the cash in any event);

(c) costs which are not of a cash nature, for example depreciation, notional rent and notional interest;

(d) absorbed overheads. Only cash overheads incurred are relevant to a decision.

The relevant cost of a unit of production is usually the variable cost of that unit plus (or minus) any change in the total expenditure on fixed costs.

2.3 The assumption used is that in the end profits earn cash. Reported profits and cash flow are not the same in any period for various reasons, such as the timing differences caused by giving credit and the accounting treatment of depreciation. In the long run, however, a profit that is earned will eventually produce a net inflow of an equal amount of cash. Hence accounting for decision making looks at cash flow as a means of measuring profits. As we have seen before, the assumption in many cases is that profit before depreciation is equated to cash unless in our studies we are specifically told otherwise.

Differential costs, incremental costs, avoidable costs

2.4 Differential costs are the differences in relevant costs between two alternative courses of action. If option A will cost an extra £300 and option B will cost an extra £360, the differential cost is £60, with option B being more expensive.

2.5 Similarly, *differential costing* is a technique used to prepare *ad hoc* information for decision making, in which only the differences in costs and income between the alternative courses of action are stated. Hence we simply look at one option and ask what costs and benefits we incur or receive by doing this rather than choosing the alternative.

2.6 Suppose that there is a choice between two methods of repairing a small machine, and the *relevant* costs of each option are as follows.

		£
(a)	*Option A: repair on site*	
	Spare parts cost	300
	Labour cost	80
	Loss of output resulting in lost contribution of	250
(b)	*Option B: repair in workshop*	
	Spare parts cost	300
	Labour cost	50
	Loss of output, resulting in lost contribution of	320

2.7 A differential cost statement would look like this.

	£
Extra cost of repairs on site (spare parts and labour)	(30)
Smaller loss of contribution from repairs on site	70
Differential benefits of option A	40

2.8 *Incremental costs* are relevant costs which are simply the additional costs incurred as a consequence of a decision. Whereas differential costs compare the differences in cost between two alternative courses of action, incremental costs are a way of stating the relevant costs when three or more options are compared.

2.9 The incremental costs of each option can then be listed side by side and compared. Incremental costing can be defined as a technique used in the preparation of *ad hoc* information where consideration is given to a range of graduated or stepped changes in the level or nature of activity and the additional costs and revenues likely to result from each degree of change are presented.

2.10 *Avoidable costs* is a term usually associated with shutdown or disinvestment decisions, but it can be applied to control decisions too. They are defined as: 'those costs which can be identified with an activity or sector of a business and which would be avoided if that activity or sector did not exist'.

Opportunity costs

2.11 Relevant costs may also be expressed as opportunity costs.

An *opportunity cost* is the benefit forgone by choosing one opportunity instead of the next best alternative.

Sunk costs, committed costs and notional costs (or imputed costs): irrelevant costs

2.12 A number of terms are used to describe costs that are *irrelevant* for decision making because they are either not future cash flows or they are costs which will be incurred anyway, regardless of the decision that is taken.

2.13 The principle underlying decision accounting is that 'bygones are bygones'. What has happened in the past is done, and cannot be undone. Management decisions can only affect the future. In decision making, managers therefore require information about future costs and revenues which would be affected by the decision under review, and they must not be misled by events, costs and revenues in the past, about which they can do nothing. Past expenditures, in decision making terms, are *sunk costs* which may be one of two types.

(a) They may have already happened and been accounted for.

(b) Alternatively they will be accounted for in a future period, although the expenditure has already been incurred (or the expenditure decision irrevocably taken). An example of this type of cost is depreciation. If the fixed asset has been purchased, depreciation may be charged for several years but the cost is a sunk cost, about which nothing can now be done.

2.14 Examples of sunk costs include the following.

(a) *Development costs already incurred.* Suppose that a company has spent £250,000 in developing a new service for customers, but the marketing department's most recent findings are that the service might not gain customer acceptance and could be a commercial failure. The decision whether or not to abandon the development of the new service would have to be taken, but the £250,000 spent so far should be ignored by the decision makers because it is a sunk cost. (Yet in spite of this, it might be tempting for managers to talk about 'throwing money down the drain' or 'putting to waste all the efforts so far'.)

(b) *Dedicated fixed assets.* Suppose a company purchased an item of computer equipment two years ago for £20,000. It has been depreciated to a net book value of £7,000 already, but in fact it already has no resale value because of developments in computer technology. The equipment can be used for its existing purpose for at least another year, but the company is considering whether or not to purchase more modern equipment with additional facilities and so scrap the existing equipment now.

In terms of decision making and relevant costs, the existing equipment, which initially cost £20,000 but now has a net book value of £7,000, is a sunk cost. The money has been spent and the asset has no alternative use. 'Writing off' the asset and incurring a 'paper' loss on disposal of £7,000 would be irrelevant to the decision under consideration.

2.15 A *committed cost* is a future cash outflow that will be incurred anyway, whatever decision is taken now about alternative opportunities. Committed costs may exist because of contracts already entered into by the organisation, which it cannot get out of. Property developers will often be faced with this type of cost because expenditure will be committed for some years ahead. However, there are often windows in any development contract to allow a delay in the contract and this process may allow a decision to be made based on uncommitted costs alone.

3. FIXED COSTS AND VARIABLE COSTS: ATTRIBUTABLE COSTS

3.1 As a general rule we can usually assume that variable costs will be relevant costs but fixed costs will be irrelevant to a decision. This is not always the case and you should therefore always question in your own mind how fixed costs will change as a direct result of the decision you are faced with.

3.2 There might be occasions when a fixed cost is a relevant cost, and you must be aware of the distinction between 'specific' or 'directly attributable' fixed costs, and general fixed overheads.

(a) Directly attributable fixed costs are those costs which, although fixed within a relevant range of activity levels, or regarded as fixed because management has set a budgeted expenditure level (for example advertising costs are often treated as fixed) would in fact either:

(i) increase if certain extra activities were undertaken; or

(ii) decrease/be eliminated entirely if a decision were taken to reduce the scale of operations or shut down entirely.

(b) General fixed overheads are those fixed overheads which will be unaffected by decisions to increase or decrease the scale of operations, perhaps because they are an apportioned share of the fixed costs of items which would be completely unaffected by the decisions. An apportioned share of head office charges is an example of general fixed overheads for a local office or department.

3.3 You should appreciate that whereas directly attributable fixed costs will be relevant to a decision, general fixed overheads will not be.

4. OTHER RULES FOR RELEVANT COST IDENTIFICATION

4.1 What materials are to be used up in the production of a product and they would not be replaced when we can identify a relevant cost. In theory, the costs which would be present would be the greater of:

(a) their existing resale value;
(b) their value if they were put an alternative use.

4.2 In practice you are likely to be given the cost of the materials and you should take this as the relevant cost. All you then need to decide is whether the cost is relevant to the decision making process. The following diagram may help your thought process.

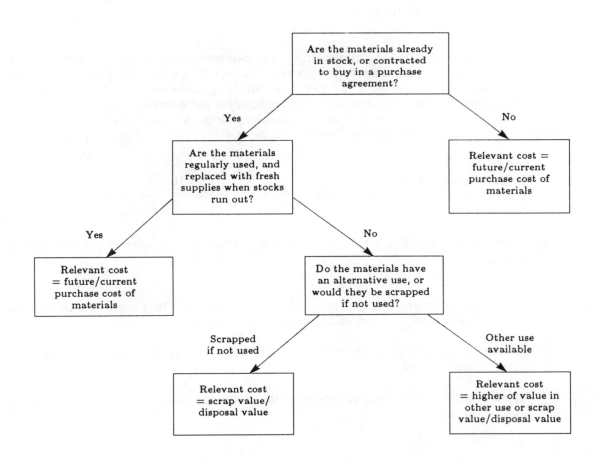

4.3 Another area where there may be difficulty in assessing the relevant cost is where machinery is used. We have already identified that depreciation is not relevant since it refers to the purchase of an asset some time back and therefore is in effect a sunk cost. However, using machinery will involve some additional costs, known as *user costs*. They may include hire charges and any fall in the resale value of the asset result directly from its use in the decision facing the manager.

Scarce resources and opportunity costs

4.4 A scarce resource is defined here as a resource (materials, labour, machine time, cash and so on) which is in short supply, so that the total opportunities that exist for making profitable use of the resource exceed the amount of the resource available.

4.5 When a decision maker is faced with an opportunity which would call for the use of a scarce resource, the total incremental cost of using the resource will be higher than the direct cash cost of purchasing it. This is because the resource could be used for other purposes, and so by using it in one way, the benefits obtainable from using it another way must be forgone.

4.6 If this seems a confusing explanation, a numerical example may help to clarify it. Suppose that a customer has asked whether your company would be willing to undertake a contract for him. The work would involve the use of certain equipment for five hours and its running costs would be £2 per hour. However, your company faces heavy demand for usage of the equipment which earns a contribution of £7 per hour from this other work. If the contract is undertaken, some of this work would have to be forgone.

4.7 The contribution obtainable from putting the scarce resource to its alternative use is its opportunity cost (sometimes referred to as its 'internal' opportunity cost). Quite simply, since the equipment can earn £7 per hour in an alternative use, the contract under consideration should also be expected to earn at least the same amount. This can be accounted for by charging the £7 per hour as an opportunity cost to the contract and the total relevant cost of five hours of equipment time would be as follows.

	£
Running costs (5 × £2)	10
Internal opportunity cost (5 × £7)	35
Relevant cost	45

It is important to notice that the variable running costs of the equipment are included in the total relevant cost.

4.8 A rule for identifying the relevant cost of a scarce resource is that the total relevant cost of the resource consists of the *sum* of the following two costs:

(a) the contribution/incremental profit forgone from the next-best opportunities for using the scarce resource; and

(b) the variable cost of the scarce resource (the cash expenditure to purchase the resource).

Exercise

Try to identify the relevant costs of labour and overheads in the following exercise.

Vanderbilt Ltd has been offered £21,000 by a prospective customer to make some purpose-built equipment. The extra costs of the machine would be £3,000 for materials. There would also be a requirement for 2,000 labour hours. Labour wages are £4 per hour, variable overhead is £2 per hour and fixed overhead is absorbed at the rate of £4 per hour.

Labour, however, is in limited supply, and if the job is accepted, workers would have to be diverted from other work which is expected to earn a contribution of £5 per hour towards fixed overheads and profit.

Should the contract be undertaken?

Solution

Fixed costs are ignored because there is no incremental fixed cost expenditure.

	£
Materials	3,000
Labour (2,000 hours × £4)	8,000
Variable overhead (2,000 hours × £2)	4,000
	15,000
Opportunity cost	
Contribution forgone from other work (2,000 hours × £5)	10,000
Total costs	25,000
Revenue	21,000
Net loss on contract	(4,000)

The contract should not be undertaken.

---

5.   LIMITING FACTOR ANALYSIS

5.1   One of the more common decision-making problems is a budgeting decision in a situation where there are not enough resources to meet the potential sales demand, and so a decision has to be made about using what resources there are as effectively as possible. The definition of a limiting factor or key factor is 'a factor which at any time or over a period may limit the activity of an entity, often one where there is shortage or difficulty of supply. The limiting factor may change from time to time for the same entity or product. Thus when raw materials are in short supply, performance or profit may be expressed as per kilo of material, or, in a restricted skilled labour market, as per skilled labour hour. Alternatively, the limiting factor may be one critical process in a chain'.

5.2   There might be just one limiting factor (other than maximum sales demand) but there might also be several scarce resources, with two or more of them putting an effective limit on the level of activity that can be achieved. In this chapter, however, we shall concentrate on single limiting factor problems and a technique for resolving these. Situations in which there are two or more limiting factors (other than sales demand) call for the application of an operational research technique known as linear programming, which is outside the scope of the syllabus.

5.3 The limiting factor is often sales demand itself, in which case the business should produce enough goods or services to meet the demand in full, provided that sales of the goods earn a positive contribution towards fixed costs and profits.

However, when the limiting budget factor is a production resource, the business must decide in its budget which part of sales demand it should meet, and which part must be left unsatisfied. This is a short term problem and assumes no other production capacity is readily available.

5.4 If fixed costs are constant, regardless of the level of output and sales within a relevant range of output, marginal costing principles should lead us to the conclusion that profits will be maximised if total contribution is maximised.

5.5 If there is a shortage of one particular production resource, it is inevitable that all the available supply of that resource will be used up. For example, if a business has a chronic shortage of skilled manpower, it will plan to use all the skilled manpower that it does have available. Total contribution will be maximised if the maximum possible contribution is obtained per unit of that scarce resource. In other words, a business should get the best possible value out of the scarce resources that it uses up.

5.6 In dealing with a limiting factor problem, the steps to be taken are as follows.

(a) Identify the possibility that there may be a limiting budget factor other than sales demand. An examination question would refer to the maximum availability of one (or more) resources, so that sales demand cannot be met. This is done quite simply as follows.

(i) Calculate the volume of resources required to produce enough units to satisfy budgeted sales demand.

(ii) Calculate the volume of resources available.

(iii) Compare the two totals. If (i) exceeds (ii) there is a limiting factor.

(b) If there is only one such limiting factor, the next step is to calculate the contribution earned by each product per unit of the scarce resource. The product(s) with the highest contribution per unit of scarce resource should receive priority in the allocation of the resource in the production budget.

Example: limiting factor problem

5.7 Haydn Gott Nutting Ltd manufactures and sells three products, X, Y and Z.

	X		Y		Z	
Budgeted sales demand	300 units		500 units		200 units	
	£	£	£	£	£	£
Unit sales price		16		18		14
Variable costs: materials	8		6		2	
labour	4		6		9	
		12		12		11
Contribution		4		6		3

112

All three products use the same direct materials and the same type of direct labour. In the next year, the available supply of materials will be restricted to £4,800, and the available supply of labour to £6,600. What would be the profit-maximising budget?

Solution

5.8 The profit-maximising budget is assumed to be contribution-maximising (so fixed costs are unaffected by the decision).

(a) Is there a limiting factor, several limiting factors, or none?

	Units of demand	Required materials cost £	Required labour cost £
X	300	2,400	1,200
Y	500	3,000	3,000
Z	200	400	1,800
Total required		5,800	6,000
Total available		4,800	6,600
(Shortfall)/Surplus		(1,000)	600

Materials are a limiting factor, but labour is not.

(b)

	X £	Y £	Z £
Unit contribution	4	6	3
Cost of materials	8	6	2
Contribution per £1 of materials	£0.50	£1.00	£1.50
Priority for manufacture	3rd	2nd	1st

Z should be manufactured up to the limit of sales demand, then Y second and X third, until the sales demand for each or the amount of materials available has been used up.

		Product	Units	Materials cost £	Unit contribution £	Total contribution £
(i)	1st	Z	200	400	3	600
(ii)	2nd	Y	500	3,000	6	3,000
(iii)	3rd	X	175	1,400 (balance)	4	700
				4,800		4,300

The profit maximising budget would be to make and sell 200 units of Z, 500 units of Y and 175 units of X, to earn a contribution of £4,300.

6. MAKE OR BUY PROBLEMS

6.1 A make or buy problem involves a decision by an organisation about whether it should make a product or carry out an activity with its own internal resources, or whether it should pay another organisation to make the product or carry out the activity, buying from 'outside'.

Examples of make or buy decisions could be as follows.

(a) Whether a company should manufacture its own components, or else buy the components from an outside supplier.

(b) Whether a construction company should do some work with its own employees, or whether it should sub-contract the work to another company.

(c) Whether the design and development of a new computer system should be entrusted to in-house data processing staff or whether an external software house should be hired to do the work.

(d) Whether maintenance and repairs of certain items of equipment should be dealt with by 'in-house' engineers, or whether a maintenance contract should be made with a specialist organisation.

Make or buy decisions: no limiting factors

6.2 If an organisation has the freedom of choice about whether to make internally or buy externally and has no scarce resources that put a restriction on what it can do itself, the relevant costs for the decision will be the differential costs between the two options.

Suppose, for example, that Shellfish Ltd makes four components, W, X, Y and Z, for which costs in the forthcoming year are expected to be as follows.

	W	X	Y	Z
Production (units)	1,000	2,000	4,000	3,000
Unit marginal costs	£	£	£	£
Direct materials	4	5	2	4
Direct labour	8	9	4	6
Variable production overheads	2	3	1	2
	14	17	7	12

Directly attributable fixed costs per annum and committed fixed costs are as follows.

	£
Incurred as a direct consequence of making W	1,000
Incurred as a direct consequence of making X	5,000
Incurred as a direct consequence of making Y	6,000
Incurred as a direct consequence of making Z	8,000
Other fixed costs (committed)	30,000
	50,000

A sub-contractor has offered to supply units of W, X, Y and Z for £12, £21, £10 and £14 respectively.

Should Shellfish Ltd make or buy the components?

Solution

6.3 (a) The relevant costs are the differential costs between making and buying, and they consist of differences in unit variable costs plus differences in directly attributable fixed costs. Sub-contracting will result in some fixed cost savings.

	W £	X £	Y £	Z £
Unit variable cost of making	14	17	7	12
Unit variable cost of buying	12	21	10	14
	(2)	4	3	2
Annual requirements (units)	1,000	2,000	4,000	3,000
	£	£	£	£
Extra variable cost of buying (per annum)	(2,000)	8,000	12,000	6,000
Fixed costs saved by buying	1,000	5,000	6,000	8,000
Extra total cost of buying	(3,000)	3,000	6,000	(2,000)

(b) The company would save £3,000 pa by sub-contracting component W (where the purchase cost would be less than the marginal cost per unit to make internally) and would save £2,000 pa by sub-contracting component Z (because of the saving in fixed costs of £8,000).

(c) In this example, relevant costs are the variable costs of in-house manufacture, the variable costs of sub-contracted units, and the saving in fixed costs.

(d) Important further considerations would be as follows.

(i) If components W and Z are sub-contracted, the company will have spare capacity. How should that spare capacity be profitably used, ie are there hidden benefits to be obtained from sub-contracting? Would the company's workforce resent the loss of work to an outside sub-contractor, and might such a decision cause an industrial dispute?

(ii) Would the sub-contractor be reliable with delivery times, and would he supply components of the same quality as those manufactured internally?

(iii) Does the company wish to be flexible and maintain better control over operations by making everything itself?

Note that we have now introduced other aspects of decision making which cannot be quantified financially but which can be far reaching in their implications. The ability to alienate our workforce because of the subcontracting of some work may take our industrial relations policy 'over the top' and result in future strike action. The opportunity cost here might be enormous so it is essential that all disciplines are consulted when what would appear to be a relatively uncomplicated decision is about to be made. Similarly, because you are currently working in a financial discipline, do not ignore the basics of your marketing background. Under a SWOT analysis we would usually identify the weaknesses and threats of a position or discussion. What about the macro environmental factors which might affect our decision? How will competitors react?

(iv) Are the estimates of fixed cost savings reliable? In the case of Product W, buying is clearly cheaper than making in-house. In the case of product Z, the decision to buy rather than make would only be financially beneficial if the fixed cost savings of £8,000 could really be 'delivered' by management. All too often in practice, promised savings fail to materialise!

(v) The 'make' option should give management more direct control over the work, but the 'buy' option often has the benefit that the external organisation has a specialist skill and expertise in the work.

Make or buy decisions and scarce resources

6.4 One reason for buying products or services from another organisation is that the scarcity of resources prevent everything being done 'in house'. A company might want to do more than it has the resources for, and so it would have to choose between one of the following.

(a) To make the best use of the resources it has got, and ignore the opportunities to buy help from outside.

(b) To combine internal resources with buying externally so as to do more and increase profitability further.

6.5 Buying help from outside is justifiable if it adds to profits. However, a further decision is then how to split the work between internal and external effort, ie what parts of the work should be given to suppliers or sub-contractors so as to maximise profitability?

6.6 In a situation where a company must sub-contract work to make up a shortfall in its own in-house capabilities, its total costs will be minimised where the extra marginal cost of buying out from a sub-contractor is least for each unit of scarce resource 'saved' by buying out.

Example: make or buy decisions

6.7 Ancient Mariner Ltd manufactures three components, the shotter, the alba and the tross using the same machines for each. The budget for the next year calls for the production and assembly of 4,000 of each component. The following information is available.

The variable production cost per unit of the final product, the coal ridge is as follows.

	Machine hours	Variable cost
		£
1 unit of Shotter	3	20
1 unit of Alba	2	36
1 unit of Tross	4	24
Assembly		20
		100

Only 24,000 hours of machine time will be available during the year, and a sub-contractor has quoted the following unit prices for supplying components.

Shotter £29;   Alba £40;   Tross £34.

Required

Advise Ancient Mariner Ltd.

Solution

6.8 (a) The company's budget calls for 36,000 hours of machine time, if all the components are to be produced in-house. Only 24,000 hours are available, and there is a shortfall of 12,000 hours of machine time, which is therefore a limiting factor. The shortage can be overcome by subcontracting the equivalent of 12,000 machine hours' output to the subcontractor.

(b) The assembly costs are not relevant costs because they are unaffected by the make or buy decision. The units sub-contracted should be those which will add least to the costs of Ancient Mariner Limited. Since 12,000 hours must be sub-contracted, the cheapest policy is to sub-contract work which adds the least extra costs per hour of time saved.

(c)

	Shotter	Alba	Tross
	£	£	£
Variable cost of making	20	36	24
Variable cost of buying	29	40	34
Extra variable cost of buying	9	4	10
Machine hours saved by buying	3 hrs	2 hrs	4 hrs
Extra variable cost of buying per hour saved	£3	£2	£2.5

It is cheaper to buy Albas than to buy Tross and it is most expensive to buy Shotters. The priority for making the components in-house will be in the reverse order.

Make: *first*   Shotter
         second   Tross
         third   Alba

There are enough machine hours to make all 4,000 units of Shotter (12,000 hours) and to produce 3,000 units of Tross (another 12,000 hours).

12,000 hours' production of Tross and Alba must be sub-contracted.

(d) The cost-minimising and so profit-maximising make and buy schedule is as follows.

Component	Machine hours	Number of units	Unit variable cost	Total variable cost
Make			£	£
Shotter	12,000	4,000	20	80,000
Tross	12,000	3,000	24	72,000
	24,000			152,000
Buy	*Hours saved*			
Tross	4,000	1,000	34	34,000
Alba	8,000	4,000	40	160,000
	12,000			

Total variable cost of components, excluding assembly costs   346,000

7.   ACCEPTING OR REJECTING ORDERS

7.1   An order will probably be accepted if it increases contribution and profit, and rejected if it reduces profit. Examination questions may set problems relating to the acceptance or rejection of a special order. The understanding of contribution and profitability is fundamental to this process, remembering that in most cases the maximisation of profit is one of the corporate objectives.

Example: accept or reject an order

7.2 Belt and Braces Ltd makes a single product which sells for £20, and for which there is great demand. It has a variable cost of £12, made up as follows.

	£
Direct material	4
Direct labour (two hours)	6
Variable overhead	2
	12

The labour force is currently working at full capacity and no extra time can be made available. A customer has approached the company with a request for the manufacture of a special order, for which he is willing to pay £5,500.

The costs of the order would be £2,000 for direct materials, and 500 labour hours will be required.

Should the order be accepted?

Solution

7.3 (a) Labour is a limiting factor. By accepting the order, work would have to be diverted away from the standard product, and contribution will be lost, so there is an *opportunity cost* of accepting the new order, which is the contribution forgone by being unable to make the standard product. The contribution from the standard product is £4 per labour hour [(£20 – £12) ÷ 2 hrs]

(b) Direct labour pay costs £3 per hour, but it is also usually assumed that variable production overhead varies with hours worked, and must therefore be spent in addition to the wages cost of the 500 hours.

	£	£
(c) Value of order		5,500
Cost of order		
Direct materials	2,000	
Direct labour (500 hours × £3)	1,500	
Variable overhead (500 hours × £1)	500	
Opportunity cost (500 hours × £4 contribution forgone)	2,000	
Relevant cost of the order		6,000
Loss incurred by accepting the order		(500)

(In other words, although accepting the order would earn a contribution of £1,500 (£5,500 – £4,000), the lost production of the standard product would reduce contribution earned elsewhere by £2,000.)

8. SHUTDOWN PROBLEMS

8.1 Shutdown problems involve decisions about the following problems.

(a) Whether or not it is best to close down a factory, department, product line or other activity, either because it is making losses or because it is too expensive to run.

(b) If the decision is to shut down, whether the closure should be permanent or temporary.

8.2 In practice, shutdown decisions will involve longer-term considerations, and capital expenditures and revenues.

    (a) A shutdown should result in savings in annual operating costs for a number of years into the future.

    (b) Closure will probably release unwanted fixed assets for sale. Some assets might have a small scrap value, but other assets, in particular property, might have a substantial sale value.

    (c) Employees affected by the closure must be made redundant or re-located, perhaps after retraining, or else offered early retirement. There will be lump sum payments involved which must be taken into account in the financial arithmetic. For example, suppose that the closure of a regional office would result in annual savings of £100,000, fixed assets could be sold off to earn income of £2 millions, but redundancy payments would be £3 millions. The shutdown decision would involve an assessment of the net capital cost of closure (£1 million) against the annual benefits (£100,000 pa).

8.3 It is possible, however, for shutdown problems to be simplified into short run decisions, by making either of the following assumptions.

    (a) Fixed asset sales and redundancy costs would be negligible.

    (b) Income from fixed asset sales would match redundancy costs and so these capital items would be self-cancelling.

In such circumstances the financial aspect of shutdown decisions would be based on short-run relevant costs.

Example: closure problem

8.4 Abandon Ship Ltd makes four products, A, B, C and D. The budget for the forthcoming year is as follows.

	A £	B £	C £	D £	Total £
Direct materials	5,000	6,000	4,000	8,000	23,000
Direct labour	4,000	8,000	6,000	4,000	22,000
Variable overheads	1,000	2,000	1,500	1,000	5,500
	10,000	16,000	11,500	13,000	50,500
Sales	20,000	15,000	14,000	20,000	69,000
Contribution	10,000	(1,000)	2,500	7,000	18,500
Share of fixed costs	6,000	4,000	4,000	2,000	16,000
Profit/(loss)	4,000	(5,000)	(1,500)	5,000	2,500

8.5 (a) Manufacture of product B should cease, because revenue does not cover variable costs and the contribution is negative.

    (b) Product C makes a positive contribution, but fails to cover its share of fixed costs:

(i) If fixed costs of £2,500 or more (ie equal to or greater than the contribution earned) could be saved by ceasing to make product C, the product should be closed down.

(ii) If the saving in fixed costs from shutdown of product C is less than £2,500 it will remain profitable to continue to make the product until a more profitable alternative use arises for the production resources.

8.6 If we suppose that fixed costs are not stepped costs, and will remain at £16,000 if any products are closed down, then product B only should be abandoned. Profits will then increase by £1,000 as follows.

	A £	C £	D £	Total £
Direct materials	5,000	4,000	8,000	17,000
Direct labour	4,000	6,000	4,000	14,000
Variable overheads	1,000	1,500	1,000	3,500
	10,000	11,500	13,000	34,500
Sales	20,000	14,000	20,000	54,000
Contribution	10,000	2,500	7,000	19,500
Fixed costs (new apportionment unknown)				16,000
Profit				3,500

8.7 Since the company now has spare capacity from the shutdown of product B, it would be recommended that management should look for an alternative use for the available resources which would earn a positive contribution, and thereby increase profit still further.

9. ASSUMPTIONS AND QUALITATIVE FACTORS

9.1 Relevant costs are future costs. Whenever anyone tries to predict what will happen in the future, the predictions could well be wrong. Managers have to make the best forecasts of relevant income and costs that they can, and at the same time recognise the assumptions on which their estimates are based. A variety of assumptions will be made, and you ought to be aware of them.

In particular, if you make an assumption in answering an examination question and you are not sure that the examiner or marker will appreciate or recognise the assumption you are making, you should explain it in narrative in your solution.

9.2 Some of the assumptions that are typically made in relevant costing are as follows.

(a) Cost behaviour patterns are known; so that if a department closes down, for example, the attributable fixed cost savings would be known.

Similarly, if a factory increases its capacity significantly, any change in fixed cost expenditure or in the variable cost per unit would also be known. This is not necessarily so, and it is always important to question assumptions of this nature.

(b) The amount of fixed costs, unit variable costs, sales price and sales demand are known with certainty.

It is possible to apply risk and uncertainty analysis to decisions and so recognise that what will happen in the future is not certain. Various approaches to risk and uncertainty analysis are described in another chapter.

(c)   The objective of decision making in the short run is to maximise 'short-term profit'. However, there are many qualitative factors or financial considerations, other than those of profit, which may influence a final decision.

(d)   The information on which a decision is based is complete and reliable.

9.3   Qualitative factors in decision making are factors which might influence the eventual decisions but which have not been quantified in terms of relevant income or costs. They may stem from non-financial objectives, or from factors which might be quantifiable in money terms, but which have not been quantified, perhaps because there is insufficient information to make a reliable estimate.

9.4   Qualitative factors in decision making will inevitably vary with the circumstances and nature of the opportunity being considered. Insofar as it is possible to categorise such factors, the following 'list' is indicative.

(a)   *Availability of cash:* an opportunity may be profitable, but there must be sufficient cash to finance any purchases of equipment and build-up of working capital. If cash is not available, new sources of funds (for example an overdraft or loan) must be sought.

(b)   *Inflation:* the effect of inflation on the prices of various items may need to be considered, especially where a fixed price contract is involved in the decision, ie if the income from an opportunity is fixed by contract, but the costs might increase with inflation, the contract's profitability would be over-stated unless inflation is taken into account.

(c)   *Employees:* any decision involving the shutdown of plant, creation of a new work shift, changes in work procedures or location and so on will require acceptance by employees, and ought to have regard to employee welfare.

(d)   *Customers:* decisions about new products or product closures, the quality of output or after-sales service and so on will inevitably affect customer loyalty and customer demand. It is also important to remember that a decision involving one product may have repercussions on customer attitudes towards a range of company products. For example, a company which sells a range of garden tools and equipment under a single brand name should consider the effects on demand for the entire brand range if one product (for example a garden rake) is deleted, or a new product of poor quality is added.

(e)   *Competitors:* in a competitive market, some decisions may stimulate a response from rival companies. For example, the decision to reduce selling prices in order to raise demand may not be successful if all competitors take similar counter-action.

(f)   *Timing factors:* timing factors should not be ignored in decision making.

There might be a choice in deciding when to take up an opportunity. The choice would not be 'accept or reject'; it would be one of the following.

(1) Accept an opportunity now.
(2) Do not accept the opportunity now, but wait until a later time before doing so.
(3) Reject the opportunity.

Deferring a decision, or leaving it on a 'back burner' until later, is common management practice and it is only being realistic to recognise this fact.

(g) *Suppliers:* some decisions will affect suppliers, whose long-term goodwill may be damaged by a decision to close a product line temporarily. Decisions to change the specifications for bought-out components, or change stockholding policies so as to create patchy, uneven demand might also put a strain on suppliers. In some cases, where a company is the supplier's main customer, a decision to reduce demand or delay payments for goods received might drive the supplier out of business.

(h) *Feasibility:* a proposal may look good on paper, but technical experts or departmental managers may have some reservations about their ability to carry it out in practice.

(i) *Political pressures:* some large companies must recognise that there might be political pressure applied by the government to influence their investment or disinvestment decisions.

(j) *Legal constraints:* a decision might occasionally be rejected because of doubts about the legality of the proposed action.

10. CONCLUSION

10.1 (a) In making decisions about the future, the only costs which are relevant are those which will be affected by the decision. Sunk costs and past costs are irrelevant and should be excluded.

(b) An opportunity cost is the benefit forgone by selecting one course of action in preference to the most profitable available alternative.

(c) Fixed costs which are affected by a decision are called directly attributable fixed costs.

(d) Where a limiting factor exists, the course of action must be that which gives the maximum possible contribution per unit of limiting factor.

(e) In a shutdown decision, only those costs which would actually be saved by a shutdown are relevant.

10.2 In this chapter we have looked at a number of specific decision problems. The next chapter goes on to look at one more type of decision for which the management accountant is often asked to provide information: pricing decisions.

TEST YOUR KNOWLEDGE

The numbers in brackets refer to paragraphs of this chapter

1   What is the definition of 'contribution'? (1.4)

2   Define a 'relevant cost'. (2.2)

3   Distinguish between avoidable costs and sunk costs (2.10, 2.13)

4   What is an opportunity cost? (2.11)

5   What is a committed cost? (2.15)

6   What is the rule for identifying the relevant cost of a scarce resource? (4.8)

7   What qualitative considerations might be relevant in a make or buy decision? (6.3(d))

Now try question 6 at the end of the text

Chapter 7

COSTING SYSTEMS: STANDARD COSTING

This chapter covers the following topics.

1. Costing systems: standard costing
2. Standard costs and budgetary control
3. Determining standards and performance
4. Advantages of standard costing

---

1. COSTING SYSTEMS: STANDARD COSTING

1.1 One method of budgetary control needs to be examined specifically: standard costing. It is unlikely that you would be asked to compute a standard costing within your studies but you will need to be aware of what it represents, why it is used and it sets out to achieve. Those of you who work in a manufacturing environment will almost certainly meet them in practice.

Definitions

1.2 A *standard cost* is an estimated unit cost, prepared in advance and calculated from management's expectations of:

(a) efficiency levels in the use of materials and labour;
(b) the expected price of materials, labour and expenses;
(c) budgeted overhead costs and budgeted volumes of activity.

It is a planned cost, and so is the cost that should be incurred in making the unit.

1.3 *Standard costing* is the preparation of standard costs:

(a) for use in cost accounting as a means of valuing stocks and the cost of production; it is an alternative method of valuation to FIFO, LIFO, replacement costing, and so on;

(b) for use in budgetary control (variance analysis).

Again we shall note and then set on one side the stock valuation arguments.

1.4 The definitions set out below are important to our understanding of the standard costing process. Particularly important to note is the degree of subjective judgement which has to be used in the establishing of standards and standard costs.

7: COSTING SYSTEMS: STANDARD COSTING

(a) *Standard:* 'A predetermined measurable quantity set in defined conditions against which actual performance can be compared, usually for an element of work, operation or activity. While standards may be based on unquestioned and immutable natural law or facts, they are finally set by human judgement and consequently are subject to the same fallibility which attends all human activity. Thus a standard for 100 per cent machine output can be fixed by its geared input/output speeds, but the effective realisable output standard is one of judgement.'

(b) *Standard cost:* 'A predetermined calculation of how much costs should be under specified working conditions. It is built up from an assessment of the value of cost elements and correlates technical specifications and the quantification of materials, labour and other costs to the prices and/or wage rates expected to apply during the period in which the standard cost is intended to be used. Its main purposes are to provide bases for control through variance accounting, for the valuation of stock and work in progress and, in some cases, for fixing selling prices.'

(c) *Standard costing:* 'A technique which uses standards for costs and revenues for the purpose of control through variance analysis.'

2. STANDARD COSTS AND BUDGETARY CONTROL

2.1 Standard costing and budgetary control are interlinked. When standard costs have been determined it is relatively easy to compute budgets for production costs and sales. On the other hand, in determining standard costs it is necessary to ascertain the budgeted level of output for the period in order to prepare a standard fixed production overhead cost per unit.

2.2 When actual costs differ from standard costs we call these differences *cost variances.* Similarly, we get sales variances when actual sales are different from budgeted sales either due to the number sold (volume variance) or to a different price (price variance). These variances will affect our budgeted profit because our budgeted profit is based on standard costs and standard selling prices.

2.3 We have already seen in earlier chapters that variances and standard costing can be used in several different situations. Detailed analysis of variances is described more fully in a later chapter.

3. DETERMINING STANDARDS AND PERFORMANCE

3.1 The responsibility for setting standard costs should be shared between managers able to provide the necessary levels of expected efficiency, prices and overhead costs.

3.2 It is common for standard costs to be revised once a year to allow for changes in prices, wage rates and any expected alterations in such factors as volume of output, efficiency levels and standard practices.

Standard cost rates

3.3 (a) Direct materials costs per unit of raw material will be estimated by the purchasing department from their knowledge of:

       (i)   purchase contracts already agreed;

       (ii)   the forecast movement of prices in the market;

       (iii)   the availability of bulk purchase discounts.

(b)   Direct labour rates per hour will be set by reference to the payroll and to any agreements on pay rises with the Trade Union:

       (i)   a separate hourly rate will be set for each different labour grade/type of employee;

       (ii)   the hourly rate will probably be an average to incorporate not only basic hourly wages, but also bonus payments, holiday pay, employers' National Insurance contributions and so on;

       (iii)   an average rate will be applied for each grade (even though rates of pay of individual employees may vary according to age and experience).

(c)   The production overhead absorption rate is usually a direct labour hours rate, so that the standard cost per unit is usually:

Standard labour hours × (standard) absorption rate per hour.

Performance standards

3.4   It is also necessary to estimate the materials required to make each product (material usage) and also the labour hours required (labour efficiency).

Technical specifications must be prepared for each product by production experts (either in the production department or the work study department).

(a)   The 'Standard Production Specification' for materials must list the quantities required per unit of each material in the product. These standard input quantities must be made known to the operators in the production department (so that control action by management to deal with excess material wastage will be understood by them).

(b)   The 'Standard Operation Sheet' for labour will specify the expected hours required by each grade of labour in each department to make one unit of product. These standard times must be carefully set (for example by work study) and must be understood by the labour force. Where necessary, standard procedures or operating methods should be stated.

3.5   Standards are averages. Even under ideal working conditions, it would be unrealistic to expect every unit of activity or production to take exactly the same time, using exactly the same amount of materials, and at exactly the same cost. Some variations are inevitable, but for a reasonably large volume of activity, it would be fair to expect that on average, standard results should be achieved.

3.6   This averaging will and must be included in the standards. They should reflect what would happen under what management would consider to be normal circumstances. Hence during production of our product those variables would be the quantity of materials used in the production of one unit, the amount of labour time spent on the production of that unit and the efficiency with which the workforce is achieving in completing the unit of production. Hence the system will be able to identify:

(a) *standard material usage* as 'the quantity of material or rate of use required as an average, under specified conditions, to produce a specified quantity of output';

(b) *standard performance for labour* as 'the rate of output which qualified workers can achieve as an average over the working day or shift, without over-exertion, provided they adhere to the specified method and are motivated to apply themselves to their work';

(c) *standard time* as 'the total time (hours and minutes) in which a task should be completed at standard performance, ie basic time plus contingency allowance plus relaxation allowance'.

3.7 A further problem arises in standard setting because there are basically four types of performance standard.

(a) *Ideal standards*: these are based on perfect operating conditions, with no wastage, no inefficiencies, no idle time and no breakdowns. Variances from ideal standards are useful for pinpointing areas where a close examination may result in large savings, but they are likely to have an unfavourable motivational impact. Employees will often feel that the goals are unattainable and they will not work so hard.

(b) *Attainable standards:* these are based on the hoped-for improvements in operation conditions. Some allowance is made for wastage, inefficiencies and so on. Well-set attainable standards provide a useful psychological incentive and, for this reason, should be introduced whenever possible. The consent and co-operation of employees involved in improving the standard are required.

(c) *Current standards:* these are standards based on current working conditions (current wastage, current inefficiencies). The disadvantage of current standards is that they do not attempt to improve on current levels of efficiency, which may be poor and capable of significant improvement.

(d) *Basic standards*: these are standards which are kept unaltered over a long period of time, and may be out-of-date. These are used to show changes in efficiency or performance over a long period of time. Basic standards are perhaps the least useful and least common type of standard in use.

Exercise

A company has 50 workers who each work a 40 hour week. It is expected that unavoidable idle time will be 5% of attendance time.

It is also expected that current efficiency levels are only 80% of attainable levels.

If idle time could be eliminated and the workforce could achieve 100% efficiency, a unit of production would take 19 hours to make.

What are the ideal, attainable and current standard times per unit?

Solution

Attendance hours per week of workforce (50 × 40)	2,000 hrs
Idle time (5%)	100 hrs
Working time	1,900 hrs

At 80% efficiency working, this represents only 1,520 hours of output at 100% efficiency.

Time per unit at 100% efficiency, and no idle time	19 hrs
Add idle time allowance	1 hr
	20 hrs
Allow for 80% efficiency level (× 20/80)	5 hrs
Current expected time	25 hrs

Summary

Ideal standard time	19 hrs
Attainable standard time	20 hrs
Current standard time	25 hrs

Revision of standards

3.8 When there is a sudden change in economic circumstances, the standard cost will no longer be accurate. In practice, changing standards frequently is an expensive operation and can cause confusion. For this reason standard cost revisions are usually only made once a year. From the point of view of providing a target, however, an out-of-date standard is useless and some revision may be necessary.

3.9 At times of rapid price inflation, many managers have felt that the high level of inflation forced them to change price and wage rate standards continually. This, however, leads to a reduction in the value of the standard as a criterion. At the other extreme is the adoption of 'basic' standards which will remain unchanged for many years. They provide a constant base for comparison, but this is hardly satisfactory when there is technological change in working procedures and conditions.

Problems of setting standard costs

3.10 The problems involved in setting standard costs, apart from the inevitable problems of forecasting errors, include:

(a) deciding how to incorporate inflation into planned unit costs;

(b) agreeing a labour efficiency standard (for example should current times, better-than-current times or ideal times be used in the labour efficiency standard?);

(c) deciding on the quality of materials to be used, because a better quality of material will cost more, but perhaps reduce material wastage;

(d) deciding on the appropriate mix of component materials, where some change in the mix is possible (for example, in the manufacture of foods and drink);

(e) estimating materials prices where seasonal price variations or bulk purchase discounts may be significant;

(f) possible 'behavioural' problems; managers responsible for the achievement of standards might resist the use of a standard costing control system for fear of being 'blamed' for any adverse variances;

(g) the cost of setting up and maintaining a system for establishing standards.

Management by exception

3.11 A standard cost, when established is an *average expected unit cost*. Because it is only an average, actual results will vary to some extent above and below the average. Variances should only be reported where the difference between actual and standard is significant, ie the principle of *reporting by exception* should be used.

4. ADVANTAGES OF STANDARD COSTING

4.1 The advantages of having a standard costing system in operation can be summarised as follows.

(a) Carefully planned standards are an aid to more accurate budgeting.

(b) Standard costs provide a yardstick against which actual costs can be measured, so that control information can be provided.

(c) The setting of standards involves determining the best materials and methods which may lead to economies.

(d) A target efficiency is set for employees to reach and cost consciousness is stimulated.

(e) Variances can be calculated which enable the principle of 'management by exception' to be operated. Only the variances which exceed acceptable tolerance limits need to be investigated by management with a view to control action.

(f) Standard costs can provide a valuable aid to management in determining prices and formulating policies. However, great care must be taken in this area; standard costs can be misleading for purposes of making pricing decisions.

(g) Standard costs simplify the process of bookkeeping in cost accounting, because they are easier to use than LIFO, FIFO, weighted average costs and so on.

(h) Standard times simplify the process of production scheduling (in the production planning department).

(i) Motivation: standard performance levels might provide an incentive for individuals to achieve targets for themselves at work.

4.2 You will have realised that when setting standards, managers must be aware of two requirements, the need to establish a useful control measure, and the need to set a standard that will have the desired motivational effect. These two requirements are often conflicting, so that the final standard cost might be a compromise between the two.

4.3   Marketing managers should be aware of standard costing systems because of the need to link the production process with the marketing and sales effort. It is important that you appreciate whether the costing system is based on marginal or absorption costing. It is important to understand where efficiencies in the production process are planned and over what time period. It is important to be aware of this costing procedure because your ability to sell a product in the market place at a given price can have far reaching effects on the profitability of the product and on the achievement of the corporate objectives in the short term.

5.   CONCLUSION

5.1   (a)   A standard cost is an estimated unit cost used for planning and control purposes.

(b)   A standard cost card shows full details of the standard cost of each product.

(c)   Differences between actual and standard costs are called variances.

(d)   There are four types of performance standard: ideal, expected, current and basic.

(e)   A standard cost is set as an average expected unit cost. The actual cost of individual items may fluctuate around this average.

(f)   Managers should only receive information of significant variances. This is known as 'management by exception'.

TEST YOUR KNOWLEDGE

The numbers in brackets refer to paragraphs of this chapter

1   What is a standard cost card? (1.2, 1.4)

2   How will standard costs for materials and labour be calculated? (3.3)

3   Give a brief description of each of the four different types of standard. (3.7)

4   What are the problems involved in setting standard costs? (3.10)

5   What is 'reporting by exception'. (3.11)

6   What are the advantages of standard costing? (4.1)

Now try question 7 at the end of the text

Chapter 8

COSTING SYSTEMS: ABSORPTION AND MARGINAL COSTING

This chapter covers the following topics.

1. Attributing overheads to products and services
2. Overhead allocation and apportionment
3. Overhead absorption
4. What is marginal (incremental) costing?
5. Marginal costing and absorption costing compared

---

1. ATTRIBUTING OVERHEADS TO PRODUCTS AND SERVICES

1.1 Management is about decision making and the analysis of financial data is one of the disciplines which may provide an insight into which alternatives would best suit the achievement of the corporate objectives in both the short and longer term. In order to arrive at the financial input to this decision making process we need to understand the process by which the finance team will assess their options. One of the areas on which specific attention to the financial detail must be focused is the area of costing. We will look at costing then move onto the pricing decision and from there on to factors which affect both short term and longer terms decision making.

1.2 A manufacturing company has the objective of producing a product which can be sold so as to generate a profit for the company; similarly, the main objective of a service company is to provide a particular service at a price which will more than cover the costs incurred. The problem is that many of the costs incurred by companies are not directly attributable to the product or service (outputs) provided. This makes it difficult to set up a direct comparison between the revenue earned from an output, and the costs of providing it.

1.3   Costs which can be directly attributed to a product or service are called *direct costs*, and costs which cannot be directly attributed to a product or service are called *indirect costs* or *overheads*.

1.4 An understanding of overheads is vital to an understanding of absorption costing so some examples are given below.

(a) In the case of manufacturing companies, *production overheads*. These may include the rent, rates and depreciation on a factory building, the depreciation and insurance of plant and equipment, repairs and maintenance costs, the costs of factory heating and lighting and the salaries of production supervisors.

(b) *Administration overheads*. These may include the costs of office premises (rent, depreciation, insurance, repairs and maintenance, heating and lighting and so on) and the salaries of administrative staff.

(c) *Selling and distribution overheads*. These may include the costs of warehouse premises, depreciation on delivery vans and salesmen's cars, and the salaries of warehouse and selling staff.

1.5 One of the reasons why these overheads are difficult to attribute to products or services, is that they often relate to periods of time rather than output levels. For instance, the rates charge is for one year, and the rates charged for a whole year are greater than for, say, six months.

This is quite different from variable costs (direct costs and any other costs which can be linked directly to the production of an item), which vary not with time but with the level of output.

1.6 A company must pay money to cover overhead costs, and this must somehow be reflected in the calculation of profit earned. For costing purposes, two main methods are in use to do this.

(a) *Marginal costing*, where overheads are deducted as a total sum to arrive at a profit figure. We will look in more detail at marginal costing in the next chapter.

(b) *Absorption costing*, where an attempt is made to allocate overhead costs to individual units of output. To calculate the cost of a unit of output we add to its prime cost a proportion of the total overheads incurred by the company. (This process is referred to as *absorbing* overheads into units of output, and the system is consequently known as absorption costing. The cost of a unit of output under this system is referred to as its *fully absorbed cost*.)

Absorption costing: a definition

1.7 To arrive at a figure of net profit in a system of absorption costing the basic principle is to compare sales revenue with the fully absorbed cost of goods sold. You should keep this basic principle firmly in mind as you get to grips with the details of absorption costing, even though in practice there will be complications.

1.8 The main practical problem is that of estimation: to absorb overheads accurately, management needs to know the total overheads incurred and the number of units of output to which they should be allocated. Neither is known for certain until the end of an accounting period, and in the meantime estimates must be made. In calculating net profit, adjustments will need to be made in respect of differences between overheads actually incurred and overheads absorbed.

1.9 We will now look in more detail at the mechanics of absorption costing, beginning with a definition of absorption costing, as follows.

'A principle whereby fixed as well as variable costs are allotted to cost units and total overheads are absorbed according to activity level. The term may be applied where:

(a) production costs only, or
(b) costs of all functions are so allotted'.

1.10 The distinguishing feature of absorption costing is that the cost of an item is calculated by adding (or 'absorbing') a share of fixed overhead costs. This distinguishes absorption costing from variable costing or direct costing, when *variable* overheads are the only indirect costs included in the cost of an item.

1.11 The procedure for building up the cost of a unit in absorption costing is as follows.

(a) Ascertain and charge the items of prime cost (direct materials, direct labour and so on). *direct expenses*

(b) Charge the appropriate amount of production overhead.

(c) The sum of (a) and (b) is the total production cost.

(d) Charge the appropriate amount of administration overhead.

(e) Charge the appropriate amounts of selling and distribution overhead.

(f) The sum of (c), (d) and (e) will be the total cost of sales. Absorption costing might only go as far as (c): it might apply to production costs only, with administration and selling and distribution costs being treated as a period charge against profits.

1.12 Suppose that a company makes and sells 100 units of a product each week. The prime cost per unit is £6 and the unit sales price is £10. Production overhead costs £200 per week, and administration, selling and distribution overhead costs £150 per week. The weekly profit could be calculated as follows.

	£	£
Sales (100 units × £10)		1,000
Prime costs (100 × £6)	600	
Production overheads	200	
Administration, selling and distribution costs	150	
		950
Profit		50

(Here prime costs mean the direct costs of production, namely the direct material costs that go to making the product, the direct labour costs involved in that process and so on).

1.13 In absorption costing, overhead costs will be added to each unit manufactured and sold.

	£
Prime cost per unit	6
Production overhead (£200 per week for 100 units)	2
Full production cost	8

The weekly profit would be as follows.

	£
Sales	1,000
Less production cost of sales	800
Gross profit	200
Less administration, selling and distribution costs	150
Net profit	50

1.14 The reasons for using absorption costing have traditionally been identified as follows.

(a) It provides, according to many accountants, a superior basis for valuing stock.
(b) It is a useful guide in taking pricing decisions.
(c) It helps to establish the profitability of different products.

Closing stock valuations

1.15 When there is closing stock at the end of an accounting period (and opening stock at the beginning of a period) the stock must be valued for balance sheet purposes and to calculate the correct profit for the period.

In our example, closing stocks might be valued at prime cost (£6), but in absorption costing, they would be valued at a fully absorbed production cost, at £8 per unit.

1.16 Of these three arguments, the problem of valuing closing stocks is perhaps the most significant because absorption costing is recommended in *financial* accounting by SSAP 9 *Stocks and long-term contracts*. SSAP 9 deals with financial accounting systems and not with cost accounting systems. The cost accountant is (in theory) free to value closing stocks by whatever method seems best, but where companies integrate their financial accounting and cost accounting systems into a single system of accounting records, the valuation of closing stocks will be determined by SSAP 9.

1.17 SSAP 9 states that 'costs' of stock should comprise those costs which have been incurred in the normal course of business in bringing the product (or service) to its 'present location and condition'. These costs incurred will include all related production overheads. In other words, in financial accounting, closing stocks should be valued at full production cost, and it may therefore be convenient and appropriate to value stocks by the same method in the cost accounting system.

1.18 Despite the fact that absorption costing is the required basis for stock valuation in financial accounts, we will see later that for management accounting purposes variable costing has many advantages. Consideration of fixed cost is often misleading, particularly in the context of decision making.

Pricing decisions

1.19 Many companies attempt to fix prices by calculating the full cost of production or sales of each product, and then adding a margin for profit. In our example, the company might have fixed a gross profit margin at 25% on production cost, or 20% of the sales price, in order to establish the unit sales price of £10. 'Full cost plus pricing' can be particularly useful for companies which do jobbing work or contract work, where each job or contract is different, so that a standard unit sales price cannot be fixed. Pricing will be discussed in detail in a later chapter.

Establishing the profitability of different products.

1.20 This argument in favour of absorption costing is more contentious, but is worthy of mention here. If a company sells more than one product, it will be difficult to judge how profitable each individual product is, unless overhead costs are shared on a fair basis and charged to the cost of sales of each product.

2. OVERHEAD ALLOCATION AND APPORTIONMENT

2.1 Ultimately, the objective of an absorption costing system is to attribute all production overheads (and possibly administration, selling and distribution overheads as well) to units of output. But it is not possible to allocate overhead costs in this way the moment they are incurred. The necessary procedure is to allocate most overhead costs initially to cost centres.

2.2 Examples of cost centres used in overhead allocation and apportionment include the following.

(a) A production department (for example the machining department in a factory).

(b) A service department (stores, repairs and maintenance) within the factory area.

(c) An administrative department (such as personnel).

(d) A selling or distribution department (for example a warehouse).

(e) 'Functional' cost centres for items of expense which are shared by several departments (for example rent, rates, heating and lighting, insurance, canteen).

2.3 It may be possible to allocate some overhead costs directly to cost units. Otherwise, as overheads are incurred they are initially allocated to an appropriate cost centre such as those identified above. The next step after allocation is *apportionment of costs*. This is the process by which cost items or costs originally allocated to service department or functional cost centres are apportioned between the other cost centres, so that all overheads are eventually charged to production, administration and selling and distribution departments.

2.4 Finally, overheads are absorbed into the cost of finished units, jobs or processes. Overhead absorption is sometimes called overhead recovery.

Overhead apportionment

2.5 Overhead apportionment follows on from overhead allocation. The first stage of overhead apportionment is to identify all overhead costs as production department, production service department, administration or selling and distribution overhead. This means that the costs in paragraph 2.2(e) must be shared out between the other cost centres.

Bases of apportionment

2.6 It is important that overhead costs should be shared out on a fair basis. You will appreciate that because of the complexity of items of cost it is rarely possible to use only one method of apportioning costs to the various departments of an organisation. Some examples of apportionment bases are given below.

Overhead item	Basis of apportionment
Rent, rates, heating and light, repairs and depreciation of buildings	Floor area occupied by each cost centre
Depreciation, insurance of equipment	Cost or book value of equipment in cost centre
Personnel office, canteen, welfare, wages and cost offices, first aid	Number of employees, or labour hours worked in each cost centre
Heating, lighting (see above)	Volume of space occupied by each cost centre
Carriage inwards	Value of material issues to each cost centre

2.7 An examination question may be set which calls for the apportionment of overhead items. In the majority of cases the basis to be used is obvious, but you may encounter one or two items for which two (or more) bases may appear to be equally acceptable. Always indicate the basis of apportionment you have chosen, and in any case of doubt explain why you chose one basis in preference to another.

2.8 Whatever the method adopted for the allocation and apportionment of overheads, one fundamental principle must completely understood. In all cases we will have assumed that a given number of units will be produced. For example, in an exam question 10,000 units of production may be assumed and an overhead cost (say the material stores department) may be expected to be £10,000 over the same period. Hence on fully absorbing this overhead we will assume that the unit cost of each product must include £1 to cover this overhead. Now what happens if we actually produce 12,000 units in the period because our marketing of the product has been so successful? Based on our costing or pricing model we will have effectively lower absorbed £12,000 of overheads. Similarly the actual costs of the material stores department may have been only £9,000. Now where do we go?

3. OVERHEAD ABSORPTION

3.1 Having allocated and/or apportioned all overheads, the next stage in the costing of overheads is to add them to, or absorb them into, the cost of production or sales.

(a) Production overheads are added to the cost of production (work in progress) and are included in the value of stocks of finished goods.

(b) Administration overheads are usually (and preferably) added as a cost of sales and are not added to the value of stocks of finished goods.

(c)   Selling and distribution overheads are a part of the cost of sales.

Use of a predetermined absorption rate

3.2   For various reasons, it is inconvenient to collect data about actual costs and to absorb overheads on the basis of actual costs.

(a)   Goods are produced and sold throughout the year, but actual overheads are not known until the end of the year. It would be inconvenient to wait until the year end in order to decide what overhead costs per unit should be.

(b)   An attempt to calculate overhead costs more regularly (for example each month) is possible, although estimated costs must be added for occasional expenditures such as rent and rates (perhaps incurred once or twice a year). The difficulty with this approach would be that actual overheads from month to month would fluctuate randomly; therefore, overhead costs charged to production would depend to a certain extent on random events and changes. A unit made in one week might be charged with £4 of overhead, in a subsequent week with £5, and in a third week with £4.50. Such changes are considered misleading for costing purposes and administratively inconvenient to deal with.

3.3   All overheads are therefore usually added to cost using a pre-determined overhead absorption rate which is calculated from the budget. Businesses establish their overhead absorption for the forthcoming accounting year by the following method:

(a)   estimating the overhead likely to be incurred during the coming year;
(b)   estimating the activity level for the year; and
(c)   dividing estimated overhead by the budgeted activity level.

Over or under absorption of overheads

3.4   Because the rate of overhead absorption is based on estimates (of both numerator and denominator) it is almost inevitable that at the end of the accounting year there will have been an over-absorption or under-absorption of the overhead actually incurred.

3.5   Suppose that the budgeted overhead in a production department is £80,000 and the budgeted activity is 40,000 direct labour hours. The overhead absorption rate, using a direct labour hour basis, would be £2 per direct labour hour.

Actual overheads in the period are, say £84,000, and 45,000 direct labour hours are worked.

	£
Overhead incurred (actual)	84,000
Overhead absorbed (45,000 × £2)	90,000
Over-absorption of overhead	6,000

3.6   In this example, the cost of produced units or jobs has been charged with £6,000 more than was actually spent. An adjustment to reconcile the overheads charged to the actual overhead is necessary, and the over-absorbed overhead will be written off as a credit to the profit and loss account at the end of the accounting period.

3.7 The overhead absorption rate is predetermined from budget estimates of overhead cost and the expected volume of activity. Under or over-recovery of overhead will occur if:

    (a) actual overhead costs; or
    (b) the actual activity volume; or
    (c) both

differ from budget.

Absorption of production overheads into factory cost

3.8 The process of apportionment ends when all production overheads have been spread among the different production departments. This is how the 'actual overheads incurred' by any department would be calculated when actual costs are analysed by the cost department. A similar process is used to calculate budgeted costs.

3.9 Example of the different bases of absorption which may be used are:

    (a) a percentage of direct materials cost;
    (b) a percentage of direct labour cost;
    (c) a percentage of prime cost;
    (d) a rate per machine hour;
    (e) a rate per direct labour hour;
    (f) a rate per unit;
    (g) a percentage of factory cost (administration overhead);
    (h) a percentage of sales or factory cost (for selling and distribution overhead).

3.10 Which basis should be used for production overhead depends largely on the organisation concerned. Percentages of materials cost, wages or prime cost should be adopted only where the value of the materials and/or wages is considered for all products to have some relationship with the overhead.

3.11 For example, it is safe to assume that the indirect costs for producing brass screws are similar to those for producing steel screws, but the cost of brass is very much greater than that of steel. Consequently, the overhead charge for brass screws would be too high and that for steel screws too low, if a percentage of cost of materials rate were to be used.

3.12 Again, if the overhead actually attributable to units was incurred on a time basis, but one skilled (and consequently more highly-paid) employee was engaged on one task, while a less skilled (and lower-paid) employee was producing another item, the overhead charged to the first job using the percentage of wages rate might be too high while the amount absorbed by the second job might be too low. A direct labour hour rate might be considered more 'fair'.

3.13 It is for this reason that many factories use the direct labour-hour rate or machine-hour rate in preference to a rate based on a percentage of direct materials cost, wages or prime cost. A machine-hour rate would be used in departments where production is controlled or dictated by machines.

3.14 A rate per unit would be effective only if all units were homogeneous (the same).

3.15 Work through the following example carefully and be sure that you understand how the allocation and apportionment of the various tasks has been arrived at.

Example: different bases of absorption

3.16 Strictly Ltd is a manufacturing company which produces three types of burglar alarms, model 1, model 2 and model 3, made in three production departments 1, 2 and 3 respectively. During the third quarter of 19X8, Strictly Ltd budgets for the following overheads costs.

	£
Depreciation (factory)	800
Repairs and maintenance (factory)	250
Office costs	1,000
Depreciation (equipment)	450
Insurance costs (equipment)	150
Heating	200
Lighting	250
	3,100

Strictly Ltd comprises three production departments (1, 2 and 3), and one service department. Information relating to these departments is:

	Production department			Service department
	1	2	3	
Floor area (sq metres)	1,000	1,000	1,500	750
Volume (cubic metres)	3,150	3,350	4,500	2,250
Number of employees	25	25	32	13
Book value of equipment (£)	10,000	12,000	17,000	11,000

The service department spends 40% of its time working for production department 3, 35% for production department 2, and only 25% for production department 1.

Other budgeted figures for the third quarter are:

	Production department		
	1	2	3
Direct materials cost	£15,000	£17,000	£25,000
Direct labour cost	£16,500	£16,500	£23,500
Machine hours	700	700	700
Output (units)	1,000	900	750

Required

Calculate the full cost of each unit, for each of departments 1, 2 and 3, absorbing overheads:

(a) on a machine-hour basis;
(b) on a units of output basis.

Solution

3.17 The first step is to apportion the various overheads to the four departments.

Item of cost	Basis of apportionment	Total cost	Department 1	2	3	Service
		£	£	£	£	£
Factory depreciation	Floor area	800	188	188	282	142
Factory repairs and maintenance	Floor area	250	59	59	88	44
Office costs	Number of employees	1,000	263	263	337	137
Equipment depreciation	Book value	450	90	108	153	99
Insurance costs	Book value	150	30	36	51	33
Heating	Volume	200	48	51	68	33
Lighting	Floor area	250	59	59	88	44
		3,100	737	764	1,067	532

3.18 The second step is to apportion the service department overhead allocation to the production departments in the ratio 25 : 35 : 40.

Production department	Previously apportioned overheads	Apportioned from Service department	Total
	£	£	£
1	737	133	870
2	764	186	950
3	1,067	213	1,280
		532	3,100

3.19 The final step is to absorb the total apportioned overheads for each of the departments, and add the results to the direct costs, to reach the full cost for each unit produced.

(a) *Using machine hours as absorption basis*

	Model 1	Model 2	Model 3
	£	£	£
Direct materials per unit	15.00	18.89	33.33
Direct labour per unit	16.50	18.33	31.33
Absorbed overhead per unit (overhead ÷ machine hours)	1.24	1.36	1.83
Full cost	32.74	38.58	66.49

(b) *Using output as an absorption basis*

	Model 1 £	Model 2 £	Model 3 £
Direct materials per unit	15.00	18.89	33.33
Direct labour per unit	16.50	18.33	31.33
Absorbed overhead per unit (overhead ÷ output)	0.87	1.06	1.71
Full cost	32.37	38.28	66.37

3.20 The apportioned cost bases is relatively straightforward (although the arithmetic is sometimes a little tricky). Remember there is no right way of apportioning the costs. What we are doing here is to find a method of attributing various costs as fairly and as reasonably as possible. The apportionment of the service department overheads has been done on the basis of the time it spends servicing the different production departments. Is this reasonable? Well its probably better than apportioning the costs on the basis of the outputs of each department because it more carefully represents how the effort was put into those cases. So again there is no right or wrong, but there is a fairly logical allocation method available which does add to those elements which should bear that cost in the most equitable way.

3.21 Now we will turn our attention to the main alternative to absorption costing, marginal or direct costing.

4. WHAT IS MARGINAL (INCREMENTAL) COSTING?

4.1 Marginal costing is an alternative method of costing to absorption costing. Whereas in absorption costing an attempt is made to apportion all overhead costs to units of production, in marginal costing only costs which vary directly with production are allocated to units of production.

4.2 The marginal or incremental cost per unit of production of an item usually consists of:

(a) direct materials;
(b) direct labour;
(c) variable production overheads.

4.3 The basic idea of marginal costing is that if an extra item is produced, then the total of the costs in the above paragraph will all go up slightly. It therefore makes sense to identify those costs as the costs of production, or the *marginal* or *incremental* costs. On the other hand, overheads such as rent, rates, heating etc, will remain the same even if an extra item is produced. They are 'fixed' costs, and are not linked directly to the level of production.

4.4 In marginal costing, only variable costs are included in our calculation of the unit cost of a product. The marginal cost is therefore the variable cost of one unit of a product or a service, a cost which would be avoided if the units was not produced or provided. As a result of this definition we can calculate the profit attributable to one additional unit of production (a unit at the margin) by deducting from its sales value the variable cost of production. This will result in a contribution to fixed overheads. In essence we are now determining that certain costs are fixed and some will vary as we change our levels of production at the margin. As a result we can determine for example how many units of production will need to be sold at a given price in order to completely cover the fixed costs of the business.

Marginal costing principles

4.5 The principles of marginal costing are set out below.

(a) Since period fixed costs are the same, no matter what the volume of sales and production (provided that the level of activity is within a 'relevant range') it follows that by selling an extra item of product, or service:

   (i)   revenue will increase by the sales value of the item sold;

   (ii) costs will increase only by the variable cost per unit;

   (iii) therefore the increase in profit will equal the sales value minus variable costs, defined as the amount of *contribution* earned from the item.

(b) Similarly, if the volume of sales falls by one item, the profit will fall by the amount of contribution earned from the item.

(c) Profit measurement should therefore be based on an analysis of total contribution. Since fixed costs relate to a period of time, and do not change with increases or decreases in sales volume, it is misleading to charge units of sale with a share of fixed costs. Absorption costing is therefore misleading, and it is more appropriate to deduct fixed costs from total contribution for the period to derive a profit figure.

(d) When a unit of product is made, the extra costs incurred in its manufacture are the variable production costs. Fixed costs are unaffected, and no extra fixed costs are incurred when output is increased. It is therefore argued that the valuation of closing stocks should be at production variable cost (direct materials, direct labour, direct expenses (if any) and variable production overhead) because these are the only costs properly attributable to the product. (If variable production overhead cannot be measured, stocks would be valued at direct production cost; direct materials and direct labour, plus direct expenses, if any.)

4.6 We will not concentrate any more on stock valuation since this is subject to some interpretation and will be left to the accountants to work out. However, marginal costing has major impacts on the marketing manager because of its implications to both pricing and decision making, so we will look at a simple example of marginal costing.

Example: marginal costing

4.7 Rain Until September Ltd makes a product, the Splash, which has a variable production cost of £6 and a sales price of £10. It also expects to spend £1 per unit on marketing the product. Fixed costs for the month are £45,000 (administration, sales and distribution).

What is the contribution to fixed costs and the profit for the month of sales cost as follows:

(a) 10,000 splashes
(b) 15,000 splashes
(c) 20,000 splashes

Solution

4.8 Firstly we identify the variable costs and deduct them from the sales value to derive the contribution. We then deduct the fixed costs to arrive at profit.

	10,000 Splashes £	15,000 Splashes £	20,000 Splashes £
Sales revenue	100,000	150,000	200,000
Variable costs			
Production	60,000	90,000	120,000
Marketing	10,000	15,000	20,000
Contribution	30,000	45,000	60,000
Fixed costs	45,000	45,000	45,000
Profit (loss)	(15,000)	Nil	15,000
Profit (loss) per unit	£(1.50)	£Nil	£1.50
Contribution per unit	£3.00	£3.00	£3.00

4.9 The conclusions which may be drawn from this example are as follows.

(a) The profit per unit varies at differing levels of sales, because the average fixed overhead cost per unit changes with the volume of output and sales.

(b) The contribution per unit is constant at all levels of output and sales. Total contribution, which is the contribution per unit multiplied by the number of units sold, increases in direct proportion to the volume of sales.

(c) Since the contribution per unit does not change, the most effective way of calculating the expected profit at any level of output and sales would be:

(i)   calculate the total contribution; then
(ii) deduct fixed costs as a period charge in order to find the profit.

(d) In our example the expected profit from the sale of 17,000 Splashes would be:

	£
Total contribution (17,000 × £3)	51,000
Less fixed costs	45,000
Profit	6,000

4.10 (a) If total contribution exceeds fixed costs, a profit is made.

(b) If total contribution exactly equals fixed costs, no profit and no loss is made; *breakeven point* is reached.

(c) If total contribution is less than the fixed costs, there will be a loss.

5.   MARGINAL COSTING AND ABSORPTION COSTING COMPARED

5.1   Marginal costing as a cost accounting system is significantly different from absorption costing. It is an *alternative* method of accounting for costs and profit, which rejects the principles of absorbing fixed overheads into unit costs.

(a)   In marginal costing:

(i)   closing stocks are valued at marginal production cost;
(ii)   fixed costs are charged in full against the profit of the period in which they are incurred.

(b)   In absorption costing, (sometimes referred to as full costing):

(i)   closing stocks are valued at full production cost, and include a share of fixed production costs;

(ii)   this means that the cost of sales in a period will include some fixed overhead incurred in a previous period (in the opening stock values) and will exclude some fixed overhead incurred in the current period but carried forward in closing stock values as a charge to a subsequent accounting period.

5.2   In marginal costing, it is necessary to identify variable costs, contribution and fixed costs. In absorption costing it is not necessary to distinguish marginal costs from fixed costs (except in preparing the budget, when the overhead absorption rate is based on expected expenditure).

Marginal costing versus absorption costing: which is better?

5.3   *Arguments in favour of absorption costing*

(a)   Fixed production costs are incurred in order to make output; it is therefore *fair* to charge all output with a share of these costs.

(b)   *Closing stock values*, by including a share of fixed production overhead, will be valued on the principle required by SSAP 9 for the financial accounting valuation of stocks.

The explanatory notes to SSAP 9 (paragraph 3) state that 'in order to match costs and revenue 'costs' of stocks and work in progress should comprise that expenditure which has been incurred in the normal course of business in bringing the product or service to its present location and condition. Such costs will include all related production overheads, even though these may accrue on a time basis'.

(c)   A problem with calculating the contribution of various products made by a company is that it may not be clear whether the contribution earned by each product is enough to cover fixed costs, whereas by charging fixed overhead to a product we can decide whether it is *profitable* or not.

5.4   *Arguments in favour of marginal costing*

(a)   Fixed costs will be the same regardless of the volume of output, because they are *period costs*. It makes sense, therefore, to charge them in full as a cost to the period.

(b)   The cost to produce an extra unit is the variable production cost. It is *realistic* to value closing stock items at this directly attributable cost.

(c)   As we have seen, the size of total contribution varies directly with sales volume at a constant rate per unit. For management purposes, *better information* about expected profit is obtained from the use of variable costs and contribution in the accounting system.

(d)   Because marginal costing yields better management information about expected profit, it is a better tool for *planning* purposes. In particular, it can be used in cost - volume - profit analysis, which we will look at in the next chapter.

5.5   Again we have encroached on the stock valuation argument which you should be aware of but thereafter we will leave it to the technical experts.

5.6   There are, however, far reaching implications of these different methods of costing which will be very relevant to your studies and in practice. You may, for example, be faced with a situation where you must decide whether in the short term to produce one of two products from your existing factory.

5.7   You may be the brand manager for a mature product which hasn't increased its sales volume for the last three years. How would you assess the potential benefits for the company if you increased your promotional support and reduced the price? These styles of question will be dealt with in a later chapter.

Exercise

What are the most important features which distinguish marginal costing from absorption costing?

Solution

The features which distinguish marginal costing from absorption costing are as follows.

(a)   In absorption costing, items of stock are costed to include a 'fair share' of fixed production overhead, whereas in marginal costing, stocks are valued at variable production cost only. Closing stocks will therefore have a higher value in absorption costing than in marginal costing.

(b)   As a consequence of carrying forward an element of fixed production overheads in closing stock values, the cost of sales used to determine profit in absorption costing will:

(i)   include some fixed production overhead costs incurred in a previous period but carried forward into opening stock values of the current period;

(ii)   exclude some fixed production overhead costs incurred in the current period by including them in closing stock values.

In contrast marginal costing charges the actual fixed costs of a period in full into the profit and loss account of the period. (Marginal costing is therefore sometimes known as period costing.)

(c) In absorption costing, 'actual' fully absorbed unit costs are reduced by producing in greater quantities, whereas in marginal costing, unit variable costs are unaffected by the volume of production (ie provided that variable costs per unit remain unaltered at the changed level of production activity). Profit in any period can be affected by the actual volume of production in absorption costing; this is not the case in marginal costing.

(d) In marginal costing, the identification of variable costs and of contribution enables management to use cost information more easily for decision-making purposes (for example in budget decision making). It is easy to decide by how much contribution (and therefore profit) will be affected by changes in sales volume. (Profit would be unaffected by changes in production volume).

In absorption costing, however, the effect on profit in a period of changes in both production volume and sales volume is not easily seen, because cost behaviour is not analysed and incremental costs are not used in the calculation of actual profit.

---

6. CONCLUSION

6.1 In absorption costing, it is usual to add overheads into product costs by applying a predetermined overhead absorption rate. This is 'normal costing'.

6.2 The predetermined rate is set annually, in the budget. To work out the absorption rate, budgeted overheads are allocated to cost centres, and then apportioned so that:

(a) all production overhead is identified with departments engaged directly in production;

(b) administration overhead and selling and distribution overhead are also separately identified.

6.3 The absorption rate is calculated by dividing budgeted overhead for the department by the budgeted level of activity. For production overheads, the level of activity is often budgeted direct labour hours or budgeted machine hours.

6.4 At the end of the accounting period (year) actual overhead for production departments, administration or selling and distribution are worked out by applying the process of allocation and apportionment to actual overhead costs incurred. The actual overheads thus calculated for each production department (or administration, selling and distribution) are compared with the overheads which have been absorbed, using the pre-determined rates.

6.5 There will be a discrepancy between overheads incurred and overheads absorbed.

(a) If overheads absorbed exceed overheads incurred, the cost of production (or sales) will have been too high. The amount of over-absorption will be written as a 'favourable' adjustment to the profit and loss account, to compensate for the excessive overhead charges in products.

(b) Similarly, if overheads absorbed are lower than the amount of overheads incurred the cost of production (or sales) will have been too low. The amount of under-absorption will be written as an 'adverse' adjustment to the profit and loss account, to compensate for the under-charging of overheads in product costs.

6.6 Under- or over-absorbed overhead is inevitable in normal absorption costing because the pre-determined overhead absorption rates are based on forecasts about:

(a) overhead expenditure; and
(b) the level, or volume, of activity.

6.7 A company may 'mix' the systems:

(a) use absorption costing techniques for the valuation of closing stocks and measurement of profit;

(b) use marginal costing techniques for variance analysis, planning and decision-making.

6.8 Marginal costing and absorption costing are different techniques for assessing profit in a period.

6.9 Marginal cost is the variable cost of one unit of product or service.

6.10 Contribution is an important measure in marginal costing and it is calculated as the difference between sales value and marginal or variable cost.

6.11 In marginal costing, fixed production costs are treated as period costs and written off as they are incurred. In absorption costing, fixed production costs are absorbed into the cost of units, and are carried forward in stock to be charged against sales for the next period.

6.12 In your examination, you may be asked to calculate a profit for an accounting period using either of the two methods of accounting. Absorption costing is more traditional but marginal costing provides better information for planning and decision-making by management.

6.13 From a general viewpoint we should be aware of when to use one method of costing or another. It would be fair to use absorption costing in any decision making process where the market or product concerned is mature and where total market share is unlikely to be changed. A good example here is in the brewing industry where the major brewers have been competing for a slightly declining market for a couple of decades. Although tastes are changing and new products are constantly being introduced, the total sales volumes and production remain fairly constant and as a result absorption costing is often used.

6.14 Marginal costing is, however, used at the margin. The utilisation of excess capacity is a classic example where marginal costing is most relevant. Hence the introduction of own label products is a classic case for the use of a marginal approach.

TEST YOUR KNOWLEDGE
The numbers in brackets refer to paragraphs of this chapter

1   Define absorption costing. (1.7-1.10)

2   Why is absorption costing used? (1.14)

3   What are over-absorbed overheads? (3.4-3.7)

4   Define marginal costing. (4.3)

5   List three examples of absorption costing and four advantages of marginal costing. (5.4)

Now try question 8 at the end of the text

Chapter 9

COST-VOLUME-PROFIT ANALYSIS (BREAKEVEN ANALYSIS)

This chapter covers the following topics.

1. Breakeven analysis and the breakeven point
2. The margin of safety
3. Breakeven charts

---

1. BREAKEVEN ANALYSIS AND THE BREAKEVEN POINT

1.1 Accounting is concerned not just with recording historic costs, and with budgetary control, but also with the provision of information which will help managers to make decisions for the future. For example, managers would like to be able to assess and plan their future profits (profit planning), so they need to be able to forecast future costs. And to forecast future costs, we must know about the cost behaviour of all cost items.

1.2 One way of providing information about expected future costs and revenues for management decision-making is breakeven analysis. Breakeven analysis is an application of marginal costing techniques and is sometimes called CVP or cost-volume-profit analysis, which is often used in budget planning, by marketing managers as well as by accountants.

The breakeven point

1.3 You should now understand that by using marginal costing techniques, it is possible to ascertain the contribution per unit. The total contribution from all sales during a period can be compared with the fixed costs for that period; any excess or deficiency of contribution over fixed costs represents the profit or loss respectively for the period.

1.4 The management of an organisation usually wishes to know not only the profit likely to be made if the aimed-for production and sales for the year are achieved, but also the point at which neither profit nor loss occurs (the breakeven point), and the amount by which actual sales can fall below anticipated sales without a loss being incurred.

The breakeven point can be calculated arithmetically. The number of units needed to be sold in order to 'break even' will be the total fixed costs divided by the contribution per unit. This is because the contribution required to break even must be an amount which exactly equals the amount of fixed costs. The breakeven point will be expressed as the number of units of sales required to break even.

$$\text{Breakeven point} = \frac{\text{required contribution}}{\text{contribution per unit}} = \frac{\text{total fixed costs}}{\text{contribution per unit}}$$

Example: breakeven point

1.5 Expected sales: 10,000 units @ £8 = £80,000
     Variable cost: £5 per unit
     Fixed costs: £21,000

Compute the breakeven point.

Solution

1.6 The contribution per unit is £ (8 - 5)   =   £3
     Breakeven point (BEP)   =   £21,000 ÷ £3
                                  =   7,000 units
     In revenue, BEP   =   (7,000 × £8) = £56,000

Sales above £56,000 will result in profit of £3 per unit of additional sales and sales below £56,000 will mean a loss of (7,000 units - actual units sold) × £3, which means that profit will improve or worsen by the amount of contribution per unit.

	Sales	
	7,000 units	7,001 units
	£	£
Revenue	56,000	56,008
Less variable costs	35,000	34,005
Contribution	21,000	21,003
Less fixed costs	21,000	21,000
Profit	– (= Breakeven)	3

A formula approach to breakeven arithmetic

1.7 (a) At the breakeven point, sales revenue equals total costs, and there is no profit.

$$S = V + F$$
where
     S = Sales revenue
     V = Total variable costs
     F = Total fixed costs

(b) Subtracting V from each side of the equation, we get:

$$S - V = F, \text{ or}$$

Total contribution = Fixed costs

Example: formula approach

1.8 Butterfingers Ltd makes a product which has a variable cost of £7 per unit. If fixed costs are £63,000 per annum, what must the selling price per unit be if the company wishes:

(a) to break even; and
(b) to sell 12,000 units of the product?

Solution

1.9 Required contribution to break even = £63,000
      (= Fixed costs)

		£
Volume of sales = 12,000 units		
Required contribution per unit $(S-V)$ = £63,000 ÷ 12,000 =		5.25
Variable cost per unit (V) =		7.00
Required sales price per unit (S) =		12.25

Target profits

1.10 A similar formula may be applied where a company wishes to achieve a certain profit during a period. To achieve this profit, sales must cover all costs and leave the required profit.

$$S = V + F + P, \text{ where}$$
$$P = \text{required profit.}$$

Subtracting V from each side of the equation, we get:

$$S - V = F + P \therefore$$

Total contribution required = F + P

First example: target profits

1.11 Seven League Boots Ltd wishes to sell 14,000 units of its product, which has a variable cost of £15 to make and sell. Fixed costs are £47,000 and the required profit is £23,000. What should the sales price per unit be?

Solution

1.12

Required contribution	=	Fixed costs plus profit
	=	£47,000 + £23,000
	=	£70,000
Required sales		14,000 units
Required contribution per unit sold		£ 5
Variable cost per unit		£15
Required sales price per unit		£20

Second example: target profits

1.13 Tripod Ltd makes and sells three products, X, Y and Z. The selling price per unit and costs are as follows.

	X	Y	Z
Selling price per unit	£80	£50	£70
Variable cost per unit	£50	£10	£20
Fixed costs per month		£160,000	

The maximum sales demand per month is 2,000 units of each product and the minimum sales demand is 1,000 of each.

Required

(a) Comment on the potential profitability of the company.

(b) Suppose that there is a fixed demand for X and Y of 1,500 units per month, which will not be exceeded, but for which firm orders have been received. How many units of Z would have to be sold to achieve a profit of at least £25,000 per month?

Solution

1.14 (a) When there is no indication about whether marginal or absorption costing is in use, it is simpler (and more informative too) to assess profitability with contribution analysis and marginal costing. This is the requirement in part (a) of the problem. The obvious analysis to make is a calculation of the worst possible and best possible results.

| | | Best possible | | | Worst possible | |
Product	Sales units	Cont'n per unit £	Total contribution £	Sales units	Cont'n per unit £	Total contribution £
X	2,000	30	60,000	1,000	30	30,000
Y	2,000	40	80,000	1,000	40	40,000
Z	2,000	50	100,000	1,000	50	50,000
Total contribution			240,000			120,000
Fixed costs			160,000			160,000
Profit/(loss)			80,000			(40,000)

The company's potential profitability ranges from a profit of £80,000 to a loss of £40,000 per month.

(b) The second part of the problem is a variation of a 'target profit' calculation.

	£	£
Required (minimum) profit per month		25,000
Fixed costs per month		160,000
Required contribution per month		185,000
Contribution to be earned from		
Product X 1,500 × 30	45,000	
Product Y 1,500 × 40	60,000	
		105,000
Contribution required from Product Z		80,000

Contribution per unit of Z	£50
Minimum required sales of Z per month = $\dfrac{£80,000}{£50}$ =	1,600 units

The contribution to sales ratio (C/S ratio)

1.15 An alternative way of calculating the breakeven point is:

$$\frac{\text{Required contribution} \ (= \text{fixed costs})}{\text{Contribution/sales ratio (or C/S ratio)}}$$

(The C/S ratio is also sometimes called a profit/volume ratio or P/V ratio).

The resulting breakeven point will be expressed in terms of sales revenue at the breakeven point.

1.16 Since the contribution per unit is the same at all sales volumes, given no change in the unit sales price, there must be a consistent relationship between contribution and sales; the contribution earned per £1 of sales revenue must be constant. The contribution/sales ratio (sometimes called the profit/volume or PV ratio or even the contribution margin ratio) can be important in marginal costing calculations for this reason.

1.17 The contribution/sales ratio is a measure of how much contribution is earned from each £1 of sales. A C/S ratio of 37.5% for example, means that for every £1 of sales, a contribution of 37.5p is earned. Thus, in order to earn a total contribution of £21,000 and if contribution increases by $37\frac{1}{2}$p per £1 of sale, sales must be:

$$\frac{£1}{37\frac{1}{2}\text{p}} \times £21,000 = \frac{£21,000}{37\frac{1}{2}\text{p}} \text{ or } £56,000$$

2. THE MARGIN OF SAFETY

2.1 The *margin of safety* is a measure by which the budgeted volume of sales is compared with the volume of sales required to break even. It is the difference in units between:

(a) budgeted sales volume; and
(b) breakeven sales volume

and it is sometimes expressed as a percentage of the budgeted sales volume. (It may also be expressed as the difference between the budgeted sales revenue and breakeven sales revenue, expressed as a percentage of the budgeted sales revenue).

Exercise

Mal de Mer Ltd makes and sells a product which has a variable cost of £30, and which sells for £40. Budgeted fixed costs are £70,000 and budgeted sales are 8,000 units.

What is the breakeven point and what is the margin of safety?

Solution

(a) Breakeven point $=$ $\dfrac{\text{Fixed costs (required contribution)}}{\text{Contribution per unit}}$ $=$ $\dfrac{£70,000}{£(40-30)}$

$$= \quad 7,000 \text{ units}$$

(b) Margin of safety $\quad = \quad$ 8,000 - 7,000 units $\quad = \quad$ 1,000 units

It may be expressed as $\quad \dfrac{1,000 \text{ units}}{8,000 \text{ units}} \times 100\% \quad = \quad 12\frac{1}{2}\%$

(c) The margin of safety indicates to management that actual sales can fall short of budget by 1,000 units or $12\frac{1}{2}\%$ before the breakeven point is reached and no profit at all is made.

Decisions to change sales price or costs

2.2 You may come across a problem in which you will be expected to offer advice as to the effect of altering the selling price, variable cost per unit or fixed cost. These problems are slight variations on basic breakeven arithmetic, and some examples will be used to illustrate typical questions.

First example: price rise

2.3 Stomer Cakes Ltd bake and sell a single type of cake. The variable cost of production is 15p and the current sales price is 25p. Fixed costs are £2,600 per month, and the annual profit for the company at current sales volume is £36,000. The volume of sales demand is constant throughout the year.

The sales manager, Ian Digestion, wishes to raise the sales price to 29p per cake, but considers that a price rise will result in some loss of sales.

What is the minimum volume of sales required each month to justify a rise in price to 29p?

Solution

2.4 The minimum volume of demand which would justify a price of 29p is one which would leave total profit at least the same as before, at £3,000 per month. Required profit should be converted into required contribution, as follows.

	£
Monthly fixed costs	2,600
Monthly profit, minimum required	3,000
Current monthly contribution	5,600

The minimum volume of sales required after the price rise will be an amount which earns a contribution of £5,600 per month, ie no worse than at the moment. The contribution per cake at a sales price of 29p would be 14p.

$$\text{Required sales} = \frac{\text{Required contribution}}{\text{Contribution per unit}} = \frac{£5,600}{14\text{p}}$$

$$= 40,000 \text{ cakes per month.}$$

Second example: cost changes

2.5 Close Brickett Ltd makes a product which has a variable production cost of £8 and a variable sales cost of £2 per unit. Fixed costs are £40,000 per annum, the sales price per unit is £18, and the current volume of output and sales is 6,000 units.

The company is considering whether to have an improved machine for production. Annual hire costs would be £10,000 and it is expected that the variable cost of production would fall to £6 per unit.

Required

(a) How many units must be produced and sold to achieve the same profit as is currently earned, if the machine is hired?

(b) What would be the annual profit with the machine if output and sales remain at 6,000 units per annum?

Solution

2.6 The current unit contribution is £(18 - (8 + 2)) = £8

		£
(a)	Current contribution (6,000 × £8)	48,000
	Less current fixed costs	40,000
	Current profit	8,000

With the new machine fixed costs will go up by £10,000 to £50,000 per annum. The variable cost per unit will fall to £(6 + 2) = £8, and the contribution per unit will be £10.

	£
Required profit (as currently earned)	8,000
Fixed costs	50,000
Required contribution	58,000
Contribution per unit = £10	
Sales required to earn £8,000 profit = 5,800 units	

(b)	*If sales are 6,000 units*	£	£
	Sales (6,000 × £18)		108,000
	Variable costs: production (6,000 × £6)	36,000	
	sales (6,000 × £2)	12,000	
			48,000
	Contribution (6,000 × £10)		60,000
	Less fixed costs		50,000
	Profit		10,000

	£
Alternative calculation	
Profit at 5,800 units of sale (see (a))	8,000
Contribution from sale of extra 200 units (× £10)	2,000
Profit at 6,000 units of sale	10,000

Sales price and sales volume

2.7 It may be clear by now that, given no change in fixed costs, total profit is maximised when the total contribution is at its maximum. Total contribution in turn depends on the unit contribution and on the sales volume.

2.8 An increase in the sales price will increase unit contribution, but sales volume is likely to fall because fewer customers will be prepared to pay the higher price. A decrease in sales price will reduce the unit contribution, but sales volume may increase because the goods on offer are now cheaper. The optimum combination of sales price and sales volume is arguably the one which maximises total contribution.

Example: maximising profit

2.9 Cymbeline Ltd has developed a new product which is about to be launched on to the market. The variable cost of selling the product is £12 per unit. The marketing department has estimated that at a sales price of £20, annual demand would be 10,000 units.

However, if the sales price is set above £20, sales demand would fall by 500 units for each 50p increase above £20. Similarly, if the price is set below £20, demand would increase by 500 units for each 50p stepped reduction in price below £20.

What is the price which would maximise Cymbeline Ltd's profit in the next year?

Solution

2.10 At a price of £20 per unit, the unit contribution would be £(20 - 12) = £8. Each 50p increase (or decrease) in price would raise (or lower) the unit contribution by 50p. The total contribution is calculated at each sales price by multiplying the unit contribution by the expected sales volume.

Unit price contribution £	*Unit contribution* £	*Sales volume* units	*Total* £
20.00	8.00	10,000	80,000
(a) *Reduce price*			
19.50	7.50	10,500	78,750
19.00	7.00	11,000	77,000
(b) *Increase price*			
20.50	8.50	9,500	80,750
21.00	9.00	9,000	*81,000
21.50	9.50	8,500	80,750
22.00	10.00	8,000	80,000
22.50	10.50	7,500	78,750

*The total contribution would be maximised, and therefore profit maximised, at a sales price of £21 per unit, and sales demand of 9,000 units.

3. BREAKEVEN CHARTS

3.1 The breakeven point can also be determined graphically. A breakeven chart is prepared showing on the horizontal axis the sales (in units or in value) and on the vertical axis values for sales and costs. The following lines are then drawn:

(a) the *sales line*, which starts at the origin and ends at the point which signifies the expected sales;

(b) the *fixed costs* line which runs above and parallel to the horizontal axis, at a point on the vertical axis denoting the total fixed costs;

(c) the *total costs line*, which starts at the point where the fixed costs line meets the vertical axis, and ends at the point which represents, on the horizontal axis, the anticipated sales in units, and on the vertical axis the sum of the total variable cost of those units plus the total fixed costs.

3.2 The breakeven point is the intersection of the sales line and the total cost lines. By projecting the lines horizontally and vertically from this point to the appropriate axes, it is possible to read off the breakeven point in sales units and sales value.

3.3 The number of units represented on the chart by the distance between the breakeven point and the expected (or budgeted) sales, in units, indicates the 'margin of safety'.

Example: breakeven chart

3.4 The budgeted annual output of a factory is 120,000 units. The fixed overhead amounts to £40,000 and the variable costs are 50p per unit. The average sales price is £1 for each unit.

Construct a breakeven chart showing the current breakeven point and profit earned up to the present maximum capacity.

Solution

3.5 *Budget*	£
Sales (120,000 units)	120,000
Variable costs	60,000
Contribution	60,000
Fixed costs	40,000
Profit	20,000

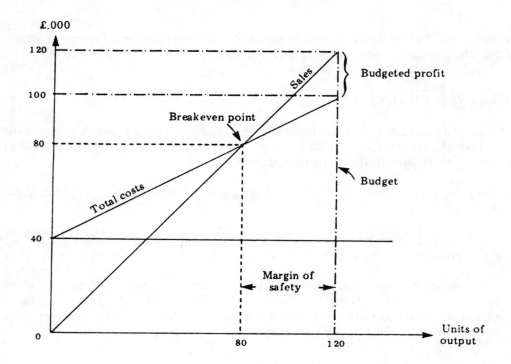

The chart is drawn as follows.

(a)   The Y axis represents money (costs and revenues); and the X axis represents the level of activity, production and sales.

(b)   The fixed costs are a straight line parallel to the Y axis (in our example, at £40,000).

(c)   The variable costs are added 'on top' of fixed costs, to give total costs.

To draw the straight line of costs, only two points need to be plotted and joined up. Perhaps the two most conventional points to plot are total costs at zero output, and total costs at the budgeted output and sales.

(i)   At zero output, costs are equal to the amount of fixed costs only, £40,000, since there are no variable costs;

(ii)   At the budgeted output of 120,000 units costs are:

	£
Fixed costs	40,000
Variable costs (120,000 × 50p)	60,000
Total costs	100,000

Therefore the total costs line can be drawn by joining up the points (0, 4,000) and (120,000, 100,000)

(d)   The revenue 'line' is also drawn by plotting two points and joining them up.

(i)   At zero sales, revenue is nil.
(ii)   At the budgeted output and sales of 120,000 units, revenue is £120,000.

3.6 The breakeven point is where total costs are matched exactly by total revenue. From the chart, this can be seen to occur at output and sales of 80,000 units, when revenue and costs are both £80,000. This breakeven point can be proved mathematically as:

$$\frac{\text{Required contribution = fixed costs}}{\text{Contribution per unit}} = \frac{£40,000}{50\text{p per unit}} = 80,000 \text{ units}$$

3.7 The margin of safety can be seen on the chart as the difference between the budgeted level of activity and the breakeven level.

The value of breakeven charts

3.8 Breakeven charts may be helpful to management in planning the production and marketing of individual products, or the entire product range of their company. A chart gives a visual display of:

(a) how much output needs to be sold to make a profit;

(b) what the likelihood would be of making a loss if actual sales fell short of the budgeted expectations.

3.9   It is necessary to realise the following, however.

    (a)   A breakeven chart is a means of showing, in 'picture' form the cost-volume-profit 'arithmetic' of sales revenues, fixed costs and variable costs. In practice, management is more likely to use the arithmetical techniques of CVP analysis without bothering to draw charts as a visual aid.

    (b)   Although the cost line starts at zero output and can be extended to costs at very high volumes of output and sales, cost accountants would claim that the estimates of fixed plus variable costs are not accurate over the entire range of output, but only within a 'relevant' or 'normal' range of output. It is generally assumed that this relevant range will include both the breakeven point and the budgeted output; therefore for all practical purposes, the breakeven chart is accurate enough.

Alternative presentation

3.10 As an alternative to drawing the fixed cost line first, it is possible to start with the line for variable costs. This is shown below using the graph from the last example.

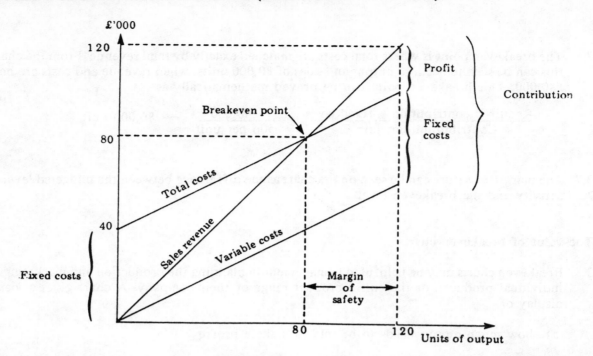

One of the advantages of this presentation is that it shows clearly the contribution for different levels of production (indicated here at 120,000 units, the budgeted level of output), as the 'wedge' shape between the sales revenue line and the variable costs line. At the breakeven point, the contribution equals fixed costs exactly. At levels of output above the breakeven point, the contribution is larger, and not only covers fixed costs, but also leaves a profit. Below the breakeven point, the loss is the amount by which contribution fails to cover fixed costs.

Variations in the use of breakeven charts

3.11 Breakeven charts can be used to show variations in the possible sales price, variable costs or fixed costs. Suppose that a company sells a product which has a variable cost of £2 per unit. Fixed costs are £15,000. It has been estimated that if the sales price is set at £4.40 per unit, the expected sales volume would be 7,500 units; whereas if the sales price is lower, at £4 per unit, the expected sales volume would be 10,000 units.

Required

Draw a breakeven chart to show the budgeted profit, the breakeven point and the margin of safety at each of the possible sales prices.

Solution

3.12 *Workings*

Budgeted costs	Sales price £4.40 per unit		Sales price £4 per unit
	£		£
Fixed costs	15,000		15,000
Variable costs			
(7,500 × £2)	15,000	(10,000 × £2)	20,000
Total costs	30,000		35,000
Budgeted revenue			
(7,500 × £4.40)	33,000	(10,000 × £4)	40,000

160

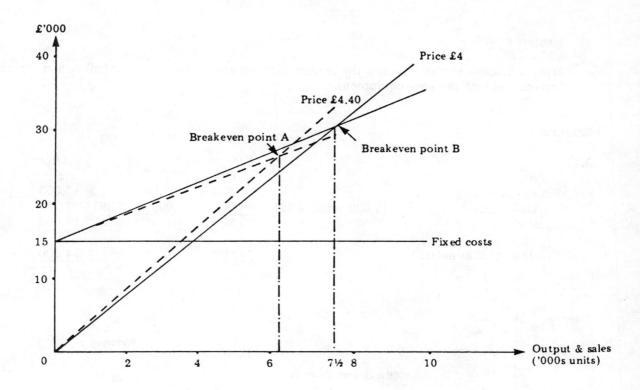

(a) Breakeven point A is the breakeven point at a sales price of £4.40 per unit, which is 6,250 units or £27,500 in costs and revenues.

(check: $\dfrac{\text{Required contribution to break even}}{\text{Contribution per unit}} = \dfrac{£15,000}{£2.40 \text{ per unit}} = 6,250 \text{ units})$

The margin of safety (A) is 7,500 units - 6,250 units = 1,250 units or 16.7% of expected sales.

(b) Breakeven point B is the breakeven point at a sales price of £4 per unit which is 7,500 units or £30,000 in costs and revenues:

(check: $\dfrac{\text{Required contribution to break even}}{\text{Contribution per unit}} = \dfrac{£15,000}{£2 \text{ per unit}} = 7,500 \text{ units})$

The margin of safety (B) = 10,000 units - 7,500 units = 2,500 units or 25% of expected sales.

3.13 Since a price of £4 per unit gives a higher expected profit and a wider margin of safety, this price will probably be preferred even though the breakeven point is higher than at a sales price of £4.40 per unit.

Further example: variation in fixed and variable costs

3.14 Streamline Ltd budgets each year to sell 5,000 units of its product at a price of £4.80 per unit. Until this year, the variable cost of sale per unit had been £2 and fixed costs £9,800 per annum. With the introduction of new electronic equipment, however, variable costs have now been reduced to £1.40 per unit, although annual fixed costs have risen to £12,000.

Required

Draw a breakeven chart to show the breakeven point and budgeted profit before and after the introduction of the new equipment.

Solution

3.15

		Before £		*After* £
Fixed costs		9,800		12,000
Variable costs	(5,000 units × £2)	10,000	(5,000 × £1.40)	7,000
Total costs		19,800		19,000
Revenue (5,000 units)		24,000		24,000

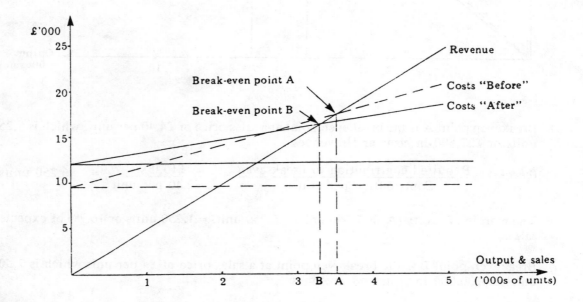

(a)   Before the changeover, annual profit would be budgeted as £4,200 and the breakeven point (A) would be 3,500 units or £16,800.

(b)   After the changeover, annual profit should be £5,000, and the breakeven point (B) will be 3,333.3 units or £16,000.

Final example: variation in variable costs

3.16   Musketeer Ltd purchases its raw materials from a single supplier, and uses 2 metres of the material in each unit of its finished product. Variable costs of the finished product, at output below 5,000 units p.a., are £4.20 per unit, of which £2 is the raw material cost. The supplier offers a discount of 10% on *all* purchases, if Musketeer Ltd buys at least 10,000 metres each year, and a *further* discount of 10 pence per metre on the *additional* purchases only above 16,000 metres per annum. The sales price of the finished product is £6 per unit and fixed costs are £12,000 per annum.

Required

Draw a breakeven chart.

Solution

3.17

	Cost of 5,000 units (10,000 metres) No discount £		Cost of 5,000 units (10,000 metres) 5% discount £
Material costs (× £2)	10,000	(× £1.8)	9,000
Other variable cost (× £2.2)	11,000	(× £2.2)	11,000
Total variable costs	21,000		20,000
Fixed costs	12,000		12,000
Total costs	33,000 (point W)		32,000 (point X)

	Cost of 8,000 units (16,000 metres) £		Cost of 10,000 units (20,000 metres) £
Material costs (£1.8 per unit)	14,400	(8,000 units)	14,400
Material costs (£1.6 per unit)	–	(2,000 units)	3,200
	14,400		17,600
Other variable costs (£2.20)	17,600		22,000
Total variable costs	32,000		39,600
Fixed costs	12,000		12,000
Total costs	44,000 (point Y)		51,600 (point Z)

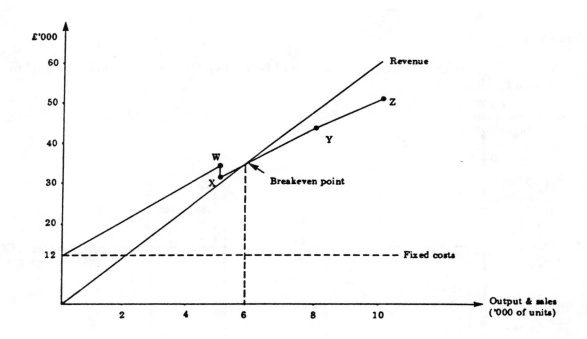

The breakeven point is 6,000 units of sale (£36,000 of costs and revenues)

The PV chart

3.18 The PV (profit/volume) chart is a variation of the breakeven chart which provides a simple illustration of the relationship of costs and profit of sales, and of the margin of safety. A PV chart is constructed as follows.

   (a) The horizontal axis comprises either sales volume in units, or sales value.

   (b) The vertical axis comprises contribution in value, extending above and below the horizontal axis with a zero point at the intersection of the two axis, and the negative section below the horizontal axis representing fixed costs. This means that at zero production, the firm is incurring a loss equal to the fixed costs.

   (c) The profit-volume line is a straight line drawn with its starting point (at zero production) at the intercept on the vertical axis representing the level of fixed cost, and with a gradient of contribution/unit (or the PV ratio of sales value is used rather than units). The PV line will cut the horizontal axis at the breakeven point of sales volume. Any point on the PV line above the horizontal axis represents the profit to the firm (as measured on the vertical axis) for that particular level of sales.

Example: PV chart

3.19 Cabbage Patch Ltd makes and sells a single product which has a variable cost of sale of £5. Fixed costs are £15,000 per annum. The company's management estimates that at a sales price of £8 per unit, sales per annum would be 7,000 units.

   Required

   Construct a PV chart.

Solution

3.20 At sales of 7,000 units, total contribution will be 7,000 × £(8 – 5) = £21,000, and total profit will be £6,000.

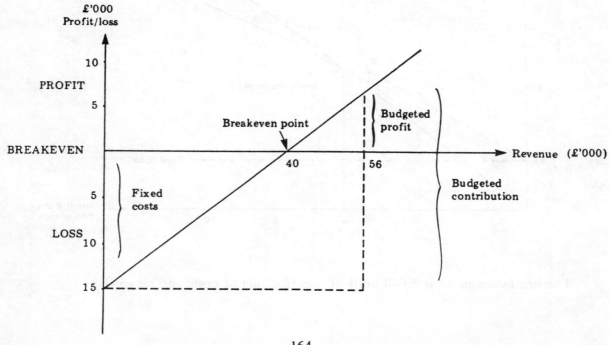

9: COST-VOLUME-PROFIT ANALYSIS (BREAKEVEN ANALYSIS)

Limitations of breakeven charts

3.21 Breakeven charts and breakeven arithmetic should be used carefully. The major limitations of breakeven charts are as follows.

(a) A breakeven chart can apply to one single product or a single mix (ie. fixed proportions) of a group of products. This restricts its usefulness.

(b) It is assumed that fixed costs are the same in total and variable costs are the same per unit at all levels of output. This assumption is a great simplification.

It is important to remember that although a breakeven chart is drawn on the assumption that fixed costs and the variable cost per unit are constant, this is only correct within a normal range or *relevant range of output*. It is generally assumed that both the budgeted output and also the breakeven point of sales lie within this relevant range.

(c) It is assumed that sales prices will be constant at all levels of activity. This may not be true, especially at higher volumes of output, where the price may have to be reduced to win the extra sales.

(d) Production and sales are assumed to be the same; therefore the consequences of any increases in stock levels (when production volumes exceed sales) or 'de-stocking' (when sales volumes exceed production levels) are ignored.

(e) Uncertainty in the estimates of fixed costs and unit variable costs is often ignored in breakeven analysis, and in any case some costs are not always easily categorised or divided into fixed and 'variable'.

3.22 In spite of its limitations, however, breakeven analysis is a useful technique for managers in planning sales prices, the desired sales mix, and profitability. CVP arithmetic should be used with a full awareness of its limitations, but can usefully be applied to provide simple and quick estimates of breakeven volumes or profitability, given variations in sales price, variable and fixed costs and sales volumes, within a 'relevant range' of output/sales volumes.

The problem of the sales mix for CVP analysis

3.23 Perhaps the most serious drawback to CVP analysis is that in a multi-product business, the sales mix is assumed to be constant. Consider the following example.

3.24 Tredgett Ltd sells two products, Widgets and Splodgets, for which the following budgeted information is available.

Sales	*Widgets* 2,000 units		*Splodgets* 6,000 units		*Both products* 8,000 units
	Per unit	Total	Per unit	Total	
	£	£	£	£	£
Revenue	8	16,000	9	54,000	70,000
Variable costs	4	8,000	8	48,000	56,000
Contribution	4	8,000	1	6,000	14,000

Total fixed costs are expected to be £7,000. What is the breakeven point?

165

3.25 One solution might be that by selling 7,000 Splodgets but no Widgets, the company would earn contribution of £1 × 7,000 = £7,000 and so break even. However, in CVP analysis, the sales mix is assumed to be constant, in the budgeted proportions.

Budgeted total contribution	£14,000
Budgeted sales	8,000 units for £70,000 revenue
Budgeted contribution per unit (average per unit)	£1.75
Budgeted (joint) C/S ratio	20%

Breakeven: $\dfrac{\text{Required contribution}}{\text{Contribution per unit}}$ or $\dfrac{\text{Required contribution}}{\text{C/S ratio}}$

$\dfrac{\text{£7,000}}{\text{£1.75}}$ $\dfrac{\text{£7,000}}{20\%}$

4,000 units   or   £35,000

Since there are two different products, the breakeven position would be better expressed in revenue than in units. But the breakeven point of 4,000 units means in this case 1,000 Widgets and 3,000 Splodgets, given a budgeted sales mix ratio of 1:3

4. CONCLUSION

4.1 If you think that you understand the principles of CVP analysis (breakeven analysis), you may be able to work out your own solutions to the following questions. Notice, by the way, that the questions deal with changes in selling prices, sales volumes, variable costs and fixed costs – hence the term 'cost-volume-profit' analysis.

(a) If a company reduces its selling prices by 20% to 80/100 of their former level, but increases its sales volumes by 20% as a consequence of the price reduction, then profits will be unchanged.

True or false?

(b) If a company introduces automation into its work practices, so that:

(i)   unit variable costs fall; but
(ii)   fixed costs increase substantially; so that
(iii) profitability at current sales volumes remains unchanged,

then the decision to automate would have been irrelevant to the future profitability of the company.

True or false?

Solution

4.2 (a)   False.

The problem should be considered in terms of contribution, and it is helpful to use algebra.

Let   the current sales price be   s
      the variable unit cost be   v
      and the sales quantity be   q

Total contribution = Contribution per unit (s–v) × Volume of sales (q)
                    = (s – v)q
                    = qs – qv.

With the reduction in sales price to 0.8s and the increase in sales volume to 1.2q, total contribution would be
                    (0.8s – v)1.2q
                    = 0.96qs – 1.2qv.

Total contribution would be less, because sales revenue would fall (qs to 0.9qs) and total variable costs would rise (qv to 1.2qv).

If you do not follow the algebra, then put actual figures in for the factors in the question and work it through.

(b)   False.

Although total contribution and profits are unchanged at the current sales volume, the automation will have important consequences for any increase or fall in sales demand in the future, because the *ratio of contribution to sales has increased*. An increase in sales volume will now result in a faster rate of increase in profits (just as a fall in sales volume would reduce profitability at a faster rate).

4.3   The purpose of CVP analysis is:

(a)   to provide information to management about cost behaviour, for routine planning and 'one-off' decision-making;

(b)   to determine what volume of sales is needed at any given budgeted sales price in order to break even; and to identify the 'risk' in the budget by measuring the margin of safety;

(c)   to calculate the effects on profit of changes in variable costs, PV ratios, sales price and volume.

4.4   However:

(a)   CVP analysis is only valid within a 'relevant range' of output volumes; and

(b)   it measures profitability, but does not consider the volume of capital employed to achieve such profits (and so ignores Return on Capital Employed);

(c)   is subject to certain other limitations described earlier in this chapter.

TEST YOUR KNOWLEDGE
The numbers in brackets refer to paragraphs of this chapter

1   If fixed costs are £200,000 and contribution per unit is £4, what is the breakeven point? (see below)

2   If target profits are £10,000 and fixed costs are £90,000, what is target contribution? (see below)

3   Variable costs of Product X are £15 and its sale price is £20. What is the PV ratio? (see below)

4   Product Y has a PV ratio of 25%. If fixed costs are £100,000, what is the breakeven point? (see below)

5   Budgeted sales revenue of Product Z is £9,000 and breakeven sales revenue is £6,000. What is the margin of safety? (see below)

6   Describe two ways of presenting a breakeven chart. (3.1, 3.10)

7   Why are breakeven charts of limited practical importance? (3.9)

8   What is a PV chart? (3.18)

9   Product Omega has variable costs per unit of £10. Demand at a sales price of £15 per unit would be 4,000 pa and 3,600 at £16 per unit. Which sales price would maximise profit? (see below)

Now try question 9 at the end of the text

Solutions

1   50,000 units.

2   £100,000

3    $\dfrac{20 - 15}{20} = 25\%$

4    $\dfrac{£100,000}{0.25} = £400,000$

5   £3,000 or $33\frac{1}{3}\%$

9

	£15/unit	£16/unit
	£	£
Revenue	60,000	57,600
Variable costs	(40,000)	(36,000)
	20,000	21,600

A sales price of £16 per unit would maximise profit.

Chapter 10

PRICING DECISIONS

This chapter covers the following topics.

1. Pricing decisions
2. Marginal cost plus pricing
3. Other cost-based pricing models
4. A demand-based approach
5. Pricing decisions and inflation
6. Transfer pricing

1. PRICING DECISIONS

1.1 The ability to fix the price of a product or service is something which is frequently determined by the marketing manager. Pricing decisions must take account of a range of factors, including demand and cost. We will consider a demand-based approach to pricing later in this chapter but for now we will concentrate on cost. Pricing decisions must have some regard for cost, and the selling price of a product should exceed its average unit cost in order to make a profit. In the long term, the selling cost of products must exceed the average unit cost because without this equation being satisfied a business will ultimately fail. There are, of course, short term situations where pricing is deliberately kept low, to the extent that the finance department will start feeling that a product is loss making. 'Loss leaders' are, however, justified in the sense that they are designed to attract other revenues. Any newsagent will tell you that he makes little or no profit from the sale of cigarettes but once in the shop people will purchase items such as chocolate and newspapers on impulse and these are extremely profitable items.

Full cost plus pricing

1.2 A 'traditional' approach to pricing products is *full cost plus pricing*, whereby the sales price is determined by calculating the full cost of the product and then adding a percentage mark-up for profit. The term *target pricing* is sometimes used, which means setting a price so as to achieve a target profit or return on capital employed. Target pricing is therefore quite rigid, in the sense that a fixed, predetermined mark-up is added to cost so as to achieve the targeted profit or return.

1.3 In full cost plus pricing, the full cost may be a fully absorbed *production* cost only, or it may include some absorbed administration, selling and distribution overhead. The full cost might also include some *opportunity costs* as well, such as the opportunity cost of a production resource that is in short supply, so that 'full cost' need not merely be the cost as it might be established in the historical cost-based accounts.

1.4 A business might have an idea of the percentage profit margin it would like to earn and so might decide on an average profit mark-up as a general guideline for pricing decisions. This would be particularly useful for businesses that carry out a large amount of contract work or jobbing work, for which individual job or contract prices must be quoted regularly to prospective customers. However, the percentage profit mark-up does not have to be rigid and fixed, but can be varied to suit the circumstances. In particular, the percentage mark-up can be varied to suit demand conditions in the market.

1.5 Full cost pricing has been frequently condemned, but businessmen persist in a belief that full cost plus pricing is the correct way to fix selling prices.

1.6 The cost plus approach to pricing is commonly used in practice, but varying the size of the profit mark-up gives the pricing decisions much-needed flexibility so as to adapt to demand conditions.

1.7 The basic principles and some of the practical problems with full cost plus pricing are illustrated in the following example. You might wish to attempt your own solution before reading ours.

Example: full cost plus pricing

1.8 Slidescale Ltd is about to quote a price for a contract which it is quite keen to win, provided that the price gives a reasonable profit on the work. If the company wins the contract, there is a good chance that a number of repeat orders will be made by the same customer within the next 18 months to two years.

The estimated costs of the contract would be as follows.

	£
Direct labour	2,500
Direct materials	6,000
Hire of equipment	500
Subcontractors' charges	1,200
Other direct expenses	300
Overheads	7,500
	18,000

The company sets is prices by adding a percentage mark-up for profit on to the full estimated cost of the contact, and the mark-up on its work for other customers tends to vary between 10% and 18%.

What price should Slidescale quote for this particular contract?

Solution

1.9 There is really only one issue involved in this example, namely the size of the profit mark-up. The percentage profit margin is variable and presumably determined by management judgement, which in turn will be influenced by the following:

(a) the wish to win the contract, perhaps in the face of competition from rival companies;

(b)   the likelihood of repeat orders and so further profits in the future; and

(c)   whether the company has idle capacity or a full order book. When the company is busy, it can opt to quote higher prices, so that the profit margins on work that it obtains will be higher.

1.10 There is no 'correct' price, but the following points could be made.

(a)   The price should exceed full cost. Companies must operate at a profit to survive and this means earning revenue that more than covers direct costs and a share of overheads. Only in exceptional circumstances would a price below full cost (but above opportunity costs) be offered.

(b)   The company must make a judgement about demand conditions (competition, probability of repeat orders), the company's workload and order book, and even the nature of the work itself (for example is it likely to be easy or difficult to do properly? Is the workforce skilled enough to do it well or does it involve work below their usual standard of skill and quality?)

1.11 In this example, if we were to assume that Slidescale Ltd had some spare capacity and was quite keen to win the contract, a profit margin of around 10% might be recommended, giving a price of 110% × £18,000 = £19,800. But we should not ignore the other contract that is being offered. If the size of the repeat is much larger and we feel that it is important to obtain it, then we may be tempted to reduce our price still further.

Problems with full cost plus pricing

1.12 There are several serious problems with relying on a full cost approach to pricing, some of which have already been mentioned. These are as follows.

(a)   The need to adjust prices to market and demand conditions.

(b)   Budgeting output volume, which is a key factor in the fixed overhead absorption rate.

(c)   Selecting a suitable basis for overhead absorption, especially where a business produces more than one product.

1.13 Perhaps the most important criticism of cost plus pricing is that it fails to recognise that since sales demand may be determined by the sales price, *there will be a profit-maximising combination of price and demand.* A cost plus based approach to pricing will be most unlikely, except by coincidence of luck, to arrive at the profit-maximising price.

Example: cost plus pricing

1.14 Tiger Ltd has budgeted to make 50,000 units of its product, timm. The variable cost of a timm is £5 and annual fixed costs are expected to be £150,000.

The financial director of Tiger Ltd has suggested that a profit margin of 25% on full cost should be charged for every product sold.

The marketing director has challenged the wisdom of this suggestion, and has produced the following estimates of sales demand for timms.

Price per unit £	Demand units
9	42,000
10	38,000
11	35,000
12	32,000
13	27,000

Required

(a)   What would be the profit for the year if a cost plus price were charged with a 25% profit mark-up?

(b)   What would be the profit for the year if a profit-maximising price were charged?

Assume in both (a) and (b) that 50,000 units of timm are produced regardless of sales volume.

Solution

1.15   The full cost per unit is £5 variable cost plus £3 fixed costs = £8 in total. A 25% mark-up on this cost gives a selling price of £10 per unit so that sales demand would be 38,000 units. (Production is given as 50,000 units). The profit, using absorption costing to measure it, would be as follows.

	£	£
Sales		380,000
Cost of production (50,000 units)		
Variable (50,000 × £5)	250,000	
Fixed (50,000 × £3)	150,000	
	400,000	
Less increase in stocks (12,000 units × £8)	(96,000)	
Cost of sales		304,000
Profit		76,000

1.16   Profit using variable costing instead of absorption costing, so that closing stock is valued at marginal cost (£5) and fixed overhead costs are written off in the period in which they occur, would be as follows.

	£
Contribution (38,000 × £(10 − 5))	190,000
Fixed costs	150,000
Profit	40,000

Since the company cannot go on indefinitely producing an output volume in excess of sales volume, this profit figure is more indicative of the profitability of timms in the longer term.

1.17   A *profit-maximising price* is one which gives the greatest net (relevant) cash flow which, in this case, is the contribution-maximising price.

Price	Unit contribution	Demand	Total contribution
£	£	units	£
9	4	42,000	168,000
10	5	38,000	190,000
11	6	35,000	210,000
12	7	32,000	224,000
13	8	27,000	216,000

The profit maximising price is £12, with annual sales demand of 32,000 units. However, in year 1, if production is 50,000 units and sales only 32,000 units, profit would be as follows.

(a) *Absorption costing*   £

Sales (32,000 × £12)	384,000
Increase in stocks (18,000 units × £8)	144,000
	528,000
Costs of production	400,000
Profit	128,000

(b) *Variable costing*

Contribution	224,000
Fixed costs	150,000
Profit	74,000

This profit figure in (b) is more indicative of the longer-term profitability of timms, if demand conditions remain the same in the future.

1.18 Full cost pricing can be criticised for a number of other shortcomings. Where products are produced by the company we need to know the level of production activity necessary to meet the needs of the market and the full costs will be assessed accordingly. But we know how difficult it is to budget accurately and a sudden slump in demand will result in difficulties in achieving the overall profit levels that were budgeted because the overhead absorption rate (see chapter on absorption costing) will now under recover the actual costs which will be incurred. We would not need to raise price on a revised sales volume to achieve the necessary level of profits, but this may lower the impact of a further fall in demand.

1.19 Another criticism arises when a company produces more than one product. The accountants will have to allocate the fixed costs of production to the different products. This is usually a fairly subjective allocation and will result in the market profitability of each product being almost interdependent. If demand varies for each product during the year we may be tempted to alter the cost plus price. However, this may in turn change demand. Our price is now being determined by internal factors and not by market conditions.

1.20 Further objections to full cost plus pricing can be listed as follows.

(a) *It fails to allow for competition.* A company may need to match the prices of rival firms when these take a price-cutting (or price-raising) initiative.

(b)　A full cost plus price is a means of ensuring that in the long run, a company succeeds in covering all its fixed costs and making a profit out of revenue earned. However, *in the short term,* it is inflexible.

　　(i)　A firm tendering for a contract may quote a cost-plus price that results in the contract going elsewhere, although a lower price would have been sufficient to cover all incremental costs and opportunity costs. 'Costing tends to concentrate on expenditures of a given work programme. It seems to ignore the alternatives open to the enterprise, or to assume that the alternative is idleness. Yet displaced opportunities are vital in making a business decision which might indeed be defined as the process of selecting among alternatives.' *(Baxter and Oxenfeldt)*

　　(ii)　In the short term, rapidly-changing environmental factors might dictate the need for lower (or higher) prices than long-term considerations would indicate. Since the sales price is part of the marketing/sales mix of the company's policy, rigid price setting is too restrictive for marketing management.

1.21　The advantages of full cost plus pricing are as follows.

(a)　Since the size of the profit margin can be varied at management's discretion, a price in excess of full cost should ensure that a company working at normal capacity will cover all its fixed costs and make a profit. Companies may benefit from cost plus pricing in the following circumstances.

　　(i)　If they carry out large contracts which must make a sufficient profit margin to cover a fair share of fixed costs.

　　(ii)　If the company must justify their prices to potential customers (for example for government contracts).

　　(iii)　If the company finds it difficult to estimate expected demand at different sales prices.

(b)　It is a simple, quick and cheap method of pricing.

2.　MARGINAL COST PLUS PRICING

2.1　Instead of pricing products or services by adding a profit margin on to *full* cost, a business might add a profit margin on to *marginal* cost (either the marginal cost of production or else the marginal cost of sales). This is sometimes called 'mark-up' pricing, which is another form of target pricing.

2.2　In practice, mark-up pricing is used in businesses where there is a readily-identifiable basic variable cost. Retail industries are the most obvious example, and it is quite common for the prices of goods in shops to be fixed by adding a mark-up (20% or 33.3%, say) to the purchase cost. For example, a department store might buy in items of pottery at £3 each, add a mark-up of one-third and resell the items at £4.

2.3 There are, of course, drawbacks to marginal cost plus pricing.

    (a) Although the size of the mark-up can be varied in accordance with demand conditions, it is not a method of pricing which ensures that sufficient attention is paid to demand conditions, competitors' prices and profit maximisation.

    (b) It ignores fixed overheads in the pricing decision, but the sales price must be sufficiently high to ensure that a profit is made after covering fixed costs. Pricing decisions cannot ignore fixed costs altogether.

3. OTHER COST-BASED PRICING MODELS

3.1 Other approaches to pricing decisions can be taken. Many of these are demand-oriented, but some are cost-based. Two cost-based approaches that are worth considering further are minimum pricing and limiting factor pricing.

Minimum prices

3.2 A minimum price is the price that would have to be charged so as to just cover the incremental costs of producing and selling the item and the opportunity costs of the resources consumed.

A minimum price would leave the business no better or worse off than if it did not sell the item.

Minimum pricing, based on relevant costs, might be used as a starting point for setting prices for special orders from customers, for which a 'standard' price is not available.

3.3 Two essential points to understand immediately about a minimum price are as follows.

    (a) It is based on relevant costs. Relevant costs have already been described in a previous chapter.

    (b) It is unlikely that a minimum price would actually be charged because if it were, it would not provide the business with any incremental profit. However, the minimum price for an item shows the following.

        (i) An absolute minimum below which the price should not be set.

        (ii) The incremental profit that would be obtained from any price that is actually charged in excess of the minimum. For example, if the minimum price is £200 and the actual price charged is £240, the incremental profit on the sale would be £40.

3.4 If there are no scarce resources and a company has spare capacity, the minimum price of a product would be an amount which equals the incremental costs of making it. Any price in excess of this minimum would provide an incremental contribution towards profit. If there are scarce resources and a company makes more than one product, minimum prices would include an allowance for the *opportunity cost* of using the scarce resources. This form of pricing is often used in distress pricing when demand is very low.

Limiting factor pricing

3.5 Another approach to pricing might be taken when a business is working at full capacity, and is restricted by a shortage of resources from expanding its output further. By deciding what target profit it would like to earn, it could establish a mark-up per unit of limiting factor.

3.6 For example, suppose that Serflike Services Ltd provides a window cleaning service to offices and factories. Business is brisk but the company is restricted from expanding its activities further by a shortage of window cleaners. The workforce consists of 12 window cleaners, each of whom works a 35 hour week. They are paid £4 per hour. Variable expenses are £0.50 per hour. Fixed costs are £5,000 per week.

The company wishes to make a contribution of at least £15 per hour.

3.7 The minimum charge per hour for window cleaning would then be as follows.

	£ per hour
Direct wages	4.0
Variable expenses	0.5
Contribution	15.0
Charge per hour	19.5

The company has a total workforce capacity of (12 x 35) 420 man hours per week, and so total contribution would be £6,300 per week, leaving a profit, after fixed costs, of £1,300 per week.

Learning curves

3.8 The Boston Consulting Group research (in the USA) has identified substantial empirical evidence to support the theory that costs are related to the learning or experience curve.

The implications of the learning curve for pricing are as follows.

(a) New products often hold their price in their early stages of life, while costs are going down, creating increasing profit margins.

(b) A policy of reducing prices as costs fall can help a company to win a dominant share of the market and pursue a strategy of overall cost leadership.

3.9 The calculation of a learning curve and a discussion about the effect of the learning curve or costing and pricing have occurred in this examination. We will therefore examine the mechanics of the learning curve calculation and look at some of its relevance and limitations. As we do so, you should bear in mind the relationship with pricing given in Paragraph 3.8.

3.10 The predominant assumption so far has been that total costs can be estimated using a straight-line formula where total cost = fixed costs + (variable cost x number of units produced). This might not always be the case and, sometimes, total costs might be *non-linear*. One cause of non-linear costs is the learning curve phenomenon.

3.11 Whenever an individual starts a job which is fairly repetitive in nature, and provided that his speed of working is not dictated to him by the speed of machinery (such as on a production line), he is likely to become more confident and knowledgeable about the work as he gains experience, to become more efficient, and to do the work more quickly. Eventually, however, when he has acquired enough experience, there will be nothing more for him to learn, and so the learning process will stop.

3.12 In a large work force, with a regular labour turnover, there will be a mix of experienced people and people who are still gaining experience, but on average, the standard level of efficiency for the work force as a whole will remain roughly the same over time.

3.13 In some industries and in some situations, however, the *work force as a whole* may gain experience in certain work, and become more efficient as it gains experience. Learning curve theory applies to these situations, where the work force as a whole improves in efficiency with experience.

3.14 This speeding up of a job with repeated performance is known as the learning effect or learning curve effect, and the reduction in the required direct labour time for a job may be quantified.

3.15 'Where it occurs, our knowledge of its effects can supply management with much better information for a variety of planning and control applications, including production scheduling, budgeting, setting standard costs and analysing variances, pricing and a host of special decisions.' (Louderback and Hirsch *Cost Accounting: Accumulation, Analysis and Use*)

Where does learning curve theory apply?

3.16 Learning curve theory was first developed in the United States aircraft industry in the 1920s and 1930s. Since then, the learning curve concept has been extended to other industries and it has been found that the time required to do most tasks of a repetitive nature gets shorter as the tasks are done more and experience in doing them is built up. The concept of a learning curve or 'experience curve' has been extended to non-production activities, such as marketing efforts.

3.17 Direct labour time should be expected to get shorter, with experience, in the production of items *which are made largely by labour effort rather than by a highly mechanised process,* and which are either:

(a) relatively short-lived products with a high rate of obsolescence, because the learning process does not continue indefinitely and so new products must be continually introduced if the learning curve phenomenon is to be a permanent feature of the industry; or

(b) products which are complex and made in small quantities for special orders.

3.18 'The learning effect is not an automatic natural phenomenon. Not all production processes will show increased efficiency, and amongst those that do, the differences in learning rates will be substantial....In general, the higher the labour content, the more opportunity for learning. Highly-automated processes offer relatively little opportunity for improvement....A high rate of learning (say, a 70% or so learning curve) might not be sustainable for long because it partly reflects rushing into production and getting some of the bugs out, as well as the learning effect.' (Louderback and Hirsch).

3.19 You should note that the learning curve effect applies to a group of workers doing the same job repetitively with the same equipment and machinery. Improvements in efficiency from better machinery or better materials and so on would *not* be the result of the learning effect.

The learning rate

3.20 The cumulative average time per unit produced is assumed to fall by a constant percentage every time total output of the product doubles.

By cumulative average time, we mean the *average time per unit for all units produced so far*, back to and including the first unit made.

The 80% learning curve

3.21 An 80% learning curve will be used for illustration, since 80% appears to be a learning factor which commonly applies.

Where an 80% learning effect occurs, the *cumulative average time required* per unit of output is reduced to 80% of the previous cumulative average time when output is *doubled*.

(The doubling of output is an important feature of the learning curve measurement. With a 70% learning curve, the cumulative average time per unit of output will fall to 70% of what it was before, every time output is doubled).

3.22 It is also *essential* to note that the cumulative average time per unit is the average time for all units made to date.

3.23 If, for example, the first unit of output requires 100 hours and an 80% learning curve applies, the production times would be:

Number of units produced	Cumulative avg time required per unit hours		Total time required hours		Incremental time for additional unit hours	
1		100.0	(× 1)	100.0		
2*	(80%)	80.0	(× 2)	160.0	60.0	(for 1 *extra unit)
4*	(80%)	64.0	(× 4)	256.0	96.0	(for 2 extra units)
8*	(80%)	51.2	(× 8)	409.6	153.6	(for 4 extra units)

* Output is being doubled each time.

3.24 This effect can be shown in a graph, or learning curve either for

    (a)   unit times; or

    (b)   cumulative total times or costs.

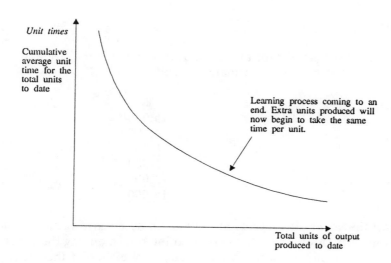

3.25 The curve becomes horizontal once a sufficient number of units have been produced - ie the learning effect is lost and production time should become a constant standard, to which a standard efficiency rate may be applied.

The formula for this learning curve is $y = ax^b$
where   y is the cumulative average time per unit
                  x is the number of units made so far
                  a is the time for the first unit
                  b is the learning factor. With an 80% learning curve, $b = -0.322$.

(*Note:* 'b' may be taken from the logarithm of 0.8.)

Using learning curve theory

3.26 Learning curve theory can be used:

    (a)   to calculate the marginal (incremental) cost of making extra units of a product;

    (b)   to quote selling prices for a contract, where prices are calculated at cost plus a percentage mark-up for profit;

    (c)   to prepare realistic production budgets;

    (d)   to compare budgeted and actual costs, and report cost variances.

3.27 When a company operates in a competitive industry, where contracts are won by the companies who quote the best prices and yet where quoted prices must be high enough to give the contractor a reasonable profit, an awareness of the learning curve can make all the difference between winning contracts and losing them, or between making profits and selling at a loss-making price.

Example: learning curve

3.28 Captain Kitts Ltd has designed a new type of sailing boat, for which the cost and sales price of the first boat to be produced has been estimated as follows.

	£
Materials	5,000
Labour (800 hrs × £5 per hr)	4,000
Overhead (150% of labour cost)	6,000
	15,000
Profit mark-up (20%)	3,000
Sales price	18,000

It is planned to sell all the yachts at full cost plus 20%. An 80% learning curve is expected to apply to the production work. A customer has expressed interest in buying the yacht, but thinks £18,000 is too high a price to pay. He might want to buy 2, or even 4 of the yachts during the next six months.

He has asked the following questions.

(a) If he paid £18,000 for the first yacht, what price would he have to pay later for a second yacht?

(b) Could Captain Kitts Ltd quote the same unit price for two yachts, if the customer ordered two at the same time?

(c) If the customer bought two yachts now at one price, what would be the price per unit for a third and a fourth yacht, if he ordered them separately later on?

(d) Could Captain Kitts Ltd quote a single unit price for:

(i) four yachts;
(ii) eight yachts;

if they were all ordered now.

Assuming that there are no other prospective customers for the yacht, how would these questions be answered?

Solution

3.29 Workings

Number of yachts		Cumulative average time per yacht hours		Total time for all yachts to date hours		Incremental time for additional yachts hours
1		800		800.0		-
2	(× 80%)	640	(× 2)	1,280.0	(1,280 - 800)	480.0
4	(× 80%)	512	(× 4)	2,048.0	(2,048 - 1,280)	768.0
8	(× 80%)	409.6	(× 8)	3,276.8	(3,276.8 - 2,048)	1,228.8

(a) *Separate price for a second yacht*

	£
Materials	5,000
Labour (480 hrs × £5)	2,400
Overhead (150% of labour cost)	3,600
Total cost	11,000
Profit (20%)	2,200
Sales price	13,200

(b) *A single price for the first two yachts*

	£
Materials cost for two yachts	10,000
Labour (1,280 hrs × £5)	6,400
Overhead (150% of labour cost)	9,600
Total cost for two yachts	26,000
Profit (20%)	5,200
Total sales price for two yachts	31,200
Price per yacht (÷2)	15,600

(c) *A price for the third and fourth yachts*

	£
Materials cost for two yachts	10,000
Labour (768 hours × £5)	3,840
Overhead (150% of labour cost)	5,760
Total cost	19,600
Profit (20%)	3,920
Total sales price for two yachts	23,520
Price per yacht (÷2)	11,760

(d) *A price for the first four yachts together and for the first eight yachts together*

		First four yachts £		First eight yachts £
Materials		20,000		40,000
Labour	(2,048 hrs)	10,240	(3,276.8 hrs)	16,384
Overhead (150% of labour cost)		15,360		24,576
Total cost		45,600		80,960
Profit (20%)		9,120		16,192
Total sales price		54,720		97,152
Price per yacht	(÷ 4)	13,680	(÷ 8)	12,144

10: PRICING DECISIONS

Example: 90% learning curve

3.30 Try your own solution to this example.

Bortamord Ltd anticipates that a 90% learning curve will apply to the production of a new item. The first item will cost £2,000 in materials, and will take 500 labour hours. The cost per hour for labour and variable overhead is £5.

Required

Calculate the total cost for the first unit and for the first 8 units.

Solution

3.31

Units		Cumulative average time per unit		Total time for all units produced to date
			hours	*hours*
1			500	500
(double) 2	(90%)		450	
(double) 4	(90%)		405	
(double) 8	(90%)		364.5	(× 8) 2,916

	Cost of 1st unit		Cost of 1st 8 units
	£		£
Materials	2,000		16,000
Labour and variable overhead			
(500 hours)	2,500	(2,916 hours)	14,580
	4,500		30,580
Average cost/unit	4,500		3,822.5

What costs are affected by the learning curve?

3.32 Direct labour time and costs are obviously affected by the learning curve effect and output capacity increases as the workforce gains experience.

Variable overhead costs will also be affected by the learning effect, but only to the extent that variable overheads vary with direct labour hours worked.

Materials costs are usually unaffected by learning among the workforce, although it is conceivable that materials handling might improve, and so wastage costs be reduced.

The relevance of learning curve effects

3.33 You should be well aware by now that where the learning curve effect applies, there are important consequences for:

(a) the direct labour budget;

(b) variable overheads;

(c) setting standard costs (there cannot be a regular standard time until the learning effect has worn off, unless a separate standard (budget) is estimated for each job);

(d) pricing decisions;

(e) output capacity.

3.34 The further considerations that should be borne in mind are as follows.

(a) *Sales projections, advertising expenditure and delivery date commitments.* Identifying a learning curve effect should allow an organisation to plan its advertising and delivery schedules to coincide with expected production schedules. Production capacity obviously affects sales capacity and sales projections.

(b) *Budgeting with standard costs.* Companies that use standard costing for much of their production output cannot apply standard times to output where a learning effect is taking place. This problem can be overcome in practice by:

   (i) establishing standard times for output, once the learning effect has worn off or become insignificant; and

   (ii) introducing a supplementary cost or 'launching cost' budget for the product for the duration of the learning period.

(c) *Cash budgets.* Since the learning effect reduces unit variable costs as more units are produced, it should be allowed for in cash flow projections.

(d) *Work scheduling and overtime decisions.* To take full advantage of the learning effect, idle production time should be avoided and work scheduling/overtime decisions should pay regard to the expected learning effect.

(e) *Pay.* Where the workforce is paid a productivity bonus, the time needed to learn a new production process should be allowed for in calculating the bonus for a period. When learning is still taking place, it would be unreasonable to compare actual times with the standard times that ought eventually to be achieved when the learning effect wears off.

(f) *Recruiting new labour.* When a company plans to take on new labour to help with increasing production, the learning curve assumption will have to be reviewed. For example, in 1980/81 the Lockheed Company took on an extra 11,000 staff to help with the production of the Tristar aircraft and this large influx of inexperienced labour led to a *fall* in productivity of 50%.

(g) *Market share.* The significance of the learning curve is that by increasing its share of the market, a company can benefit from shop-floor, managerial and technological 'learning' to achieve economies of scale.

Limitations of learning curve theory

3.35 The limited use of learning curve theory is due to several factors.

(a) The learning curve phenomenon is not always present. There ought to be evidence of a learning curve effect in previous experience with similar work before it can be assumed that a learning rate can be applied to estimating production times and costs for new items of production.

(b) It assumes stable conditions at work (for example of the labour force and labour mix) which will enable learning to take place. This is not always practicable (say because of labour turnover).

(c) It must also assume a certain degree of motivation amongst employees.

(d) Breaks between repeating production of an item must not be too long, or workers will 'forget' and the learning process would have to begin all over again.

(e) It might be difficult to obtain enough accurate data to decide what the learning curve is.

(f) There will be a cessation to learning eventually, once the job has been repeated often enough.

(g) The trade unions might not readily agree to a gradual reduction in production times per unit, in which case management might try to establish a low standard time per unit from the outset, and accept adverse efficiency variances until the learning effect has taken place.

(h) If the work force is paid a productivity bonus, there might be dissatisfaction amongst employees at the gradual reduction in standard times for production, because this might appear to be a threat to the size of the bonuses they earn.

(i) Production techniques might change, or product design alterations might be made, so that it takes a long time for a 'standard' production method to emerge, to which a learning effect will apply.

4.   A DEMAND-BASED APPROACH

4.1 We have now looked at a variety of cost-based approaches to pricing, making the point that they have the inherent weakness of not fully recognising demand factors. In practice, businesses do seem to use cost-based pricing, with adjustments made to allow for demand factors. However, we have not yet considered demand-based approaches to pricing.

4.2 A difficulty with a demand-based approach to pricing is to draw a balance between theory and practice.

(a) Price theory or demand theory is based on the idea that a connection can be made between price, quantity demanded and sold, and total revenue. Demand varies with price, and so if an estimate can be made of demand at different price levels, it should be possible to derive either a profit-maximising price or a revenue-maximising price.

The theory of demand cannot be applied in practice, however, unless realistic estimates of demand at different price levels can be made.

(b) In practice, businesses might not make estimates of demand at different price levels, but they might still make pricing decisions on the basis of demand conditions and competition in the market. The marketing department should be able to deduce the demand levels from research and past experience.

4.3 Some larger organisations go to considerable effort to estimate the demand for their products or services at differing price levels. For example a large transport authority such as the London Regional Transport Authority might be considering an increase in bus fares or underground fares.

The effect on total revenues and profit of the fares increase could be estimated from a knowledge of the demand for transport services at different price levels. If an increase in the price per ticket caused a large fall in demand then total revenues and profits would fall, whereas a fares increase when demand does not vary much with price movements would boost total revenue, and since a transport authority's costs are largely fixed, this would probably boost total profits too.

4.4 Many businesses enjoy a monopoly position in their market or something akin to a monopoly position, even in a competitive market. This is because they develop a unique marketing mix, for example a unique combination of price and quality, or a monopoly in a localised area. The significance of a monopoly situation is as follows.

(a) The business does not have to 'follow the market' on price, it is not a 'price-taker', but has more choice and flexibility in the prices it sets.

   (i) At higher prices, demand for its products or services will be less.
   (ii) At lower prices, demand for its products or services will be higher.

(b) There will be a selling price at which the business can maximise its profits.

Exercise

Moose Ltd sells a product which has a variable cost of £8 per unit. The sales demand at the current sales price of £14 is 3,000 units. It has been estimated by the marketing department that the sales volume would fall by 100 units for each addition of 25 pence to the sales price.

Required

Is the current price of £14 the optimal price which maximises contribution?

Solution

Sales price £	Unit contribution £	Sales volume units	Total contribution £
13.00	5.00	3,400	17,000
13.25	5.25	3,300	17,325
13.50	5.50	3,200	17,600
13.75	5.75	3,100	17,825
14.00	6.00	3,000	18,000
14.25	6.25	2,900	18,125
14.50	6.50	2,800	18,200
14.75	6.75	2,700	18,225*
15.00	7.00	2,600	18,200

* Contribution would be maximised at a price of £14.75, and sales of 2,700 units.

The current price is not optimal.

Competitors' prices

4.5 Our analysis of the demand-based approach to pricing has so far avoided any mention of the prices charged by competitors for the same or similar products. When competitors sell exactly the same product in the same market, price differences are likely to have a significant effect on demand.

4.6 This is the case with oil companies and the price of petrol at filling stations: different companies sell the same product and so within a local area, the prices charged at each station (whether BP, Shell, Esso or Texaco) will be much the same. If they were not, customers would go to the cheapest place to buy.

4.7 When companies sell similar products which are not exactly identical, or where the geographical location of the sales point is of some significance, there is more scope for charging different prices. Even so, what competitors charge cannot be ignored altogether. Price differences can be achieved in a number of ways.

(a) *Through product quality*. A product or service of a higher quality than the competition can be priced higher, provided that customers perceive the quality.

(b) *Through design differences*. Similar products can vary in design and features. Motor cars are an obvious example, and fashion goods another.

(c) *Through geographical location*. Petrol prices were referred to earlier: prices tend to vary between local markets. Similarly, the prices of crossing the Channel by ferry might be varied between different ports of departure (Dover, Folkestone and so on).

(d) *Through brand loyalty*. Some companies might promote a brand, largely through advertising, and build up a consumer following. Customers loyal to the brand will buy goods with the brand name in preference to rival brands, or non-branded goods, even at a higher price.

5. PRICING DECISIONS AND INFLATION

5.1 An organisation should recognise the effects of inflation on its pricing decisions. When its costs are rising, it must try to ensure that its prices are increased sufficiently and regularly enough to make an adequate profit (in the case of a profit-making concern) or to cover its costs (in the case of non-profit making activities where it is only necessary to break even).

5.2 There are several simple guidelines to pricing review during a period of inflation.

(a) *Fixed price long-term contracts should be avoided*. Long term contracts should include a price variation clause, which allows the supplier to raise the contract price to cover any escalation in his costs due to inflation.

A long term contract might have a fixed price which includes a safety margin for cost inflation, but estimating inflation is often a matter of guesswork, and this approach to contract pricing is not recommended.

(b) When one organisation sets its prices, it should decide how long it will be until the next price review. If prices are published in price lists or brochures and circulars, this can be important.

(c) *Prices should be reviewed regularly.* The more rapid the rate of inflation becomes, the more frequent the price reviews ought to be.

(d) An organisation cannot assume that it can pass on its cost increases to its customers by raising prices to cover the extra costs (and the extra return required on the additional cost of capital invested).

(i) In a competitive market, competitors might opt to trim their profit margins and try to control costs.

(ii) Customers might resist higher prices, and so price increases would result in some fall in demand.

(e) When prices are reviewed, management must recognise that costs are likely to continue to rise, and so the new price levels ought to anticipate *future* cost increases up to the time of the next price review, not just current cost levels.

6. TRANSFER PRICING

6.1 So far in this chapter we have concentrated on pricing to third parties. This is in essence a business decision to determine how to maximise revenues and profitability in the long term, although there may be short term constraints as well. One element of pricing has not been discussed so far and that is pricing of goods and services within the company or within a group of companies. This subject is important in assessing value added to a product or service, in motivation of segments of the workforce and in the measurement of the use of assets in producing the final product. Hence it is equally important to pricing decisions as it is to budgeting, motivation and cost control, performance evaluation and the achievement of the corporate objective.

6.2 It is particularly important in the case of transferred goods that a proper transfer price should be charged. A proper system of accounting demands that goods should be costed as they progress through work in progress to finished goods and so the need for a transfer cost or transfer price should be clear.

6.3 A transfer price is defined as 'a price related to goods or other services transferred from one process or department to another or from one member of a group to another. The extent to which costs and profit are covered by the price is a matter of policy'.

6.4 A transfer price may be based upon:

(a) marginal cost;
(b) full cost;
(c) market price (perhaps with a small deduction for cost savings);
(d) negotiated price.

6.5 A transfer based on cost might be at marginal cost or full cost (with no profit or contribution margin) but in a profit centre system of divisionalisation it is more likely to be a price based on marginal cost or full cost plus a margin for contribution or profit.

6.6 When goods or services are passed between different profit centres of one business the use of transfer prices is extremely common. You should be aware that if these different profits centres are companies within one group and if they are based in different countries, then transfer pricing becomes much more technical because by underpricing goods or services, management can ensure that profits in that country are minimised. This may be useful to the company if the tax rate in the country concerned is extremely high. The tax authorities, however, tend to take a different view and hence a commercial price has to be negotiated in many cases.

The responsibilities of a transfer price

6.7 Why are transfer prices important?

'The presence of divisional profit centres requires a system of pricing of internal transfers between divisions, such prices affecting the profits of both the buying and selling division. Under these circumstances the transfer prices (although not directly affecting the corporation's aggregate profit) will not be neutral in their impact on the behaviour and attitude of managers whose personal incomes and job security may correlate closely with the profits their divisions make or are permitted to make.'(Choudhury: *Accountancy* August 1979) Managers of individual profit centres are tempted to take decisions that are harmful to other divisions and are not *congruent* with the goals of the organisation as a whole, the problem is likely to emerge in disputes about the transfer price.

6.8 Ideally, a transfer price should be set at a level that overcomes any problems.

(a) The transfer price should provide an 'artificial' selling price that enables the transferring division to earn a reasonable return for its efforts, and the receiving division to incur a fair cost for benefits received.

(b) The transfer price should be set at a level that enables profit centre performance to be measured 'commercially'. This means that the transfer price should be a fair commercial price.

(c) If possible the transfer price should encourage profit centre managers to agree on the amount of goods and services to be transferred, which will also be at a level that is consistent with the aims of the organisation as a whole (for example maximising company profits).

We shall now consider the various types of transfer price, with a view to identifying what transfer price would most suitably fulfil all these functions, in particular (b) and (c).

6.9 You should remember that the transfer prices charged by a supply division must cover the fixed and variable costs of the supply division, but that they represent purely variable costs to the buying division.

6.10 We shall begin by looking at the guidelines for transfer pricing when there are constant unit variable costs and market prices, regardless of the volume of output. An example will be used to illustrate the principles involved.

Example: transfer pricing

6.11 As a simple illustration, suppose a company has two profit centres, A and B. Centre A sells half its output on the open market, and transfers the other half of its output to B. Costs and revenues in an accounting period are as follows.

	A £	B £	Total £
Sales	8,000	24,000	32,000
Costs of production in the division	12,000	10,000	22,000
Profit			10,000

There are no opening or closing stocks. It does not matter, for this illustration, whether marginal costing or absorption costing is used. For the moment, we shall ignore the question of whether the current output levels are profit-maximising and congruent with the goals of the company as a whole.

6.12 We shall consider in turn each of the following values for goods transferred from A to B.

    (a)   The transfer price is at cost.
    (b)   The transfer price is at cost plus a profit margin of 25%.
    (c)   The transfer price is at market value.

Solution

6.13 *Transfer price at cost (constant unit variable costs and sales prices)*
If the transfer price is at cost, A in our example would have 'sales' to B of £6,000. This would be a cost to B, as follows.

	A £	A £	B £	B £	Company as a whole £
Open market sales		8,000		24,000	32,000
Transfer sales		6,000		-	
Total sales, inc transfers		14,000		24,000	
Transfer costs		-	6,000		
Own costs	12,000		10,000		22,000
Total costs, inc transfers		12,000		16,000	
Profit		2,000		8,000	10,000

The transfer sales of A are self-cancelling with the transfer costs of B so that total profits are unaffected by the transfer items. The transfer price simply spreads the total profit of £10,000 between A and B.

6.14 The obvious drawback to the transfer price at cost is that A makes no profit on its work, and the manager of division A would much prefer to sell output on the open market to earn a profit, rather than transfer to B, regardless of whether or not transfers to B would be in the best interests of the company as a whole. Division A needs a profit on its transfers in order to be motivated to supply B; therefore transfer pricing at cost is inconsistent with the use of a profit centre accounting system.

10: PRICING DECISIONS

6.15 *Transfer price at cost plus (constant unit variable costs and sales prices)*
If the transfers are at cost plus a margin of, say, 25%, A's sales to B would be £7,500.

	A		B		Total
	£	£	£	£	£
Open market sales		8,000		24,000	32,000
Transfer sales		7,500		-	
		15,500		24,000	
Transfer costs	-		7,500		
Own costs	12,000		10,000		22,000
		12,000		17,500	
Profit		3,500		6,500	10,000

6.16 Compared to a transfer price at cost, A gains some profit at the expense of B. However, A makes a bigger profit on external sales in this case because the profit mark-up of 25% is less than the profit mark-up on open market sales. The choice of 25% as a profit mark-up was arbitrary and unrelated to external market conditions, and in this case the transfer price might have the following effects.

(a) Arguably, it does not give a fair revenue to A or charge B a reasonable cost, and so their profit performance is distorted. It might be unfair, for example, to compare A's profit with B's profit.

(b) The transfer price would seem to give A an incentive to sell more goods externally and transfer less to B. This may or may not be in the best interests of the company as a whole.

(c) On the other hand, internal transfers may be less costly than external sales, because of savings on costs such as distribution, advertising and bad debts. It might therefore be argued that A is in fact being given a fair reward for the transfers to B, since the transfer price is marginally lower than the external selling price.

6.17 *Transfer price at standard cost plus*
It is also worth noting that when a transfer price is based on cost plus, *standard* cost plus should be used, not *actual* cost plus.

A transfer price of actual cost plus 25% would encourage the manager of A to overspend because this would increase the divisional profit, even though the company as a whole (and division B) suffers.

6.18 For example suppose that A's costs should have been £12,000, but actually were £16,000. Transfers (50% of output) would cost £8,000 actual, and the transfer price would be £8,000 × 125% = £10,000.

	A		B		Total
	£	£	£	£	£
Market sales		8,000		24,000	32,000
Transfer sales		10,000		-	
		18,000		24,000	
Transfer costs	-		10,000		
Own costs	16,000		10,000		26,000
		16,000		20,000	
Profit		2,000		4,000	6,000

A's overspending by £4,000 has reduced the total profits from £10,000 to £6,000, but division B has suffered a much larger fall in profit than division A.

6.19 Division B must bear much of the cost of A's overspending, which is clearly unsatisfactory for responsibility accounting.

If, however, the transfer price were at standard cost plus instead of actual cost plus, the transfer sales would have been £7,500, regardless of A's overspending.

	A		B		Total
	£	£	£	£	£
Market sales		8,000		24,000	32,000
Transfer sales		7,500		-	
		15,500		24,000	
Transfer costs		-	7,500		
Own costs	16,000		10,000		26,000
		16,000		17,500	
Profit/(loss)		(500)		6,500	6,000

6.20 The entire cost of the overspending by A of £4,000 is now borne by division A itself, as a comparison with the figures in the transfer price at cost plus will show.

6.21 *Transfer price at market value*
If an external market price exists for transferred goods, profit centre managers will be aware of the price they could obtain or the price they would have to pay for their goods on the external market, and they would inevitably compare this price with the transfer price.

6.22 In our example, if the transfer price is at market price, A would be happy to sell the output to B for £8,000, which is what the division would get by selling it externally instead of transferring it.

	A		B		Total
	£	£	£	£	£
Market sales		8,000		24,000	32,000
Transfer sales		8,000		-	
		16,000		24,000	
Transfer costs		-	8,000		
Own costs	12,000		10,000		22,000
		12,000		18,000	
Profit		4,000		6,000	10,000

6.23 (a) Division A earns the same profit on transfers as on external sales. Division B must pay a commercial price for transferred goods, and both divisions will have their profit measured in a fair way.

(b) Division A will be indifferent about selling externally or transferring goods to B because the profit is the same on both types of transaction. B can therefore ask for and obtain as many units as it wants from A. We do not know what the profit-maximising of the company is: perhaps there are production limiting factors in A that prevent it from making more units, or perhaps there is a limit to external market sales demand for A's output or B's output. A market value transfer price would seem to ensure, however, that the company's profit-maximising output level will be achieved.

6.24 In this case, it would therefore appear that the following conclusions can be drawn.

(a) A market-based transfer price is the ideal transfer price. (In practice, the transfer price might be slightly less than market price, so that A and B could share the cost savings from internal transfers compared with external sales).

(b) Agreement between the profit centre managers on this price and on output levels should be reachable with a minimum of intervention from head office.

The advantages of market value transfer prices

6.25 Market value transfer prices have several important advantages.

(a) In a decentralised company, divisional managers should have the opportunity to make output, selling and buying decisions which appear to be in the best interests of the division's performance. (If every division optimises its performance, the company as a whole must inevitably achieve optimal results.) Thus a transferor division should be given the freedom to sell output on the open market, rather than to transfer them within the company. The reason for this option is that the 'seller' might find more profitable opportunities to sell other products, so that if output is switched to this new option, the transferee division is able to replace the halted internal supply by buying on the open market.

(b) 'Arm's length' transfer prices, which give profit centre managers the freedom to negotiate prices with other profit centres as though they were independent companies, will tend to result in a market-based transfer price.

(c) In most cases where the transfer price is at market price, internal transfers should be expected, because the buying division is likely to benefit from a better quality of service, greater flexibility, and dependability of supply. Both divisions may benefit from cheaper costs of administration, selling and transport. A market price as the transfer price would therefore result in decisions which would be in the best interests of the company or group as a whole.

(d) Where a market price exists, but the transfer price is a different amount, (say, at standard cost plus), divisional managers will argue about the volume of internal transfers. Suppose division X is expected to sell output to division Y at a transfer price of £8 per unit when the open market price is £10, the manager will decide to sell all output on the open market. The manager of division Y would resent the loss of his cheap supply from X, and would be reluctant to buy on the open market. A wasteful situation would arise where X sells on the open market at £10, where Y buys at £10, so that administration, selling and distribution costs would have been saved if X had sold directly to Y at £10, the market price.

(e) In some cases, the failure to select market value as a transfer price might result in even more serious inter-departmental disputes. Returning to an example of a garage and car sales company, suppose there are three profit centres:

(i)   new car sales;
(ii)   used car sales;
(iii) garage work, repairs and inspections.

The manager of the new car sales division might sell a car for £8,000 to a customer who trades in his old vehicle for £3,000. The new car sales division must transfer the old car to the used car sales division, but if the manager of this division could buy a similar car for £2,500, he would refuse the transfer. Similarly, the garage must carry out tests on the new car for the customer, but if the transfer price/rate for the work is below the market price of work to outside customers, the manager of the garage would be most reluctant to do the tests. Where the interdependence of divisions is very strong, as it would be in the example just described, a discrepancy between the transfer price and market value would place intolerable burdens on the co-ordination and integration between the separate divisions.

The disadvantages of market value transfer prices

6.26 Market value as a transfer price does have certain disadvantages.

(a) The market price may be a temporary one, induced by adverse economic conditions, or 'dumping', or the market price might depend on the volume of output supplied to the external market by the profit centre.

(b) A transfer price at market value might, under some circumstances, act as a disincentive to use up any spare capacity in the divisions. A price based on incremental cost, in contrast, might provide an incentive to use up the spare resources in order to provide a marginal contribution to profit.

(c) Many products do not have an equivalent market price, so that the price of a suitable 'nearly the same' product might be chosen. In such circumstances, the option to sell or buy on the open market does not exist.

(d) There might be an imperfect external market for the transferred item, so that if the transferring division tried to sell more externally, it would have to reduce its selling price.

(e) Internal transfers are often cheaper than external sales, with savings in selling costs, bad debt risks and possibly transport/delivery costs. It would therefore seem reasonable for the buying division to expect a discount on the external market price, and to negotiate for such a discount.

Transfer pricing when there is no external market for the transferred item

6.27 When there is no external market for the transferred item, a transfer price can be one of the following.

(a) The price of a similar item that does have an external market.
(b) At cost (ideally, standard cost).
(c) At cost plus (ideally, standard cost plus).

6.28 If there is no similar item sold on an external market, and if the transferred item is a major product of the transferring division, there is a strong argument for suggesting that profit centre accounting is a waste of time. Profit centres cannot be judged on their commercial performance because there is no way of gauging what a fair revenue for their work should be. It would be more appropriate, perhaps, to treat the transferring 'division' as a cost centre, and to judge performance on the basis of cost variances.

6.29 However, if profit centres are established, in the absence of a market price, the optimum transfer price is likely to be one based on standard cost plus, but only provided that the variable cost per unit and sales price per unit are unchanged at all levels of output. A standard cost plus price would motivate divisional managers to increase output and to reduce expenditure levels.

Example: transfer price calculation

6.30 Motivate Ltd has two profit centres, P and Q. P transfers all its output to Q. The variable cost of output from P is £5 per unit, and fixed costs are £1,200 per month. Additional processing costs in Q are £4 per unit for variable costs, plus fixed costs of £800. Budgeted production is 400 units per month, and the output of Q sells for £15 per unit.

From what range of prices should the transfer price (based on standard full cost plus) be selected, in order to motivate the managers of both profit centres to both increase output and reduce costs?

Solution

6.31 Any transfer price based on standard cost plus will motivate managers to cut costs, because favourable variances between standard costs and actual costs will be credited to the division's profits. Managers of each division will also be willing to increase output (above the budget) provided that it is profitable to do so.

(a) Division P will increase the output provided that the transfer price exceeds the variable cost of £5 per unit.

(b) Division Q will increase purchases provided that the transfer price is less than the difference between the fixed selling price (£15) and the variable costs in Q itself (£4), ie provided that the transfer price is less than £11 per unit.

The correct range of prices is therefore between £5.01 and £10.99. The fixed overhead absorption rate is irrelevant to the price-fixing, if the under/over absorbed overhead is debited/credited to the profit centre's results.

6.32 This may be checked. Suppose the transfer price is £9. What would divisional profits be if output and sales are:

(a) 400 units;
(b) 500 units?

6.33 (a) *At 400 units*

	P £	Q £	Total £
Sales	–	6,000	6,000
Transfer sales	3,600	–	
Transfer costs		3,600	
Own full cost of sales	3,200	2,400	5,600
	400	0	400
Under/over absorbed overhead	0	0	0
Profit/(loss)	400	0	400

The full cost of sales is £(5 + 3) in division P and £(4 + 2) in division Q, plus transfer costs of £9.

(b) *At 500 units*

	P £	Q £	Total £
Sales	–	7,500	7,500
Transfer sales	4,500	–	–
Transfer costs	–	4,500	–
Own full cost of sales	4,000	3,000	7,000
	500	0	500
Over absorbed overhead	300	200	500
Profit/(loss)	800	200	1,000

Increasing output improves the profit performance of both divisions and the company as a whole, and so decisions on output by the two divisions are likely to be goal congruent.

Negotiated transfer prices

6.34 A transfer price based on opportunity cost is often difficult to identify, for lack of suitable information about costs and revenues in individual divisions.

6.35 When authority is decentralised in an organisation to the extent that divisional managers negotiate transfer prices with each other, the agreed price may be finalised from a mixture of accounting arithmetic, politics and compromise. It may be, for example, that a negotiated price is based on market value, but with some reductions to allow for the internal nature of the transaction, which saves external selling and distribution costs.

6.36 Where one division receives near-finished goods from another, a negotiated price might be based on the market value of the end product, minus an amount for the finishing work in the receiving division.

6.37 'The main strength of the negotiated approach, however, lies in its scope and versatility. Interdivisional conflict frequently does not relate solely to transfer pricing, but is multidimensional, encompassing other facets, like product design, quality control, production and delivery schedules.

The process of negotiation will therefore operate on several planes and agreement may be achieved on a trade-off between several conflict variables. For instance, the buying division may be willing to meet the asking price, provided the selling division incorporates some design improvements and promises early delivery.' (Choudhury).

6.38 The process of negotiation will be improved if adequate information about each division's costs and revenues is made available to the other division involved in the negotiation. By having a free flow of cost and revenue information, it will be easier for divisional managers to identify opportunities for improving profits, to the benefit of both divisions involved in the transfer.

6.39 Even so, inter-departmental disputes about transfer prices are likely to arise and these may need the intervention or mediation of head office to settle the problem. Head office management may then impose a price which maximises the profit of the company as a whole. On the other hand, head office management might restrict their intervention to the task of keeping negotiations in progress until a transfer price is eventually settled. The more head office has to impose its own decisions on profit centres, the less decentralisation of authority will be and the less effective the profit centre system of accounting will be for motivating divisional managers.

Optimum transfer prices: guiding rules

6.40 The examples so far have been intended to lead up to the following guiding rules for identifying the optimal transfer price.

(a) The ideal transfer price should reflect the opportunity cost of sale to the supply division and the opportunity cost to the buying division (ie purchase price available externally and/or the contribution obtainable from the extra output that could be made and sold with the transferred items).

(b) When unit variable costs and unit selling prices are constant and an external market price exists, the opportunity cost of transfer will be:

    (i)   external market price; or
    (ii) external market price less savings in selling costs.

(c) In the absence of an external market price for the transferred item, but when unit variable costs are constant, and the sales price per unit of the end-product is constant, the ideal transfer price should reflect the opportunity cost of the resources consumed by the supply division to make and supply the item.

    (i)   In some cases, this may simply be the standard variable cost of production.

    (ii) When there is a scarce production resource, the transfer price might be the variable cost of production plus the contribution forgone by using the scarce resource instead of putting it to its most profitable alternative use.

(d) When unit variable costs and/or unit selling prices are not constant, either in the intermediate market or the end-market, a more difficult problem arises, and the ideal transfer price will only be found by sensible negotiation and careful analysis.

    The starting point should be to establish the output and sales quantities that will optimise the profits of the company or group as a whole.

Having done this, the next step is to establish the transfer price at which both profit centres, the supply division and the buying division, would maximise their profits at this company-optimising output level.

(e) There may be a range of prices within which both profit centres can agree on the output level that would maximise their individual profits and the profits of the company as a whole. Any price within the range would then be 'ideal'. However, in some circumstances, there may be just one ideal transfer price.

6.41 As a result of these various arguments regarding how to set a realistic and acceptable transfer price we can suggest that:

(a) Transfer prices ought to be competitive.

(b) There should be a company policy on decisions to buy from outside rather than 'buy' internal transfers. A suitable policy might be as follows.

(i) Internal supply divisions must be given the opportunity to tender a selling price for goods that a buying division wants to acquire, and which the supply division could provide.

(ii) If the transfer price is not as competitive as an external supplier's price, the buying division should be free to buy externally; however, the supply division should be given a chance to reconsider its transfer price, and quote a lower price if it wishes.

(iii) If a buying division does buy externally instead of taking transferred goods, its manager must be prepared to justify the decision to senior management if the decision is challenged.

(c) Even though incorrectly based transfer prices can motivate divisional managers to take decisions which are against the company's interests and so which are decisions that central management would not take in the same circumstances, it would nevertheless be wrong for central management to impose transfer prices arbitrarily on its profit centres. This is because head office interference would remove the autonomy of profit centre managers and destroy their profit incentive.

(d) The market price or a market price equivalent should be the basis for setting a transfer price. In the absence of a market price or market equivalent price, a negotiating procedure should be adopted by the trading divisions, and a price agreed in advance of any work being done. Head office intervention in the price negotiations should be kept to a minimum, for example to providing arbitration on request in cases where divisional managers cannot agree on a price.

7. CONCLUSION

7.1 There are two main approaches to external pricing decisions.

(a) A cost-based approach, for example cost plus pricing.
(b) A demand-based approach, for example selecting a profit-maximising price.

7.2 In theory the two approaches are very different and can result in different price recommendations. However in practice they can be combined and are not necessarily in conflict. In contrast the transfer price ought to reflect the opportunity cost of transfer, in order that the following are achieved:

(a) The transferring division receives at least as much for a transferred item that it could get for the same item on an external market.

(b) The receiving division should pay no more for a transferred item than it would have to pay for the same item on an external market. Additionally, where the receiving division could earn marginally higher revenues from producing more units, the cost of transfers should not exceed the marginal revenues obtainable from the higher output, less the marginal costs of making the output in the receiving division itself (ie ignoring the transfer price).

7.3 The ideal transfer price will often be the external market price of the transferred product (or a price negotiated just below this market price) because this is often the opportunity cost of transfer.

7.4 In all cases, however, because the transfer price should help to achieve agreement between divisions on a profit-optimising level of output and sales for the company as a whole, the transfer price should ideally be agreed within the framework of already having established what is best for the company as a whole.

TEST YOUR KNOWLEDGE
The numbers in brackets refer to paragraphs of this chapter

1 List four criticisms of full cost plus pricing. (1.20)

2 What are the advantages of full cost plus pricing? (1.21)

3 What are the implications of the learning curve for pricing? (3.8)

4 What relevance does the learning curve effect have? (3.33, 3.34)

5 What factors may enable companies to charge different prices for similar products? (4.2-4.4)

6 What general guidelines should a company follow when reviewing selling prices during a period of inflation? (5.2)

7 Suggest four possible bases for determining a transfer price. (6.4)

8 What functions should a transfer price fulfil? (6.8)

9 What are the drawbacks of using cost as a transfer price? (6.14)

10 What are the advantages of market value transfer prices? (6.25)

11 What are the disadvantages of market value transfer prices? (6.26)

Now try question 10 at the end of the text

Chapter 11

DECISION-MAKING TECHNIQUES

This chapter covers the following topics.

1. Long term decision making
2. Appraisal methods
3. The time value of money
4. Discounted cash flow: net present value (NPV)
5. Annuities
6. Profitability ratio
7. Discounted cash flow: internal rate of return (IRR)
8. Mutually exclusive projects
9. The real rate and the money (nominal) rate of return
10. Introducing risk
11. Methods of treating risk
12. Decision trees

---

1. LONG TERM DECISION MAKING

1.1 Not all decisions are made in the short term. Businesses will need to assess proposals which will affect the long term health of the company and which may be competing for a scarce resource: cash. In such circumstances financial considerations will have an impact on the decision making process. Managers need to assess each project to determine its suitability in terms of the corporate objectives and then to determine how, whether and when to invest the available funds. This decision making process will usually involve the investment in a capital item (an item which will add to the capacity of the business to generate revenue and profits). The capital asset investment decision would usually involve the following considerations.

    (a) Once paid for, the asset cannot be re-sold quickly at a profit. The capital is tied up for several years.

    (b) The investment will earn profits (or returns) over this period of several years.

    (c) At the end of this time, the investment might have some re-sale or scrap value, but it might also be worthless.

1.2 Capital expenditure projects usually involve comparatively large amounts of money and a long timescale. This means that a formalised procedure must be adopted for their appraisal and authorisation.

1.3   The proposal to insist on a project is usually a detailed document which is presented either to the board of directors or to a senior committee. it will contain a summary of the proposal, the rationale for its acceptance, the strategic reasons for the investment, the strengths and weaknesses of the project (a SWOT analysis) and a financial justification.

2.   APPRAISAL METHODS

2.1   The principal methods of evaluating a capital project are:

(a)   the return on investment method (or accounting rate of return);
(b)   the payback method;
(c)   discounted cash flow (DCF) techniques.

Before looking at each of these methods in turn it is worth considering one problem common to all of them, that of estimating future cash flows.

2.2   Cash flow forecasting is never easy, but in capital budgeting the problems are particularly acute. This is because the period under consideration may not be merely a year or two, but five, ten, perhaps twenty years. It is therefore important that decision makers should consider how variations in the estimates they have made might affect their decision. For the time being, however, it is assumed that future cash flows are known with certainty.

Accounting rate of return

2.3   A capital investment project may be assessed by calculating the *return on investment* (ROI) or *accounting rate of return* (ARR) and comparing it with a pre-determined target level. A formula for ARR which is common in practice is:

$$\text{ARR} = \frac{\text{Estimated average profits}}{\text{Estimated average investment}} \times 100\%$$

Other formulae use total profits for the numerator, or initial investment for the denominator. Various combinations are possible, but the important thing is to be consistent once a method has been selected.

Example: accounting rate of return

2.4   Bee Ltd is contemplating the purchase of a new machine and has two alternatives.

	Machine X	Machine Y
Cost	£10,000	£10,000
Estimated residual value	£2,000	£3,000
Estimated life	4 years	4 years
Estimated future profits before depreciation		
Year 1	£5,000	£2,000
2	£5,000	£3,000
3	£3,000	£5,000
4	£1,000	£5,000
Total profits	£14,000	£15,000

Based on the ARR method which of the two machines would be purchased?

Solution

2.5

	X	Y
	£	£
Total profits before depreciation	14,000	15,000
Total depreciation	8,000	7,000
Total profits after depreciation	6,000	8,000
Average profits (4 years)	1,500	2,000
Value of investment initially	10,000	10,000
Eventual scrap value	2,000	3,000
	12,000	13,000
∴ Average value of investment (÷ 2)	6,000	6,500

The accounting rates of return are:

$$X = \frac{£1,500}{£6,000} = 25\%$$

$$Y = \frac{£2,000}{£6,500} = 31\%$$

Machine Y would therefore be chosen.

2.6 This method of assessing an investment is a measure of profitability and its major advantage is that it is easily understood and the data needed for forecasting purposes is readily available. But basing our decision on profits alone without considering cash flows can be extremely dangerous and this method of appraisal falls short of the necessary controls required for such a long term decision. For example, if we look at the profits generated by the two alternatives given above, as much emphasis is placed in the profits generated in year one as those generated in year four. If, instead of profits, these were actually cash flows we could make an incorrect decision, particularly if the management of Bee Ltd needed a quick return on its cash invested.

The payback method

2.7 The payback method is one which gives greater weight to cash flows generated in earlier years. The payback period is the length of time required before the total cash inflows received from the project is equal to the original cash outlay. In other words, it is the length of time the investment takes to pay itself back.

2.8 In the previous example, machine X pays for itself within two years and machine Y in three years. Using the payback method of investment appraisal, machine X is preferable to machine Y.

2.9 The payback method has obvious disadvantages. Consider the case of two machines for which the following information is available:

	Machine P £	Machine Q £
Cost	10,000	10,000
Cash inflows year 1	1,000	5,000
2	2,000	5,000
3	6,000	1,000
4	7,000	500
5	8,000	500
	24,000	12,000

Machine Q pays back at the end of year two and machine P not until early in year four. Using the payback method machine Q is to be preferred, but this ignores the fact that the total profitability of P (£24,000) is double that of Q.

2.10 Despite the disadvantages of the payback method it is widely used in practice, though often only as a supplement to more sophisticated methods. The argument in its favour is that its use will tend to minimise the effects of risk and aid liquidity. This is because greater weight is given to earlier cash flows which can probably be predicted more accurately than distant cash flows.

2.11 A more scientific method of investment appraisal is the use of discounted cash flow (DCF) techniques. Before DCF can be understood it is necessary to know something about the time value of money.

3. THE TIME VALUE OF MONEY

3.1 Money is spent to earn a profit. For example, if an item of machinery costs £6,000 and would earn profits (ignoring depreciation) of £2,000 per year for three years, it would not be worth buying because its total profit (£6,000) would only just cover its cost.

3.2 Clearly then, items of capital expenditure must earn profits or make savings to justify their costs, but we would also say that the *size of profits or return must be sufficiently large* to justify the investment. In the example above, if the machinery costing £6,000 made total profits of £6,300 over three years, the return on the investment would be £300, or an average of £100 per year. This would be a very low return, because it would be much more profitable to invest the £6,000 somewhere else (for example, on deposit at a bank).

3.3 We must therefore recognise that if a capital investment is to be worthwhile, it must earn at least a minimum profit or return so that the size of the return will compensate the investor (the business) for the *length* of time he must wait before the profits are made. (For example, if a company could invest £6,000 now to earn revenue of £6,300 in one week's time a profit of £300 in seven days would be a very good return. If it takes three years to earn the revenue, however, the return would be very low).

3.4 When capital expenditure projects are evaluated, it is therefore appropriate to decide whether the investment will make enough profits to allow for the 'time value' of capital tied up. DCF is an evaluation technique which takes into account the time value of money and also the total profitability over a project's life. DCF is therefore a superior method of investment appraisal to both ARR and payback.

What is discounting?

3.5 Discounting is simply compounding in reverse. We have all seen compound interest rates at work. if we borrow £1,000 now at 10% interest rate and repay nothing for two years, then at the end of year one, provided interest is only calculated at the end of the year, we will owe

£1,000 plus 10% = £1,000 (1 + 10%) = £1,000 × 1.10 = £1,100

If again we do not repay anything in the second year and interest is calculated at the end of the year the balance on the loan will be:

£1,100 × 1.10 = £1,210

The original borrowing has grown as follows.

£1,000 × 1.10 × 1.10 = £1,000 × $(1.10)^2$ = £1,210

This would continue forever if we left the whole balance (interest and original capital) untouched. Hence after five years we would owe:

£1,000 × $(1.10)^5$ = £1,611

3.6 Discounting simply reverses this process. it says that if we owed £1,611 in five years time whilst paying interest of 10% per annum, what did we borrow today? Or more usually 'what is the present value of a given sum of money held in the future?' For those of you who are mathematically minded the present value calculation is:

$$P = F \times \frac{1}{(1 + R)^n} \quad \text{or} \quad P = F \times (1 + R)^{-n}$$

when   P = present value of sum required
             F = future value of sum
             r = rate of interest expressed as a fraction of one
             n = number of years invested.

Hence in our example

$$£1,000 = £1,611 \times \frac{1}{(1 + 0.1)^5}$$

Example: discounting

3.7 A good example of this technique is shown where a businessman has two sons who are just 18 years and 17 years old. He wishes to give them £10,000 each on their 20th birthdays and he wants to know how much he must invest now at 8% interest to pay this amount.

Solution

3.8   The following table is relevant, giving values r = 8% or 0.08.

Year n	Future value of £1 $(1 + r)^n$	Present value of £1 $(1 + r)^{-n}$
1	1.080	0.926
2	1.166	0.857
3	1.260	0.794
4	1.360	0.735

3.9   The investment must provide £10,000 after two years for the elder son and £10,000 after three years for the younger son.

Son	After n years n =	Discount factor at 8%		Amount provided £		Present value £
Elder	2	0.857	×	10,000	=	8,570
Younger	3	0.794	×	10,000	=	7,940
Total investment required						16,510

Proof

After two years the investment of £16,510 will be worth £16,510 × 1.166 = £19,251. After paying £10,000 to the elder son, £9,251 will be left after two years. This will earn interest of 8% in year three, to be worth £9,251 × 1.08 = £9,991 at the end of the year. This is almost enough to pay £10,000 to the younger son. The difference (£9) is caused by rounding errors in the table of discount (present value) factors and compound (future value) factors.

Note. Discount table extracts are included at the end of this chapter.

Example: project investment

3.10 We can extend this example to consider a company's investment decisions. A company is wondering whether to invest £15,000 in a project which will pay £20,000 after two years. It will not invest unless the return from the investment is at least 10% per annum. Is the investment worthwhile?

The present value of £1 in two years time at 10% interest is 0.826.

Solution

3.11 The return of £20,000 after two years is equivalent to an investment now at 10% of £20,000 × 0.826 = £16,520.

In other words, in order to obtain £20,000 after two years, the company would have to invest £16,520 now at an interest rate of 10%. The project offers the same payment at a cost of only £15,000, so that it must provide a return in excess of 10% and it is therefore worthwhile.

	£
Present value of future profits at 10%	16,520
Cost of investment	<u>15,000</u>
The investment in the project offers the same return, but at a cost lower by	<u>1,520</u>

3.12 A very common use of discounted cash flow is seen in the promotional offers we often get through our front doors. We are asked to choose our cash prize (should we win!) as either £10,000 every year until we are 65 or £100,000 now. The company will have worked out how much it needs to invest now to produce £10,000 every year at the current interest rates. From the individual's viewpoint he would need to assess his use for the money, his age against the 65 year barrier and the value of money. If the winner is young then it is probably preferable to accept the £10,000 a year for life since its present value will exceed £100,000; the older one gets the less likely that this option is preferable. Remember, £10,000 in 10 years time is worth only £3,855 at 10%! There may of course be other considerations that each individual should consider, not just the real value of money. 'do I need cash now?' is a primary consideration.

4. DISCOUNTED CASH FLOW: NET PRESENT VALUE (NPV)

4.1 Discounted cash flow or DCF is a technique of evaluating capital investment projects, using discounting arithmetic to determine whether or not they will provide a satisfactory return. A typical investment project involves a payment of capital for fixed assets at the start of the project and then there will be profits coming in from the investment over a number of years.

4.2 The word 'profits' however, is not really appropriate in DCF, for two main reasons.

(a) The cost of a fixed asset is charged against profits each year as depreciation in the normal financial accounts. In DCF, however, depreciation must be ignored because the full cost of the asset is treated as a capital investment at the start of the project. It would therefore be wrong to charge depreciation against profits as well because this would be 'double-counting' the cost.

(b) The return on an investment only occurs when the investor receives payments in cash. There is a difference between:

(i) accounting profits; and
(ii) cash receipts less cash payments

and in DCF it is the cash flows which are considered more relevant. For example, suppose that a company makes profits of £5,000 before depreciation during one year, but in that time increases its debtors by £1,000. The cash received in the year would not be £5,000, but only £4,000. In DCF, the return for the year would be taken as the cash flow of £4,000, not the profit of £5,000.

4.3 DCF can be used in either of two ways:

(a) the net present value method;
(b) the internal rate of return (sometimes called DCF yield, DCF rate of return) method.

We will now look at each method in turn.

The net present value (NPV) method of DCF

4.4 The net present value (NPV) method of evaluation is as follows.

(a) Determine the present value of costs. In other words, decide how much capital must be set aside to pay for the project. Let this be £C.

(b) Calculate the present value of future cash benefits from the project. To do this we take the cash benefit in each year and discount it to a present value. (This shows how much we would have to invest now to earn the future benefits, if our rate of return were equal to the cost of capital.) By adding up the present value of benefits for each future year, we obtain the total present value of benefits from the project. Let this be £B.

(c) Compare the present value of costs £C with the present value of benefits £B. The net present value is the difference between them: £(B - C).

(d) If the NPV is positive, the present value of benefits exceeds the present value of costs. This in turn means that the project will earn a return in excess of the cost of capital.

(e) If the NPV is negative, this means that it would cost us more to invest in the project to obtain the future cash receipts than it would cost us to invest somewhere else, at a rate of interest equal to the cost of capital, to obtain an equal amount of future receipts. The project would earn a return lower than the cost of capital and would not be worth investing in.

Example: net present value (NPV) method

4.5 Suppose that a company is wondering whether to invest £18,000 in a project which would make extra profits (before depreciation is deducted) of £10,000 in the first year, £8,000 in the second year and £6,000 in the third year. Its cost of capital is 10% (in other words, it would require a return of at least 10% on its investment). Is the project worth undertaking?

4.6 In DCF we make several assumptions. One such assumption is that discounted cash flows (payments or receipts) occur on the last day of each year. For example, although profits are £10,000 during the course of year 1, we assume that the £10,000 is not received until the last day of year 1. Similarly, the profits of £8,000 and £6,000 in years 2 and 3 are assumed to occur on the last day of years 2 and 3 respectively. The cash payment of £18,000 occurs 'now' at the start of year 1. To be consistent, we say that this payment occurs on the last day of the current year which is often referred to as year 0.

4.7 The NPV is now calculated with discounting arithmetic. Present value tables give us the following values:

Year n	Present value of £1 $(1 + r)^{-n}$ where r = 0.10
1	0.909
2	0.826
3	0.751

Year	Cash flow £	Present value factor at 10%	Present value £
0	(18,000)	1.0	(18,000)
1	10,000	0.909	9,090
2	8,000	0.826	6,608
3	6,000	0.751	4,506
		NPV	+2,204

The NPV is positive, which means that the project will earn more than 10%. (£20,204 would have to be invested now at 10% to earn the future cash flows; since the project will earn these returns at a cost of only £18,000 it must earn a return in excess of 10%.)

Note. The discount rate should reflect investors' requirements or expectations of the returns they should get. For this reason, we talk about the *cost of capital*, which is the level of return required by the providers of capital, and the discount rate for investment decisions should be based on a firm's cost of capital.

4.8 A second assumption we have made is that the profits generated before depreciation are the same as cash flows. This is not unreasonable since it is unlikely that there are major timing differences between the recognition of the activities required to generate profit (sales, purchases and their related expenses) and the cash flows associated with them. It is also reasonable because we have no other information and hence an assumption must be made. Unless you are told otherwise in your studies, this is an assumption that is frequently made.

5. ANNUITIES

5.1 In DCF the term 'annuities' refers to an annual cash payment which is the same amount every year for a number of years, or else an annual receipt of cash which is the same amount every year for a number of years.

Consider an example where a capital proposal involves a capital outlay of £24,000 and profits before depreciation of £5,000 each year for six years. If the cost of capital is 12% then the usual contribution would be:

Year	Cash flow £	Present value factor at 12%	Present value £	
0	(24,000)	1.000	(24,000)	
1	5,000	0.893	4,465	
2	5,000	0.797	3,985	
3	5,000	0.712	3,560	£20,560
4	5,000	0.636	3,180	
5	5,000	0.567	2,835	
6	5,000	0.507	2,535	
		NPV	(3,440)	

The NPV is negative and so the project is not worthwhile.

Note that the present value factor can be looked up in tables (which will be given to you during your studies) or worked out using the $\frac{1}{(1 + r)^n}$ formula.

5.2 In the example above, the profits are an annuity of £5,000 per annum for six years. The present value of profits (£20,560 as shown in the solution above) is the present value of an annuity of £5,000 per annum for six years at a discount rate of 12%.

5.3 When there is an annuity to be discounted, there is a short cut method of calculation. You may already have seen what it is, from the previous example.

Instead of multiplying the cash flow each year by the present value factor for that year, and then adding up all the present values (as shown in the solution above) we can multiply the annuity by the sum of the present value factors.

Thus we could have multiplied £5,000 by the sum of (0.893 + 0.797 + 0.712 + 0.636 + 0.567 + 0.507) = 4.112. We then have £5,000 × 4.112 = £20,560.

5.4 Annuity tables which do this addition for your may also be available. An extract is included at the end of this chapter.

5.5 Two further example will help your understanding of the annuity shortcut. By using annuity tables you would discover that the discount factor for years one to three at 10% is 2.487 and for years four to six it is 1.868. Similarly the discount factor for years 1-5 at 10% is 3.791.

Example: annuities

5.6 (a) A project costs £39,500. It will earn £10,000 per year for the first three years and then £8,000 per year for the next three years. The cost of capital is 10%. Is the project worth undertaking?

(b) Another project costs £75,820. If its life is expected to be five years and the cost of capital is 10%, what are the minimum annual savings required to make the project worthwhile?

Solution

5.7 (a) The discount factor for the annual receipts of £8,000 from years 4 - 6 can be calculated as follows.

	£
Present value of £1 per annum, years 1-6	4.355
Less present value of £1 per annum, years 1-3	2.487
Gives present value of £1 per annum, years 4-6	1.868

Year	Cash flow £	Discount factor at 10%	Present value £
0	(39,500)	1.0	(39,500)
1 - 3	10,000 pa	2.487	24,870
4 - 6	8,000 pa	1.868	14,944
		NPV	+ £314

The NPV is positive, but only just (£314). The project therefore promises a return a little above 10%.

If we are confident that the estimates of cost and benefits for the next six years are accurate, the project is worth undertaking. However, if there is some suspicion that earnings may be a little less than the figures shown, it might be prudent to reject it.

(b) The project will just be worthwhile if the NPV is 0. For the NPV to be 0 the present value of benefits must equal the present value of costs, £75,820.

The PV of benefits = Annual savings × Present value of £1 per year for 5 years (at 10%)

£75,820 = Annual savings × 3.791

$$\text{Annual savings} = \frac{£75,820}{3.791} = £20,000$$

This example shows that annuity tables can be used to calculate an annual cash flow from a given investment.

5.8 You will notice that a little short cut is used in calculating the annuity factor for years four to six in example (a) above. To establish this we effectively add up the discount factors for years one to six (giving 4.355) and deduct the sum of the factors for years one to three (2.487). This short cut is very useful when we have a constant stream of cash flows for a number of years, which do not conveniently start in year 1.

DCF and relevant costs

5.9 The cash flows to consider in decision-making are only those that are directly relevant to the decision under consideration.

5.10 A relevant cost is a future cash flow arising as a consequence of a decision. It follows that:

(a) any costs incurred in the past; or

(b) any committed cost which will be incurred regardless of whether or not an investment is undertaken;

are not relevant cash flows because they have occurred, or will occur whatever investment decision is taken.

5.11 When considering the amount of the cash flows during the life of a project the annual cash flows used for the DCF calculation will differ from the values of profits plus depreciation. This is not because different basic figures are used, but because the DCF cash flows will be allocated to the years in which the cash movement takes place so that the time value of money is taken into account. This is always the case but in many practical situations you may need to make assumptions about cash flows and profit before depreciation.

5.12 If a decision is whether to accept project A or no project at all, the cash flows are the capital outlay and running costs of the project and the *cash savings* or *additional cash receipts*. The cash flows are, in effect, being compared with zero cash flows (from rejecting the project).

5.13 If a decision is about which of two projects to accept, project A or project B, one method of evaluation would be to use the differences in the cash flows between the projects, namely the *relative* or *differential* cash flows.

Example: relevant costs

5.14 A good example of using relevant costs may occur when a business has already incurred £100,000 research and development costs. It has resulted in two new products which will need investment in machinery of £50,000 and £70,000 respectively. The cash benefits to accrue (before depreciation) are £15,000 for each year for five years under project A, and £20,000 each year for five years under project B.

Which project should be undertaken if the cost of capital is 10%?

Solution

5.15 The matter of importance is that the R & D expenditure has already happened and does not affect the decision of which project to undertake. Hence we only use the relevant costs and cash inflows.

	Project A	Project B
Cash investment year 0 (£)	(50,000)	(70,000)
Cash inflows years 1-5 (£)	15,000	20,000
Discount factor (£)	3.791	3.791
Present value of cash inflows (£)	56,865	75,820
Net present value (£)	+ 6,865	+ 5,820

6. PROFITABILITY RATIO

6.1 We have another problem. Although one project gives a greater NPV than the other, both projects in our example above give a positive NPV and so both should be considered as good projects in that they meet the financial criteria set by the group. If we only had enough cash to take up one of them, which should we choose?

6.2 On available method of ranking the projects is by using the profitability index. This is calculated as follows.

$$\text{Profitability index} = \frac{\text{Present value of future cash flows}}{\text{Total investments}}$$

6.3 In our example the present value of the future cash flows are:

Project A	£56,865
Project B	£75,820

The profitability index is therefore:

Project A = $\dfrac{£56,865}{£50,000}$ = 1.137

Project B = $\dfrac{£75,820}{£70,000}$ = 1.083

Project A should therefore be chosen because it is the most efficient use of funds.

Example: profitability ratios

6.4   Six projects require investments and produce cash returns as follows.

	A	B	C	D	E	F
Initial investment (£m)	(15)	(15)	(100)	(15)	(40)	(30)
Future cash benefits (£m)						
Year 1	-	-	15	(3)	15	-
2	5	-	25	2	5	-
3	5	-	30	4	10	-
4	5	5	30	5	10	-
5	2	10	30	5	10	25
6	1	10	30	5	15	25
7	-	10	30	5	15	25
8	10	-	30	5	15	25
Present value of future cash flows (£m)	17.43	20.40	142.26	16.16	61.48	54.13
Net present value (£m)	2.43	5.40	42.26	1.16	21.48	24.13
Profitability index	1.16	1.36	1.42	1.08	1.54	1.80

The cost of capital is 10%

Solution

6.5   With unlimited funds we would want to do every project, since they all show a positive net present value. We would then get a good return for the owners. But cash may be limited. If we only had £100 million to spend we could spend it all on project C and get an NPV of £42.26 million. However, we could also invest in a mixture of the other projects as follows.

Project	Profitability index	Initial investment £m	Net present value £m
F	1.80	30	24.13
E	1.54	40	21.48
B	1.36	15	5.40
A	1.16	15	2.43
		100	53.44

6.6 We have now managed to invest the same £100 million and improved the present value to £53.44 million. This indicates that we should look at all our options and not simply select the one with the highest NPV. (Work through the example yourself to ensure you understand how to use the tables.)

6.7 During this example you also met one convention which is used extensively. All cash investments are detailed as figures in brackets indicating an outflow of funds. Project D also has an outflow of funds in its first year and so this is also shown in brackets. It is discounted in the same way and again will result in a negative cash flow. This will happen in projects which require considerable capital development followed by significant injections of working capital over a period of time. If the project is slow in its returns in the initial years, the outflows will exceed the inflows.

Annual cash flows in perpetuity

6.8 By simply looking at the discount factor tables (see end of this chapter) you will note that the present value of £1 in future years gets smaller and smaller. For example, using the 10% cost of capital table £1 in year 15 is only worth $6\frac{1}{2}$ pence today. From this you can deduce that the impact of later years gets less and less significant and eventually will become nothing! We can see that at 10% £1 invested annually for 5 years is worth £3.79, for 10 years is worth £6.14 in today's value and for 15 years is worth £7.60. If we went on forever this would reach a limit. This limit is defined arithmetically as:

$$\text{NPV of £1 in perpetuity} = \frac{1}{r}$$

when r is the rate of investment/cost of capital. Hence at 10% the present value of £1 invested annually is

$$\frac{1}{0.10} = £10.$$

7. DISCOUNTED CASH FLOW: INTERNAL RATE OF RETURN (IRR)

7.1 The internal rate of return method of DCF involves:

(a) calculating the rate of return which is expected from a project;
(b) comparing the rate of return with the cost of capital.

7.2 If a project earns a higher rate of return than the cost of capital, it will be worth undertaking (and its NPV would be positive). If it earns a lower rate of return, it is not worthwhile (and its NPV would be negative).

If a project earns a return which is exactly equal to the cost of capital, its NPV will be 0 and it will only just be worthwhile.

Example: calculating the internal rate of return (IRR)

7.3　Suppose that a project would cost £20,000 and the annual net cash inflows are expected to be:

Year	Cash flow (£)
1	8,000
2	10,000
3	6,000
4	4,000

Table of factors for the present value of £1

Years	10%	11%	12%	13%	14%	15%	16%	17%	18%	19%	20%
1	0.909	0.901	0.893	0.885	0.877	0.870	0.862	0.855	0.847	0.840	0.833
2	0.826	0.812	0.797	0.783	0.769	0.756	0.743	0.731	0.718	0.706	0.694
3	0.753	0.731	0.712	0.693	0.675	0.658	0.641	0.624	0.609	0.593	0.579
4	0.683	0.659	0.636	0.613	0.592	0.572	0.552	0.534	0.516	0.499	0.482
5	0.621	0.594	0.567	0.543	0.519	0.497	0.476	0.456	0.437	0.419	0.402

What is the internal rate of return of the project?

Solution

7.4　The IRR is a rate of interest at which the NPV is 0 and the discounted (present) values of benefits add up to £20,000.

We need to find out what interest rate or cost of capital would give an NPV of 0.

7.5　The way we do this is to guess what it might be, and calculate the NPV at this cost of capital. It is most unlikely that the NPV will turn out to be 0, but we are hoping that it will be nearly 0.

7.6　We repeat this exercise until we find two rates of return:

(a)　one at which the NPV is a small positive value, where the actual IRR will be higher than this rate of return; and

(b)　one at which the NPV is a small negative value, where the actual IRR will be lower than this rate of return.

The actual IRR will then be found (approximately) by using the two rates in (a) and (b).

7.7　In our example, we might begin by trying discount rates of 10%, 15% and 20%.

Year	Cash flow	Discount factor at 10%	Present value at 10%	Discount factor at 15%	Present value at 15%	Discount factor at 20%	Present value at 20%
0	(20,000)	1.000	(20,000)	1.000	(20,000)	1.000	(20,000)
1	8,000	0.909	7,272	0.870	6,960	0.833	6,664
2	10,000	0.826	8,260	0.756	7,560	0.694	6,940
3	6,000	0.751	4,506	0.658	3,948	0.579	3,474
4	4,000	0.683	2,732	0.572	2,288	0.482	1,928
Net present value			2,770		756		(994)

The IRR is more than 15% but less than 20%. We could try to be more accurate by trying a discount rate of 16%, 17%, 18% or 19%, but in this solution we will use the values for 15% and 20%.

7.8   To estimate the IRR, we now assume that the NPV falls steadily and at a constant rate between £756 at 15% and £(994) at 20%. This represents a fall of £(756 + 994) = £1,750 in NPV between 15% and 20%. This is an average fall of:

$$\frac{£1,750}{(20-15)\%} = \text{£350 in NPV for each 1\% increase in the discount rate.}$$

Since the IRR is where the NPV is 0, it must be $\frac{£756}{£350} \times 1\%$ above 15% = approximately 2.2% above 15% = 17.2%.

7.9   We could show this process graphically to indicate approximately where we believe the IRR would fall. From the example we know IRR is between 15% and 20% which gives NPV's of 756 and (994) respectively. Then:

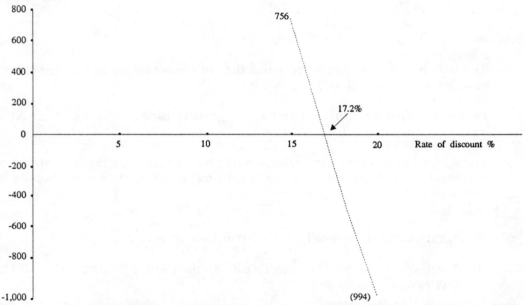

7.10   The IRR ratio where NPV is zero is often referred to as the yield of the project. Companies will often have internal limits or 'hurdle ratios' below which they will determine that a project is not worth investing in. In the case above and given that the company hurdle rate is 15% the decision is likely to be 'that the project is worthwhile since it has a yield of 17.2%, and an initial capital outlay of £20,000. This exceeds the target yield of 15% for investments.

Exercise

A manager is faced with two investment opportunities, A and B.

Each requires an initial outlay of £37,000, which is all that is currently available in the manager's budget. The anticipated net cash flows from the projects over their expected useful lives are as follows.

	A £	B £
Year 1	15,000	6,000
Year 2	15,000	6,000
Year 3	15,000	6,000
Year 4	-	6,000
Year 5	-	40,000
Total	45,000	64,000

Which project would you recommend on the basis of the following evaluation techniques?

(a) Payback.
(b) Net present value.
(c) Internal rate of return.

Take the appropriate discount rate as being 12%.

Solution

(a) Project A recoups the initial outlay of £37,000 in year 3. Assuming the cash flows are generated at a steady rate, the payback period is 2 7/15 years (£15,000 + £15,000 + £7,000 = £37,000).

Project B recoups its initial outlay in year 5. Assuming the cash flow in year 5 is at an even rate, the payback period is 4 13/40 years (£6,000 + £6,000 + £6,000 + £6,000 + £13,000 = £37,000).

The payback period of project A is shorter than that of project B. Project A should therefore be recommended.

(b) *Project A*

Year	Cash flow £	Discount factor at 12%	Present value £
0	(37,000)	1.000	(37,000)
1-3	15,000 pa	2.402	36,030
		NPV	(970)

Project B

Year	Cash flow £	Discount factor at 12%	Present value £
0	(37,000)	1.000	(37,000)
1-4	6,000 pa	3.037	18,222
5	40,000	0.567	22,680
			3,902

Project B should be recommended since it has a positive NPV (whereas project A has a negative NPV).

(c)   The only way to calculate IRR is by trial and error.

Project A

We might begin by trying a discount rate of 10% for project A.

Year	Cash flow £	Discount factor at 10%	Present value £
0	(37,000)	1.000	37,000
1-3	15,000 pa	2.487	37,305
		NPV	305

In (a) above, the NPV of project A was negative at 12%, but calculated at 10% it is positive. We can therefore interpolate between 10% and 12% to find the discount rate which produces NPV = 0.

The formula for estimating the IRR by interpolation is as follows.

$$IRR = A + \left[\frac{N_A}{N_A + N_B} (B - A) \right]$$

Where   A is the rate of return with a positive NPV.
   B is the rate of return with a negative NPV.
   N_A is the positive NPV at discount rate A.
   N_B is the negative NPV at discount rate B.

Let us apply the formula.

$$IRR_A = 0.10 + \frac{305}{305 + 970} (0.12 - 0.10) = .1048 = 10.48\%.$$

Project B

Let us try a discount rate of 15% for project B.

Year	Cash flow £	Discount factor at 12%	Present value £
0	(37,000)	1.000	(37,000)
1-4	6,000 pa	2.855	17,130
5	40,000	0.497	19,880
		NPV	10

We could use the formula to refine our answer further but it is sufficient to use 15% as the IRR of project B since a NPV of ten is sufficiently close to a NPV of zero.

Project B should be recommended since it has a higher IRR than project A.

8. MUTUALLY EXCLUSIVE PROJECTS

8.1 Now we must consider mutually exclusive projects. These are projects which are effectively competing for the same scarce resource, namely cash. We have already seen one method of calculating the alternatives using the profitability ratio. The exercise described here is known as 'capital rationing'.

Example: mutually exclusive projects

8.2 Suppose that a company is considering two mutually exclusive options, option A and option B. The cash flows for each would be:

Year		Option A £	Option B £
0	Capital outlay	(10,200)	(35,250)
1	Net cash inflow	6,000	18,000
2	Net cash inflow	5,000	15,000
3	Net cash inflow	3,000	15,000

The company's cost of capital is 16%.

Solution

8.3 The NPV of each project is calculated below:

Year	Discount factor 16% £	Option A Cash flow £	Option A Present value £	Option B Cash flow £	Option B Present value £
0	1.000	(10,200)	(10,200)	(35,250)	(35,250)
1	0.862	6,000	5,172	18,000	15,516
2	0.743	5,000	3,715	15,000	11,145
3	0.641	3,000	1,923	15,000	9,615
		NPV =	+610	NPV =	+1,026

However, the IRR of option A is 20%, and the IRR Of option B is only 18%.

8.4 On a comparison of NPVs, option B would be preferred, but on a comparison of IRRs, option A would be preferred.

8.5 Using the profitability ratio, option A would have a ratio of 1.06 and option B a ratio of 1.03 so again option A would be chosen. Now this is a little confusing. However, we can say that option B *is better* if we can only do either option A or option B. This is because the *differences in the cash flows* between the two options, when discounted at the cost of capital of 16%, show that the present value of the incremental benefits from option B compared with option A exceed the PV of the incremental costs.

This can be re-stated in the following ways.

(a) The NPV of the differential cash flows is positive, and so it is worth spending the extra capital to get the extra benefits; also

(b) The IRR of the differential cash flows exceeds the cost of capital 16%, and so it is worth spending the extra capital to get the extra benefits.

8.6 Year	Option A cash flow £	Option B cash flow £	Difference £	Discount factor at 16%	Present value of difference £
0	(10,200)	(35,250)	(25,050)	1.000	(25,050)
1	6,000	18,000	12,000	0.862	10,344
2	5,000	15,000	10,000	0.743	7,430
3	3,000	15,000	12,000	0.641	7,692
				NPV of difference	416

The NPV of the difference, of course is the difference between the NPV of option A (£610) and the NPV of option B (£1,026).

The IRR of the differential cash flows is a little over 18%.

8.7 We would use the profitability ratio when we have a finite amount of capital to invest. In the above case it would suggest that if we have £35,250 to invest, then being able to invest in three option A's instead of one option B would be preferable because both the total NPV and the IRR of all three projects would exceed the NPV and IRR of option B above. Note that the profitability ratio of each project A will remain the same.

8.8 The lesson to learn here is that none of the techniques is current in its own right. They each give a different emphasis to the elements affecting the future cash flows and the company must decide how important the various aspects of each project are within the overall corporate objective. A high NPV but with profits only being made from year five onwards and with a heavy initial investment may not allow the corporate objectives to be achieved in the meantime. These techniques are therefore only indicators, not decision makers in their own right.

8.9 From a purely arithmetical viewpoint, in using there techniques, we can draw conclusions. If capital is rationed or limited in one year and projects can be divided or duplicated (for example, if a project is said to cost £50,000 and we only have £25,000 available, then we can effectively invest in half the project and get half the benefits; similarly if we have £50,000 to spend and our project costs £25,000 then we can do two projects of the same type) the we would wish to maximise the return. This is done by using the profitability index. You will find this will always give the same ranking of projects as the use of IRR. The ranking of projects with different capital outlays and benefits by using the absolute NPV generated will mislead management from the most efficient use of funds.

Limitations of capital rationing techniques

8.10 There are various limitations to the use of the techniques described in this section. The most significant of these are that:

(a) It has been assumed that fractions of projects may be accepted, whereas in practice, this might not be so.

(b) No account has been taken of the risk associated with the various projects, and the attitudes towards risk of a company's management and shareholders.

(c)   Interdependencies between projects have not been accounted for: for example, if Project A is undertaken without Project B, the costs of Project A might be higher (or revenues lower) than if Project B were undertaken at the same time.

(d)   Linear relationships are assumed, so that if a fraction of Project X were undertaken, the costs and benefits would be earned in the same proportion, to give a proportional NPV. In practice, there might be economies (or diseconomies) of scale, so that if, say, one half of Project X were undertaken, the NPV might be only, say, one quarter of the NPV of the entire project. This is because the *differences in the cash flows* between the two options, when discounted at the cost of capital of 16%, show that the present value of the incremental benefits from option B compared with option A exceed the PV of the incremental costs.

9.   THE REAL RATE AND THE MONEY (NOMINAL) RATE OF RETURN

9.1   So far we have not considered the effect of inflation on the appraisal of capital investment proposals. As the inflation rate increases so will the minimum return required by an investor. For example, you might be happy with a rate of return of 5% in an inflation-free world, but if inflation was running at 15% you would expect a considerably greater yield.

What level of return should you choose? We will examine this by looking at an example.

Example: real rate of return

9.2   A company wishes to invest in a machine at a cost of £50,000 which will generate sales of £20,000 pa for five years and for which the additional costs of running the machine will be £5,000 pa.

(a)   Assuming inflation is running at 6% pa and the company's real cost of money is 10%, should the project be accepted?

(b)   If sales prices are expected to rise at 2% and costs at 7% and the company's money cost of capital is 16%, should the investment be made?

Solution

9.3   (a)   Under the first case we are given the real cost of capital and told of a general rate of inflation. We must therefore inflate the sales and additional costs by 6% pa (remember this is cumulative) before discounting. To get to the approximate money cost of capital we will add the general inflation rate to the real cost of capital giving a money rate of 16% (10 + 6).

The calculation is:

Year	Capital cost + sales less Discount costs £	Inflated (6%) £	Discount factor	NPV £
0	(50,000)	(50,000)	1	(50,000)
1	15,000	15,900	$1/1.16$	13,707
2	15,000	16,854	$1/1.16^2$	12,525
3	15,000	17,865	$1/1.16^3$	11,445
4	15,000	18,937	$1/1.16^4$	10,459
5	15,000	20,073	$1/1.16^5$	7,557
			NPV	5,693

The project should go ahead.

(b) Under part (b) the elements of cash flow are inflated at different ratios, and we are given the money cost of capital. Here we simply follow the guidelines.

Year	Cash outlay + costs £	Inflated (7%) £	Sales inflated (2%) £	Net cash flows £	NPV £
0	(50,000)	(50,000)		(50,000)	(50,000)
1	(5,000)	(5,350)	20,400	15,050	12,974
2	(5,000)	(5,725)	20,808	15,083	11,209
3	(5,000)	(6,125)	21,224	15,099	9,673
4	(5,000)	(6,554)	21,649	15,095	8,337
5	(5,000)	(7,013)	22,082	15,069	7,175
				NPV	(632)

Now the project is not worth doing!

9.4 In your studies you will either be given the money cost of capital and asked to inflate the cash streams or be asked what impact a general rate of inflation will have on the real cost of capital and the cash strains. The method adopted is the first part of the example above is not absolutely correct, but the approximation used is sufficient for the purposes of your studies. If you follows the rules laid out in the example you will have no problems.

Points to note on DCF

9.5 It might be tempting to suppose that DCF is a technique which is always used in capital expenditure evaluations, because it allows for the time value of money. In practice, many firms (especially small firms) make their capital investment decisions without first checking to find the NPV or IRR of the project. There might be several reasons for this, but two in particular seem to be most relevant.

(a) Capital expenditure might be invested in a project with a very long life, such as the purchase of buildings or major items of plant and machinery. Such a project might have a positive NPV and a high IRR, but it could be many years before these benefits are fully realised. Companies might think that their business cannot afford to wait a long time for a good return, and that it is more important that profits should 'pay back' the capital invested as quickly as possible. In such circumstances, use of the payback method might be preferred to DCF.

(b) One of the biggest problems in trying to evaluate a capital expenditure project is forecasting the future with accuracy. It is difficult to decide what savings or profits might arise from a capital project for the next five or ten years. Indeed, it is often difficult to decide how long a project might last. Given such uncertainties, an NPV or IRR can only be an approximate guess or estimate of the value of a project. Companies might therefore take the view that DCF should only be used either:

(i) if the uncertainties about the future are carefully analysed and quantified;

(ii) if the payback period is also considered, and the project is expected to pay back its costs fairly quickly.

10. INTRODUCING RISK

10.1 In the previous section we noted that the future is difficult to predict. As a result when we analyse projects we do so with only one certainty, that our forecast will be wrong! The degree to which our forecasts are inaccurate may be a reflection of the risk factor. Two different projects may have exactly the same capital requirement and the same present value. However, one may be extremely uncertain compared with one where we are confident of our predictions. For example, a retail store chain in the UK may wish to open its 100th store in the UK. At the same time it may review the possibility of opening its first store in Hong Kong. These two options may need to be assessed in a totally different light.

10.2 Risk is part of every management decision. The ability of management to understand the elements of risk involved and be able to act accordingly will often determine the success of any strategy. Risk in any project can be divided into three main elements.

(a) *The inherent risk of the industry or market itself.* For example, the fashion industry is a higher risk industry than the food processing industry; and to a UK firm, export markets in the Third World are likely to be higher risk markets than the UK market.

(b) *The stage in the product's life cycle.* Every product has a life cycle, and the 'classical' product life cycle consists of four stages.

(i) introduction;
(ii) growth;
(iii) maturity;
(iv) decline.

When an investment is made in a product which is in its introductory phase, there is a high risk that it will fail to win market acceptance, and will have a very short market life. When an investment is made in a declining product, the risk of a rapid decline in sales is also high.

(c) *Proportion of fixed costs in total costs.* When an investment involves a high proportion of fixed costs (costs which are not dependent on the level of volume of production), it will need to achieve greater sales volume just to break even, and so the business risk will be higher.

11. METHODS OF TREATING RISK

11.1 The methods of treating or analysing risk for capital expenditure projects include the following.

(a) Adjusting the discount rate to allow a premium on the cost of capital for risk.

(b) Expecting projects to pay back, or achieve a positive net present value within a certain time limit.

(c) Sensitivity analysis.

(d) Using probability estimates of cash flows.

(e) Simulation modelling.

Adjusting the discount rate

11.2 In this method of allowing for risk, a premium is added to the discount rate as a safety margin.

By adding a safety margin into the discount rate, marginally profitable projects (the riskiest projects) are less likely to have a positive NPV. For example, if a company's true cost of capital is, say, 10% all capital projects might be evaluated against a discount rate of, say, 15%. Projects which would have a positive NPV at a discount rate of 10% but a negative NPV at 15% would then be considered too risky to undertake.

11.3 The merit in this method is that it gives recognition to the idea that risky investments ought to earn a higher return as reward for the risks that are taken. However, if the same topped-up discount rate is applied to all the proposed capital projects, no distinction would be made between more risky and less risky investments. And how is the size of the risk premium decided anyway?

Payback period: applying a time limit

11.4 A view can be taken that estimates of future cash flows are difficult to make at the best of times, and estimates of cash flows several years ahead are quite likely to be inaccurate. It is also difficult to control capital projects over a long period of time, to ensure that the expected benefits are fully realised.

11.5 A method of limiting the risk on a capital project is to apply a payback time limit, so that a project should not be undertaken unless it pays back within, say, 4 years.

11.6 There are two ways of applying a payback time limit.

(a) A project might be expected to pay back within a certain time limit, and in addition show a positive NPV from its net cash flows.

(b) Alternatively, a project might be expected to pay back *in discounted cash flow terms* within a certain time period. For example, a project might be required to have a positive NPV on its cumulative cash flows before the end of year 4.

Sensitivity analysis

11.7 One method of applying sensitivity tests to a project is to re-calculate the NPV if:

(a) the initial cost of the investment were, perhaps, 5% higher than expected;

(b) running costs were, say, 10% higher, or savings/benefits were, perhaps 10% lower than estimated;

(c) costs were, say, 5% higher and savings 5% lower.

Thus sensitivity analysis is applied by varying the expected cash flows of a project, to measure what would happen if the outcome of the investment was different to that expected.

11.8 If the NPV is negative when costs are increased by a small margin, or benefits reduced a little, the project would be rejected on the grounds that it is too sensitive to variations in one or more key cost or revenue items.

11.9 Sensitivity analysis is widely used in businesses as the primary assessor of risk, if only because it is relatively easy to change a financial model to indicate the importance of one or more of the variables. It can, for example, vary the sales revenue if demand is lower than currently anticipated because of a recession. Imagine how sales forecasts made in 1986 would appear under today's economic climate if the project being evaluated then had been the launch of a new type of brick for use in industrial construction.

11.10 The use of sensitivity analysis in many cases may be used to determine just how much the major variables in the equation can individually vary before the NPV becomes negative. Equally it can be used to vary the timing of our cash inflows. Suppose we had predicted that a project would only start generating cash two years after the initial cash investment. We may now vary that assumption and rework the model on the assumptions that the project does not generate cash until the end of the third year.

11.11 One final area to examine for our sensitivity analysis is the concept of the *residual values*. An investment decisions may involve the building of, say, a factory and result in a property based assets. Our project evaluation will ascribe a value to that asset at the end of the period under review and thus residual value is crucial to the decision making process. The asset will have a useful life which will generally far exceed the period over which we are assessing the project. Hence we will attribute a value as at the end of the review period.

11.12 In calculating our sensitivity analysis it is important to remember that we are evaluating an ongoing project and determining if it is particularly susceptible to changes in our basic assumptions for the trading environment. We are trying to assess the risk factor and not determining a worst case or disaster situation. However, it is worthwhile being reasonably cautious in ascribing residual values to a property based asset. Too bullish a prediction will result in the business becoming a property investment company and will hide the marketing success or failure of the proposal.

11.13 There are two main weaknesses of sensitivity analysis.

(a) In spite of the possibility of checking the sensitivity of a project's NPV to changes in the cash flows from two or more items in conjunction, it is more usual for sensitivity analysis to be applied to each cost or revenue item individually. This is often unrealistic, because such items are often interdependent.

(b) Sensitivity analysis does not examine the *probability* that any particular variation in costs or revenues might occur. For example how *likely* is it that running costs will be 5% or 10% higher than expected?

12. DECISION TREES

12.1 The inability of sensitivity analysis to allocate probabilities to the decision making process is addressed by using the decision tree methodology. This method requires that we identify all the stages in the decision process and that we evaluate the outcomes at each stage. We then ascribe mathematical probabilities to each potential outcome. Although this process will give us a risk-based financial result, it is most important that it identifies the decision points where management action to alter events can result in the minimisation of risk either by altering the initial strategy or by correcting mistakes. The greater the management control of the project, the lower the risk will become.

12.2 A brewing company, Best Butter Ltd, wishes to expand its small operational base by buying pubs in London. The cost of one pub chain is £15 million and it expects that there will be cash outflows in years 1 and 2 of £2 million each year. Thereafter it will make £1 million in year 3 and £12 million in years 4 to 10. The pubs will be worth £4 million at the end of the period. Assume a 10% cost of capital.

The NPV calculation would be:

Year	Cash flow £m	Discount factor	NPV £m
0	(15)	1.000	(15.00)
1	(2)	0.909	(1.82)
2	(2)	0.826	(1.65)
3	1	0.751	(0.75)
4–10	12	3.658	43.90
10	4	0.386	1.54
		NPV	27.72

12.3 As we can see the project is very rewarding but the returns do not really start to flow in until year four. Sensitivity analysis can be used to suggest that perhaps trade will not be good in year four and that we only have a cash inflow of £1m in that year so we delay the high earning years by one year. Now we can re-evaluate the NPV.

Year	Cash flow £m	Discount factor	NPV £m
0	(15)	1.000	(15.00)
1	(2)	0.909	(1.82)
2	(2)	0.826	(1.65)
3	1	0.751	(0.75)
4	1	0.683	0.68
5–10	12	2.975	35.70
10	4	0.386	1.54
		NPV	20.20

12.4 We can also determine how low the cash inflows in years 5–10 must now decline before the project becomes marginal ie has a zero NPV.

Thus: NPV above is £20.20m
Present value in years five to ten must decline by £20.20m to give an overall zero NPV for the project
Present value in years five to ten must equal £15.5m (£35.70 - £20.20m)
Annual cash inflow is hence:

$$\frac{£15.50m}{2.975} = £5.21m$$

12.5 We should now look at the decision taken for this purchase of pubs and their operational success. We can simplify the process by assuming that a similar decision process will occur every year and hence only look at one period.

12.6 We can now introduce the measurement of risk into our decision tree approach by using probabilities.

12.7 A company might be reviewing three options:

(a) launch a new product, and advertise nationally; or
(b) launch a new product, and don't advertise; or
(c) don't launch the product.

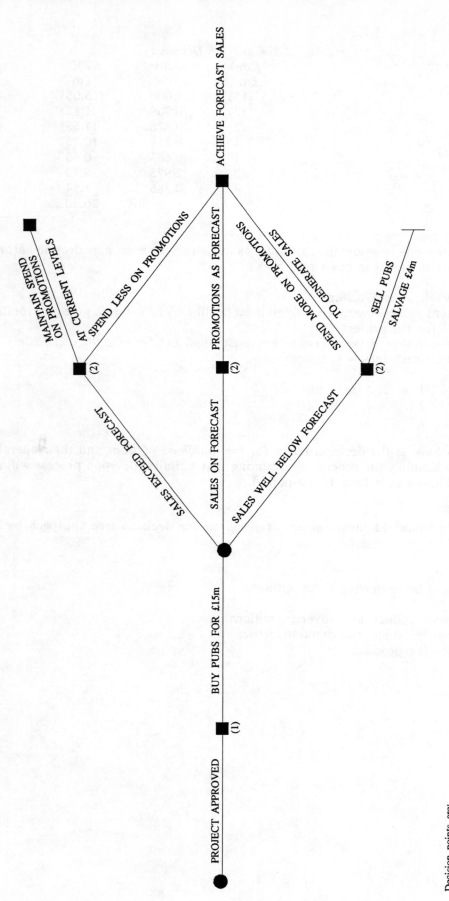

PROJECT APPROVED

BUY PUBS FOR £15m

(1)

SALES EXCEED FORECAST

SALES ON FORECAST

SALES WELL BELOW FORECAST

MAINTAIN SPEND
ON PROMOTIONS
AT CURRENT LEVELS

SPEND LESS ON PROMOTIONS

(2)

PROMOTIONS AS FORECAST

(2)

SPEND MORE ON PROMOTIONS
TO GENERATE SALES

SELL PUBS

SALVAGE £4m

(2)

ACHIEVE FORECAST SALES

Decision points are:

(1) All investment committed at once
(2) Change promotional activity to generate sales and profits in accordance with projections

This could be shown in either of two ways, (i) and (ii) below.

(i)

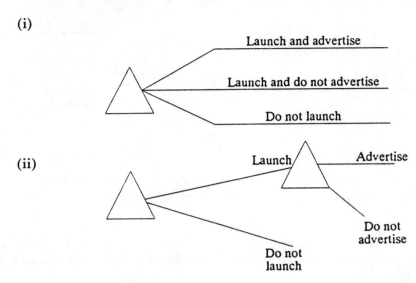

(ii)

12.8 Now suppose that a company can choose to launch a new product XYZ or not. If the product is launched, expected sales and expected unit costs might be:

Sales			Unit costs	
Units	Probability		£	Probability
10,000	0.8		6	0.7
15,000	0.2		8	0.3

The decision tree could be drawn as follows.

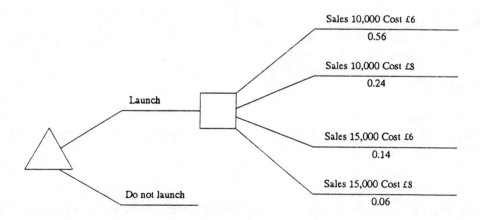

12.9 Occasionally, a decision taken now will influence another decision which might then have to be taken at some time in the future, depending on how results turn out. When this situation arises, the decision tree can be drawn as a two-stage tree, as follows:

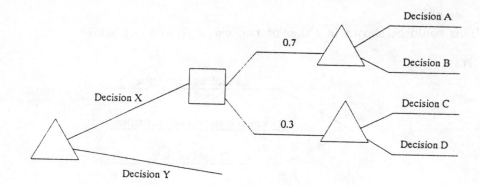

In this tree, either a choice between A and B or else a choice between C and D will be made, depending on the outcome which occurs as a consequence of choosing X.

12.10 The decision tree should be in chronological order from left to right; when there are two-stage decision trees, the first decision in time should be drawn on the left. This is the decision of immediate concern to management.

Example: drawing a decision tree

12.11 Beethoven Ltd has a new wonder product, the vylin, of which it expects great things. At the moment the company has two courses of action open to it, to test market the product or abandon it. If they test it, it will cost £100,000 and the market response could be positive or negative with respective probabilities of 0.60 and 0.40. If the response is positive the company could either abandon the product or market it full scale. If it markets the vylin full scale, the outcome might be low, medium or high demand, and the respective net payoffs would be (200), 200 or 1,000 in units of £1,000 (which means that the result could range from a net loss of £200,000 to a gain of £1,000,000). These outcomes have probabilities of 0.20, 0.50 and 0.30 respectively.

If the result of the test marketing is negative and the company goes ahead and markets the product, estimated losses would be £600,000. If, at any point, the company abandons the product, there would be a net gain of £50,000 from the sale of scrap. All the financial values have been discounted to the present.

Required

(a) Draw a decision tree.
(b) Include figures for cost, loss or profit on the appropriate branches of the tree.

Solution

12.12 The starting point for the tree is to establish what decision has to be made now. What are the options? In this case, they are:

(a) test market;
(b) abandon.

The outcome of the 'abandon' option is known with certainty. There are two possible outcomes of the option to test market, positive response and negative response.

228

Depending on the outcome of the test market, another decision will then be made, to abandon the product or to go ahead.

12.13 This is the decision tree:

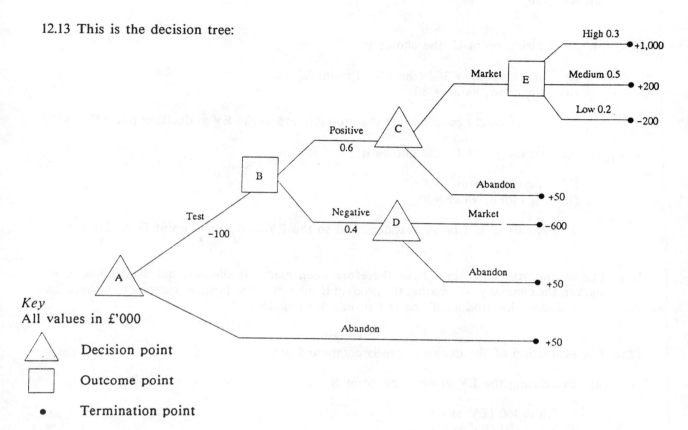

Key
All values in £'000

△   Decision point

▢   Outcome point

●   Termination point

Evaluating the decision with a decision tree

12.14 The expected value (EV) of each decision option can be evaluated, using the decision tree to help with keeping the logic properly sorted out. The basic rules are as follows.

(a) We start on the right hand side of the tree and work back towards the left hand side and the current decision under consideration.

(b) It will help if you label each decision point and outcome point on the tree, to give it an identification.

(c) Working from right to left, we calculate the EV of revenue, cost, contribution or profit at each outcome point on the tree.

12.15 In our example, the right-hand-most outcome point is point E, and the EV is:

	Profit x £'000	Probability p	px £'000
High	1,000	0.3	300
Medium	200	0.5	100
Low	(200)	0.2	(40)
		1.0	EV 360

229

This is the EV of the decision to market the product if the test market shows positive response. It may help you to write the EV on the decision tree itself, at the appropriate outcome point.

12.16 (a)   At decision point C, the choice is

    (i)   market, EV + 360 (the EV at point E); or
    (ii)   abandon, value + 50.

The choice would be to market the product, and so the EV at decision point C is +360.

(b)   At decision point D, the choice is:

    (i)   market, value -600;
    (ii)   abandon, value +50.

The choice would be to abandon, and so the EV at decision point D is +50.

12.17 The second stage decisions have therefore been made. If the original decision is to test market, the company will market the product if the test shows positive customer response, and will abandon the product if the test results are negative.

12.18 The evaluation of the decision tree is completed by:

(a)   calculating the EV at outcome point B.

$$0.6 \times 360 \text{ (EV at C)}$$
$$+ \ 0.4 \times \ 50 \text{ (EV at D)}$$
$$= 216 + 20 = 236$$

(b)   comparing the options at point A, which are:

    (i)   test: EV = EV at B minus test marketing cost = 236 - 100 = 136;
    (ii)   abandon: value 50.

The choice would be to test market the product, because it has a higher EV of profit.

12.19 It would be useful to work through the above example again. The ability to measure risk by using probability analysis is important to our assessment of any project. Its most obvious disadvantage, however, of the subjective use of that probability. Who determines that the probability of success by one route is 60% whereas the alternative will be 40%? Unfortunately no one has yet discovered the ultimate crystal ball and as a result all forecasting procedures are subjective. All we as managers can do is try to use known criteria to maximise the logical basis for any assumptions used in our forecasting.

13. CONCLUSION

13.1 A long-term view of benefits and costs must be taken when reviewing a capital expenditure project.

13.2 The return on investment method, sometimes called accounting rate of return method, calculates the estimated average profits as a percentage of the estimated average investment.

13.3 The payback period is the time taken for the initial investment to be recovered in the cash inflows from the project.

Payback method is particularly relevant if there are liquidity problems, or if distant forecasts are very uncertain.

13.4 Discounted cash flow techniques take account of the time value of money - the fact that £1 received now is worth more because it could be invested to become a greater sum at the end of a year, and even more after the end of two years etc. As with payback, discounted cash flow techniques use cash figures before depreciation in the calculations.

13.5 Annuities are an annual cash payment or receipt which is the same amount every year for a number of years.

13.6 The net present value method calculates the present value of all cash flows, and sums them to give the *net* present value. If this is positive, then the project is acceptable.

13.7 The internal rate of return technique uses a trial and error method to discover the discount rate which produces the NPV of zero. This discount rate will be the return forecast for the project.

13.8 Risk should be assessed within the decision making process. This is normally done by use of sensitivity analysis and the decision tree analysis. At the end of the day, however, we are trying to understand the points when management intervention and control will be required to determine how any project should proceed.

TEST YOUR KNOWLEDGE

The numbers in brackets refer to paragraphs of this chapter

1 How is the accounting rate of return calculated? (2.3)

2 What is one of the major disadvantages of the payback method? (2.9)

3 Why is £1 now worth more than £1 at a later time? (3.3)

4 What is an annuity? (5.1)

5 What is the profitability index? (6.2)

6 What are the limitations of capital rationing techniques? (8.10)

7 What are the three main elements of risk? (10.2)

8 A cost of £20,000 is expected to occur near the beginning of year 3. To what year should the £20,000 be allocated in DCF analysis? (see below)

9 The annuity factor at 9% for years 1–5 is 3.890, years 1–6 is 4.486 and years 1–8 is 5.535. What is the PV of £10,000 pa for years 6–8? (see below)

10 A seven year project will need working capital of £50,000 from the start of year 1. What should the cash flows be in a DCF analysis, to allow for the effects of increases or decreases in working capital on cash flows? (see below)

11 What is the PV of £9,000 pa in perpetuity, discounted at a cost of capital of 12%? (see below)

Now try question 11 at the end of the text

Solutions

1 Year 2

2 Years 6–8 = Years 1–8 minus years 1–5. (5.535 − 3.890) × £10,000 = £16,450.

3 Year 0 −£50,000. Year 7 + £50,000

4 $\dfrac{£9,000}{0.12}$ = £75,000

Present value of £1, ie $(1 + r)^{-n}$ Where r = discount rate, n = number of periods until payment.

Discount rates (r)

Periods (n)	1%	2%	3%	4%	5%	6%	7%	8%	9%	10%	
1	0.990	0.980	0.971	0.962	0.952	0.943	0.935	0.926	0.917	0.909	1
2	0.980	0.961	0.943	0.925	0.907	0.890	0.873	0.857	0.842	0.826	2
3	0.971	0.942	0.915	0.889	0.864	0.840	0.816	0.794	0.772	0.751	3
4	0.961	0.924	0.888	0.855	0.823	0.792	0.763	0.735	0.708	0.683	4
5	0.951	0.906	0.863	0.822	0.784	0.747	0.713	0.681	0.650	0.621	5
6	0.942	0.888	0.837	0.790	0.746	0.705	0.666	0.630	0.596	0.564	6
7	0.933	0.871	0.813	0.760	0.711	0.665	0.623	0.583	0.547	0.513	7
8	0.923	0.853	0.789	0.731	0.677	0.627	0.582	0.540	0.502	0.467	8
9	0.941	0.837	0.766	0.703	0.645	0.592	0.544	0.500	0.460	0.424	9
10	0.905	0.820	0.744	0.676	0.614	0.558	0.508	0.463	0.422	0.386	10
11	0.896	0.804	0.722	0.650	0.585	0.527	0.475	0.429	0.388	0.350	11
12	0.887	0.788	0.702	0.625	0.557	0.497	0.444	0.397	0.356	0.319	12
13	0.879	0.773	0.681	0.601	0.530	0.469	0.415	0.368	0.326	0.290	13
14	0.870	0.758	0.661	0.577	0.505	0.442	0.388	0.340	0.299	0.263	14
15	0.861	0.743	0.642	0.555	0.481	0.417	0.362	0.315	0.275	0.239	15

	11%	12%	13%	14%	15%	16%	17%	18%	19%	20%	
1	0.901	0.893	0.885	0.877	0.870	0.862	0.855	0.847	0.840	0.833	1
2	0.812	0.797	0.783	0.769	0.756	0.743	0.731	0.718	0.706	0.694	2
3	0.731	0.712	0.693	0.675	0.658	0.641	0.624	0.609	0.593	0.579	3
4	0.659	0.636	0.613	0.592	0.572	0.552	0.534	0.516	0.499	0.482	4
5	0.593	0.567	0.543	0.519	0.497	0.476	0.456	0.437	0.419	0.402	5
6	0.535	0.507	0.480	0.456	0.432	0.410	0.390	0.370	0.352	0.335	6
7	0.482	0.452	0.425	0.400	0.376	0.354	0.333	0.314	0.296	0.279	7
8	0.434	0.404	0.376	0.351	0.327	0.305	0.285	0.266	0.249	0.233	8
9	0.391	0.361	0.333	0.308	0.284	0.263	0.243	0.225	0.209	0.194	9
10	0.352	0.322	0.295	0.270	0.247	0.227	0.208	0.191	0.176	0.162	10
11	0.317	0.287	0.261	0.237	0.215	0.195	0.178	0.162	0.148	0.135	11
12	0.286	0.257	0.231	0.208	0.187	0.168	0.152	0.137	0.124	0.112	12
13	0.258	0.229	0.204	0.182	0.163	0.145	0.130	0.116	0.104	0.093	13
14	0.232	0.205	0.181	0.160	0.141	0.125	0.111	0.099	0.088	0.078	14
15	0.209	0.183	0.160	0.140	0.123	0.108	0.095	0.084	0.074	0.065	15

Cumulative discount factors for the PV of £1 p.a., ie

$$\frac{1 - (1 + r)^{-n}}{r} \quad \text{where r = interest rate, n = periods}$$

Interest rates (r)

Periods (n)	1%	2%	3%	4%	5%	6%	7%	8%	9%	10%	
1	0.990	0.980	0.971	0.962	0.952	0.943	0.935	0.926	0.917	0.909	1
2	1.970	1.942	1.913	1.886	1.859	1.833	1.808	1.783	1.759	1.736	2
3	2.941	2.884	2.829	2.775	2.723	2.673	2.624	2.577	2.531	2.487	3
4	3.902	3.808	3.717	3.630	3.546	3.465	3.387	3.312	3.240	3.170	4
5	4.853	4.713	4.580	4.452	4.329	4.212	4.100	3.993	3.890	3.791	5
6	5.795	5.601	5.417	5.242	5.076	4.917	4.767	4.623	4.486	4.355	6
7	6.728	6.472	6.230	6.002	5.786	5.582	5.389	5.206	5.033	4.868	7
8	7.652	7.325	7.020	6.733	6.463	6.210	5.971	5.747	5.535	5.335	8
9	8.566	8.162	7.786	7.435	7.108	6.802	6.515	6.247	5.995	5.759	9
10	9.471	8.983	8.530	8.111	7.722	7.360	7.024	6.710	6.418	6.145	10
11	10.37	9.787	9.253	8.760	8.306	7.887	7.499	7.139	6.805	6.495	11
12	11.26	10.58	9.954	9.385	8.863	8.384	7.943	7.536	7.161	6.814	12
13	12.13	11.35	10.63	9.986	9.394	8.853	8.358	7.904	7.487	7.103	13
14	13.00	12.11	11.30	10.56	9.899	9.295	8.745	8.244	7.786	7.367	14
15	13.87	12.85	11.94	11.12	10.38	9.712	9.108	8.559	8.061	7.606	15

	11%	12%	13%	14%	15%	16%	17%	18%	19%	20%	
1	0.901	0.893	0.885	0.877	0.870	0.862	0.855	0.847	0.840	0.833	1
2	1.713	1.690	1.668	1.647	1.626	1.605	1.585	1.566	1.547	1.528	2
3	2.444	2.402	2.361	2.322	2.283	2.246	1.210	2.174	2.140	2.106	3
4	3.102	3.037	2.974	2.914	2.855	2.798	2.743	2.690	2.639	2.589	4
5	3.696	3.605	3.517	3.433	3.352	3.274	3.199	3.127	3.058	2.991	5
6	4.231	4.111	3.998	3.889	3.784	3.685	3.589	3.498	3.410	3.326	6
7	4.712	4.564	4.423	4.288	4.160	4.039	3.922	3.812	3.706	3.605	7
8	5.146	4.968	4.799	4.639	4.487	4.344	4.207	4.078	3.954	3.837	8
9	5.537	5.328	5.132	4.946	4.772	4.607	4.451	4.303	4.163	4.031	9
10	5.889	5.650	5.426	5.216	5.019	4.833	4.659	4.494	4.339	4.192	10
11	6.207	5.938	5.687	5.453	5.234	5.209	4.836	4.656	4.486	4.327	11
12	6.492	6.194	5.918	5.660	5.421	5.197	4.988	4.793	4.611	4.439	12
13	6.750	6.424	6.122	5.842	5.583	5.342	5.118	4.910	4.715	4.533	13
14	6.982	6.628	6.302	6.002	5.724	5.468	5.229	5.008	4.802	4.611	14
15	7.191	6.811	6.462	6.142	5.847	5.575	5.324	5.092	4.876	4.675	15

Chapter 12

SOURCES OF FINANCE

This chapter covers the following topics.

1. Sources of finance
2. Reinvesting profits
3. Equity funding
4. Loan stock
5. Convertible loan stock
6. Bank borrowings
7. Other methods of raising finance: fixed assets
8. Smaller companies
9. Other methods of raising finance: current assets

---

1. SOURCES OF FINANCE

1.1 Once the corporate objectives have been set and agreed, and the plan to achieve those objectives have been quantified, one problem remains. How are we going to finance all those wonderful expansion plans? The company will have short, medium and long term requirements and all those aspects will need to be funded.

1.2 Businesses have three main sources of funds available to them:

(a) reinvest the profits it generates;
(b) from its shareholders, both existing and new (equity); and
(c) from borrowings.

2. REINVESTING PROFITS

2.1 You will remember the basic description of the profit and loss account of a company. After profit after taxation two further items will usually be charged: extraordinary items and dividends. There are particular technical rules defining what is an extraordinary item (as opposed to items which are ordinarily profits or losses incurred in the normal course of business) and we will leave them to the technical accountants. Dividends, however, are a way of rewarding the shareholders or owners of the business for their risk in investing in the company. In a public company the shareholders will be looking to get a benefit from the growth in the value of their shares, or income by way of a dividend, or by a mixture of them both. In most cases the dividend will not pay out all of the available retained profits. Some will be retained and will be reinvested in the business.

2.2 Retained earnings are the single most important source of finance for UK companies. For any company, the amount of earnings retained within the business has a direct impact on the amount of dividends. Profit re-invested as retained earnings is profit that could have been paid out as a dividend.

2.3 The major reasons for using retained earnings to finance new investments, rather than to pay higher dividends and then raise new equity funds for the new investments, are as follows.

(a) The management of a company might easily believe that retained earnings are funds which do not cost anything. This is not true. All sources of long term finance have a cost, including retained earnings.

However, it is true that the use of retained earnings as a source of funds does not lead to a cost of raising the funds which involves a payment of cash. Raising large sums of money outside the company will inevitably result in the payment of fees and other costs.

(b) The dividend policy of a company is determined by the directors rather than the shareholders. Directors are people who might not be shareholders themselves, and so do not benefit personally from high dividends. Director-managers will regard retained earnings as an attractive source of finance because investment projects can be undertaken without involving either the shareholders or any outsiders.

(c) The use of retained earnings avoids the possibility of a change in control resulting from an issue of new shares.

(d) Using retained earnings builds up the company's equity, and so helps to keep down the gearing of its capital structure.

2.4 A company must restrict its self-financing through retained profits at least to the extent that it must satisfy a minimum requirement by shareholders for dividends. Shareholders should be paid a reasonable dividend, in line with realistic expectations, even if the directors would rather keep the funds for re-investing.

At the same time, a company that is looking for extra funds will not be expected by investors (such as banks) to pay generous dividends, nor over-generous salaries to owner-directors in the case of proprietary companies.

3. EQUITY FUNDING

3.1 A second and often-used source of finance is to ask existing and new shareholders to invest more funds in the business. The most frequent application of this source of funds is known as a 'rights issue'. This practice gives the existing shareholders the right to buy new shares in the company in exact proportion to the existing number of shares owned (for example you may be given the right to a 1 for 8 issue, which is one new share for every eight you already hold). Because the company is looking to encourage the shareholders to accept the offer, the issue is normally sold at a discount to the price currently available on the open market. Such issues are also usually underwritten by the large City institutions. This means that in exchange for a fee the institution will guarantee that the company receives all the cash injection that they are looking for, hence eliminating the risk that the shareholders will not take up the offer. Despite this underwriting, this process is expensive to the company because of the need to contact every shareholder with a detailed explanation of the needs of the company. As a result it is only used for the raising of large sums of money for large public companies.

3.2 Another way of raising funds is by issuing new shares to new shareholders. This process is most frequently used when one company acquires another. It simply issues new shares in itself, and the shareholders in the acquired business swap their shares for those in the acquiring company.

3.3 For example, company A has 15 million shares with a value of £5 each, hence giving the company a market capitalisation of £75 million. Company B has 10 million shares with a market value of £1 each. Company A can now offer one share in itself for every 5 held by the shareholders of company B. As a result the new structure of company A is:

Old shares	15m
New shares	2m
	17m

3.4 All the shares in company A are valued now at £5 and the acquired company has been bought for £10m or its equivalent value. Effectively no cash was actually raised in this case, but then company A did not have to find £10m in cash to finance the deal. This example is a little oversimplified for the purposes of explaining the mechanics of the deal and in practice company A will usually have to pay a premium to buy the target company. Similarly the price of shares will change as a result of the transaction because of market expectations.

3.5 Both the above examples indicate that shares are generally available. Although this is not true of privately owned companies, public companies make shares available to the public and these shares can be openly traded.

3.6 A company seeking to obtain additional equity funds may be:

(a) an unquoted company wishing to obtain a stock market quotation;

(b) an unquoted company wishing to issue new shares, but without obtaining a stock market quotation;

(c) a company which is already listed on the stock market wishing to issue additional new shares.

A stock exchange quotation might be obtained on the 'main market' of the Stock Exchange (a 'listing') or on the smaller Unlisted Securities Market (USM). There are current proposals to close the USM within the next few years.

3.7 Methods by which an unquoted company can obtain a quotation on the stock market are:

(a) an offer for sale;
(b) a prospectus issue;
(c) a placing;
(d) an introduction.

Of these, (a) and (c) are the most common.

Offer for sale

3.8 An offer for sale is a means of selling the shares of a company to the public at large.

(a) An unquoted company may issue new shares, and sell them on the Stock Exchange, to raise cash for the company. All the shares in the company, not just the new ones, would then become marketable.

(b) Private shareholders in an unquoted company may sell some of their existing shares to the general public. When this occurs, the company is not raising any new funds as no new shares are being issued, but is merely providing a wider market for its existing shares (all of which would become marketable), and giving existing shareholders the chance to cash in some of their investment in their company.

3.9 When companies 'go public' for the first time, a *large* issue will probably take the form of an offer for sale (and occasionally an offer for sale by tender). A smaller issue is more likely to be a placing, since the amount to be raised can be obtained more cheaply if the issuing house or similar sponsoring firm of brokers/market makers approaches selected institutional investors 'privately'.

3.10 A company *whose shares are already listed* might issue new shares to the general public. It is likely, however, that a new issue by a quoted company will be either a placing or a rights issue, which are described later.

A prospectus issue

3.11 In a prospectus issue, or public issue, a company offers its own shares to the general public. An issuing house or merchant bank may act as an agent, but not as an underwriter. This type of issue is therefore risky, and is very rare. Well known companies making a large new issue may use this method, and the company would almost certainly already have a quotation on the Stock Exchange.

A placing

3.12 A placing is an arrangement whereby the shares are not all put on offer to the public, but instead, the sponsoring market maker arranges for *most* of the issue to be bought by a small number of investors, usually institutional investors such as pension funds and insurance companies.

Offer for sale or placing?

3.13 When a company is planning a flotation on to the USM, or to apply for a full Stock Exchange listing, is it likely to prefer an offer for sale of its shares, or a placing?

Placings are much cheaper, although most of the shares will be placed with a relatively small number of (institutional) shareholders, which means that most of the shares are unlikely to be available for buying and selling in an 'active' market after the flotation. This is a particular problem for smaller companies.

A Stock Exchange introduction

3.14 By this method of obtaining a quotation, no shares are made available to the market, neither existing nor newly-created shares; nevertheless, the Stock Exchange grants a quotation. This will only happen where shares in a large company are already widely held, so that a market can be seen to exist. It may therefore be asked why a company should want an introduction. The reasons would be a greater marketability for the shares, a known share valuation for inheritance tax purposes and easier access in the future to additional capital.

3.15 So far we have considered the issuing of ordinary shares which in most cases are classified as shares which carry a vote at the various meetings of the company. Each vote will carry equal weight, although it is possible to get different classes of ordinary shares with differing voting rights. This is outside the scope of your syllabus. Cash can be raised in addition to ordinary shares by way of preference shares and loan stocks.

Preference shares

3.16 Preference shares have a fixed percentage dividend before any dividend is paid to the ordinary shareholders. As with ordinary shares a preference dividend can only be paid if sufficient distributable profits are available, although with *cumulative* preference shares the right to an unpaid dividend is carried forward to later years. The arrears of dividend on cumulative preference shares must be paid before any dividend is paid to the ordinary shareholders. Hence preference shares are less risky as an investment because they have a fixed return (or yield) and *must* be paid before the company pays a dividend to the ordinary shareholders.

3.17 They do have the advantages that their issue does not restrict the company's borrowing power, at least in the sense that preference share capital is not secured against assets of the business, and that the non-payment of dividend does not give the preference shareholders the right to appoint a receiver, a right which is normally given to debenture holders.

3.18 From the point of view of the investor, preference shares are less attractive than loan stock because:

(a) they cannot be secured on the company's assets;

(b) the dividend yield 'traditionally' offered on preference dividends has been much too low to provide an attractive investment compared with the interest yields that have been payable on loan stock.

4. LOAN STOCK

4.1 Loan stock is long term debt capital raised by a company for which interest is paid, usually half yearly and at a fixed rate. Holders of loan stock are therefore long term creditors of the company. The loan stock has a value (the nominal value) which is the debt owed by the company and will attract a ratio of interest attached to it (the coupon yield).

4.2   *Debentures* are a form of loan stock, legally defined as the written acknowledgement of a debt incurred by a company, normally containing provisions about the payment of interest and the eventual repayment of capital.

4.3   A debenture trust deed would empower a trustee (such as an insurance company or a bank) to intervene on behalf of debenture holders if the conditions of borrowing under which the debentures were issued are not being fulfilled. This might involve:

(a)   failure to pay interest on the due dates;

(b)   an attempt by the company to sell off important assets contrary to the terms of the loan;

(c)   a situation where a company takes out other additional loans and thereby exceeds previously-agreed borrowing limits established either by the Articles or by the specific terms of the debenture trust deed. (A trust deed might well place restrictions on the company's ability to borrow more from elsewhere until the debentures have been redeemed.)

4.4   Debentures with a floating rate of interest are debentures for which the coupon rate of interest can be changed by the issuer, in accordance with changes in market rates of interest. They may be attractive to both lenders and borrowers when interest rates are volatile, and preferable to fixed interest loan stock or debentures. As a result borrowers are protected from having to pay high rates of interest on their debentures when market rates of interest have fallen, whilst lenders will benefit if the market ratio rise.

4.5   Loan stock and debentures will often be *secured*. Security may take one of two forms.

(a)   *A fixed charge.* Security would be related to a specific asset or group of assets, typically property. The company would be unable to dispose of the asset without providing a substitute asset for security, or without the lender's consent.

(b)   *A floating charge.* With a floating charge on certain assets of the company (for example, stocks and debtors), the lender's security in the event of a default of payment is whatever assets of the appropriate class the company then owns (provided that another lender does not have a prior charge on the asset). The company would be able, however, to dispose of its assets as it chose. In the event of default, the lender would probably appoint a receiver to run the company rather than lay claim to a particular asset.

5.   CONVERTIBLE LOAN STOCK

5.1   One final area of fund raising within this section is known as convertible loan stock. These are usually fixed interest securities (normally debentures but sometimes preference shares) which are issued for cash but which can be converted, on pre-determined dates and at the option of the holder, into ordinary shares of the company at a predetermined rate.

6.   BANK BORROWINGS

6.1   Borrowings from banks are an important source of finance to companies. Bank lending is still mainly short-term, although medium-term lending has grown considerably in recent years.

6.2 *Short-term borrowing* might be in the form of:

(a) an overdraft, which a company should keep within a limit set by the bank and in which interest is charged on the amount by which the company is overdrawn at a variable rate of interest;

(b) a short term loan.

6.3 *Medium term loans* are loans from a period of 3-10 years (short term loans are for less than 3 years).

6.4 The rate of interest charged on medium term bank lending to *large* companies will be set at a margin above the London Inter-Bank Offer Rate (LIBOR), with the size of the margin depending on the credit standing and riskiness of the borrower. The loans may have a fixed rate of interest or a variable interest rate, so that the rate of interest charged will be adjusted every 3, 6, 9 or 12 months in line with recent movements in the LIBOR.

6.5 Lending to smaller companies will be at a margin above the bank's base rate and at either a variable or a fixed rate of interest. (Lending on overdraft is always at a variable rate). A loan at a variable rate of interest is sometimes referred to as a *floating rate loan*.

6.6 Longer term funds will also be available from a bank, usually to purchase a long life asset such as property. The loan will normally be in the form of a mortgage. The needs of the bank in the transaction are satisfied if the following criteria are acceptable:

(a) The *purpose* of the loan. A loan request will be refused if the purpose of the loan is not acceptable to the bank.

(b) The *amount* of the loan. The customer must state exactly how much he wants to borrow. The banker must verify, as far as he is able to do so, that the full amount required has been estimated correctly.

(c) How will the loan be *repaid?* Will the customer be able to obtain sufficient income to make the necessary repayments? If not, the loan request will be refused.

(d) What would be the duration *(term)* of the loan? Traditionally, banks have lent 'short' (short term loans or overdrafts) although longer-term lending to companies (medium-term loans) and private customers (mortgages) is now much more common.

(e) Does the loan require *security?* If so, is the proposed security adequate?

Note. This forms the mnemonic PARTS.

6.7 Companies can also borrow money from international sources through the money markets and through the Eurobond and Eurocommercial paper.

Eurocurrency markets

6.8   A UK company might borrow money from a bank or from the investing public, in sterling. But it might also borrow in a foreign currency, especially when it conducts trade abroad, or if it already has assets or liabilities abroad denominated in a foreign currency.

When a UK company borrows in a foreign currency from a UK bank, the loan is known as a *eurocurrency loan.*

For example, if a UK company borrows US $50,000 from its bank, the loan will be a 'eurodollar' loan. London is a centre for eurocurrency lending and companies with foreign trade interests might choose to borrow from their bank in another currency.

6.9   The eurocurrency markets describe the depositing of funds with a bank outside the country of origin of the funds (for example, depositing Deutschmarks with a bank in London) and re-lending these funds for a fairly short term, typically 3 months. Most eurocurrency lending in fact takes place between banks of different countries, and takes the form of negotiable Certificates of Deposit.

International capital markets

6.10 Large companies will arrange borrowing facilities from their bank, in the form of bank loans or bank overdrafts. Instead, however, they might prefer to borrow from private investors. In other words, instead of obtaining a £10 million bank loan, a company might issue 'bonds', 'notes' or 'paper' in order to borrow direct from investors, with

(a)   the bank merely acting as a go-between, finding investors who will take up the bonds, notes or paper that the borrowing company issues, and

(b)   interest being payable to the investors themselves, not to a bank.

6.11 In recent years, a strong market has built up which allows very large companies to borrow this way, long term or short term, and on an international scale.

Eurobonds

6.12 A Eurobond is a bond issued in a European capital market, denominated in a currency which often differs from that of the country of issue and sold internationally. Eurobonds are long-term loans raised by international companies or other institutions in several countries at the same time. Such bonds can be sold by one holder to another. The term of a Eurobond issue is typically 10-15 years.

6.13 Eurobonds may be the most suitable source of finance for a large organisation with a top-class credit rating, such as a large successful multinational company, which:

(a)   requires a long term loan to finance a big capital expansion programme (with a loan of at least 5 years and up to 20 years);

(b) requires borrowing which is not subject to the national exchange controls of any government, (for example, a company in country X could raise funds in the currency of country Y by means of a Eurobond issue, and thereby avoid any exchange control restrictions which might exist in country X). In addition, domestic capital issues may be regulated by the government or central bank, with an orderly queue for issues. In contrast, Eurobond issues can be made whenever market conditions seem favourable.

6.14 The interest rate on a bond issue may be fixed or variable.

An issue with a variable rate of interest is known as floating rate notes (FRNs) or a floating capital notes issue, and many of these have a minimum interest rate which the note holders are guaranteed, even if market rates fall even lower. These notes convert to a fixed rate of interest when market rates do fall to this level. For this reason, they are called 'drop lock' floating rate notes.

6.15 Borrowing in a foreign currency does attract a currency risk. If a company borrows in US$. this means that the company must have a source of income in US$. As a result of this and the size of transactions necessary to make the loans worthwhile, only international companies tend to use these euromarkets for raising finance.

Exercise

Long term sources of finance for limited companies typically include shareholders' funds and debt.

Required

Compare and contrast the key characteristics of these two forms of finance.

Solution

Shareholders' funds	*Debt*
(a) Ownership if reflected.	Not related to ownership.
(b) Permanent.	Not permanent.
(c) Come in part from trading activities (revenue reserves only) and in part from financing activities.	Arises from financing activities only.
(d) Dividends do not have to be paid.	Interest (which is tax allowable) has to be paid.
(e) Shares of public limited companies can be traded. Some shareholders' funds are therefore marketable.	Some debt (debentures) is marketable.
(f) Should not affect cash flow.	Cash flow problems may arise as repayment of debt falls due.

Shareholders' funds	*Debt*
(g) Security not required.	Security may be required.
(h) Risk affects the value of the funds and hence the dividend payments. To maintain value of the company, higher dividends may have to be paid.	Interest payments do not vary.

7. OTHER METHODS OF RAISING FINANCE: FIXED ASSETS

7.1 So far we have concentrated on raising cash by means of the capital markets. Hence we have concentrated on those areas which determine the gearing of the company (see chapter on the interpretation of accounts), although bank overdrafts you will remember we only sometimes treated as gearing.

There are other ways and methods of financing our plans. If you recall, the balance sheet is made up of fixed assets, working capital and shareholders funds. The capital raised by the methods discussed so far may fund any element of the plan but raising money in the capital markets is normally done either to fund an expansion programme or to reschedule debt, where there is an opportunity to reduce the repayment burden on the company. In most circumstances a company will wish to match its funding to the asset which require that funding. Now we will examine some alternative methods available to fund the assets.

Leasing transactions

Sale and leaseback arrangements

7.2 A company which owns its own premises can obtain finance by selling the property to an insurance company for immediate cash and renting it back, usually for at least 50 years, with rent reviews every 3,4 or 5 years or so. The property itself must be non-specialised, modern, and situated in a geographical area with good long-term prospects for increases in property value, otherwise it would offer a poor investment to the insurance company, in the event that the tenant went out of business, or stopped renting the property for some other reason.

7.3 A company would raise more cash from a sale and leaseback agreement than from a mortgage, but it should only make such an agreement if it cannot raise sufficient funds any other way. The main disadvantages of sale and leaseback are that:

(a) the company loses ownership of a valuable asset which is almost certain to appreciate over time with inflation;

(b) the future borrowing capacity of the firm will be reduced, since the property if owned could be used to provide security for a loan;

(c) the company is contractually committed to occupying the property for many years ahead, and this can be restricting;

(d) the real cost is likely to be high, particularly as there will be frequent rent reviews.

Leasing

7.4   'Leasing' in the UK is historically associated with leasehold property, but we will concentrate here with leasing arrangements for goods and equipment. A lease is an agreement between two parties, the lessor and the lessee:

(a)   the lessor owns a capital asset, but grants the lessee use of it (*finance houses*, often subsidiaries of banks, act as the lessor in such arrangements);

(b)   the lessee does not own the asset, but has the use of it, and in return makes payments under the terms of the lease to the lessor, for a specified period of time.

7.5   Leasing is therefore a form of rental. Leased assets have usually been plant and machinery, and cars and commercial vehicles, but might also be computers, ships, aeroplanes, oil production equipment and office equipment etc.

There are two basic forms of lease, operating leases and finance leases.

7.6   Operating leases are rental agreements between a lessor and a lessee whereby:

(a)   the lessor supplies the equipment to the lessee;

(b)   the lessor is responsible for servicing and maintenance of the leased equipment; and

(c)   the period of the lease is fairly short, less than the economic life of the asset, so that at the end of one lease agreement, the lessor can either:

(i)   lease the same equipment to someone else, and obtain a good rental for it; or
(ii)   sell the equipment at a second–hand value.

7.7   Much of the growth in the UK leasing business in recent years has been in operating leases. With an operating lease, the lessor, often a finance house, purchases the equipment from the manufacturer and then leases it to the user (the lessee) for the agreed period. Many businessmen who obtain lease equipment in this way think of the arrangement as 'renting' rather than 'leasing' because this is what, in effect, it is.

7.8   Finance leases are lease agreements between the user of the leased asset (the lessee) and a provider of finance (the lessor) for most or all of the asset's expected useful life.

7.9   Suppose that a company decides to obtain a company car and finance the acquisition by means of a finance lease. A car dealer will supply the car. A finance house will agree to act as lessor in a finance leasing arrangement, and so will purchase the car from the dealer and lease it to the company. The company will take possession of the car from the car dealer, and make regular payments (monthly, quarterly, six monthly or annually are all typical) to the finance house under the terms of the lease.

7.10 There are other important distinguishing characteristics of a finance lease.

(a) The lessee is responsible for the upkeep, servicing and maintenance of the asset. The lessor is not involved in this at all.

(b) The lease has a primary period, which covers all or most of the useful economic life of the asset. At the end of this primary period, the lessor would not be able to take possession of the asset and lease it for a good rental to someone else, because the asset would be too well-worn or obsolete. The lessor must therefore ensure that the lease payments during the primary period pay for the full cost of the asset as well as providing the lessor with a suitable return on his investment.

(c) It is usual at the end of the primary period to allow the lessee the option to continue to lease the asset for an indefinite secondary period, in return for a very low nominal rent, sometimes called a 'peppercorn rent'. Alternatively, the lessee might be allowed to sell the asset on a lessor's behalf (since the lessor is the legal owner) and to keep most of the sale proceeds, paying only a small percentage (perhaps 10%) to the lessor.

7.11 Under some schemes, a lessor 'rents' equipment to the lessee for the main part of the equipment's life, and at the end of the lease period sells the equipment itself, with none of the sale proceeds going to the lessee.

7.12 Returning to the example of the car lease, the primary period of the lease might be 3 years, with an agreement by the lessee to make three annual payments of £6,000 each. The lessee will be responsible for repairs and servicing, road tax, insurance, garaging etc. At the end of the primary period of the lease, the lessee might be given the option either to continue leasing the car at a nominal rent (perhaps £250 per annum) or to sell the car and pay the lessor 10% of the proceeds.

7.13 What are the attractions of leases to the supplier of the equipment, the lessee and the lessor?

(a) The supplier of the equipment is paid in full at the beginning. The equipment is sold to the lessor, and apart from obligations under guarantees or warranties, the supplier is free from all further financial concern about the asset.

(b) The lessor invests finance by purchasing assets from suppliers and makes a return out of the lease payments from the lessee. Provided that a lessor can find lessees willing to pay the amounts he wants to make his return, the lessor will make good profits on his deals. He will also get capital allowances on his purchase of the equipment.

(c) Leasing might be attractive to the lessee:

(i) if the lessee does not have enough cash to pay for the asset, and may be having difficulty obtaining a bank loan to buy it, and so has to rent it in one way or another if he is to have use of the asset at all; or

(ii) if finance leasing is cheaper than a bank loan. The cost of payments under a loan *might* exceed the cost of a lease.

The lessee will be able to deduct the lease payments in computing his taxable profits.

7.14 Operating leases have the further advantages that:

(a) the leased equipment does *not* have to be shown in the company's (lessee's) published balance sheet, and so the lessee's balance sheet is kept 'clean', with no increase in its gearing ratio;

(b) the equipment is leased for a shorter period than its expected useful life. In the case of high-technology equipment, if the equipment becomes out-of-date before the end of its expected life, the user (the lessee) doesn't have to keep on using it, and it is the lessor who must bear the loss risks of having to sell out-of-date equipment on the second hand market.

7.15 Not surprisingly perhaps, the biggest growth area in operating leasing in the UK has been in computers and office equipment (photocopiers, fax machines and so on) where technology is continually improving.

Hire purchase

7.16 Hire purchase is a form of instalment credit. There are two basic forms of instalment credit, whereby an individual or business purchases goods on credit and pays for them by instalments.

(a) *Lender credit* occurs when the buyer borrows money from a lender (for example a personal loan or overdraft from a bank) and uses the money to purchase goods outright.

(b) *Vendor credit* occurs when the buyer obtains goods on credit from a seller (vendor) and agrees to pay the vendor by instalments. Hire purchase is an example of vendor credit.

Hire purchase is similar to leasing, with the exception that ownership of the goods passes to the hire purchase customer on payment of the final credit instalment, whereas a lessee never becomes the legal owner of the goods.

7.17 Hire purchase agreements nowadays usually involve a finance house, or finance company, whereby:

(a) the supplier sells the goods to the finance house; but
(b) delivers the goods to the customer who will eventually purchase them; and
(c) the hire purchase arrangement exists between the finance house and the customer.

7.18 The finance house will nearly always insist that the hirer should pay a deposit towards the purchase price, perhaps as low as 15% or even less, or as high as 33%. The size of the deposit will depend on the finance company's policy and its assessment of the hirer. This is in contrast to a finance lease, where the lessee might not be required to make any down-payment.

7.19 An industrial or commercial business can use hire purchase as one alternative source of finance. With *industrial hire purchase*, a business customer wants hire purchase finance from a finance house in order to purchase a fixed asset.

Goods bought by businesses on hire purchase include company vehicles, plant and machinery, office equipment and farming machinery. Hire purchase arrangements for fleets of motor cars are quite common, and most car manufacturers have a link with a leading finance house for point-of-sale hire purchase credit.

Government assistance

7.20 The government provides finance to companies in cash grants and other forms of direct assistance, as part of its policy of helping to develop the national economy, especially in high technology industries and in areas of high unemployment.

7.21 Government incentives might be offered on:

(a) a *regional basis*, giving help to firms that invest in an economically depressed area of the country that has been officially designated as a 'development area' or 'assisted area'; or

(b) a *selective national basis*, giving help to firms that invest in an industry that the government would like to see developing more quickly, for example robotics or fibre optics.

7.22 Government assistance is now severely limited by European Community rules on competition, which attempt to prevent distortion of markets.

Conclusion

7.23 From the above you can see that various options exist to finance assets which are usually of a long-term nature. Although those listed above are available to all companies the equity and bond market methods of raising capital and other funding are only realistically available to the large public companies. Small companies, however, have access to one or two specific sources of funds because of their size.

8. SMALLER COMPANIES

8.1 Compared to large firms, small firms have great difficulty in obtaining funds. Smaller firms are perceived as being more risky, and investors choose either not to invest or to expect a higher return on their investment, which the borrowing firm must then be able to pay.

8.2 Small and unquoted companies do not have ready access to new long-term funds, except for:

(a) retained earnings;
(b) perhaps, extra finance obtained by issuing more shares to private shareholders;
(c) some bank borrowing.

So how are small companies to overcome financial restrictions to achieve a good rate of growth?

8.3 The problems of finance for small businesses and struggling companies have received much publicity in recent years, and some efforts have been made to provide them with access to sources of funds. Most of these sources are referred to as 'venture capital'.

Venture capital

8.4 Venture capital is money put into a new enterprise which may all be lost if the enterprise fails.

A businessman starting up a new business will invest venture capital of his own, but he will quite possibly need additional funding from a source other than his own pocket. However the term 'venture capital' is more specifically associated with putting money, *usually in return for an equity stake*, into a new business start-up, a management buy-out or a major expansion scheme by a small business.

8.5 The institution that puts in the money recognises the gamble inherent in the funding – there is a serious risk of losing the entire investment, and it might take a long time before any profits and returns materialise. But there is also the prospect of very high profits and a substantial return on investment.

8.6 A venture capital organisation will not want to retain its investment in a business indefinitely, and when it considers putting money into a business venture, it will also consider its 'exit', how it will be able to pull out of the business eventually (after 5 to 7 years, say) and realise its profits, for example by a stock market flotation.

The problems of small companies and government measures

8.7 A major problem of small businesses, despite venture capital funds, is still one of finding investors prepared to lend them money at a reasonable rate of return. Some venture capital institutions specialise in lending to small firms but the total amount of funds available is relatively low.

8.8 The government introduced a few schemes in recent years to encourage more lending to small firms and these include the following.

(a) The *Business Expansion Scheme* or BES. The BES is a tax incentive scheme to encourage investors to put up 'venture capital' for certain qualifying companies. Companies have been limited to raising £750,000 a year in this way. The scheme ends on 31 December 1993.

(b) *Development agencies* and other agencies or boards set up by either central or local government (see below).

Development agencies

8.9 The UK government has set up some development agencies (the Scottish and Welsh Development Agencies) which have been given the task of trying to encourage the development of trade and industry in their area. The strategy of the agencies has been mainly to encourage the start-up and development of *small companies* in their region, although they will also give help to larger companies too.

8.10 The assistance that a development agency might give to a firm could include:

(a) free factory accommodation, or factory accommodation at a low rent;

(b) financial assistance, in the form of:

(i)   an interest relief grant for a bank loan (a company developing its business in an area might obtain a bank loan, and the development agency will agree to compensate the bank for providing the loan at a low rate of interest);

(ii) direct financial assistance in the form of equity finance, preference share finance, or loans.

9.   OTHER METHODS OF RAISING FINANCE: CURRENT ASSETS

9.1 Current assets (stocks and debtors) or by definition short term in nature and the methods of finance available are hence determined by short term requirements.

Stocks

9.2 The most obvious form of finance for stock is to buy on credit in order to minimise our drain on cash by ensuring that we turnover our stock as quickly as possible. The most evident example of this type of finance being used in industry is the large DIY supermarkets run under trade names such as Homebase, Texas Homecare. Here the concept is to buy on credit and sell the stock before payment for the stock is due. However this type of trade cycle is not typical, particularly if we examine a manufacturing company. Here payment for raw materials is due well before the finished product is sold on. The company must find a way of financing the stock holding and a widely used source of finance are 'bills of exchange' which allow the supplier to be paid without using the funds of the purchaser. These are negotiable documents rather like an uncrossed post-dated cheque. They promise to pay a specified sum on a specified date to the bearer or named supplier. The supplier can wait for his funds and cash in the bill of exchange on the due date or it can be traded in with a bank at an earlier date, but obviously at a discount. This discount will vary depending on the credit worthiness of the original company, who ultimately must pay.

9.3 This facility can be rolled over such that the bills of exchange will be renewed at the end of their maturity period, hence changing the short term funds into longer term facilities. Large companies have developed this even further and will send bank acceptance fees which are levied every time a bill is cashed in by issuing 'promissory notes' now described as commercial paper. There is now a market for this source of finance and the rates of interest are extremely competitive.

Debtors

9.4 Another major component of current assets is trade debtors. Each debtor may individually be a short term debt but on payment the debt will be replaced by another debt and so on. So again over time the level of debt will need to be financed since they represent goods or services supplied to our customers who have not paid us. Banks in this case are no longer lending money to us based on our credit worthiness but in the various levels of credit worthiness of the individual customers. This can, however, be financed by way of invoice discounting or factoring. This consists of selling the debts to a finance company who charge interest since they will not collect the cash for some time. The usual practice is that the finance house will pay between 65% and 80% of the face value of debt at the end of the month in which the sale was made. Different forms and levels of factoring are available from a full service (sell all debts) to a confidential service (where the customer is unaware of the factor being involved) to a non-recourse service (where the finance house take the risk of bad debts). The charges for these services will vary according to the type of customer, the debt periods expected and the level of service required.

Bad debts and credit control

9.5 As we are on the subject of debtors, now might be the time to consider how we minimise loss of funding through customer non-payment; in other words, how to avoid bad debts. In an earlier chapter we considered the accounting treatment of bad debts, but now we should look at the impact bad debts can have on a business, what the marketing manager should be aware of in terms of credit control and what action he or she can take to minimise the problem of bad debts.

9.6 The most important thing for a marketing professional to remember is that there is a trade off between:

(a) extending credit, so as to increase sales and therefore profits; and
(b) the interest and administrative cost of carrying debtors, and the cost of bad debts.

In simple terms, however much you want to increase sales, you must remember what those sales might cost. Not all potential customers are credit worthy. Although the control of debtors is not part of the remit of a marketing professional, he or she should appreciate the impact of the marketing decisions made on the bad debt situation of the organisation.

Formulating a policy for credit control

9.7 Several factors need to be considered by management when a policy for credit control is formulated. These include:

(a) the administrative costs of debt collection;

(b) the procedures for controlling credit to individual customers and also debt collection;

(c) the amount of extra capital required to finance an extension of total credit; there might be an increase in debtors, stocks and creditors, but the net increase in working capital must be financed;

(d) the cost of the additional finance required to increase working capital (or the savings from a reduction in working capital); this cost might be bank overdraft interest, or the cost of long-term funds (for example loan stock or equity);

(e) any savings or additional expenses in operating the credit policy (such as the extra work and extra 'chasing' of slow payers);

(f) the ways in which credit policy can be implemented; for example:

(i) credit can be eased by giving debtors a longer period in which to settle their account. The cost of credit would be the finance cost of the resulting increase in debtors;

(ii) a discount can be offered for early payment; the cost of the credit policy would then be the cost of the discounts;

(g) the effect of easing credit might be to:

(i) encourage a higher proportion of bad debts;

(ii) increase sales volume. Provided that the extra gross contribution from the increase in sales exceeds the increase in fixed cost expenses, bad debts, discounts and the finance cost of an increase in working capital, a policy to relax credit terms would be profitable.

Some of these factors involved in credit policy decisions will now be considered in more detail.

Debt collection policy

9.8 The overall debt collection policy of the firm should be that the administrative costs incurred in debt collection should not exceed the benefits received from incurring those costs.

Within a range, however, it would generally be correct to state that extra expenditure on debt collection procedures would:

(a) reduce bad debt losses;

(b) reduce the average collection period (and therefore the cost of the investment in working capital/debtors).

Beyond a certain level, however, additional expenditure on debt collection would not have a sufficiently great effect on reducing losses or on the average collection period to justify the extra administrative costs.

Credit control: individual accounts

9.9 Credit control involves the initial investigation of potential credit customers and the continuing control of outstanding accounts. The main points to note are:

(a) new customers should give two good references, including one from a bank, before being accepted;

(b) credit rating should be checked through a credit bureau, such as Dun & Bradstreet;

(c) a new customer's credit limit should be fixed at a low level and only increased if the payment record warrants it;

(d) for large value customers files should be maintained of any available financial information;

(e) aged lists of debts should be produced and reviewed at regular intervals;

(f) the credit limit for existing customers should be periodically reviewed, but should only be raised at the request of the customer and if his credit standing is good.

Debt collection

9.10 There are three main areas which need to be considered in connection with the control of debtors:

(a) paperwork;
(b) debt collection;
(c) credit control.

9.11 It is important that sales paperwork should be dealt with promptly and accurately:

(a) invoices should be sent out immediately after delivery;

(b) checks should be carried out to ensure invoices are accurate;

(c) the investigation of queries and complaints and, if appropriate, the issue of credit notes should be carried out promptly;

(d) if practical, monthly statements should be issued early so that they can be included in the customers' monthly settlement of bills.

9.12 The use of pre-printed letters to remind customers to pay their accounts is ineffective. Although it will be more expensive, it is usually better to adopt a more personal approach. A good method of positive debt collection may include the following stages:

(a) request for payment by telephone;
(b) telegram or letter;
(c) personal visit, perhaps by a sales representative;
(d) withdrawal of credit facilities;
(e) place debt in hands of a debt collection agency;
(f) legal proceedings.

Total credit

9.13 To determine whether it would be profitable to extend the level of total credit, it is necessary to assess:

(a) the additional sales volume;
(b) the profitability of the extra sales;
(c) the extra length of the average debt collection period;
(d) the required rate of return on the investment in additional debtors.

Discount policies

9.14 Varying the discount allowed for early payment of debts:

(a) shortens the average collection period;

(b) affects the volume of demand (and possibly, therefore, indirectly affects bad debt losses).

To consider whether the offer of a discount for early payment is financially worthwhile it is necessary to compare the cost of the discount with the benefit of a reduced investment in debtors.

Debtors turnover

9.15 A useful control measure in monitoring the level of debtors is the debtors turnover or the debtors collection period in days. You may already be familiar with this measure and it is calculated as follows.

$$\text{Debtors turnover} = \frac{\text{trade debtors}}{\text{turnover}} \times 365 \text{ days}$$

9.16 In summary, the marketing professional must consider the impact of credit control on the marketing strategy he or she is implementing. For example, if a new customer is granted instant credit to secure a sale, the risk of that customer not paying may be quite high and could result in a substantial loss to the company. But by waiting a few days for a credit application to be processed, the sale may be lost. This kind of risk may be quantified by estimating the risk of non-payment, but in general it is not considered good practice to give instant credit.

10. CONCLUSION

10.1 Any strategy will involve the use of funds. To remain in their chosen business, companies must generate surplus funds and this is the primary source of funding future projects. However, businesses have a variety of different ways to raise additional funds, both internal and external. They can also:

(a) raise equity from existing or new shareholders;

(b) raise debt from banks or similar institutions;

(c) refinance existing assets eg sale and leaseback of a freehold property;

(d) change their payment and receipts approach in order to maximise the timing of cash flows from working capital;

(e) apply for government grants.

10.2 All the options should be assessed in the light of the goals to be achieved and the impact of each decision on the financial security of the business. Each area of raising finance will carry its own risk and the understanding, measurement and control of that element of risk is important to the health of the business.

TEST YOUR KNOWLEDGE

The numbers in brackets refer to paragraphs of this chapter

1   What are the three main sources of funding available to a business? (1.2)

2   What methods are available to a company to issue ordinary shares? (3.1-3.7)

3   What is the difference between preference shares and ordinary shares?(3.16)

4   What characteristics distinguish loan stock? (4.1)

5   What types of bank finance are available in the short and medium term? (6.2-6.15)

6   How can companies use leasing to finance fixed asset purchases? (7.2-7.23)

7   How can companies finance their current assets? (9.2-9.4)

Now try question 12 at the end of the text

PART C
CONTROL

Chapter 13

VARIANCE ANALYSIS

This chapter covers the following topics.

1. Variance analysis
2. Sales variances
3. Production and efficiency variances
4. Interpretation of variances
5. Interdependence between variances
6. The efficiency standard
7. Inflation and price variances
8. Controllable and uncontrollable variances

---

1. VARIANCE ANALYSIS

1.1 Control is a key aspect of finance. Of course it is vital that corporate objectives are agreed and communicated; it is vital that short term and long term decision making is made with the best available knowledge of the various alternatives; it is vital that budgets are agreed and set in order for the company to achieve the goals it set out to achieve. Finance does not, however, end there, and neither does the role of the marketing manager. The decision making process is constant and therefore a key cog in the decision making circle is to identify what aspects of business life vary from that which is expected. This process is carried out by variance analysis, which is in effect a style of exception reporting. Variance analysis attempts to highlight areas where actual performance varies from that which was budgeted or forecast and then explains why the variance occurred. At this point it is up to the manager to determine whether any action is necessary to steer towards a new short term objective or whether further control and management is needed to return to the original course as communicated within the budgeting process.

1.2 Variance analysis is a means of assessing performance, but it is only a method of identifying and explaining how which vary from the anticipated path. It can therefore highlight areas of strength *and* weakness, opportunity *and* threat. It does not provide a ready made diagnosis of faults nor does it provide management with a ready made indication of what action needs to be taken. It simply highlights areas which need investigation and explanation of what has happened. The conclusion from this analysis must be drawn by the management team.

1.3   Variances might occur for several reasons.

(a)   A variance may fall within acceptable tolerance limits and should be ignored, since small favourable and adverse variances should be expected to cancel each other out over a number of control periods. Where small variances are always slightly adverse in every control period they may appear as significant in cumulative total over a longer period of time, for example when annual returns are produced.

(b)   A variance may indicate excessive (or favourable) expenditure which is *controllable*.

(c)   A variance may indicate excessive (or favourable) expenditure which is *uncontrollable*.

(i)   The variance may be uncontrollable by the manager to whom it is reported, although controllable by a different manager. In a well designed costing system, this should not happen.

(ii)   The variance may be uncontrollable by anyone because it has been caused by factors beyond the company's control.

(d)   If the standard cost is inaccurate, variances which are reported will be unreliable. A standard may be inaccurate because of poor planning, or because a deliberately unrealistic standard has been set in order to measure performance (for example setting ideal standards).

2.   SALES VARIANCES

2.1   We will concentrate initially on sales based variances since these are the ones which the marketing manager must understand. All sales revenue is the product of a quantity of sales multiplied by the unit sales price. The actual total sales revenue can then be compared with the budgeted sales revenue and the difference will indicate whether we have overachieved (a favourable variance) or underachieved the expected level of performance (an adverse variance). But why did the variance occur? Was it due to price variance, or to volume variances or a mixture of both? In multi-product companies this can be further complicated by the mix of product sold. Initially we will look at price and volume variances. These will be described as variances of actual performance against a standard or budgeted level.

Sales price variance

2.2   This is perhaps the variance with the most óbvious meaning. A sales price variance indicates by how much actual selling prices of products or services have exceeded or been less than standard (or budget).

2.3   Sales price variances will be common. Many companies sell their products to customers at a discount, with the size of the discount depending on the size of the order or who the customer is. (For example, regular customers might be given a minimum discount on their purchases, regardless of order quantity). The standard selling price might ignore discounts altogether, or it might have an allowance for the average expected discount. In either event, the actual sales prices and standard sales prices will usually differ.

Sales volume variance

2.4   In contrast a sales volume variance expresses how much of a total revenue variance is due to changes in levels of sales volume from that anticipated in the standards or budgets. In its most basic form a sales revenue variance can only be due to either changes in price or changes in volume and hence the sum of these two elements must be equal to the change in total revenue. In any budgeting process the marketing manager will be asked to estimate how may units of a product will be sold during the year and at what price. The actual performance will be different in the vast majority of cases and it is the difference in the sales volumes at the budgeted price that determines the change in revenue.

2.5   This concept of variance analysis can equally well be described graphically by simply looking at how revenue has changed.

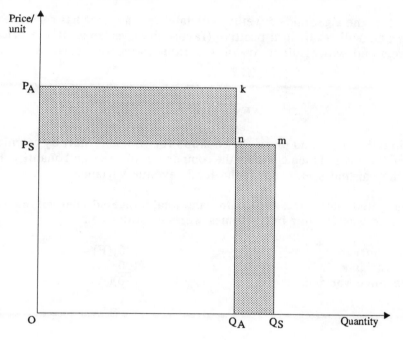

2.6   Revenue is a function of price and quantity. If price is charged on the vertical axis and quantity on the horizontal axis then we can show the total sales revenue as the product of the number of units sold multiplied by the price per unit. In our standard or budget let us assume that P_s is the standard price and Q_s is the standard volume of sales. Now

$$\text{TOTAL SALES REVENUE} = P_s \times Q_s$$

2.7   Those of you who remember basic geometry will note that the areas defined by the rectangle $O\,P_s\,M\,Q_s$ is measured by multiplying the length of the rectangle by the width: $P_s \times Q_s$. Hence revenue is simply the area under the given sales and quantity as defined as by the points on the graph.

2.8   If actual price per unit exceeds the standard level but quantity, as a result, is a little lower than budget, then actual revenue is described by the new rectangle $OP_a\,kQ_A$. This area is $P_A \times Q_A$.

2.9 So what is the difference in the revenues? Effectively the two areas clearly show the difference. As a result of the increased price a new 'rectangle' of revenue has been created defined at $P_s P_A kn$ which is the areas $(P_A - P_s) \times Q_A$.

2.10 Similarly, as a result of reduced quantity being sold some revenue has been lost and is defined by another rectangle $(Q_A - Q_s) \times P_s$.

2.11 So in terms of changes in revenue we have now defined the variances as:

Price = change in price per unit × actual quantity sold

Volume = change in units sold × budget or standard price per unit.

Remember as well that the algebraic convention dictates that as price has risen the change in price is particular and will result in a positive (favourable) variance. If the price fell this is a negative change and will result in an unfavourable (adverse) variance.

Exercise

Put some figures into the graph and prove the equation for yourself. Start by calculating what the total revenue variance is and then compute the components of price and quantity. Remember that the total of the variances *must* equal the total revenue variance.

For example, if budgeted sales price was £5/unit and total budgeted sales volume is 100 units and actual sales price was £6/unit but volumes were 80 units then:

Sales price variance	80 (F)
Sales volume variance	(100)(A)
Total sales revenue variance	(20)(A)

Sales volume (margin) variance

2.12 This type of analysis shown above is often adopted in sales and marketing organisations which do not produce goods and to whom the elements of variable and fixed costs are not as clearly defined as they could or should be. However, it is evident that if sales volumes change this will effect other variable costs. So perhaps we should look at the impact on margins rather than simply sales revenues.

2.13 Sales volume variances can be measured in terms of sales revenues, or in terms of standard profit margins or standard contribution margins, and any reported sales volume variance cannot be interpreted properly until it is established exactly what the variance is showing.

2.14 An example might help to illustrate this point. Suppose that Volauvent Ltd had the following budgeted and actual results for one of its products.

	Budget	*Actual*
Sales	5,000 units	6,000 units
Sales price per unit	£10	£10
Marginal cost per unit	£6	£6
Fixed costs	£10,000	£10,000
Fixed cost per unit	£2	

2.15 The sales volume variance in units is the difference between the budgeted and actual sales, which in this case is 1,000 units (F).

This variance could be expressed in terms of standard sales revenue. In other words, given that the volume variance is 1,000 units (F), how much extra sales revenue should have been earned? The volume variance should be converted from units into sales value at the *standard sales price*. (Any price variance is dealt with separately as the sales price variance).

2.16 Converting the sales volume variance from units into standard sales revenue can be helpful as management information, especially when there are two or more different products in the sales budget. This is because a volume variance of one unit for one product cannot be compared with a volume variance of one unit for another, different product, but the sales volume variance of the two products *can* be compared or combined using sales revenue as a common factor.

2.17 A sales volume variance will result in higher-than-expected sales revenue if it is favourable, but there will be an off-setting increase in the cost of sales. Similarly, an adverse sales volume variance will result in lower-than-expected sales revenue, but there will be an offsetting reduction in the cost of sales.

2.18 The net effect of a sales volume variance is an increase or reduction in profitability, which is valued as follows:

(a)   in terms of profit margin, when a standard *absorption* costing system is in use;
(b)   in terms of contribution margin, when a standard *marginal* costing system is in use.

2.19 In our example, if a standard absorption costing system were used, the sales volume variance should be a profit margin variance.

Budgeted sales	5,000 units
Actual sales	6,000 units
Sales volume variance in units	1,000 units (F)
Standard profit margin	£2 *
Sales volume (profit) variance	£2,000 (F)

   * £(10 - 6 - 2) per unit.

2.20 If standard marginal costing were used, the sales volume variance should be a contribution margin variance.

Sales volume variance in units	1,000 units (F)
Standard contribution per unit	£4
Sales volume (contribution margin) variance	£4,000 (F)

2.21 In terms of our graphical representation of the analysis of variances it makes no difference if we calculate the variances based on total revenue or on the total contributions.

Sales mix and quantity variances

2.22 A company selling two or more products is often able to control the quantity and mix of its sales, perhaps by adjusting expenditures on advertising, sales promotion and direct selling effort. Variance analysis can inform managers of the effect of such changes by analysing the overall sales volume variance into a sales mix variance and a sales quantity variance.

2.23 The sales mix variance calculates whether the actual proportions of each product sold represent a more or less profitable mix than the standard (budgeted) proportions. For example if proportionately more of the most profitable products are sold then there will be a favourable sales mix variance.

2.24 The sales quantity variance measures the standard average profit gained or lost as a result of achieving a higher or lower level of sales than budgeted, regardless of the mix of sales.

2.25 Before we look at the details of the variances you should realise that a sales mix variance and a sales quantity variance would only be meaningful where management can exercise control over the proportions of the products sold.

Example: unit method

2.26 Just Desserts Ltd makes and sells two products, Bland Fete and Gotters Dew. The budgeted sales and profit are as follows.

	Sales	Revenue	Costs	Profit	Profit per unit
	units	£	£	£	£
Bland Fete	400	8,000	6,000	2,000	5
Gotters Dew	300	12,000	11,100	900	3
				2,900	

Actual sales were as follows.

Bland Fete	280 units
Gotters Dew	630 units

The company management is able to control the relative sales of each product through the allocation of sales effort, advertising and sales promotion expenses.

Required

Calculate the sales volume (profit), sales mix and quantity variances.

264

Solution

2.27 A sales volume (profit) variance is calculated for each separate product in the usual way.

	Bland Fete	Gotters Dew
Budgeted sales	400 units	300 units
Actual sales	280 units	630 units
Sales volume variance	120 units (A)	330 units (F)
× Standard profit per unit	£5	£3
	£600 (A)	£990 (F)
Total sales volume variance		£390 (F)

2.28 When we look at the mix of sales in this example it is apparent that a bigger proportion than budgeted of the less profitable Gotters Dew has been sold, therefore the sales mix variance will be adverse. The method for calculating the variance is as follows.

(a) We take the *actual* total volume of sales and convert this total into a *standard mix*, on the assumption that sales should have been in the budgeted proportions or mix.

(b) The difference between actual sales and 'standard mix' sales for each product is then converted into a profit variance or contribution variance, as shown below.

	Actual mix of sales units	Standard mix units	Mix variance units	Standard profit per unit £	Mix variance £
Bland Fete	280	(4) 520	240 (A)	5	1,200 (A)
Gotters Dew	630	(3) 390	240 (F)	3	720 (F)
	910	910			480 (A)

The sales mix variance is £480 adverse: the standard profit would have been £480 higher if the 910 units sold had been in the standard mix of 4:3.

2.29 The sales quantity variance is the total sales volume variance of all the products combined. It is valued at the weighted average standard profit per unit.

The weighted average profit per unit is calculated from the budgeted level of sales activity and the budgeted profit per unit. Hence:

	Units	Profit per unit	Total profit
Bland Fete	400	5	2,000
Gotters Dew	300	3	900
	700		2,900

Now Bland Fate and Gotters Dew together will generate £2,900 for 700 units sold or £2,900/700 per unit. So now:

Budgeted sales (in total)	700 units
Actual sales (in total)	910 units
Sales quantity variance	210 units (F)
× £29/7 =	£870 (F)

13: VARIANCE ANALYSIS

Summary

	£
Sales mix variance	480 (A)
Sales quantity variance	870 (F)
Sales volume variance	390 (F)

2.30 You will note that we have not mentioned any change in selling price. This is because it is irrelevant to this part of our analysis since we are trying to understand the impact of changes in volume mix and quantity of units sold. We have changed the volume of each product sold, the total quantity of units sold and the mix of product sold within that actual sales total.

	Bland Fete	Gotters Dew	Total
	£	£	£
Total budgeted profits	2,000	900	2,900
Total actual profits	1,400	1,890	3,290
	(600) A	990 F	390 F

We have now proved that the total volume variance can be subdivided into the sales mix and sales quantity variances.

So how does this type of analysis help the marketing manager? Lets us go back to basic information again in another example.

Comprehensive example

2.31 A company sells three products and prepares a budget based on variable and fixed costs (ie a standard costing system). Results for a period can be summarised as follows:

	Budget	Actual	Variance
	£	£	£
Sales revenue	105,000	140,000	35,000
Expenses	(77,000)	(100,000)	(23,000)
Profit	28,000	40,000	12,000

2.32 This really does not help the decision making process. We can tell that revenue has improved but which product caused this increase and why? Are costs totally out of control? Should we continue producing all these products in the same proportion? If we look at more detailed analysis of the budget we see the following.

	A	B	C	Budget total	Actual total	Variance
Sales (units)	2,000	4,000	5,000	11,000	14,000	3,000
Budget per unit	£	£	£	£	£	£
Selling price	10	15	5			
Variable cost	5	5	3			
Contribution	5	10	2			
Totals						
Sales revenue	20,000	60,000	25,000	105,000	140,000	35,000
Variable costs	10,000	20,000	15,000	45,000	63,000	(18,000)
Contribution	10,000	40,000	10,000	60,000	77,000	17,000
Fixed costs: direct	-	20,000	5,000	25,000	30,000	5,000
	10,000	20,000	5,000	35,000	47,000	12,000
Fixed costs: indirect	-	5,000	2,000	7,000	7,000	-
Profit	10,000	15,000	3,000	28,000	40,000	12,000

The volume (quantity) variance

2.33 The first item of particular importance to notice in this exercise is that the actual sales activity is well ahead of the level predicted by the original budget. At this stage we could analyse the variances immediately, although more detailed results would be needed. However, it would be slightly more useful if we flexed the budget so that the budget has identified the difference between variable costs and fixed costs. If we make the assumption that the fixed costs would not increase for this level of volume activity increase, then only the variable costs will move in line with the sales. We should therefore flex the budget up to the new 'actual' sales level. This results in a volume variance of £28,636 caused by changing the quantity of units sold at budgeted rates.

	Original budget	Flexed budget	Variance
Sales volume (units)	11,000	14,000	3,000
Sales revenue	105,000	133,636	28,636
Variable costs	45,000	57,273	(12,273)
Contribution	60,000	76,363	16,363
Fixed costs: direct	25,000	25,000	-
Fixed costs: indirect	7,000	7,000	-
Profit	28,000	44,363	16,363

Volume (mix) variance

2.34 We can now analyse the critical sales volumes against the flexed budget.

	A £	B £	C £	Total £
Actual volumes	2,000	4,000	8,000	14,000
Flexed budget volumes	2,545	5,091	6,364	14,000
Variances	(545)	(1,091)	1,636	-

2.35 Sales volumes are well ahead of budget in the original form. We can see that the average selling price per unit in the original budget is £9.55. Applying this rate to the actual level of activity (the revised flexed budget) indicates that revenues should be £133,636 whereas in fact they were £140,000. This is due partly to the actual mix of products sold as opposed to that included in the flexed budget. We can quantify this by multiplying the actual product volumes by the budgeted selling price to see what revenue we would have expected from this actual mix.

	A	B	C	Total	Flexed Budget
Actual volumes	2,000	4,000	8,000	14,000	14,000
Budget selling price per unit (£)	10	15	5	–	–
Total revenue (£)	20,000	60,000	40,000	120,000	133,636

We now see that the actual volume would have been expected to result in revenues of £133,626 but in fact only resulted in revenue of £120,000 because of the change of mix of products sold.

The price variance

2.36 The rate of the variance must be due to changes in price. So now we need to analyse the price details of the actual sales and compare it with the anticipated sales as for the budget.

	A	B	C	Total
Actual sales revenue	30,000	52,000	48,000	140,000
Actual price/unit	15	15.50	6	
Budget price/unit	10	15.00	5	
Variance per unit	5	0.50	1	
Revenue variance	10,000	2,000	8,000	£20,000

2.37 Now we can see the changes in the price have increased our sales revenues by £10,000 above that which our budget would have expected.

2.38 We have new analysed the sales revenue variance into its component parts.

	£
Volume (quantity) of 32,000 units at average budgeted price per unit	28,636
Sales mix: actual mix of products at budgeted price/unit gave a lower revenue than expected	(13,636)
Volume variance	15,000
Increase in prices: prices have risen overall and hence increased revenues	20,000
Total variance	35,000

2.39 The first two variances, based on quantity and mix, are in total equal to the volume variance. This can be proved by taking each product separately and applying our originally stated formula for such variances, that total volume variance is equal to the change in volume recorded at budgeted price per unit. Hence:

	A	B	C	Total
Original volume	2,000	4,000	5,000	11,000
Actual volume	2,000	4,000	8,000	14,000
Change in volume	-	-	3,000	3,000
Budgeted price/unit	£10	£15	£5	
Volume variance	-	-	15,000	15,000

2.40 This style of analysis has now answered the main question of why things have happened. We already know that by selling 3,000 more units, we increased revenue by £35,000. We can now make statements about the impact of our policy of selling more units of product C at a slightly increased price. We can now see that changes in price of units A and B have not effected volume sales at all; so can we afford to raise prices further without losing any sales volume? Now the decision making process has some relevant empirical evidence on which to base its conclusions.

2.41 In the above example we worked purely on sales revenue as the important factor. We could have worked equally well on contribution or on profitability because we are aware that changes in the levels will affect variable costs as well as sales revenues.

Exercise

Using the above example work out the same variances at the contribution level. Remember fixed costs will not change and we are therefore assuming that we do not increase our marketing support for product C despite increasing its sales volume by 3,000 unit. You will need to know that actual volumes are as stated above but that actual contributions are:

	£
A	12,000
B	45,000
C	20,000
	77,000

Solution

	A	B	C	Total	Flexed Budget
Budgeted contribution per unit (£)	5.00	10.50	2.00	5.45	-
Actual sales (units)	2,000	4,000	8,000	14,000	14,000
Contribution expected (£)	10,000	40,000	16,000	66,000	76,364
Actual contribution per unit (£)	6.00	11.25	2.50		

Variances at:

				£	£
Volume	(1)	Quantity	: flexed budget	76,364	
			: original budget	(60,000)	
					16,364
	(2)	Mix	: flexed budget	76,364	
			: expected contribution with actual mix	(66,000)	
					(10,364)
Price		Change in contribution per unit multiplied by actual volumes			
	A	£1.00 × 2,000		2,000	
	B	£1.25 × 4,000		5,000	
	C	£0.50 × 8,000		4,000	
					11,000
Total variance					17,000

Note that the total original budget contribution is £60,000 and the actual contribution total is £77,000 giving a total variance of £17,000

---

3. PRODUCTION AND EFFICIENCY VARIANCES

3.1 The example you have just worked through has stopped short of understanding variances caused by the changes in the various elements that are utilised to make any product. Those elements are primarily materials and labour. In any budgeting and costing system these resources will be utilised in given or anticipated proportions to produce the product. In the same way that the sales price and volume will be different when actual events occur, so too will this resource utilisation be different and give rise to variances which will need explanation; the cost or price of these resources may also change. Instead of price and volume sales variances we will now have material price and usage variances, (do not worry too much about the terminology, the explanation for them is exactly the same as in the sales revenue variance analysis).

Material cost variances

3.2 The direct material cost variances consist of two sub-variances.

(a) *A direct materials price variance,* which is the difference between the standard price and the actual purchase price for the actual quantity of material used or purchased.

A price variance can be calculated when the materials are purchased, or when they are used in production. The 'matching concept' would suggest that the variance ought to be calculated when the materials are used in production. But it is preferable to calculate the price variance at the time of purchase, for two reasons.

(i) Control information about price variances ought to be reported as soon as it becomes available. This is when the materials are first bought.

(ii) By calculating a variance at the time of purchase, stocks of materials can be valued in store at standard price. This is administratively simpler than using actual price in the stock records.

(b) *A direct materials usage variance,* which is the difference between the standard quantity of materials that should have been used, and the actual quantity of materials used, valued at the *standard* price of material purchases.

3.3 The formulae for the direct material variances are as follows.

(a) Material price variance = actual quantity x (standard price - actual price)
(b) Material usage variance = standard price x (standard quantity - actual quantity)

Example: material cost variances

3.4 Suppose that product A has a standard direct material cost as follows.
5 kilograms of material M at £2 per kg = £10 per unit of A

During April 19X3, 600 kilograms of M were purchased, which cost £1,140. 100 units of product A were manufactured, using 520 kilograms of material M.

Required

Calculate the following variances:

(a) direct material price; and
(b) direct material usage.

Solution

3.5 (a) *Material price variance*

This will be calculated on quantities purchased.

	£
600 kg of M: should cost (× £2)	1,200
did cost	1,140
Material M price variance	60 (F)

(*Note*. The unused M, 600 - 520 = 80 kg, will be held as closing stock, valued at the standard price of £2 per kg = £160).

(b) *Material usage variance*

100 units of product A should use (× 5)	500 kg of M
did use	520 kg
Usage variance, in kg	20 kg (A)
Standard price per kg of M	£2
Usage variance in £	£40 (A)

Labour cost variances

3.6 The direct labour cost variance in total is the difference between the standard direct labour cost of the output produced and the actual direct labour cost.

3.7 The total direct labour cost variance is sub-analysed into two subsidiary variances.

(a) A *direct labour rate variance*. This is similar to a materials price variance. It is the difference between the standard direct labour rate per hour and the actual direct labour rate per hour, multiplied by the actual total hours worked. In other words, was the rate per hour paid to the direct labour force more or less than standard?

A formula for the rate variance is as follows.

$$AH \ (ALR - SLR)$$

where   AH is the actual hours worked
ALR is the actual rate of pay per hour
SLR is the standard rate of pay per hour.

(b) A *direct labour efficiency variance*. This is similar to the materials usage variance. It is the difference between the actual hours taken to produce the output, and the standard number of hours that this output should have taken, multiplied by the standard rate per hour.

A formula for the efficiency variance is as follows.

$$SLR \ (AH - SH)$$

where   SLR is the standard rate of pay per hour
AH is the actual hours taken
SH is the standard number of hours that should have been taken.

Example: labour cost variances

3.8 The standard direct labour cost of product B is

4 hours of grade S labour at £3 per hour = £12 per unit of product B.

During May 19X3, 200 units of product B were made, and the direct labour cost of grade S was £2,440 for 785 hours of work.

Required

Calculate the following variances:

(a) total direct labour cost;
(b) direct labour rate;
(c) direct labour efficiency.

Solution

3.9 (a) *The total direct labour cost variance*

	£
Actual direct labour cost for 200 units of B	2,440
Standard direct labour cost for 200 units of B (× 12)	2,400
Total direct labour cost variance	40 (A)

(b) *The direct labour rate variance*

		£
785 hours of work	should cost (× £3 per hr)	2,355
	did cost	2,440
Direct labour rate variance		85 (A)

(c) *The direct labour efficiency variance*

200 units of B	should take (× 4)	800 hrs
	did take	785 hrs
Efficiency variance, in hours		15 hrs (F)
Standard rate per hour		£3
Efficiency variance in £		£45 (F)

(d) *Summary*

	£
Labour rate variance	85 (A)
Efficiency variance	45 (F)
Direct labour total cost variance	40 (A)

3.10 We have now entered into an analysis of the second basic resource used in production, that of labour. You will see that labour has again been separated into two main variances, one related to the pay ratio or price of labour and one related to the efficient usage of that labour (which is equivalent to the sales revenue volume variance). Again the calculations follow exactly the same pattern and methodology but the names of the variances change to equate more logically to the resource we are trying to measure.

3.11 We can continue this type analysis even further because under many existing systems the production costs will have been divided into direct and indirect costs, being both fixed and variable. In most situations the total costs of the production facility can be broken down into direct costs of production and overhead costs (those costs which can not be directly associated with the production of one product but which are nevertheless necessary to the production facility). These overhead costs can again be split into their variable and fixed elements. Analysis of variances can therefore look into these elements of cost control as well.

Variable production overhead variances

3.12 Variable production overheads are indirect production costs that are usually assumed to vary with the labour hours worked.

3.13 The total variable production overhead variance is the difference between the actual variable production overhead cost of the output and the standard variable production overhead cost of the output.

In other words, did the output produced cost more or less than it should have done in variable production overhead costs?

3.14 In the same way as for direct materials and direct labour, the total variable production overhead variance can be sub-divided into two subsidiary variances.

(a) A *variable overhead expenditure variance*. This is the difference between the actual rate per hour for variable production overhead expenditure and the standard rate per hour, multiplied by the actual hours worked (ignoring any idle time hours). A formula for the variable production overhead expenditure variance is:

AH (SVOR - AVOR)

where   AH is the actual hours worked, excluding idle time
        SVOR is the standard variable overhead rate per hour
        AVOR is the actual variable overhead rate per hour

(b) A *variable overhead efficiency variance*. This will be the same *in hours* as the direct labour efficiency variance (ignoring idle time hours, if there are any, because it is usually assumed that variable overheads are not incurred during idle time, only during active working hours). It is valued at the standard rate per hour for variable production overhead. A formula for the variable production overhead efficiency variance is:

SVOR (ALH - SLH)

where   SVOR is the standard variable production overhead rate per hour
        ALH is the actual labour hours worked, excluding any idle time
        SLH is the standard number of labour hours that should have been worked to produce the actual output.

Example: variable production overhead variances

3.15 Suppose that the variable production overhead of product D is as follows.

2 hours at £1.50 = £3 per unit.

During July 19X3, 400 units of product D were made. The labour force worked 820 hours, of which 60 hours were recorded as idle time. The variable overhead cost was £1,230.

Required

Calculate the following variances:

(a)   total variable overhead cost;
(b)   variable overhead expenditure;
(c)   variable overhead efficiency.

Solution

3.16 (a)   *Total variable overhead cost variance*

	£
Actual variable overhead cost of 400 units of D	1,230
Standard variable overhead cost of 400 units of D (× 3)	1,200
Variable production overhead, total cost variance	30 (A)

(b) *Variable overhead expenditure variance*

(820 - 60) = 760 hours were active working hours.

	£
760 hours should cost, in variable overhead (× £1.5)	1,140
did cost	1,230
Variable overhead expenditure variance	90 (A)

(c) *Variable overhead efficiency variance*

400 units of D should take (× 2)	800 hours
Ignoring idle time, they did take	760 hours
Efficiency variance in hours	40 hrs (F)

Standard variable overhead rate in hour	£1.50

Variable production overhead efficiency variance in £	£60 (F)

(d) *Summary*

	£
Variable overhead expenditure variance	90 (A)
Variable overhead efficiency variance	60 (F)
Total variable overhead	30 (A)

Fixed production overhead variances

3.17 The *total* fixed production overhead cost variance is the total under- or over-absorbed fixed production overhead in the period.

3.18 Fixed overheads often cause difficulties for students, and there are some features of absorption costing that you need to be aware of.

 (a) Fixed overheads are fixed costs. The total amount of fixed overhead expenditure ought to be unchanged, regardless of the volume of production.

 (b) However, in absorption costing, we must add an amount to unit production costs for fixed overhead. Adding a share of fixed overheads to unit costs is the process of *absorbing* fixed overheads into the cost of production.

 (c) Fixed overheads are not usually absorbed by sharing actual fixed overhead expenditure between actual output. It might seem sensible and logical that the fixed overhead cost per unit ought to be:

$$\frac{\text{Actual fixed overhead expenditure}}{\text{Actual units produced}}$$

But we don't do it this way!

 (d) Fixed overheads are absorbed into the cost of production at a pre-determined or standard rate.

$$\frac{\text{Budgeted fixed overhead expenditure}}{\text{Budgeted production}}$$

(e)   In standard absorption costing, the standard fixed overhead cost per unit is

   SH × SFOR

where   SH is the standard hours to make one unit
           SFOR is the standard fixed overhead rate per hour, calculated as

   $$\frac{\text{Budgeted fixed overhead expenditure}}{\text{Budgeted hours of work}}$$

(f)   A further feature of standard absorption costing is that fixed overheads are absorbed into the cost of production at a *unit* rate, at the *standard fixed overhead cost per unit*.

3.19   Under- or over-absorbed fixed overhead occurs because the absorbed fixed overhead is unlikely to be exactly the same as the actual fixed overhead expenditure.

Example: fixed production overhead variances

3.20   A numerical example may help to explain these points.

Suppose that Speckles Ltd makes a single product, product Z, for which the fixed overhead budget is £100,000. The company plans to make 5,000 units of Z, which ought to take four hours each to make.

The standard fixed overhead rate per hour will be

   $$\frac{£100,000}{(5,000 \times 4)} = £5 \text{ per hour}$$

The standard fixed overhead cost per unit of Z will be 4 hrs × £5 per hour = £20. This standard cost is the fixed overhead cost per unit that will be absorbed into every unit of Z that is made.

3.21   Now suppose that actual production in the period is 5,200 units of Z, made in 19,600 hours of work. The actual fixed overhead expenditure is £115,000.

The total fixed overhead variance will be as follows.

	£
Standard (absorbed) fixed overhead for 5,200 units of Z (× 20)	104,000
Actual fixed overhead expenditure	115,000
Fixed overhead total cost variance (under-absorbed overhead)	11,000 (A)

Under-absorbed overhead is an adverse variance.
Over-absorbed overhead would be a favourable variance.

Fixed overhead expenditure and volume variances

3.22   We can explain the under-absorbed overhead in some more detail by calculating subsidiary variances.

3.23 The budgeted standard fixed overhead cost per unit was based on the budgeted fixed overhead expenditure and the budget output volume. Either, or both, of these budgeted amounts could be different from the actual amounts, and we can calculate two variances which explain the differences:

(a) an expenditure variance; and
(b) a volume variance.

3.24 The *fixed overhead expenditure variance* is the difference between the budgeted fixed overhead expenditure and the actual fixed overhead expenditure. The actual fixed overhead expenditure ought to be the same as the budget, regardless of output volume.

3.25 In our example the fixed overhead expenditure variance would be calculated as follows.

	£
Budgeted fixed overhead expenditure	115,000
Actual fixed overhead expenditure	100,000
Fixed overhead expenditure variance	15,000 (A)

Actual spending exceeded the budget, so the variance is adverse.

3.26 The total fixed overhead variance is also partly attributable to the difference between the budgeted production output and the actual output.

3.27 In our example this part of the total variance is calculated as follows.

Budgeted output of Z	5,000 units
Actual output of Z	5,200 units
Difference in output in units	200 units (F)
Standard fixed cost per unit	£20
Variance in £	£4,000 (F)

This variance is favourable, because actual output volume (in units or standard hours) exceeded the budget, therefore more overhead would have been absorbed.

3.28 *Summary so far*

	£
Fixed overhead expenditure variance	15,000 (A)
Fixed overhead variance due to difference between budgeted and actual output	4,000 (F)
Total fixed overhead variance	11,000 (A)

Fixed production overhead efficiency and volume variances

3.29 The analysis of fixed overhead variances can be taken one stage further, by sub-analysing the fixed production overhead output variance into an efficiency variance and a volume variance.

3.30 Why was actual production output different from the budgeted output? There are two possible reasons.

(a) The work force might be more or less efficient than budgeted, and so might produce more or less output than standard in the time they work. This can be quantified as a *fixed overhead efficiency variance*, which will be the same *in hours* as the labour efficiency variance and the variable overhead efficiency variance, but will be valued at the standard fixed overhead rate per hour.

Fixed overhead efficiency variance = SFOR (ALH − SLH):

where   SFOR is the standard fixed overhead rate per hour
           ALH is the actual labour hours worked (exclude any idle time)
           SLH is the standard labour hours to produce the actual output.

(b) The work force might have worked more hours than budgeted, and so would have had more time in which they should have produced more output. Alternatively, the work force might have worked fewer hours than budgeted, and so wouldn't have had enough time to achieve the budgeted output, if they worked at the standard rate of efficiency.

This can be quantified as a *fixed overhead volume variance* which is the difference between the budgeted hours of work and the actual hours worked (excluding any idle time) multiplied by the fixed overhead rate per hour.

Fixed overhead volume (capacity) variance = SFOR (BLH − ALH):

where   SFOR is the standard fixed overhead rate per hour
           BLH is the budgeted labour hours
           ALH is the actual labour hours.

3.31 In our example, we have the following.

5,200 units of Z should take (× 4 hrs)	20,800 hrs
did take	19,600 hrs
Efficiency variance, in hours	1,200 hrs (F)
Standard fixed overhead rate per hour	£5
Fixed production overhead efficiency variance	£6,000 (F)
Budgeted hours of work (5,000 units × 4 hrs)	20,000 hrs
Actual hours of work	19,600 hrs
Volume variance in hours	400 hrs (A)
Standard fixed overhead rate per hour	£5
Fixed production overhead volume variance	£2,000 (A)

Actual hours were less than budgeted, meaning that fewer units were produced than might have been, and this is an adverse variance.

3.32 *Summary*

Fixed production overhead variances	£
Expenditure variance	15,000 (A)
Efficiency variance	6,000 (F)
Volume variance	2,000 (A)
Total fixed overhead cost variance	11,000 (A)

What do fixed overhead variances signify?

3.33 Fixed overhead variances are different from variable cost variances, because they are concerned with under- or over-absorbed overheads, not actual expenditure.

3.34 The fixed overhead expenditure variance is a 'true' expenditure variance, in the sense that it compares actual spending with what spending should have been. But the volume variance is not related to spending matters at all, only to the absorption of fixed overheads into production costs.

3.35 It helps management to know whether actual production volume was more or less than budgeted, whether the work force was more or less efficient than standard, and whether actual hours worked (capacity) were more or less than budgeted. But the money value given to these fixed overhead variances should be treated with caution. They certainly do not on their own, represent 'cash flows' gained or lost because the variance has occurred.

Marginal costing systems

3.36 If an organisation uses standard marginal costing instead of standard absorption costing, there will be two differences in the way that variances are calculated.

(a) Since fixed overheads are not absorbed into production costs, there will be *no fixed overhead volume or efficiency variances*. There will, however, be a fixed overhead expenditure variance.

(b) The *sales volume margin variance* will be valued at standard contribution margin, not standard profit margin.

4. INTERPRETATION OF VARIANCES

4.1 We have now seen a complete family of the types of variances which go together to complete a picture of the operating performance of a company compared to a budget. Some variances will in practice be small and will thus be ignored whilst on an exception reporting basis the large variances will be highlighted. It is important that we emphasise the fact that variance analysis is only a technique used in the control and evaluation of performance. It is only one step in that control procedure. Good computer systems will usually facilitate this control but communication of the results is equally important. It is essential that the information gained from this control exercise is brought to the attention of each appropriate manager in an accurate and presentable way and in a timely fashion: the right information must be in the right place at the right time. It is only then that decisions can be made based on the evidence presented. It may, of course, be true that some variances are outside the control of any particular manager and the process should not be viewed as the 'ultimate measure of success or failure'. It is only an indication of what has happened in order that appropriate explanations can be sought and decisions made.

4.2 Before continuing we will recap on the meaning of the various types of variance we have encountered and look at their significance.

Price/rate/expenditure variances

4.3 *Material price variances*. Material price variances are intended to show differences between the actual price paid for materials and their standard price. An adverse price variance would suggest that the managers responsible for buying decisions have paid too much for the materials, and should be more careful in future.

There are reasons why a large adverse or favourable price variance might occur, however, which are outside the buying management's control. These include the following.

(a) *Inflation*. This is discussed more fully later.

(b) *Seasonal variations in prices*. If material prices fluctuate seasonally, the standard price might be an average price for the year as a whole, on the assumption that it is impractical to buy a whole year's supply in the cheap season and store it until needed. In such a situation, price variances should be favourable for purchases in the cheap season and adverse for purchases in the more expensive season.

(c) *Rush orders*. If buying managers are asked to make an order for immediate delivery, they might have to forgo a bulk purchase discount, or pay more for the quick supply lead time. The responsibility for the resulting adverse price variance might then properly belong to whoever made the rush order necessary in the first place.

4.4 It is also worth remembering that price variances should be reported in the period when the purchases are made, not when the materials are issued from stores and used. This is mainly because control information about price variances ought to be made available as soon as possible after the buying decision which gave rise to the variance, ie when the materials are bought.

4.5 *Labour rate variances*. Labour rate variances are the difference between the actual rate per hour paid to the workforce, and the standard rate per hour. It might be tempting to think that the rate variance is something that operational managers can do little about, since rates of pay will be agreed at a senior level between the board of directors and trade union officials. However, a rate variance might occur for the following reasons:

(a) the unexpected overtime working, with overtime paid at a premium rate;
(b) the productivity bonuses added on to basic rates.

To some extent, these should be controllable by operational managers.

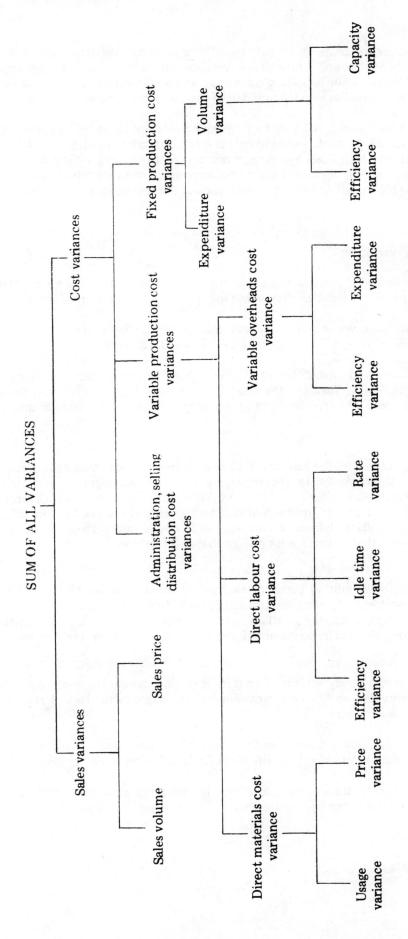

4.6   *Overhead expenditure variances.* Overhead expenditure variances can occur with both variable and fixed overhead items. Adverse expenditure variances might relate to salary payments, rates of pay for other indirect labour including marketing and administration staff, indirect materials costs, power costs, depreciation, accommodation costs and other items of overhead expenditure.

For overhead expenditure variances to have any practical value as a control measure, the expenditure variances for each overhead cost centre need to be calculated, and reported to the managers responsible. Within each overhead cost centre, the manager should be able to analyse the total variance into indirect materials cost variances, indirect labour cost variances and excess or favourable spending on other items, such as depreciation, postage, telephone charges and so on.

Usage and efficiency variances

4.7   *Materials usage variance.* A materials usage variance indicates that the quantity of materials consumed was larger or smaller than standard. It could indicate the following:

(a)   materials wastage was higher or lower than it should have been;
(b)   the quantity of rejects was above or below standard.

Wastage costs money, and should obviously be kept down to a minimum. The size of a materials usage variance, however, just like the size of a labour efficiency variance, depends on the standard rate of usage (or efficiency) and whether the standard was attainable, current or ideal.

4.8   *Labour efficiency variance.* The labour efficiency variance indicates that the actual production time needed to do the work in the reporting period was longer or less than expected. Inefficiency costs money: after all, if it takes three hours to make a unit of product instead of two hours, the unit cost of production will be higher and the profit from selling the unit will be less. Controlling labour efficiency is a key control issue in labour-intensive industries, and one that bristles with the problems of labour relations.

4.9   A standard time for labour to produce an item of work will normally take into account contingency allowances for down time and rest periods. In a production industry based on batch production or jobbing work, the standard time will include an allowance for setting up times for each batch or job, and clearing up times after each batch or job has been finished.

4.10   An adverse labour efficiency variance might indicate poor labour productivity in a period, for which a badly-motivated workforce or weak supervision might be to blame, but other causes of a variance might be as follows.

(a)   Excessively high down times, due to a serious machine break down, or a bottleneck in production which left many of the workforce idle and waiting for work.

(b)   Shorter batch runs than expected, which increase the amount of setting up time and cleaning up time between batches, when no physical output is being produced.

4.11 *Variable overhead efficiency variance.* A variable overhead efficiency variance arises because labour is either more or less efficient than standard. Variable production overheads tend to be incurred in direct proportion to production hours worked, and so if the workforce spends too much time on a job, it will incur not only more labour cost than it should, but also more variable overhead cost too.

Fixed overheads and the volume variance

4.12 Fixed production overhead variances have been described in the chapter on variance analysis as the under- or over-absorbed production overheads in a period, which can be divided into an expenditure variance, an efficiency variance and a volume variance. The fixed overhead volume variance and the fixed overhead efficiency variance are perhaps misleading as variances for management control, because unlike expenditure variances or variable cost efficiency variances, they are not a true reflection of the extra or lower cash spending by an organisation as a result of the variance occurring. This non-association with cash flow sets the fixed overhead volume variance and efficiency variance aside from all other cost variances.

4.13 However, the fixed overhead efficiency and volume variances are of some relevance for control. They provide some measurement of the difference between budgeted production volume and actual production volume, and management should obviously be interested in whether budgeted output was achieved, and if not, why not (efficiency and volume variances). The existence of a fixed overhead variance can be important; and it is only the monetary value given to the fixed overhead variance that can be misleading to managers.

5. INTERDEPENDENCE BETWEEN VARIANCES

5.1 Quite possibly, individual variances should not be looked at in isolation. One variance might be inter-related with another, and much of it might have occurred only because the other, inter-related, variance occurred too.

5.2 When two variances are interdependent (interrelated) one will usually be adverse and the other one favourable. Here are some examples.

5.3 *Materials price and usage.* It may be decided to purchase cheaper materials for a job in order to obtain a favourable price variance, possibly with the consequence that materials wastage is higher and an adverse usage variance occurs. If the cheaper materials are more difficult to handle, there might be some adverse labour efficiency variance too.

If a decision is made to purchase more expensive materials, which perhaps have a longer service life, the price variance will be adverse but the usage variance might be favourable.

5.4 *Labour rate and efficiency.* If employees in a workforce are paid higher rates for experience and skill, using a highly skilled team to do some work would incur an adverse rate variance, but should also obtain a favourable efficiency variance. In contrast, a favourable rate variance might indicate a larger-than-expected proportion of inexperienced workers in the workforce, which could result in an adverse labour efficiency variance, and perhaps poor materials handling and high rates of rejects too (adverse materials usage variance).

5.5 *Sales price and sales volume.* The connection between sales price and sales volume is perhaps an obvious one. A reduction in the sales price might stimulate bigger sales demand, so that an adverse sales price variance might be counterbalanced by a favourable sales volume variance. Similarly, a price rise would give a favourable price variance, but possibly at the cost of a fall in demand and an adverse sales volume variance.

5.6 It is therefore important in analysing an unfavourable variance that the overall consequence should be considered, ie has there been a counterbalancing favourable variance as a direct result of the unfavourable one?

5.7 Because management accountants analyse total variances into component elements, materials price and usage, labour rate, idle time, efficiency, and so on, they should not lose sight of the overall 'integrated' picture of events, and any interdependence between variances should be reported whenever it is suspected to have occurred.

6. THE EFFICIENCY STANDARD

6.1 The efficiency variance reported in any control period, whether for materials or labour and overhead, will depend on the efficiency level in the standard cost.

6.2 If an *ideal standard* is used, variances will always be adverse.

6.3 If an *attainable standard* is used, or a current standard, we should expect small variances around the standard from one period to the next, which may not necessarily be significant.

6.4 Management might set a target standard above the current standard but below the ideal standard of efficiency. In such a situation, there will probably be adverse efficiency variances, though not as high as if ideal standards were used. However, if there is support from the workforce in trying to improve efficiency levels to the new standard, management would hope to see the adverse efficiency variances gradually diminish period by period, until the workforce eventually achieves 100% efficiency at the target standard level.

6.5 It is therefore necessary to make a judgment about what an adverse or favourable efficiency variance signifies, in relation to the 'toughness' of the standard set. *Trends* in efficiency variances, gradual improvements or deteriorations in efficiency, should be monitored, because these might be more informative than the variance in a single control period.

7. INFLATION AND PRICE VARIANCES

7.1 Standard costs are usually based on either of the following.

(a) Expected average price levels for the period in question (normally one year).
(b) Current price levels.

If there is no inflation, (a) and (b) should be the same.

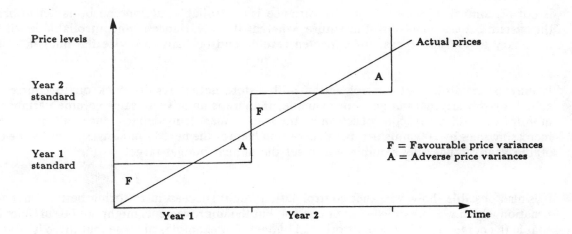

Average price levels might be used for material costs in a period of fairly high inflation.

7.2 If the standard cost is based on current price levels, the effect of inflation on actual prices will be to create ever-increasing adverse price variances as inflation progresses over time. The use of current price levels might be prudent for the following items.

(a) *Labour rates*. Management may be uncertain about the size of future pay settlements during the course of the year. When new wages and salary levels are finally agreed, the size of the expected monthly labour rate variance can be measured (or alternatively, the standard cost could be revised) so that management is made aware of how much of the total rate variance is due to the pay settlements and how much to other causes.

(b) *Materials prices*. In a period of fairly low inflation the adverse price variances which occur due to inflation ought to remain within a tolerance limit which is fairly close to the standard price, otherwise they might warrant investigation.

8. CONTROLLABLE AND UNCONTROLLABLE VARIANCES

8.1 Just as there are controllable and uncontrollable costs, so too might the causes of some variances be controllable and others uncontrollable. Uncontrollable variances are taken here to include the following.

(a) Small variances that are insignificant and completely irrelevant, since a standard cost is really only an *average* expected cost and is not a rigid specification. Some variances either side of this average must be expected to occur.

(b) Larger variances arising for reasons outside management's control.

8.2 Since a variance compares historical actual costs with standard costs, it is a statement of what has gone wrong (or right) in the past. By taking control action, managers can do nothing about the past, but they can use their analysis of past results to identify where the 'system' is out of control. If the cause of the variance is controllable, action can be taken to bring the system back under control in future, whereas if the variance is uncontrollable it will be necessary to revise forecasts of expected results, and perhaps to revise the budget.

8.3   It may be possible that control action will restore actual results back on to course for achieving the original budget. For example, if there is an adverse sales volume variance in month 1 of 1,100 units, control action by the sales or marketing department might succeed in increasing sales by 100 units per month above budget for the next 11 months, so that by the end of the year, actual sales volume will meet the annual budget target.

8.4   It is also possible, however, that control action might succeed in restoring better order to a situation which was previously out of control, but the improvements might not be sufficient to enable the company to achieve its original budget. For example, suppose that there is adverse labour efficiency in a production department, so that the cost per unit of output is, say, £8 instead of a standard cost of £5. Control action might succeed in improving efficiency, so that unit costs are reduced to £7, £6 or even £5, but the earlier excess spending means that the profit in the master budget will not be achieved.

8.5   Control action may take immediate effect, or it may take several weeks or months to implement. The effect of control action might be short-lived, lasting for only one control period; but it is more likely to have lasting effects into the longer term future. The benefits of control action might therefore be the discounted value of all future (cash) savings which arise as a result of the control action that is taken.

8.6   Management must use their experience to judge the likely cost of an investigation and the benefits which will arise if the investigation is successful in correcting the variance. Clearly, an investigation is not worthwhile if the expected costs exceed the expected benefits.

9.   CONCLUSION

9.1   We have now dealt with all the major aspects of financial control which are established through budgets or standards. In isolation the analysis is meaningless; it is the explanation of the variances that is important and the management action that is taken as a result which make variance analysis worthwhile. To the marketing manager the process is extremely informative.

9.2   What is the importance to marketing of all the analysis of production and expenditure variances? The answer lies in the corporate *raison d'etre*. The objective of most organisations is to make money. This may well be coupled with other objectives but without profitability and cash generation the company will fail in the long run. The analysis of the market place and the likely reactions to our marketing strategies are an essential part of this decision making process. But to concentrate entirely on revenue or sales volume is to ignore that basic concept: loss leaders are only used to catch a bigger fish in the long term. If loss leaders lead to a depression in the market expectations of price and result in an inability to increase price or to gain the longer term benefits intended, then the company needs to look carefully at its strategy.

9.3   Profitability or contribution is an essential part of the understanding of the marketing manager. Ultimately it will be of very little value if the marketing manager believes he can sell an excellent product at £10 per unit as the low price will create a high volume of sales and we discover that we can only produce the product for £11 per unit. The decision making process in this case needs to examine the options. Can the unit cost be reduced? Can we sell at a higher price by selling a different competitive advantage? At what point do sales production and finance come together in achieving the corporate goals? How does the short term profitability and strategy of the company get affected by the options open to us?

9.4   We can summarise by stating the following.

Variances provide control information, and should be reported to the managers responsible for the costs or revenues concerned.

9.5   A manager must then decide whether or not to take control action. To do this, the manager needs to consider the following points.

(a)   Whether the results have been recorded accurately.

(b)   Whether there is any possible interdependence between variances.

(c)   The type of efficiency standard in operation.

(d)   Whether a favourable price variance at the beginning of the year is likely to be offset by an adverse price variance caused by inflation during the year.

(e)   The likely cost of an investigation and whether it exceeds the expected benefits from correcting the variance.

(f)   Whether the variance is controllable or uncontrollable.

(g)   Whether the variance falls within established tolerance or control limits.

TEST YOUR KNOWLEDGE
The numbers in brackets refer to paragraphs of this chapter

1   How does variance analysis help to keep control within a business? (1.1 - 1.2)

2   What elements will make up a total sales revenue variance? (2.11)

3   How do sales volume variances and sales volume (margin) variances differ? (2.4, 2.13)

4   How is sales mix variance get calculated? (2.28)

5   Describe the calculation of the two main variances related to materials costs. (3.2 - 3.5)

6   How do fixed overhead variances get calculated under standard absorption costing? (3.18(e))

7   What kind of information can be gained from:

    (i)   material price variances (4.3); and
    (ii) labour efficiency variances (4.8-4.10)

8   How might the following variances affect each other?

    (a)   Materials price and materials usage variances. (5.3)
    (b)   Sales price and sales volume variances. (5.5)

9   How do controllable and uncontrollable costs variances impact the management control action? (8.2)

Now try question 13 at the end of the text

Chapter 14

MEASURING PERFORMANCE

1.   MEASURING PERFORMANCE

1.1   We have now established that control is necessary within any business to act as the third arm of the decision making process.

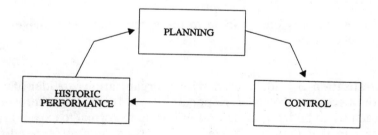

1.2   Without the proper allocation of responsibility for the various costs and revenues which the assets of the business are to generate, the concept of control may not be effective. In this chapter we will look at the concept of responsibility accounting and at how managers will be recognised as decision making units in their own right. It is necessary to monitor and report on the effectiveness and efficiency of the performance of an individual manager or group of managers in terms of their control in order that the basic information for the decision makers is available to identify whether action is necessary. But before performance can be monitored it is of fundamental importance to establish who is responsible for what.

2.   RESPONSIBILITY ACCOUNTING

2.1   Responsibility accounting is the term used to describe decentralisation of authority, with one aspect of performance of the decentralised units measured in terms of accounting results. It is a system which recognises that decisions are made in the short term throughout the organisation and that these decision will impact the profitability of the organisation. The system therefore segregates the revenues and costs into areas of personal responsibility in order to assess performance.

2.2   Responsibility accounting attempts to associate costs (revenues, assets and liabilities) with the managers most capable of controlling them. As a system of accounting, it therefore distinguishes between controllable and uncontrollable costs. Briefly:

(a)   most variable costs within a department are thought to be controllable in the short term, because managers can influence the efficiency with which resources are used, even if they cannot do anything to raise or lower price levels;

(b)   there is a tendency for managers to spend too much time in trying to improve their 'revenues' by raising the *transfer price* for goods or services given to another department; similarly, managers may attempt to reduce their costs by arguing about the transfer price of goods received from another department;

(c)   many fixed costs are uncontrollable (or committed) in the short term, although some fixed costs may be discretionary;

(d)   many fixed costs are *directly attributable* to a department or profit centre in that although they are fixed (in the short term) within the relevant range of output, a drastic reduction (or increase) in the department's output, or closure of the division entirely, would reduce or remove these costs; the existence of directly attributable fixed costs is an important factor in responsibility accounting reporting systems;

(e)   assets and liabilities are only controllable to the extent that the manager has authority to increase or reduce them.

2.3   This type of decentralisation is widely used within organisations to identify the decision makers and attach the necessary levels of responsibility to them. It is therefore sensible to adopt a similar approach when budgeting. As a result it is quite normal to expect brand managers to be budget managers in that they will be responsible for a level of expenditure which is agreed as necessary to support the sales of the product concerned. It is equally sensible in this environment to attempt to motivate managers with targets which are under their direct control. It is thus not unusual for senior management to be rewarded (and hence hopefully motivated) by including elements which are not under their direct control but which are essential if the company is to achieve its overall objectives. For example, part of the brand manager's bonus may include an element based on sales of the brand which his budget is intended to support, even though this will depend partly on external factors over which he will have very little control. Care must be exercised with this type of motivational incentive, to ensure that the element of communication of corporate goals included in any individual's budget- based bonus does not outweigh the extent to which the budget relates to that person's own performance, to activities over which he or she has direct control.

2.4 This decentralisation of the decision making responsibility has various advantages:

   (a) better quality decisions, because the divisional manager is more familiar with local conditions and can make a more informed judgement;

   (b) motivation of divisional managers, because they are given the authority to act to improve their measures of performance (profit, ROCE, added value and so on);

   (c) the head office 'bureaucracy' should be reduced in size, because many administrative decisions will be decentralised;

   (d) where transfer pricing schemes are in operation, there is a greater awareness of market conditions and market prices, since these often provide the basis for determining what the transfer price should be.

2.5 The disadvantage of decentralisation is 'dysfunctional decision-making', which is where decisions made at a local level by a divisional manager profit his own division, but create greater off-setting losses (or benefits forgone) to the company as a whole. Dysfunctional decision-making is most likely where the divisions in the organisation are highly interdependent, where decisions affecting one part of the organisation influence the decisions and performance of another part. If interdependence is great then co-ordination is needed to obtain optimum decisions for the organisation as a whole. There will be great interdependence where divisions transfer goods between each other, or perform services for each other, and it is often therefore the transfer price which becomes the focal point of inter-divisional arguments and dysfunctional decisions.

2.6 Responsibility accounting aims to provide accounting reports so that every manager is made aware of all the items which are within his area of authority so that he is in a position to explain them. There are three types of responsibility accounting unit, or responsibility centre. A responsibility centre is 'a unit or function of an organisation headed by a manager having direct responsibility for its performance'.

Type of unit	Manager has control over	Principal performance measurement
Cost centre	Costs (only controllable cost items)	Variance analysis Efficiency measures
Profit centre	Costs (controllable costs) Sales prices (including transfer prices) Output volumes	Profit
Investment centre	Costs (controllable costs) Sales prices (including transfer prices) Output volumes Investment in fixed and current assets	Return on investment (ROI) Residual income Other financial ratios

Cost centre

2.7　To recap, a cost centre is a 'location, function or items of equipment in respect of which controls may be ascertained and related to cost units for control purposes'. The term is more widely used to indicate a department or function in an organisation to which costs are allocated. A brand manager may be considered a cost centre if he has responsibility for all marketing support for that brand.

Profit centres

2.8　A profit centre is any sub-unit of an organisation (such as a division of a company) to which both revenues and costs are assigned, so that the profitability of the sub-unit may be measured.

In many organisations, the manager in charge of a profit centre is made accountable and responsible for the profits achieved. There are some highly centralised organisations where managers are held responsible for the profits of their division but are not given sufficient authority (or power) to make planning decisions which will improve profitability. It is preferable, however, that managers of profit centres should have sufficient authority to make such decisions themselves, and profit centre accounting ought to be associated with decentralised authority.

2.9　The only areas of businesses that have control of both sales revenues and costs are within the defined responsibility of one group of managers are vertical subdivisions of the business. These divisions will have their own products and their own markets and are hence self contained businesses. Strategic Business Units (SBU's) come into the category and indeed most large companies will structure themselves with smaller divisional responsibilities. It is possible of course to further divide businesses so that not all the divisions have external sales but supply other parts of the same business. Here a system of transfer pricing will evolve in order to transfer goods and services at a price from one division to another.

Investment centres

2.10　Where a divisional manager of a company is allowed some discretion about the amount of investment undertaken by the division, assessment of results by profit alone is clearly inadequate. The profit earned must be related to the amount of capital invested. Such divisions are sometimes called 'investment centres' for this reason. Performance is measured by return on capital employed (ROCE), often referred to as return on investment (ROI), and other subsidiary ratios, or by residual income (RI).

An investment centre is therefore a profit centre in which inputs are measured in terms of expenses, and outputs are measured in terms of revenue, and in which assets employed are also measured, the excess of revenue over expenditure then being related to assets employed.

Investment centre managers therefore have responsibility (and ideally authority too) for costs, revenues *and* assets employed.

Investment centres, profit centres, cost centres and responsibility accounting

2.11 In a system of responsibility accounting, responsibility centres will consist of investment centres, profit centres and cost centres. You should be aware, however, that an investment centre, profit centre or cost centre is only a responsibility centre if the principles of responsibility accounting are applied: personal responsibilities for costs, revenues and asset utilisation must be properly identified.

2.12 Within an organisation, it is quite possible to have investment centres, profit centres and cost centres all within the same accounting system. The sketch below gives a brief outline of how this might occur.

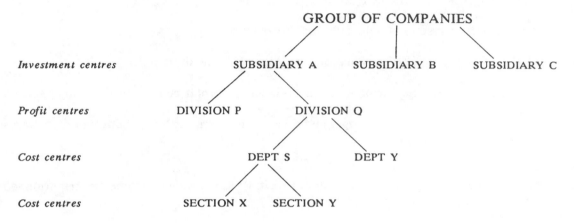

2.13 Managers of subsidiary companies will be treated as investment centre managers, accountable for profits and capital employed. Within each subsidiary, the major divisions might be treated as profit centres, with each divisional manager having the authority to decide the prices and output volumes for the products or services of the division. Within each division, there will be departmental managers, section managers, group foremen and so on, who can all be treated as cost centre managers. Every manager should receive regular, periodic performance reports for his area of responsibility.

2.14 The manager of a decentralised responsibility centre might be given the authority to decide matters relating to:

(a) the introduction of new products;

(b) all aspects of marketing (sales pricing, sales promotion and advertising etc);

(c) plant replacement decisions and the initiation of new investment schemes;

(d) stock carrying decisions;

(e) employment of personnel in the division;

(f) short-term operational decisions, such as sub-contracting work, overtime working, productivity standard setting etc;

(g)   short-term financing arrangements;

(h)   obtaining new equipment and disposing of ageing equipment;

(i)   borrowing;

(j)   granting credit to customers.

However, (h), (i) and (j) would only apply to an investment centre and (a) and (b) to a profit centre or investment centre.

3.   SEGMENT PERFORMANCE MEASUREMENT

3.1   An information system should attempt to report on:

(a)   the controllable performance of a manager, in the short term;

(b)   the controllable performance of a division, or profit centre, in the longer term;

(c)   the performance of the manager and division, measured against a budget or other yardstick of achievement.

3.2   Should performance be judged in terms of profit, ROCE, residual income, contribution, added value, or other quantitative ratios?

There is a variety of ratios available for use by management not necessarily in an investment centre, and their comparative merits and de-merits are discussed below.

Ratio analysis for control measures

3.3   Ratios are useful in that they provide a means of comparison of actual results with:

(a)   a budget, or desired target;

(b)   ratios of previous years' results, in order to detect trends;

(c)   ratios of other companies or divisions, in order to learn whether current actual results are better or worse than those of other similar business units.

3.4   Although financial accounting ratios are perhaps the most important, other useful ratios, which will be considered in more detail later, are:

(a)   the contribution/sales ratio;
(b)   added value ratios;
(c)   non-financial ratios.

Use of finance ratios

3.5 We have already seen in the chapter on interpretation of accounts how ratio analysis can be used to analyse business performance. In the case of an investment centre, ratio analysis can be used to judge the divisions performance. We can use ROCE as the basic measure of performance and break this down further into different elements involving both the profit and loss account and the balance sheet. Hence we can summarise the ratios as follows:

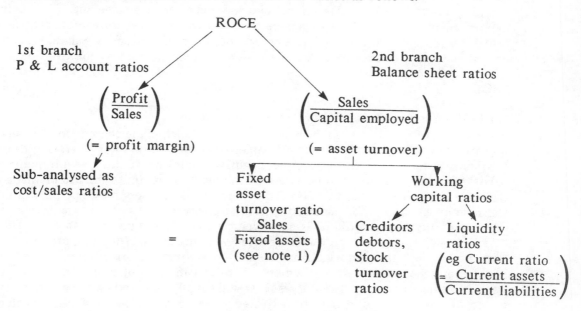

Note. A business invests in fixed assets in order to generate sales. Their ability to achieve this aim is the best measure of their real worth.

3.6 The principal ratios for analysing the profit and loss account are:

(a) $\dfrac{\text{production cost of sales}}{\text{sales}}$

(b) $\dfrac{\text{distribution and marketing costs}}{\text{sales}}$

(c) $\dfrac{\text{administrative costs}}{\text{sales}}$

3.7 When particular areas of weakness are found subsidiary ratios are used to examine them in greater depth. For example, for production costs the following ratios might be used:

(a) $\dfrac{\text{material costs}}{\text{sales value of production}}$

(b) $\dfrac{\text{works labour cost}}{\text{sales value of production}}$

(c) $\dfrac{\text{production overheads}}{\text{sales value of production}}$

3.8 We must always remember when using ratio analysis that a ratio in isolation is relatively meaningless. It is the trend over time that gives us a feeling for the level of performance. Similarly we must be careful to ensure that the ratios are consistently calculated. It would be pointless for us to compare two different divisions by using ratio analysis if they adopted very different policies. For example, one division may own all its retail outlets on a freehold basis where another may decide to adopt a sale and leaseback policy. The property owning division would probably have much higher profits and a vastly greater level of net assets (all other things being equal). The division that has adopted a sale and leaseback policy will be paying rent and hence reducing its profitability, but equally it will have much lower net asset values. If the divisions were measured purely on ROCE as a performance indicator, we may be tempted to believe that the division with the higher ROCE was the better performer but this would ignore the entirely different policies adopted by the management. It is usually better to look at all the aspects of performance that one would attribute to cost centres as well as profit centres and investment centres before judging performance. We should also try to assess only that part of overall performance which the management of the division can control.

Residual income

3.9 One measure of performance which has not been included in the chapter on ratio analysis is the use of residual income (RI). Many companies do not allow their operating divisions total autonomy as they cannot, for example, negotiate their own funding requirements with third parties. But they will need to be aware of the need to maximise the use of the assets which they are using. However, the division of the physical assets may not be straightforward. Consider an example where a company has two operating divisions each with one product and separate markets. Each product is, however, produced from the same factory. The operating divisions will now have their own identified working capital (debtors, creditors, stocks) but their main asset, the factory, is not instantly divisible. In this circumstance the divisions may be charged an interest cost which will reflect the cost of money invested in the assets which produce the goods. The interest cost will usually be based on the average cost of funds to the overall group, and may be adjusted to indicate the level of risk involved in each operation. Now the divisional profit will be calculated after the deduction of the interest charge, giving a *residual income*.

3.10 This concept can be taken a step further. If a division cannot negotiate funding from third parties but does have the control over its own assets (such as a dedicated factory, salesforce, cars and so on) then under the principle of responsibility accounting that division should be aware of the cost of money. If the managers of the division are allowed to buy and sell assets then they should know that the control of those assets to maximise profit is an essential objective of the business. Assets must be funded and hence the concept of a notional interest charge is frequently used.

3.11 Why should notional interest be charged on capital employed?

(a) Notional interest can be charged to derive a residual income figure. The *profit* centre or *investment* centre would be charged with the notional interest in order to reflect a cost for the value of the capital investment in that part of the business. This might help senior managers to compare the results of one department against another. In the same way, charging notional interest to a *cost* centre would help managers to judge the full cost of operating the centre, allowing for the opportunity cost of interest on capital invested.

(b) Notional interest must be recognised as a cost for which the centre's manager ought to be, or ought not to be, held responsible. The concept of responsibility accounting and controllable costs should apply and managers should only be charged directly with costs over which they have some control and so for which they should be held responsible.

(i) If a manager has the authority to purchase and sell fixed assets for his division, or to decide the level of his division's working capital investment, then it is reasonable to charge him and his investment centre with the notional cost of interest (since this reflects the opportunity cost of tying up capital in the investment centre).

(ii) If a manager has no authority over the size of his investment, and asset purchase and disposal decisions are made by his superiors, then it might be useful for comparison purposes to attribute notional interest charges to the cost centre or profit centre, but the manager of the centre should not be held personally responsible for them.

The advantages and weaknesses of residual income measurement compared with ROI

3.12 The advantages of using RI are that:

(a) residual income will increase when:

(i) investments earning above the cost of capital are undertaken; and
(ii) investments earning below the cost of capital are eliminated;

(b) residual income is more flexible since a different cost of capital can be applied to investments with different risk characteristics.

The weakness of RI is that it does not facilitate comparisons between investment centres nor does it relate the size of a centre's income to the size of the investment. In this respect, ROI is a better measure of performance. However, it is better still if several measures are used.

Usefulness of profit to sales ratio

3.13 The profit to sales ratio provides a measure of performance for management and investigation of unsatisfactory profit margins would enable control action to be taken, either to reduce excessive costs or, possibly, to raise selling prices.

Example: profit to sales ratio

3.14 A company compares its 19X1 results with 19X0 results as follows.

	19X1	19X0 (previous year)
	£	£
Sales	160,000	120,000
Cost of sales		
Direct materials	40,000	20,000
Direct labour	40,000	30,000
Production overhead	22,000	20,000
Marketing overhead	42,000	35,000
	144,000	105,000
Profit	16,000	15,000
Profit to sales ratio	10%	12½%

Solution

3.15 Ratio analysis would show that there is a decline in profitability in spite of the £1,000 increase in profit, because the profit margin is less in 19X1 than 19X0. Closer investigation would show that higher direct materials are the probable cause of the problem.

	19X1	*19X0*
Material cost/sales	25.0%	16.7%

Other cost/sales ratio have remained the same or improved.

Limitations of profit to sales ratio and advantage of the C/S ratio

3.16 The profit/sales ratio is a measure of overall profitability, but it must not be misused.

(a) It cannot be used to measure the effect on profit of changes in sales volume.
(b) It cannot provide a clear guide for decision-making.

Example: contribution to sales ratio

3.17 Annie Ball Ltd makes two products, the Crossan and the Halp. Results for each product in September were as follows:

	Crossan		*Halp*	
	£	£	£	£
Sales		300,000		200,000
Direct materials	140,000		60,000	
Direct labour	95,000		80,000	
Variable overhead	20,000		20,000	
Fixed overhead	15,000		24,000	
		270,000		184,000
Profit		30,000		16,000
Profit to sales ratio		10%		8%

During October, the company expects to have extra production capacity, and sales demand exists for additional volume of either product at the current sales price. Production levels of both the Crossan and the Halp must be at least the same in October as in September, to meet existing orders.

With the extra capacity, it would be possible to make units of Crossan to the sales value of £50,000 or units of Halp to the sales value of £40,000. Which product should be made and sold into this additional capacity?

Solution

3.18 The profit to sales ratio would suggest that Crossan is more profitable, and would earn 10% of £50,000 = £5,000; whereas making the Halp would earn profit of 8% of £40,000 = £3,200. This, of course, is nonsense, because fixed costs would be unaffected by the increase in volume. The contribution/sales ratio (C/S) is required for this decision. The C/S ratio is 15% for the Crossan and 20% for the Halp. Profit from additional sales of the Crossan would be 15% of £50,000 = £7,500, whereas the sales of Halp would earn 20% of £40,000 = £8,000, £500 more.

3.19 An alternative approach to the solution would be to identify the limiting factor(s) among the production resources and select the product which earns the *higher contribution per unit of scarce resource.*

4. MARKETING PROFITABILITY AND PRODUCTIVITY

4.1 The need to understand, monitor, control and measure the effectiveness of marketing is extremely important. The marketing plan is usually designed to maximise the value to the business of its products by understanding and meeting the needs of the market place. Because of this we will need information that relates both to the products and to markets. For example a sales team will often be responsible for a geographic area, but within that area they will be responsible for a range of products.

Profitability analysis

4.2 Internal information should be available to meet these matrix-based needs in order to determine the levels of performance. Of course, external information will be available and will give us a feeling for general trends such as market size, geographic segmentation, population trends (for example Media Expenditure Analysis Ltd, Mintel, Target Group Index) but these databases will not be sufficiently specific to provide the level of detail on the competition that we may require. In general terms we can get a feel for competitor activity and performance by constantly monitoring published data (such as financial accounts) from shared customers and from an analysis of their organisational locations, strengths and weaknesses. This style of detailed analysis is always undertaken before any corporate acquisition but unless specific information is supplied, the level of detail should be kept fairly global because of the difficulty of getting reliable information at a lower level of the organisation under scrutiny.

4.3 We have already mentioned the need for product profitability analysis. Similarly, original analysis can be taken down to its lowest level, such as outlet or customer profitability. This style of analysis is extremely important if we are dealing with fast moving consumer goods (fmcg) businesses, because it is easy to discount price away in an attempt to raise volumes. If we concentrate entirely on raising revenues and ignore profitability the results can be disastrous unless an eye is kept on what objectives have been set and how they are being achieved.

4.4 A good example is the use of own label products which normally have been used to use up excess capacity in production facilities. Since most costs in a factory are fixed, the costs of producing one more item of a product are comparatively low and as a result the product is sold at a large discount. Consider, however, the situation where the retailer decides to change his buying policy because the own label you supply is selling very well. As a result he reduces purchases of your branded products and increases the purchases of the own label. Now you are left in the position that the overall volume sold may have risen but revenues will have dropped and margins eroded. Brand profitability and outlet profitability exercises will identify this trend at an early stage. What started out as a sensible management decision on your part to utilise excess production capacity has, in the short term, resulted in a change in selling policy and resulted in a margin squeeze. Management must determine whether this is a route that they wish to pursue.

4.5 In determining brand and outlet or customer profitability we must consider how best to determine profits. We must now concentrate therefore on direct and indirect costs. Direct costs have been defined before and it is interesting to note that what is a direct cost of the product may not be a direct cost of the outlet. All direct costs attributable to getting a product to its place of sale (or distribution point) should be allocated to the product. Similarly any cost attributable to getting the product sold, such as promotional support, advertising and so on should be allocated to the product. In this way we can build a picture of how profitable a brand is to sell in differing geographic sectors or markets.

4.6 What then of indirect costs? These are costs that are incurred by the business but which cannot be directly attributable either to the product or to the market. Examples are costs such as the managing director, the head office team, central office costs and so on. Because allocation to either the product or the market is arbitrary, there is a tendency to ignore these costs altogether. This is dangerous. Indirect costs are still costs and the sale of our products or services must still cover these costs if we are to be profitable. It is therefore suggested that they should at least be recognised in any product/market sector performance analysis either by arbitrary allocation or by deduction as a 'one line' expense in order that they are not forgotten. Simply ignoring them because they are outside the control of the sales and marketing teams can lead to incorrect pricing decisions.

Marketing productivity

4.7 How then do we measure *marketing productivity?* In a general sense this is not particularly easy, but in specific circumstances it can be measured. Consider a sales promotion in a particular geographic area. By measuring sales volumes and revenues over a period which precedes the promotional period, covers the period itself and a similar period after the promotional activity, a trend can be established. Sales for the entire period may be compared over the same period in the previous year, if the circumstances are sufficiently similar. The measurement is not difficult since we are trying to assess the productivity of an action by comparing the extra benefit generated by sales against the input (the cost of the sales promotion) which is an immediately defined additional or incremental expense. No problems of cost apportionment of indirect costs exist. We should, however, be careful to include all additional costs such as extra sales commissions, returns, coupon redemption and so on.

4.8 Trying to make decisions based on product or market profitability or on marketing productivity is, in most cases, a little difficult and extreme caution should be taken. The difficulty of how costs are apportioned and the causal relationship between marketing activity, sales revenue and variable costs makes this analysis extremely sensitive. Care is advised to ensure that every time the analysis is done a review of the cost apportionment in *the light of the object of the exercise* should be completed and questioned by at least one independent manager.

4.9 A favourite method of understanding the effectiveness and efficiency of the marketing costs/activities is the use of *market share analysis.* Indeed, within the world of branded product finance advertising this is often taken further to determine the 'share of voice' achieved in media related activities, provided that message is recognised and supported by research. It can be an extremely useful indicator of awareness. Market share and market growth statistics, however, remain as the most frequently used sector performance indicator. Marketing objectives are usually clearly defined in the marketing plan, subject to the markets in which each product is being sold and where the product is placed in its life cycle. This is not always as easy as it sounds since the determination of a market in terms of value, particularly for new products, is subjective in the extreme. Thus defining your marketing spend in terms of revenues for a new product might not be acceptable to management because you could overestimate the potential market dramatically and as a consequence overspend and cause a loss for the product.

4.10 Understanding your market share over time is the subject of a type of project known as *profit impact over time* (PIMS). Competitor returns on capital employed against the various different marketing strategies are measured and reported confidentially. This can be a useful tool in setting a required standard. Notice that the measures employed are both of growth in market share and in profitability. One of the difficulties of setting objectives solely in terms of market share is that being the biggest in a particular market does not ensure financial survival. Commercial history is littered with companies who had this as their sole objective and went into liquidation because of the inability to understand the need for cash generation and profitability.

4.11 Having established our goals we may wish to have some performance indicators available in the short term to determine our relative segmental performance over time. The most normal feature of this type of short term analysis is the identification of ratios. For marketing departments this may ideally link the marketing activity to sales revenues. This does not in itself introduce profitability into the equation. However, if our product pricing has been carefully understood and the element of variable marketing expenditure fully identified then it is possible to use such an indicator in the full knowledge that increasing, say, our advertising budget will result in additional sales and hence add an incremental contribution to the profitability of the company. Provided therefore that other costs are properly monitored and controlled the short term profitability concept can be maintained.

4.12 Linking advertising spend to sales revenue can, of course, lead to incorrect decisions. If we simply used a percentage of, say, 5% as our benchmark over time it might lead us to cut our marketing activity at precisely the time that we should increase that activity. We must use the ratio only as one measure of performance. The position of our product in its life cycle and the desired level of market share must also come into the equation of performance evaluation. Similarly, the other areas which comprise the total marketing spend such as merchandising, promotional activity, sales force costs and central overheads can all be assessed by reference to ratios over time. They can also be assessed against competitor levels if accurate and reliable data can be established. Common ratios would link sales revenues and sales quantities to those specific aspects of marketing activity. It is important to ensure that the costs concerned are related specifically to the revenues generated as a consequence of the actions taken. Once again the difficulty of time lag becomes evident. The majority of marketing effort is arrived at filling a future order book whereas the uncertainty will only reorganise revenue when a sale is made. Measuring sales in one month against the marketing cost in the same month may be severely misleading. As a result it is the trend in those ratios over time that becomes important and not the specific identification of one ratio in one time period. This is entirely in keeping with the segmental approach that we have adopted. Unless we assess performance over time and specifically relate the spend to the segment which we are targeting, the analysis will be of little value.

4.13 It is often important within companies to assess performance across segments. This is not an easy task. A regional sales team in one area cannot necessarily be compared with a similar sized team in another area if there is differential pricing used for different geographic regions; if the costs related to covering one region will exceed another because, say, of geographic area; if socio-economic conditions are drastically different in the areas; and if

301

demographic conditions are different and so on. So the important measurement in these circumstances may be to measure performance against a predetermined target or standard. The concepts of budgeting are dealt with in another chapter.

4.14   One final warning on ratio analysis comes form the vary concept of ratios. If we concentrate entirely on ratios it can detract attention from the *absolute* levels of costs and revenues involved. In isolation the ratios will not give a true picture of events or the materiality of those events in the overall picture of the activities in which we are engaged. So look at the absolute levels of cost and revenue as well as the ratios.

5.   MATRIX MODELS AND MISSION ANALYSIS

5.1   If financial analysis is to be of any use in the decision making processes within a business, then the way in which it matches the decision-making structure of the organisation must be clearly identified. Hence the impact of the marketing effort must be assessed in each area of the business and the relative productivity of each alternative marketing activity must be identified and analysed.

Matrix models

5.2   A specific problem with the needs of this analysis can be presented by the type of organisation we are working within, and the organisational structure that has been adopted to ensure the best uses of resources. Similarly, organisations will change over time and the need to provide sufficiently flexible analysis for those changing needs presents its own series of problems. The organisational needs of the company will vary according to the industry, the geographic mix, the product range, the need for technological interface, the continuing need for production development and so on.

5.3   A particular example of the way in which a complex organisational structure is assessed is found in matrix management control. When a company has a multi-product portfolio which is being sold to different market segments, the organisation may require both product knowledge and market knowledge. These elements may be controlled separately. Hence the market managers may be geographically distributed to develop markets for the company products. But the central resource of product managers with specific knowledge of the capabilities and materials which will form part of the overall products may not be distributed in the same way or managed under the same structure.

5.4   For example, a company involved in natural and man made fibres, with a variety of products, may adopt a structure such as that shown below, which shows the cross over of communication and information-sharing between managers.

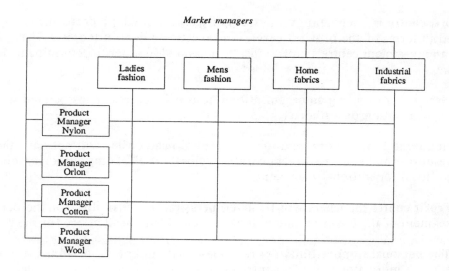

Mission analysis

5.5 Firms offering a professional service such as accountants, lawyers or advertising agencies will often adopt a pool based system of matrix management. Certain managers will specialise in industry sections to whom they offer their services. The resources to meet the needs of a specific project or assignment that is then won will be drawn from a central pool of people who are far less specialised, and who may need detailed management to complete the assignment. On completion of the project these resources can be returned to the central pool for assignment to another project.

5.6 How then should the financial analysis follow these organisational structures? The most meaningful way is to identify the mission or project for which the resource was allocated and to analyse it accordingly. The resource is only dedicated to the project for a defined period of time and hence the project must be carefully analysed so as to incorporate only those costs and resources that relate to that project, and not to those elements which are outside its scope. In theory this is fine, but in practice the underlying information may be difficult to extract. In the case of the company which has an organisation where market managers are distributed globally (possibly with their own basic organisational structure being accounted for locally) but where the product managers are located in much fewer locations and accounted for as separate sites, on different systems and using different resources, getting comparable and relevant data can become awkward. Nevertheless analysis of the mission by reference to the matrix needs of the organisation must be undertaken in order to identify the effectiveness of the marketing being undertaken. The important lesson to be learned is to ensure exactly what data is needed to preserve the effectiveness of the mission because the omission of relevant or inclusion of irrelevant data may reduce dramatically the effectiveness of the planning and control aspects of this analysis.

6. ADVANTAGES AND PROBLEMS OF A PROFIT CENTRE ORGANISATION

6.1 Having established how to measure performance of individual departments or business segments, we must now move on to the measurement of bigger segments of the business.

6.2 A profit centre is a segment of a business organisation whose performance is measured and judged in terms of the profit it earns. An investment centre, too, is a form of profit centre since an investment centre's profit must be measured in order to determine its ROI or residual income.

The reasons for dividing an organisation into profit centres are associated with the benefits of decentralisation of authority.

(a) In a large business organisation, the central head office will not have the management resources and skills to direct operations closely itself. Some authority must be delegated to 'local' operational managers.

(b) Profit centre managers will be given personal responsibility for the performance of a segment of the business, and will be accountable to head office for the results achieved.

(c) The personal responsibility for revenues, costs and profit of a business segment should act as a motivator to profit centre managers. Provided that a suitable reward structure exists (successful managers are paid more, or are given promotion incentives and so on) managers will want to achieve good results for their profit centre.

(d) Head office ought to delegate sufficient authority to profit centre managers to enable them to take what decisions they need to improve the results of their profit centre (subject to resources being available). Profit centre managers, with a good knowledge of 'local' conditions affecting their profit centre, and with a personal incentive to earn high profits, ought to be able to take decisions that improve the profits, of their segment of the business.

6.3 In summary, the advantages of profit centres are decentralisation of authority to managers with a better knowledge of local conditions in their segment of the business, and so better management decisions, reinforced by the motivating effects of personal responsibilities and rewards. Significantly, however, when a manager is made personally accountable for the results of a profit centre, he will make his prime target:

(a) achieving a satisfactory profit for the profit centre; and
(b) ideally, improving the centre's profit performance.

The profit and performance of the organisation as a whole are likely to become a lesser consideration, subordinated to the 'self-interest' of the profit centre.

6.4 A danger with profit centre accounting is that the business organisation will divide into a number of self-interested segments, each acting at times against the wishes and interests of other segments. Decisions might be taken by a profit centre manager in the best interests of his own part of the business, but against the best interests of other profit centres and possibly of the organisation as a whole.

6.5 A task of head office is therefore to try to prevent dysfunctional decision-making by individual profit centres. To do this, head office must reserve some power and authority for itself and so profit centres cannot be allowed to make entirely independent decisions. Just how much authority head office decides to keep for itself will vary according to individual circumstances. A balance ought to be kept between decentralisation of authority to provide incentives and motivation, and retaining centralised authority to ensure that the organisation's profit centres are all working towards the same target, the benefit of the organisation as a whole (in other words, retaining *goal congruence* among the organisation's separate divisions).

How might dysfunctional decisions arise?

6.6 Why might a profit centre manager take decisions that will improve his own centre's performance at the expense of other parts of the business? This fundamental problem in a profit centre system of organisation arises because:

(a) profit centre managers tend to put their own profit performance above everything else;

(b) profit centres are not isolated and separate entities, but inter-related divisions within a single organisation. Actions taken in one profit centre will have an effect on others.

   (i) Profit centres share certain resources such as head office services, and so there might be disputes about what proportion of the shared services each profit centre should be given and should be charged for.

   (ii) Profit centres might do work for each other, ie supply goods to each other or provide services for each other. Since profit centre performance is measured according to the profit they earn, no profit centre will want to do work for another and incur costs without being paid for it. Problems can and do arise in arranging payments for inter-divisional transfers of goods and services, ie in agreeing a transfer price for such work.

7. MEASURING PERFORMANCE: PROFIT OR CONTRIBUTION?

7.1 A principle of responsibility accounting is that profit centre managers should only be held accountable for those revenues and costs that they are in a position to control (or at least to explain). Short-term controllable costs are mainly variable (although there may be some fixed costs which are discretionary) and it is therefore arguable that a manager's performance should be measured in terms of total contribution, or contribution per unit of the production limiting factor.

(a) The costs he is capable of reducing (by improvements in efficiency) are mainly variable costs.

(b) Increases in production volume, within the relevant range of output, will raise profit by the amount of increase in contribution.

7.2 A divisional performance statement based on contribution might appear as follows:

	Division A	Division B	Total
	£'000	£'000	£'000
Sales	80	100	180
Less variable costs	60	50	110
Contribution	20	50	70
Less fixed costs			50
Profit			20

(a) Divisional performance can be improved by increasing the sales price, or volume of sales, or reducing the unit variable costs.

(b) The relative profitability of Divisions A and B could be compared by means of their contribution to sales ratio (in this example, 20% and 50% respectively).

(c) If there is a production limiting factor, performance could also be measured in terms of contribution per unit of limiting factor. In our example, if there is a shortage of cash for working capital acting as a restriction on output, and if Divisions A and B use £2,500 and £8,000 in working capital respectively, the contribution per £1 of working capital employed would be £8 for Division A and £6.25 for Division B (so that a transfer of some production resources from B to A might be profitable under these circumstances).

Directly attributable fixed costs

7.3 One drawback to using contribution alone as a measure of divisional performance is that although it indicates the short-term controllable results of the division, it gives no indication as to longer-term underlying profitability. Suppose, for example, that a division is closed down. Apart from the 'one-off' effects of closure, such as redundancy payments and receipts from the sale of assets, there would be a reduction of annual running costs.

The variable costs of production would be avoided, but there would also be a reduction in fixed costs. All the fixed costs which are directly attributable to the division would be saved, so that even if a contribution towards profits is being earned, it might still be profitable to close the division because directly attributable costs exceed the size of the contribution.

7.4 In the following example, closure of Division X might be justified, since there would be a net saving in annual running costs of £5,000.

	Division X £'000	Division Y £'000	Total £'000
Sales	70	120	190
Less variable costs	50	80	130
Contribution	20	40	60
Less directly attributable fixed costs	25	25	50
Profit of the division	(5)	15	10
Less fixed costs (general)			8
Company profit			2

7.5 The longer-term performance of divisions should therefore be measured after deducting directly attributable fixed costs, but contribution should also be shown, since this indicates short-term controllable results.

Charging a proportion of shared fixed costs

7.6 An argument against measuring profit on the basis of contribution less directly attributable fixed costs is that no one is made responsible for earning a sufficiently large profit to ensure that shared fixed costs are covered, and that the organisation as a whole is profitable.

To ensure that a company makes a profit overall, it is necessary to set a budget or target contribution for each division so that collectively enough contribution is earned to more than cover all fixed costs. By assigning a target contribution to each division, we are effectively allocating a share of general fixed costs. In accounting reports, it is therefore informative to charge a proportion of shared fixed costs to each division and to measure the net profit.

7.7   In the following example of an absorption costing approach, the contribution is also identified, together with the directly attributable fixed costs. In this way, short-term and long-term controllability are accounted for within the reporting framework.

	Division P £'000	Division Q £'000	Total £'000
Sales	90	110	200
Less variable costs	45	50	95
Contribution	45	60	105
Less directly attributable fixed costs	15	20	35
Divisional gross profit	30	40	70
Less apportioned general fixed costs	20	20	40
Divisional net profit	10	20	30

Exercise

Outline the problems in establishing and interpreting performance ratios for the purpose of comparing inter-divisional results and efficiency.

Solution

There are many problems in establishing and interpreting performance ratios for the purpose of comparing inter-divisional results and performance.

(a)   The accounting methods used by each division may not be the same. Unless a system of uniform costing exists, there are various items which could be treated differently in the accounts of each division and this would affect their apparent comparative performance. Examples of such items include:

   (i)   *depreciation:*   which method is used and how are the useful lives and scrap values determined?

   (ii)   *method of valuing assets:*   historical or current cost for fixed assets? FIFO, LIFO or weighted average for stocks?

   (iii) *management accounts:*   are they prepared on a marginal or absorption cost basis?

(b)   It may not be possible to compare the inter-divisional performance effectively if the divisions are in different industries. For instance, it may not be meaningful to compare the performance of labour intensive industries with that of capital intensive industries, or to compare product and service industries. In such circumstances it would be better to compare each division's performance with an industry average, rather than with the performance of the other divisions.

(c) If there are inter-divisional transfers then the apparent profitability of each division can be affected by the transfer pricing policy. Transfer prices will need to be established which enable the correct measurement of divisional performance.

(d) If profit is to be used as part of a performance measure then it will be necessary to establish the most representative profit measure - either profit after tax, profit before tax, profit before interest and tax and so on.

(e) If Return on Capital Employed (ROCE) is to be used as a performance measure, then it may not be valid to compare the performance of a division with old assets with that of a division with new assets. This is because ROCE calculated on the traditional basis tends to increase as the net book values of assets are reduced. This problem could be avoided by revaluing assets before calculating ROCE.

(f) Management must consider any potential behavioural problems which could arise from the use of different performance measures. It is important that the performance measures encourage goal congruence and do not lead managers to take actions which improve the performance of their own division at the expense of the company as a whole.

(g) Another problem is in deciding whether or not to apportion head office costs to divisions, and if so what basis should be used. Behavioural problems could arise if managers are charged with costs which are outside their control, particularly if the charge seems to be on an arbitrary basis.

---

8. CONCLUSION

8.1 Responsibility accounting is a system of accounting that makes managers responsible for a unit of the business under their authority. Accounting reports are produced regularly to help managers control their unit's operations.

8.2 A business unit might be a cost centre, a profit centre or an investment centre. Investment centre performance is judged overall according to ROI or residual income. Profit centre performance is judged overall according to profit earned. In addition variances and ratios provide further budgetary control information.

8.3 The marketing effort can be evaluated by reference to both internally generated and externally collected ratios over a period of time. However, great care must be taken to ensure that the accounting detail and marketing effort are matched, since costs are incurred by marketing managers to obtain further sales whereas accounting data tends to be historic and hence relates to prior activity. Hence the use of market share targets over time and ratios over time must be used in unison if a meaningful trend is to be established.

TEST YOUR KNOWLEDGE
The numbers in brackets refer to paragraphs of this chapter

1   Define 'responsibility accounting'. (2.1)

2   List four advantages of decentralisation. (2.4)

3   Define 'profit centre'. (2.8, 2.9)

4   What is residual income? (3.9)

5   Give two examples of how marketing productivity can be measured? (4.8, 4.9)

6   How might dysfunctional decisions arise in a profit centre organisation? (6.6)

Now try question 14 at the end of the text

310

ILLUSTRATIVE QUESTIONS
AND
SUGGESTED SOLUTIONS

ILLUSTRATIVE QUESTIONS

1 PROFIT V CASH (25 marks)

(a) Explain why a company's reported profit for a given financial year will differ from the change in its cash position over the same period. (15 marks)

(b) Why is this difference relevant to marketing managers? (10 marks)

CIM December 1990

2 BAD AND DOUBTFUL DEBTS (10 marks)

The Lax Company began trading in 19X7 and makes all its sales on credit. The company suffers from a high level of bad debts and a provision for doubtful debts of 3% of outstanding debtors is made at the end of each year.

Information for 19X7, 19X8 and 19X9 is as follows.

	Year to 31 December		
	19X7	*19X8*	*19X9*
	£	£	£
Outstanding debtors at 31 December	44,000	55,000	47,000
Bad debts written off during year	7,000	10,000	8,000

Required

(a) State the amount to be shown in the profit and loss account for bad debts and provision for doubtful debts for the years ended 31 December 19X7, 19X8 and 19X9.

(b) State the value of debtors which would be shown in the balance sheet as at 31 December each year.

3 RATIO ANALYSIS (25 marks)

The data given below relate to the most recent quarter's results for four companies in the printing industry.

	A Ltd	*B Ltd*	*C Ltd*	*D Ltd*
	£	£	£	£
Sales	2,000	1,000	1,500	2,500
Net profit after tax	300	50	225	300
Total assets	1,500	750	1,500	2,400
Shareholders' funds	1,000	5,000	1,400	1,000

(a) Calculate for each company the following performance indicators.

    (i) Asset turnover ratio
    (ii) Net profit margin
    (iii) Return on shareholders' funds (4 marks each)

(b) Given the industry averages below, evaluate each company's performance.

Asset turnover	1.4
Net profit margin	12%
Return on shareholders' funds	25%

(13 marks)
CIM December 1989

4   LIMITATIONS OF HISTORICAL COST ACCOUNTING (20 marks)

Describe the main limitations of preparing the balance sheet and profit and loss account on an historical cost accounting basis in times of inflation.

5   MARQUIS MARKETING LIMITED (25 marks)

Marquis Marketing Limited operates in a highly seasonal sector of the retail industry. The company's management is estimating its cash requirements for the third quarter of 19X9 for which the following schedule of anticipated inflows and outflows has been produced.

Month	Sales £	Purchases £
May	160,000	240,000
June	320,000	60,000
July	80,000	40,000
August	80,000	120,000
September	160,000	180,000
October	220,000	120,000
November	180,000	80,000

Sales are made on 2 months' credit, whilst suppliers allow one month's credit. Monthly salaries amount to £36,000 and the company's annual rent of £48,000 is paid quarterly in advance.

An overdraft of £112,000 is expected to exist on 30 June.

Required

(a)   Prepare a cash budget for the period July–September 19X9.   (10 marks)

(b)   Comment on the cash budget you have prepared with particular reference to the ways in which Marquis Marketing Ltd might control the seasonality of its cash requirements.
                                        (15 marks)
                                        CIM June 1989

6   RELEVANT COSTS (25 marks)

(a)   Are sunk costs ever relevant to decision-making?   (10 marks)

(b)   Felix Fashions manufacture shirts. Last month a batch of 20,000 units was found to be defective. The out-of-pocket cost of the batch was £100,000.

There appears to be two options.

(i)   The items in the batch could be sold in their present state for £4.50 per unit.

(ii)   The defects could be corrected at an estimated unit cost of £3.00 and then the batch could be sold at the normal price of £9.00 per unit.

State (with reasons) which option Felix Fashions should choose.   (7 marks)

(c)   If the correcting of the defective batch referred to in (b) above meant forgoing the manufacture of a further batch of 20,000 units, which option would then be preferable?
                                        (8 marks)
                                        CIM December 1989

ILLUSTRATIVE QUESTIONS

7 DOODLE LIMITED (15 marks)

Doodle Ltd manufactures and sells a range of products, one of which is the squiggle.

The following data relates to the expected costs of production and sale of the squiggle.

Budgeted production for the year   11,400 units

Standard details for one unit:
  direct materials   30 metres at £6.10 per metre
  direct wages
    Department P   40 hours at £2.20 per hour
    Department Q   36 hours at £2.50 per hour

Budgeted costs and hours per annum
  Variable production overhead (factory total)
    Department P   £525,000 : 700,000 hours
    Department Q   £300,000 : 600,000 hours

Fixed overheads to be absorbed by the squiggle
    Production   £1,083,000 (absorbed on a direct labour hour basis)
    Administration   £125,400 (absorbed on a unit basis)
    Marketing   £285,000 (absorbed on a unit basis)

Required

Prepare a standard cost sheet for the squiggle which includes the following costs.

(a) Standard total direct cost
(b) Standard variable production cost
(c) Standard production cost
(d) Standard full cost of sale

Calculate the standard sales price per unit which allows for a standard profit of 10% on the sales price.

8 ABSORPTION V VARIABLE COSTING (25 marks)

(a) In what ways might absorption costing be potentially helpful and potentially misleading in the context of marketing planning?   (10 marks)

(b) Production and other operating data for Napton Enterprises Ltd for last year is given below.

Sales (units)	200,000
Selling price per unit	£32
Production (units)	240,000
Opening inventory	0
Manufacturing cost per unit	
Direct costs	£20
Variable indirect costs	£2
Fixed indirect costs*	£3

315

Marketing and administrative costs

Variable	£300,000
Fixed	£500,000

*Based on an output level of 240,000 units.

Required

Calculate the company's profit under the following costing methods.

(i)   Absorption costing
(ii)   Variable costing

Explain the difference.

(15 marks)
CIM December 1989

9   ESTIMATED COSTS (20 marks)

A company which manufactures and sells a single product has estimated its costs for the forthcoming year as follows:

	Unit cost	
	100,000 units	200,000 units
	£	£
Direct wages	10.00	10.00
Direct materials	40.00	40.00
Manufacturing overheads	20.00	12.50
Administration cost	10.00	5.00
Marketing and selling costs	10.00	7.50
	90.00	75.00

The marketing manager estimates that 100,000 units could be sold annually if the unit selling price were £100, and 200,000 if the selling price were £84. Fixed costs will be unaffected by the level of output adopted.

Assume that the number of units manufactured and sold is the same (finished goods stock remains the same).

Required

(a) Calculate the annual net profit before tax if the company sells:

(i)   100,000 units;
(ii)   200,000 units.

(3 marks)

(b) Calculate the number of units that the company must sell annually to breakeven when the unit selling price is:

(i)   £100;
(ii)   £84.

(12 marks)

(c) State, with reasons, which of the two unit selling prices you would advise the company to adopt.

(2 marks)

(d) Compare the relevance of absorption costing and marginal costing in answering parts (b) and (c) above.

(3 marks)

10   MIDTOWN COMMUNITY HALL   (28 marks)

The manager of the Midtown Community Hall has asked for your assistance in determining the rates to be charged for letting the hall and the admission charge for a forthcoming popular concert. The concert is a one-night performance by the 'Nutones', a popular group of entertainers, and the direct costs of the concert, excluding the cost of hiring the hall, are estimated to be as follows.

	£
Fee to entertainers	4,000
Light, heat and general expenses	400
Advertising	1,000
Cost of tickets and stationery	300

In addition the wages of attendants and other variable costs are incurred at the rate of £0.50 per person attending.

The hall has a capacity of 1,500 and it is the policy to charge a single flat rate for concerts of this type. The manager estimates demand at different price levels to be as follows.

Admission price	Attendance
£7.00	1,000
£6.00	1,250
£5.00	1,500

Fixed costs for the hall for the coming year have recently been budgeted as follows.

	£
Rent	20,000
Light, heat and power (fixed)	2,000
Depreciation/amortisation	10,000
Insurance	3,000
Salaries of manager and assistant	18,000
Maintenance, cleaning	4,000
Postage, telephone, general expenses	3,000

There are three classes of usage of the hall.

Class A - charities, theatrical companies
Class B - meetings, social functions
Class C - popular concerts.

Class A users are charged a daily rate 10% below the average rate; Class B users are charged the average rate and Class C users are charged the average rate plus 20%. The usage of the hall in the coming year is budgeted to be as follows.

Class A: 80 days;   Class B: 120 days;   Class C: 40 days

The board of management of the hall require that the daily charges for the hall should, in total, cover all budgeted fixed costs plus a margin of 10%.

Required

(a) Give calculations to show the daily rates to be charged for the use of the hall.

(5 marks)

(b) Advise the manager of the expected results for each price level for the forthcoming concert. (5 marks)

(c) Show the breakeven point for each of the admission charges. (8 marks)

(d) The agent for the 'Nutones' has suggested that instead of a fee of £4,000 the group should be paid a guaranteed fee of £2,000 plus £1.50 for every ticket sold. Advise the manager of the effect on the results you have produced in (b) and show the new breakeven point for each price level. (10 marks)

11 BUMBLE LIMITED (25 marks)

Bumble Ltd is faced with a choice between two major projects since it only has sufficient resources to undertake one or the other. Its cost of capital is 15%.

The first alternative, project A, is based on a strategy of market development with the following characteristics.

(a) An immediate outlay of £100,000 on market research.

(b) Increased expenditure on advertising and sales promotion in years 1, 2 and 3 of £300,000, £200,000, and £100,000 respectively.

(c) Additional sales force training outlays are expected to be £200,000 in year 1 and £100,000 in year 2.

(d) An increase in debtors and stock of £500,000 will be required in year 1. This will be recoverable in year 10 when it is anticipated that there will be no further sales potential.

(e) The net proceeds from additional sales are estimated at £250,000 pa from year 1 onwards.

The second alternative, project B, reflects a strategy of product development and has the following characteristics.

(a) An immediate outlay on market research of £100,000, followed by further outlays of £50,000 in each of years 1 and 2.

(b) An immediate outlay of £200,000 on R& D plus a further outlay of £50,000 in year 1.

(c) Increased expenditure on advertising and sales promotion of £400,000 in year 1, £300,000 in year 2, £200,000 in year 3, and £100,000 in each year thereafter until the market potential disappears (which is expected to be at the end of year 10).

(d) Additional sales training will involve outlays of £100,000 in both year 1 and year 2.

(e) Recoverable investments in working capital of £300,000, £200,000 and £100,000 in years 1 to 3 respectively will be required.

(f) The net proceeds from sales of the new product are expected to be £100,000 in year 1, £300,000 in year 2, and £500,000 pa thereafter.

Required

Advise the marketing director of Bumble Ltd as to the best course of action. Justify your choice, and make any assumptions in your analysis explicit.

CIM December 1990

12 LOAN OR EQUITY

Babington has invented a radically new item of sports equipment and has financed the development and prototype stages from his own resources. Market research indicates the possibility of a large volume of demand and a significant amount of additional capital will be needed to finance production.

Required

Advise Babington on:

(a) the advantages and disadvantages of loan or equity capital from his own point of view;

(b) the various types of capital likely to be available and the sources from which they might be obtained;

(c) the method(s) of finance likely to be most satisfactory to both Babington and the supplier of funds.

13 PETER PRICE (25 marks)

Peter Price is the finance manager of Bray & Co Ltd which operates in an inflationary economy: the recent annualised rate of inflation has been running between 20% and 24%. This high rate has been accompanied by wide variations in relative price changes: some prices have been changing faster than others.

The following data has been gathered by Mr Price during December 1990 as a basis for preparing a budget for 1991.

Anticipated sales during 1991: 1,000 units

Inputs per kilo sold
   5 kg of material (M)
   10 hours of labour (L)

Current input costs
   M = £12 per kilo
   L = £5 per hour

Current selling price of output is £250 per unit.

Three alternative approaches to developing the 1991 budget are available to Mr Price.

(a)   To base it on December 1990 data.

(b)   To base it on a general increase in prices during 1991 of 20% with no change in relative prices.

(c)   To base it on the following relative changes.

    (i)   Increase in output prices of 20%
    (ii) Increase in labour rates of 16%
    (iii) Increase in material prices of 30%

Required

(a)   Calculate the anticipated profit under each of the approaches to budgeting given above.
                                                   (10 marks)

(b)   The number of units of output actually sold during 1991 was 900 at an average price of £310 per unit; the labour input was 8,750 hours at a total cost of £51,750; the material input was 4,700 kilos at a total cost of £70,265. Prepare a statement that shows actual results (using whichever approach you prefer, but make your choice explicit and justify it), and the resulting variances.
                                                   (10 marks)

(c)   Comment on the statement produced in answer to (b) above.   (5 marks)
CIM December 1990

14   RESPONSIBILITY CENTRES (25 marks)

(a)   Explain the way in which cost centres, profit centres, and investment centres might operate within a responsibility accounting system.   (13 marks)

(b)   Which type of responsibility centre (ie cost centre, profit centre, or investment centre) would you recommend for each of the following?

    (i)   Marketing director
    (ii) Distribution manager
    (iii) Sales manager

Justify your recommendations.   (12 marks)
CIM December 1990

SUGGESTED SOLUTIONS

1 PROFIT V CASH

(a) The measurement of profitability is governed by two basic concepts of accounting, those of prudence and of matching. Where these two concepts conflict, then the prudence aspect will generally be pre-eminent. Added to this is the premise that accountants will attempt to reflect the activity basis of any action or transaction within the accounts.

These fundamental concepts will regularly result in differences in timing between an activity and the result or benefit of that activity. For example, it is common business practice to sell goods on credit. The accountant will recognise a sale well before the cash has been collected. If we sell goods on very long periods of credit or even on a sale and return bases the activity of the sale will be recognised well before the cash has been received.

Similarly, the accountant will wish to rely on the prudence concept in trying to provide for or measure the extent to which a fixed asset of the business is being used up. This is known as depreciation, and it reflects the extent to which, say, a machine used in the manufacture of a product has been utilised in making that product. It is not a cash based activity but a way of identifying a need to replace assets which will lose value over time. This permanent reduction in the asset value is charged to profit but no cash will have been spent.

Finally, cash can be generated and used up in a number of ways which are not a part of the trading activities of the business. These sources and utilisations of funds would include cash movements caused by way of issuing shares or by way of loan, by the buying and selling of fixed assets such as machinery, cars or offices and by the payment of items such as company tax and dividends which are usually identified in the last years profit statement.

The net result is that profit is not synonymous with cash and the need to monitor and manage both aspects is critical to business performance.

(b) Most of a marketing manager's effort is channelled into the activity of order filling. For an existing product or service this may mean that the marketing manager will wish to spend cash now in order to generate a future benefit. The most obvious example of this is the use of current expenditure on media support, the benefit of which in term of sales activity may not be felt for some time.

The accountant will rely in this case on the concept of prudence. There may be an argument to suggest that the cost of the marketing activity (in this example advertising) should be deferred and notched against the future benefit (the sales revenue). However, because this revenue shown in the future is not absolutely certain the accountant will charge the cost immediately and only account for the sales activity when it occurs.

Similarly, a sale may be considered complete when the goods are transferred from seller to buyer. Indeed this will be reflected in the accounts of a company; but the cash may not have been collected. The inability of the company to collect that cash will result in a bad debt being incurred and this is considered a business expense which will again be reflected in the profit statement. So two transactions have been reflected in the profit statement, a sale and a bad debt, but no cash has changed hands.

One area where specific attention to the difference between cash and profit is most evident in the development of a new product. Here the marketing manager will be involved in market research, product design, product testing, product launching, asset purchasing (to perhaps expand existing production facilities) and finally product portfolio management. Many of these activities will need to be funded by a scarce resource: cash. But the benefits will only accrue at some time in the future. Some of his activity will not affect the profit statement immediately (such as buying the production assets, although they will depreciate over time as they are used). Certainly the majority of these activities will affect both cash and the current years profits but in different measures. The benefits will be shown in the profit statement of a future period.

The marketing manager must be aware of the need for cash to fund his projects and the understanding that being profitable today does not mean the business has surplus funds. He must identify his needs within the overall corporate framework.

2 BAD AND DOUBTFUL DEBTS

(a) *Initial working: provision for doubtful debts*

				£	£
31 December					
19X7	Provision required	=	£44,000 × 3%	1,320	
19X8	Provision required	=	£55,000 × 3%	1,650	
Increase in provision - charge to P & L					330
19X9	Provision required	=	£47,000 × 3%	1,410	
Decrease in provision - credit to P & L					(240)

Profit and loss account charge
Year ended 31 December

	19X7	19X8	19X9
	£	£	£
Bad debts	7,000	10,000	8,000
Provision for doubtful debts	1,320	330	(240) credit

(b)

Balance sheet extracts
as at 31 December

	19X7	19X8	19X9
	£	£	£
Debtors	44,000	55,000	47,000
Less provision for doubtful debts	1,320	1,650	1,410
Balance sheet value	42,680	53,350	45,590

3 RATIO ANALYSIS

(a)

	A Ltd	B Ltd	C Ltd	D Ltd
Asset turnover ratio	1.33	1.33	1.00	1.04
Net profit margin	15%	5%	15%	12%
Return on shareholders funds	30%	1%	16%	30%

(b) (i) *Asset turnover ratio*

This ratio is used to measure now much investment is needed in the assets of a business to generate sales revenues. All four companies are below the industry norm of 1.4 in this respect with companies C and D well below the average. This could have been caused by a very recent investment in new assets where the benefits of that investment have yet to be seen. However, the question raised is whether the companies concerned are generating sufficient revenues from their assets. Are they, for example, producing at less than full capacity or do they need to re-evaluate their pricing policy? Producing at less than full capacity would definitely reduce sales revenues. There may therefore be an opportunity to utilise the excess capacity by producing another product or producing for a particular market segment at a lower price, thereby obtaining a competitive advantage in the market place.

The problem may not be one of excess capacity, it may be one of inefficient production. Is the product being sold in a competitive market where price is already determined? A re-evaluation of the unit costs may be worthwhile to determine what can be done to reduce costs and of course the problem may simply be one of lack of quality or lack of awareness within the market. Perhaps the marketing strategy for the product needs to be re-evaluated, or the product repositioned. Perhaps a relaunch is required.

Finally, the finance director should consider reducing the asset base. Excess assets may need to be sold off whilst current assets (stock and debtors) might be better managed and therefore reduced. All of these actions, if successful, would raise the ratio towards the industry norm.

(ii) *Net profit margin*

The profit margin of all the companies except Company B look healthy against the industry average. The profit margin described is calculated as the profit after tax expressed as a percentage of sales revenue. The fact that the asset turnover ratio for Company B is closer to the industry average these two ratios together would suggest that the cost levels of Company B are higher than would be expected. This can arise for any number of reasons. General overheads may be high because of several one off costs incurred in the year under review, which may result in a more efficient organisation in the future. Equally, certain costs such as marketing research, R & D or product launch costs may have been incurred and included as a cost in the year for which the benefits have not yet been felt.

Two other aspects could have caused the apparent under-achievement in this area. Interest costs may be very high, indicating that assets are funded by borrowing or that the operation is running on bank borrowings. Alternatively, taxation costs may be high, which may suggest that the company has not invested in new fixed assets for some while (allowances given on fixed assets would decrease the taxation charge). In all the above circumstances the level of cost needs to be reviewed.

One final element in this area should be considered. The net margin may be low because the gross margin is low (the sales less cost of sales before overheads). If margins are low but the asset turnover ratio is close to the industry average it would suggest an inefficient production facility. Again a review of unit costs may be required.

(iii) *Return on shareholders funds*

This ratio is the measure which the owners of the business are likely to scrutinise closely. If the owners are the general public they are unlikely to continue to invest in a company that can not produce an acceptable return. Results below the industry average are therefore worrying.

Both Company B and Company C are poor performers in this sector. If we view this in conjunction with the other ratios, Company B must improve its net profit margin whilst Company C must increase its sales or reduce its net assets. Of course a very low return on shareholders funds can be due to the position of the main product(s) in its life cycle. A very high return may be indicative of products which are late in their life cycle and hence the return may not be sustained. Similarly a very low return may indicate a very young company who have only recently entered a market. Hence Company B may have only recently been admitted to the Stock Exchange and its business basis is relatively small. This would be borne out by the low level of absolute sales and poor profit performance. The shareholders will be unlikely to be happy, however, if the existing poor return were to continue. Cash would need to be invested wisely to improve sales without any increase in overheads if the shareholders are to be satisfied. Alternatively the company could consider a capital reconstruction to swap equity for debt, although this is not advisable without proper investigation into the detailed cause of the rather poor ratios.

Conclusion

(a) Company A seems to be a good solid performer. Its ratios are largely in line with or ahead of the industry averages. It is apparently well managed.

(b) Company B needs to improve its profitability particularly with an eye on the shareholders requirements.

(c) Company C needs to increase sales to allow its return to shareholders and its asset turnover ratio to improve. The marketing department should carefully consider its existing policies.

(d) Company D needs to improve sales without any increase in overheads or investment and again the marketing strategy needs to be reviewed.

4 LIMITATIONS OF HISTORICAL COST ACCOUNTING

The presentation of the financial affairs of a business in the form of a balance sheet and profit and loss account, using the 'historical cost convention' and generally accepted principles of accounting suffers from a number of fairly serious shortcomings at the best of times, but there are particular problems in times of inflation.

(a) The values disclosed in the financial statements are expressed in terms of an unstable measuring unit, ie sterling. Because of the continuing erosion of the purchasing power of money, historical cost values of assets bear no relation to current values. In other words, comparisons of the current trading results of a business with its results, of say, ten years ago might indicate that in money terms the business has had a satisfactory growth in profits and assets. However, when the effects of inflation have been taken into account and the money values are restated as real values it is very possible that the business is worse off now compared with its position ten years ago. The use of an unstable measuring unit is the greatest drawback of financial statements for interpretation purposes. Consider the comparison of the balance sheets of two companies, A and B.

BALANCE SHEET AS AT 31 DECEMBER 1980 (EXTRACT)

	Company A £	Company B £
Fixed assets		
Factory buildings at cost	200,000	100,000

It would appear from the balance sheets that Company A owns a factory building either twice as large or twice as valuable as the building owned by Company B. In fact, the building owned by B is exactly the same as that owned by A, but was built five years earlier, when it cost half as much to build. To be able to compare the assets owned by Company A and Company B, the historical cost convention must be abandoned, and the assets stated in terms of current market value, or replacement cost.

(b) The return on capital employed in historical cost accounts gives a misleading comparison of results over a period of years. If profits are the same each year, they are really declining in value because of inflation. This means that whereas ROCE might be constant, or even rising, year by year in the historical cost accounts, the real position might be getting worse.

(c) After paying taxation, interest and some (necessary) dividends, most companies have insufficient internally-generated funds to survive in the long term, without an improvement in real profits. (Shortages of cash are essentially the problem, which historical cost accounts do not reveal because they do not disclose the cost of replacing the assets of the business.)

(d) Accounting profits are an inadequate guide to the amount which may safely be distributed as dividend. This is because at least a part of the profit shown by the historical cost account must be ploughed back into the business just to maintain its previous operating capacity.

(e) There are difficulties in measuring profits. In historical cost accounts, holding gains on stocks are included in the gross profit figure. Such gains merely represent the amount the business would have to spend to maintain its existing level of stocks. Conversely profits or losses on holdings of monetary items are not shown.

5 MARQUIS MARKETING

(a) MARQUIS MARKETING
CASH BUDGET: JULY TO SEPTEMBER 19X9

	July £'000	August £'000	September £'000	Total £'000
Inflows				
Receipts from sales	160	320	80	560
Outflows				
Payments for purchases	60	40	120	220
Salaries	36	36	36	108
Rent	12	-	-	12
	108	76	156	340
Net movement in month	52	244	(76)	220
Opening balance	(112)	(60)	184	(112)
Closing balance	(60)	184	108	108

(b) The trading information given in the question denotes an erratic, probably highly seasonal trend. It would be more informative to have the information for at least one year, if not longer, to give a full picture of the trading cycle.

It would help to reduce the fluctuations in the monthly cash balance of the receipts from sales and the payments if purchases could be 'matched' as the sales and payments are themselves. The best way of doing this would be to reduce the length of credit term allowed to customers to one month.

It would be even more beneficial if the company could pay the suppliers after a longer period. By negotiating the company might be able to pay in two months' time rather than one.

Another option is to negotiate the rent so that it is paid monthly, which would help to spread the payment out more evenly over the year.

If the credit terms given to customers were reduced to one month and if rent was paid monthly, then the cash budget would appear as follows.

	July £'000	August £'000	September £'000	Total £'000
Inflows				
Receipts from sales	320	80	80	480
Outflows				
Payments for purchases	60	40	120	220
Salaries	36	36	36	108
Rent	4	4	4	12
	100	80	160	340
Net movement in month	220	–	(80)	140
Opening balance	(112)	108	108	(112)
Closing balance	108	108	28	28

This shows a slightly more even cash flow although obviously the same months are still better or worse than others.

6   RELEVANT COSTS

(a) In decision making as a rule, only those costs which will have an impact on the decision should be considered. By definition, sunk costs are costs which have already been incurred and therefore should not affect the decision making process. In a new product development situation research and development costs may be necessary. Before those costs are incurred they can be assessed as part of the overall decision making process. After the R & D has been completed, however, another decision may need to be taken about whether or how to proceed. At this stage the R & D cost has been incurred and should be excluded from any financial evaluation.

(b)

	Sell £	Correct £
Revenue	90,000	180,000
Costs	–	(60,000)
Profit	90,000	120,000

The out of pocket expenses incurred in manufacturing the defective batch of shirts are irrelevant. They cannot be recovered and must be eliminated from the decision making process. The two options quoted indicate that the business will generate more profit from correcting the faulty batch than by selling them immediately. The company should, however, be careful. If the market image of the goods is one of quality then selling a defective brand at low prices might harm the image. They should consider a sale under a different brand name or into markets where their image has not been developed. This presupposes that the correction will not be perfect. If that can be guaranteed, then the issue will not arise.

There may also be a production consideration as well as a financial consideration which will affect the decision. If we correct the batch will we hold up or delay the production of the next order quantity? Will this harm our customer image? Do we have the spare production capacity to cope? From a financial angle, we have already incurred the sunk costs of £100,000 without any revenue. Is there a cash shortage and does the company's liquidity become threatened if revenue is not immediately forthcoming?

(c) If we had to forgo the production of another batch of 20,000 shirts, we are foregoing a revenue stream of £180,000.

	Sell £	Correct £
Opportunity cost: lost revenue	–	(180,000)
Revenue	90,000	180,000
Costs	–	(60,000)
	90,000	(60,000)

The revenue lost by forgoing the manufacture of the next 20,000 shirts has caused the sell decision to become more profitable. This assumes that other costs associated with the manufacture are sunk costs, although if other costs were to be taken into account, they must reach £150,000 before they affect the decision. It would be more informative to consider the lost *contribution* of the next batch of shirts, rather than the lost revenue.

7   DOODLE LIMITED

Workings

The budgeted direct labour hours are 11,400 × (40 + 36) = 866,400 direct labour hours.

The fixed production overhead absorption rate = £1.25 per hour (£1,083,000 ÷ 866,400 hours).

The variable production overhead rate (both for costs incurred and absorbed) is as follows.

department P	75 pence per hour
department Q	50 pence per hour

STANDARD COST SHEET: THE SQUIGGLE

	£	£
Direct materials: 30 metres at £6.10		183
Direct wages		
Department P : 40 hours at £2.20	88	
Department Q : 36 hours at £2.50	90	
		178
Standard total direct cost		361
Variable production overhead		
Department P : 40 hours at £0.75	30	
Department Q : 36 hours at £0.50	18	
		48
Standard variable production cost		409
Fixed production overhead 76 hours at £1.25		95
Standard production cost		504
Administration overhead (note (a))		11
Marketing overhead (note (b))		25
Standard cost of sale		540
Standard profit (10% of sales price)		60
Standard sales price		600

Notes

(a) £125,400 ÷ 11,400
(b) £285,000 ÷ 11,400

8 ABSORPTION V VARIABLE COSTING

(a) The two basic methods of costing have the following two objectives.

(i) To ascertain the cost to the company of production
(ii) To act as a basis for pricing decisions

The decision as to which method of costing to use relies on identifying the relevant factors surrounding each case. Both methods have benefits and disadvantages and the circumstances of the decision have to be taken into account.

Marginal costing is an approach which identifies costs which vary with units of production, thereby indicating a unit contribution which the company can then multiply by its number of units of production. This contribution will then be set off against the fixed costs of the business in order to arrive at a true profit.

Absorption costing, on the other hand, will allocate *all* costs to the products, thereby arriving at a fully allocated unit cost. These costs will include all fixed costs which do not vary (within limits) whatever the level of production.

Fully allocating and apportioning costs will have its own difficulties. The most obvious is that the allocation of central costs to a specific product is arbitrary. By nature fixed costs are not specific to that product but are incurred because we are in business. Allocating these costs to the product may limit our ability to be flexible to the needs of the market place and result in lost sales opportunities because it will have driven selling prices up. Any unique selling point or strategic advantage may be wasted as a

328

result. This would be particularly true in a highly competitive marketplace where there is an existing market price and where our ability to compete in that market will be determined by our ability to be cost efficient at the production end.

At the same time a fully costed product will suffer in the market place if production levels change. Producing an over or under recovery of overhead from an accounting viewpoint will not help the products' competitiveness in the marketplace.

On the reverse side, however, absorption costing has some advantages. It will ensure that all overheads are covered by selling the product at the required price. At times when products are reaching the end of their life cycle this is a frequent application of this costing technique. Similarly, when factories are nearing full capacity it is a sound costing technique, since all overheads can be adequately allocated and production levels cannot rise without significant investment in new facilities.

Finally, the choice of costing method can affect stock valuation and therefore reported profit. Using absorption costing, overheads are absorbed into each unit of production. The closing stock will therefore include some fixed costs which will be carried forward to the following year. This can be used to distort or manipulate profit figures from year to year. Under marginal costing fixed costs are written off as they arise.

(b) NAPTON ENTERPRISES LIMITED

	Absorption £	*Variable* £
Unit costs		
Price/unit	32	32
Manufacturing cost		
Variable: direct	(20)	(20)
indirect	(2)	(2)
Fixed indirect	(3)	
Contribution	7	10

Profit and loss account

	£'000	£'000
Sales	6,400	6,400
Opening stock	-	-
Manufacturing cost (240,000 × 25)/(240,000 × 22)	(6,000)	(5,280)
Closing stock (40,000 × 25)/(40,000 × 22)	1,000	880
Contribution	1,400	2,000
Indirect costs: fixed (240,000 × 3)	-	(720)
	1,400	1,280
Marketing costs		
Variable	(300)	(300)
Fixed	(500)	(500)
Profit	600	480

Marketing costs, whether fixed or variable, are usually excluded from the contribution or stock valuation process. This is because they are not incurred in getting the physical goods though the production process or to their existing location for sale. The variable element, however, may be included in the contribution of the product when simply assessing the unit profitability or its contribution towards fixed costs.

In assessing these two scenarios the difference in profit is £120,000. This has arisen because we produced 40,000 more units than we sold. The profit statement will value those goods based on the two costing processes and effectively defer the cost of the product until we have the benefit of a sale. Here we are using the matching principle of accounting, trying to match the costs incurred against the related benefits. If in later periods the stock becomes obsolete or damaged it will be reduced in value. By using two different costing methods we have changed the profit. Under absorption costing we have allocated all the fixed overhead to the stock value and hence deferred the part of the fixed overhead in closing stock to a future period. The amount deferred is (40,000 × £3 = £120,000). Under variable costing the total fixed indirect costs have been charged to profit.

9   ESTIMATED COSTS

(a) (i)   *100,000 units sold*

	£'000	£'000
Sales (100,000 × £100)		10,000
Less		
Direct wages	1,000	
Direct materials	4,000	
Manufacturing overheads	2,000	
Administration cost	1,000	
Marketing and selling costs	1,000	
		9,000
Net profit		1,000

Net profit is therefore £1m. An alternative method of reaching the same result is as follows.

$$\begin{aligned} \text{Net profit} &= 100,000 \times \text{unit profit} \\ &= 100,000 \times (£100 - £90) \\ &= £1m \end{aligned}$$

(ii)   *200,000 units sold*

	£'000	£'000
Sales (200,000 × £84)		16,800
Less		
Direct wages	2,000	
Direct materials	8,000	
Manufacturing overheads	2,500	
Administration cost	1,000	
Marketing and selling costs	1,500	
		15,000
Net profit		1,800

Net profit is therefore £1.8m.

$$\begin{aligned} \text{Alternatively, net profit} &= 200,000 \times \text{unit profit} \\ &= 200,000 \times (£84 - £75) \\ &= £1.8m \end{aligned}$$

(b) Breakeven point means that fixed costs are exactly equalled by contribution (sale price less variable costs). To answer this part of the question, it is therefore necessary to calculate fixed costs as a preliminary step (using the high-low method).

Direct wages and direct materials are variable costs (by definition).

Manufacturing overheads		_Units produced_	_Cost_
			£'000
High		200,000	2,500
Low		100,000	2,000
		100,000	500

Variable manufacturing overheads for producing 100,000 units amounts to £500,000. Fixed manufacturing overheads are therefore £1.5m.

Administration cost		_Units produced_	_Cost_
			£'000
High		200,000	1,000
Low		100,000	1,000
		100,000	-

Administration cost is therefore entirely a fixed cost of £1m.

Marketing and selling costs		_Units produced_	_Cost_
			£'000
High		200,000	1,500
Low		100,000	1,000
		100,000	500

Variable marketing and selling costs for producing 100,000 units amounts to £500,000. Fixed marketing and selling costs are therefore £500,000.

Total fixed costs

	£m
Manufacturing overheads	1.5
Administrative costs	1.0
Marketing and selling costs	0.5
	3.0

(i)

	£	£
Unit selling price		100
Variable costs		
Direct wages	10	
Direct materials	40	
Manufacturing overheads	5	
Marketing and selling costs	5	
		60
Contribution/unit		40

$$\text{Breakeven point in units} = \text{£3m} \div \text{£40}$$
$$= 75,000 \text{ units}$$

(ii)

	£	£
Unit selling price		84
Variable costs		
Direct wages	10.0	
Direct materials	40.0	
Manufacturing overheads	5.0	
Marketing and selling costs	5.0	
		60
		24

Breakeven point in units =   £3m ÷ £24

                              =   125,000 units

(c) The company should adopt the selling price of £84. All the relevant pointers indicate this course of action.

(i) A selling price of £84 yields the higher profit (£1.8m as against £1m).

(ii) Manufacturing 200,000 rather than 100,000 units guarantees a bigger 'slice' of the market.

(iii) The £84 price option, with a breakeven point of 125,000, offers a 37.5% *safety factor* (125,000/200,000 × 100%) whereas the £100 option only offers a 25% safety factor.

(d) Parts (b) and (c) are answered on the basis of marginal costing as fixed costs have not been absorbed. If fixed costs *were* absorbed, it would be fact make no difference to the conclusions reached in (b) and (c), but only because the number of units manufactured and sold is the same (ie finished goods stock remains the same). If stocks are carried forward from one period to the next, profit according to marginal costing will in general be different from profit according to absorption costing (because under absorption costing, in effect some 'profit' is carried forward because it will not actually be earned until the next period).

10 MIDTOWN COMMUNITY HALL

(a) Fixed costs

	£
Rent	20,000
Light etc	2,000
Depreciation	10,000
Insurance	3,000
Salaries	18,000
Maintenance	4,000
Postage etc	3,000
	60,000
Profit margin required (10%)	6,000
Total revenue required	66,000

(*Note.* Since there are no variable costs, the required contribution equals the required revenue).

	Days		Average rate days
Class A users	80	× 90% =	72
Class B users	120	× 100% =	120
Class C users	40	× 120% =	48
			240

Average rate per day needed $\dfrac{£66,000}{240 \text{ average rate days}}$

                         = £275 per day at average rate.

Class of user	Rate per day £	No of days	Total revenue £
A (90% of £275)	247.5	80	19,800
B	275.0	120	33,000
C (120% of £275)	330.0	40	13,200
			66,000

(b)

Admission price	£7	£6	£5
Attendance	1,000	1,250	1,500
	£	£	£
Revenue	7,000	7,500	7,500
Variable costs (× £0.5)	500	625	750
	6,500	6,875	6,750
Direct costs excluding hire of hall cost (4,000 + 400 + 1,000 + 300)	5,700	5,700	5,700
Attributable profit, excluding hire of hall cost	800	1,175	1,050

It is not clear whether the hall manager will be 'charged' with a cost of hiring his own hall, of £330 which is the rate per day. If this is the case, the profit figures above should be reduced by £330.

(c) On the assumption that there is no hire cost for the hall, breakeven sales are as follows.

	£	£	£
Admission price	7.0	6.0	5.0
Less variable cost	0.5	0.5	0.5
Contribution per ticket sold	6.5	5.5	4.5
Directly attributable fixed costs	£5,700	£5,700	£5,700
Breakeven point (tickets sold)	$\frac{5,700}{6.5}$	$\frac{5,700}{5.5}$	$\frac{5,700}{4.5}$
	= 877	= 1,036	= 1,267

(d)

	£	£	£
Admission price	7.0	6.0	5.0
Variable cost per ticket sold (0.5 + 1.5)	2.0	2.0	2.0
Contribution per ticket sold	5.0	4.0	3.0
Attendance	1,000	1,250	1,500
	£	£	£
Total contribution	5,000	5,000	4,500
Direct costs (hire of hall cost taken as nil 2,000 + 400 + 1,000 + 300)	3,700	3,700	3,700
Attributable profit	1,300	1,300	800
Breakeven point	$\frac{3,700}{5}$	$\frac{3,700}{4}$	$\frac{3,700}{3}$
	= 740 tickets	925 tickets	1,233 tickets

11   BUMBLE LIMITED

The cash inflows and outflows of the two projects are as follows:

	A £'000	B £'000
Sales revenue	2,500	4,400
Research	(100)	(200)
Advertising and promotion	(600)	(1,000)
Training	(300)	(200)
Working capital	-	-
Research and development	-	(250)
Net inflow	1,500	2,750

On the face of it therefore it would seem sensible to invest in alternative B because of the greater net cash inflow. However we must take time into account. Note here that cash *inflows* are shown as negatives.

Project A

Year	Market research £'000	Advert & promotion £'000	Training £'000	Working capital £'000	Sales revenue £'000	Net cash £'000	Disc factor £'000	Discovery value £'000
0	100					100	1.0000	100.0
1		300	200		500	1,000	0.8696	869.6
2		200	100			300	0.7562	226.9
3		100				100	0.6575	65.8
10				(500)		(500)	0.2472	(123.6)
1-10					(250)	(250)	5.0190	(1,254.8)
							NPV	(116.1)

Note: Payback is after 6.4 years.

Project B

Year	Market research £'000	Research and promotion £'000	Advert & promotion £'000	Training £'000	Working capital £'000	Sales £'000	Net cash £'000	Disc factor £'000	Discounted £'000
0	100	200					300	1.0000	300.0
1	50	50	400	100	300	(100)	800	0.8696	695.7
2	50		300	100	200	(300)	350	0.7562	264.7
3			200		100		300	0.6575	197.3
4-10			100				100	2.1639	216.4
3-10						(500)	(500)	2.7357	(1,367.9)
10					(600)		(600)	0.2472	(148.3)
								NPV	157.9

Note. Payback is after 6.125 years.

It can be seen that Project A has a positive net present value at 15% whilst Project B has negative net present value. Under these circumstances it is suggested that Project A is chosen since the return is considered to be better. The management may, however, wish to take two other questions into consideration.

(a)   Risk related to each project
(b)   The cash flow returns

The riskiness of either project has not been mentioned. By using the same cost of capital we have assumed that each project is equally risky. This may not be the case. The introduction of different levels of risk would change our perception of which project is best. For example, there may be a greater risk of competitor threat and response by choosing project A and the uncertainties of future sales must then be assessed. Nor have we mentioned which markets we are entering: are they existing markets in which we operate or are we staking new geographic territories? If this is so what risk can be attached to such an action and to the economic and political certainty of the future? Perhaps we should also look at the levels of cost and sales included in our projections. What would happen if perhaps our sales returns started in year 3 rather than year 1 for project A? (The project would actually become uneconomic to perform since the NPV would reduce to -290.4, worse than project B and in any event below the return required by the company.)

Finally, we should look at the cash flow streams since these may be relevant to the company. Hence:

		Cash flows	
		A	B
		£'000	£'000
Year	0	100	300
	1	750	800
	2	50	350
	3	(150)	(200)
	4	(250)	(400)
	5	(250)	(400)
	6	(250)	(400)
	7	(250)	(400)
	8	(250)	(400)
	9	(250)	(400)
	10	(750)	(1,000)

The payback under project A is slightly slower than under project B, but this is unlikely to be significant in the decision making process.

12   LOAN OR EQUITY

(a)   *Loan capital*

The advantages of loan capital for Babington are as follows.

(i)   In the case of a new business with no record of profitability it is likely to be easier to attract than risk capital, at least if Babington is able to offer some security.

(ii)   He is likely to be able to retain greater control of his business by using loan rather than equity finance. However, he may find that potential loan investors will seek to exercise at least some measure of control over the business.

(iii)   In times of inflation, borrowing is advantageous in that the monetary liability remains fixed and the real rate of interest is low or even negative.

Equity capital

The advantages of equity capital for Babington are as follows.

(i)   The pattern of earnings for a new enterprise such as this is frequently erratic, possibly with significant losses in opening years. This might make regular loan repayments difficult to cope with.

(ii) Equity providers might be more willing to take a risk on an investment offering little security if they have the chance of a high return later.

The advantages of each type of finance correspond to disadvantages of the other type.

(b)   The various sources of finance which might be available to Babington include:

(i)   clearing banks. If the amount of capital required is small a bank might be willing to consider an overdraft or loan;

(ii) special financial institutions, such as Investors in Industry;

(iii) venture capital. Various government incentives have been introduced in recent years to encourage private investment in industry. Some financial institutions have set up machinery to bring together potential investors with businesses looking for finance. This is particularly so with the Business Expansion Scheme and Babington might be able to obtain finance from a business expansion fund.

(c)   The considerations which are relevant here are substantially those set out in part (a) above. An additional factor is the type of contribution which a supplier of capital might wish to make to the business. This might go so far as to constitute a joint venture arrangement if the supplier of capital had technical or managerial expertise and Babington was willing to relinquish a share in the running of the business.

13   PETER PRICE

(a)

	Inflation = 0%		Inflation = 20%		Relative inflation	
	£'000	£'000	£'000	£'000	£'000	£'000
Sales		250		300		300
Less: Materials, M	60		72		78	
Labour, L	50		60		58	
		(110)		(132)		(136)
		140		168		164

Workings

1   Inflation = 0%
    Material, M, used = 5 × £12 × 1,000 = £60,000
    Labour, L, used   = 10 × £5 × 1,000 = £50,000
    Sales = £250 × 1,000 = £250,000

2   Inflation = 20%
     Material, M, used = £60,000 × 120/100 = £72,000
     Labour, L, used = £50,000 × 120/100 = £60,000
     Sales = £250,000 × 120/100 = £300,000

3   Relative inflation
     Material M, used, = £60,000 × 130/100 = £78,000 (unit cost = £12 × 130/100 = £15.60)
     Labour L, used   = £50,000 × 116/100 = £58,000 (unit cost = £5 × 116/100 = £5.80)
     Sales = £300,000 (as in (2) above)

(b)

	Budget for 1,000 units	Budget for 900 units	Actual	Difference
	£	£	£	£
Sales	300,000	270,000	279,000	9,000
Materials	78,000	70,200	70,265	(65)
Labour	58,000	52,200	51,750	450
	136,000	122,400	122,015	385
Profit	164,000	147,600	156,985	9,385

The budgeted results used are those adjusted for relative inflation, because they are the most specific and detailed (and realistic). It would be quite helpful to use the figures adjusted for general inflation as they would help to avoid managers concentrating on factors which are unavoidable. However, managers need to be able to examine each component of the profit calculation separately to diagnose problems accurately. The budget was for 1,000 units produced and sold. For the sake of comparison, the budget is 'flexed' to 900 units, to be comparable with the actual results.

The differences noted above can be broken down into variances as follows, where F is favourable and A is adverse.

		£	
(i)	Sales price variance	9,000	F
(ii)	*Material variances*		
	Material price variance (4,700 × £15.60) – £70,265	3,055	F
	Material usage variance [(900 × 5) – 4,700] × £15.60	(3,120)	A
		(65)	A
(iii)	*Labour variances*		
	Labour rate variance (8,750 × £5.80) – £51,750	(1,000)	A
	Labour efficiency variance [(8,750 – (900 × 10)] × £5.80	1,450	F
		450	F

(c) *Commentary*
The overall budgeted cost figures have been remarkably accurate, with differences of less than 1% on budget for both materials and labour. The sales price variance represents a 3% rise in sales price compared to budget. This may have been due to a factor outside the control of the company.

The cost variances are worth examining in detail because, for both labour and materials, an increase in cost over budget has been offset by a saving in efficiency. This efficiency saving should be investigated. The price rise should also be investigated and the possibility of obtaining a discount should be negotiated in an attempt to bring the costs back into line with budget.

14 RESPONSIBILITY CENTRES

(a) In order to achieve its corporate objectives, a business is often broken down into subdivisions where the managers become responsible for their own defined objectives. Provided these divisional objectives have been clearly communicated, the division decision makers become a self contained responsibility centre. They will have responsibility for inputs and outputs where appropriate and will be held accountable for the achievement of the predetermined objectives. Some of these objectives will be financial and will be defined by the area of responsibility which is being managed.

Cost centres are usually subdivisions of a business which do not generate revenue or other measurable output, and where the only financial yardstick is the level of expenditure. In some circumstances the non-financial goals of the cost centre should be clearly stated and given sufficient visibility to ensure that an apparently good record of control over expenditure does not result in inability to reach the overall corporate objective. Hence failure to 'launch' a new firework by November in the UK should be more significant than the likely underspent cost centre budget that may result from this lack of achievement.

It is also important that the areas of expenditure are clearly defined when setting budgets or financial objectives and that the cost is described by reference to the benefit it is intended to bring about (if appropriate). Thus the need for a promotional campaign to support a brand should be clearly defined by how the campaign is intended to increase sales revenues over time.

Profit centres, on the other hand, are sectors of the business which have both measurable outputs and inputs. The financial objectives of the profit centre should include only those revenues and costs over which the manager has direct control and should specifically exclude any allocated costs which cannot be managed by the decision makers within the profit centre. Profit centres are usually vertical subdivisions of the business and are self contained. However, they can be created by allowing the use of transfer pricing to create an output between divisions of a company, particularly where one department provides a service to another. Provided the transfer pricing mechanism is realistic the corporate objectives can be enhanced by this type of internal pricing.

The third type of centre is an investment centre. Here we focus attention not just on profits but on maximising the funds generated from the investment in the division. These responsibility centres must be self contained divisions and they are often limited companies in their own right. They are generally characterised by having their own board of directors or at least an operating management committee who run the business and rely only on their head office for centralised services (matters such as central tax advise, treasury funding). By definition, investment centres need to be asset based and hence are not found in those service based industries where the assets are people and no capital is involved in generating profits. Again, however, the financial objective needs to be clearly defined because the simple requirement to produce a high return on investment can be subject to management abuse. As a result, group offices will often fund any investment centrally and charge the business a notional interest charge intended to measure the cost of funds and perhaps the degree of riskiness of all investment undertaken.

(b) (i) The marketing director of a business is usually responsible for the policy, procedures and resources necessary within a business to generate revenues. In a multiproduct business this would stretch across the entire product range. He may therefore be responsible for the level of sales activity for all products, the support activities and expenditure levels needed to generate those sales, and the resources necessary (by way of central marketing staff and a field sales force) to bring the product to the market. He may also be responsible for research and development.

The marketing director is not usually responsible for the efficient investment in assets required to generate the sales and he is unlikely to be considered to be an investment centre. However, the constituent parts of his areas of responsibility would suggest that he is responsible for a series of revenue centres and cost centres. In a single product business it may be possible to create one profit centre and the marketing director will be responsible for that.

Taking this to its logical conclusion the marketing director can be considered to be a profit centre manager because of his need to consider both outputs and inputs. The direct costs associated with sales generation would be offset against the revenue streams associated with that activity. However, within that profit centre is a series of revenue and cost centres for which those managers reporting to the marketing director will be responsible.

(ii) A distribution manager will have a primary duty to transfer goods from the point of production to the point of sale (or to a point where responsibility for further distribution is transferred). He will need assets to achieve this and he is likely to have a clearly defined geographic area in which he operates. His function may be to operate as a service in its own right (a distribution based company) or to be a service, provided at one end to the producer or at the other end to the wholesaler/retailer. Where a revenue stream can be clearly defined (either by sales to third parties or by a transfer pricing scheme within a company) the distribution manager may be considered as an investment centre. In practice, however, this is unlikely because of his managerial rather than his director status. This would infer that the manager is one of several managers and his area of responsibility is not sufficiently far reaching to encompasses all areas of finance and costs which go into making up the total return on the funds invested in the assets. In a stand-alone distribution company the distribution director as managing director is most likely to be the investment centre. In most areas therefore the manager will be responsible for the costs associated with running and maintaining his distribution services and he will therefore be considered as a cost centre manager. If transfer pricing where introduced this could in certain instances become a profit centre.

(iii) The sales manager is generally responsible for generating revenue by the sale of certain products in a prescribed area by the employment of a field sales force. He will never be considered as an investment centre because his responsibilities will not encompass investment in assets. He will, however, have a responsibility for output (sales revenues or, at least, the revenue value of sales orders) and inputs (direct costs incurred by achieving those sales). He could therefore be described as a profit centre.

340

INDEX

REVIEW FORM

Name: _____

How have you used this Text?

Home study (book only) ☐   With 'correspondence' package ☐

On a course: college_____ ☐   Other _____

How did you obtain this Text?

From us by mail order ☐   From us by phone ☐

From a bookshop ☐   From your college ☐

Where did you hear about BPP Texts?

At bookshop ☐   Recommended by lecturer ☐

Recommended by friend ☐   Mailshot from BPP ☐

Advertisement in _____ ☐   Other _____

Your comments and suggestions would be appreciated on the following areas.

Syllabus coverage

Illustrative questions

Errors (please specify, and refer to a page number)

Presentation

Other

Please send to: BPP Publishing Ltd, FREEPOST, London W12 8BR